Film Review

2002-2003

James Cameron-Wilson became a committed film buff when he moved to London at the age of 17. After a stint at the Webber Douglas Academy of Dramatic Art he joined *What's On In London* and took over from F. Maurice Speed as cinema editor. Later, he edited the trade newspaper *Showbiz*, was commissioning editor for *Film Review*, was consultant for *The Movie Show* on BSkyB and a frequent presenter on the Radio 2 *Arts Programme*. He is also author of the books *Hollywood: The New Generation*, *Young Hollywood*, *The Cinema of Robert De Niro* and *The Moviegoer's Quiz Book*. His film reviews are currently syndicated in *247* and the *What's On* magazines distributed in Birmingham, Manchester and Liverpool, and he has a regular column in *Film Review*, Britain's longest-running film magazine. He has also reviewed for the BBC and Talk Radio and has written frequently for the *Times*, as well as contributing to the *Sunday Times*, the *Guardian*, the *Daily Telegraph*, *Flicks* and *Shivers*. On television he made over 100 appearances on *The Movie Show* both as critic and quizmaster and has regularly popped up on CNN, Channel One and BBC Worldwide Television. He was also Britain's resident 'dial-a-film critic' for two years. Besides the cinema, James Cameron-Wilson's academic interests include face transplants, false memory syndrome and Feng Shui, while his personal interests include his wife, 11-year-old daughter, dinner parties and reading.

Includes video releases and websites

Film Review
2002-2003

JAMES CAMERON-WILSON

Founding father: F. Maurice Speed
1911-1998

Reynolds & Hearn Ltd
London

TO BILL, WHOSE LOVE OF WOMEN,
WORDS AND WINE ECHOES MY OWN

Acknowledgements

The author would like to declare his eternal appreci-
ation to the following, without whom this book
would not have been possible: David Aldridge,
Charles Bacon, Ewen Brownrigg, Juliet Cameron-
Wilson, Ian Crane, Pauline Dunham, The Joel Finler
Collection, Marcus Hearn, Adam Keen, David
Miller, Emily Mortimer, Nigel Mulock, Scot
Woodward Myers, my mother, Daniel O'Brien,
Frances Palmer, Virginia Palmer, Richard Reynolds,
Jonathan Rigby, Adrian Rigelsford, Mansel Stimpson
and David Nicholas Wilkinson. And, of course,
Cate, Gwyneth and Nicole. Till next year…

Founding father:
F. Maurice Speed, 1911-1998

First published in 2002 by
Reynolds & Hearn Ltd
61a Priory Road
Kew Gardens
Richmond
Surrey TW9 3DH

A CIP catalogue record for this book is available from the
British Library.

ISBN 1 903111 46 3

Designed by Paul Chamberlain.

Printed and bound in Great Britain by MPG Books Ltd,
Bodmin, Corwall.

Contents

Introduction

There was some criticism in the media last year about the poor quality of films produced by the major American studios. The summer in particular proved to be a creative tundra, with titles such as *Pearl Harbor*, *Planet of the Apes*, *Lara Croft: Tomb Raider*, *The Mummy Returns*, *Dr Dolittle 2*, *Swordfish* and *Scary Movie 2* regularly appearing before the critics' firing squad. Despairingly, the summer of 2002 yielded almost as many lacklustre 'tent pole' pictures: *Scooby-Doo*, *K-19: The Widowmaker*, *The Sum of All Fears*, *Windtalkers*, *Mr Deeds*, *Bad Company*. Enough already…

There was also an alarming number of sequels, such as *Star Wars: Episode II – Attack of the Clones*, *Austin Powers in Goldmember*, *Men in Black II*, *Spy Kids 2*, *Stuart Little 2*, *Halloween: Resurrection*, *Jason X* and *Red Dragon* (the last named being both a prequel and a remake). Of the latter trend, an interesting pattern emerged. The sequels often received better reviews than the so-called 'original' event pictures. *Time Out* praised *Jason X* for being, 'notably more entertaining than many of its predecessors,' while the *Times* admitted that it 'at least shows an awareness of its own absurdity.' *Stuart Little 2* was considered 'good, clean,

wonderful-to-look-at fun' by the *Mail on Sunday* and *Austin Powers in Goldmember* was hailed by the *Boston Globe* as 'the most consistently funny of the Austin Powers films.' The *Washington Post* went one step further, raving that if '*The Spy Who Shagged Me* was a string of inventive gags, puns and crudity, this movie's a couple of ropes' worth.'

Not everybody was as kind towards *Men in Black II*, though. However, I have a theory. Had *Men in Black II* opened five years earlier, and the first film was released this summer, then the situation would have been reversed. In my opinion, the sequel is no worse than its forebear, although its audience has changed dramatically. In the intervening years, the quality of special effects has jumped exponentially and the viewers' sophistication along with it. Aliens, too, have come a long way in five years.

So the question is: why bother to remake *Men in Black* at all? The answer lies securely in the record-breaking $87.2 million that the picture took over the 4th of July weekend. Hollywood, as everyone knows, is a dollar-driven animal. As stars demand ever more ludicrous sums (Arnold Schwarzenegger is getting $30 million for *Terminator 3:*

Rise of the Machines), budgets escalate and the bottom line has to be accounted for. So the closer a film is to a sure thing, the better for the bean-counters. This, in the short term, would seem to be stemming an economic haemorrhage. But as the studios repeatedly play safe, they are establishing a climate in which anything new or adventurous is immediately asphyxiated. Give an audience junk food all the time and it will never develop an appetite for anything intellectually nutritious.

There is a mentality in the Western world – a mentality Hollywood habitually feeds – which maintains that what is familiar is good. But if a viewer craves familiarity, he or she needs only to tune in to any one of the countless soap operas polluting the small screen. So, doesn't the larger screen have a bigger purpose? *Austin Powers in Goldmember* certainly has its funny moments – it may even have more laughs per minute than the previous two outings put together. But humour, as in living life in

the moment, is more potent when packed with a surprise.

And that is what is lacking in Hollywood today: the thrill of the unexpected. But it's a downward spiral. As long as mass-marketed dross like Scooby-Doo continues to dominate the multiplexes, the filmgoer will have nowhere to turn to educate his imagination. The cinema is still a wonderful place to share our dreams – and our nightmares – but it needs creative investment. When FilmFour – the indepen-

dent British company responsible for such innovative works as *My Beautiful Laundrette*, *Trainspotting*, *The Crying Game* and *East is East* – took on Hollywood at its own game (assisted by unreasonable budgets), it went bottom up. FilmFour had found a recipe that worked and then abandoned it in the kitchen. It's only a matter of time, then, before the entire restaurant closes down.

James Cameron-Wilson
August 2002

Top 20 UK Box-Office Hits
July 2001 – June 2002

1. Harry Potter and the Philosopher's Stone
2. The Lord of the Rings: The Fellowship of the Ring
3. Bridget Jones's Diary
4. Star Wars: Episode II – Attack of the Clones
5. Monsters, Inc.
6. Shrek
7. Ocean's Eleven
8. Spider-Man
9. Cats & Dogs
10. American Pie 2
11. Moulin Rouge!
12. Jurassic Park III
13. Planet of the Apes
14. About a Boy
15. Ice Age
16. Lara Croft: Tomb Raider
17. The Others
18. Bend It Like Beckham
19. Rush Hour 2
20. Gosford Park

Top 10 Box-Office Stars
Star of the Year: Hugh Grant

With the news that the late Bruce Lee is to be digitally resurrected in order to star in *Dragon Warrior*, the living, breathing actor is becoming increasingly redundant at the box-office. Indeed, the big draws in the UK over the last 12 months have been an 11-year-old wizard, a giant-footed Hobbit, an army of cloned warriors, an animated eyeball, a flatulent green ogre, a comic-strip superhero and a load of cats and dogs.

In stark contrast to the golden era of Hollywood, audiences today seem to be little interested in flesh-and-blood icons. Some may argue that the closest thing we have to a certifiable box-office star is Tom Cruise; yet even he, in *Minority Report* – directed by the most successful filmmaker on the planet – lost out at the box-office to *Lilo & Stitch*, a slapdash cartoon from Disney about a genetically engineered alien.

Still, it behoves me to scrape together a top-ten list of box-office humans and so, taking past records into account, here is the rundown. Runners-up this year include Angelina Jolie, Cameron Diaz, Jodie Foster, Brad Pitt, John Travolta, Chris Tucker, Gwyneth Paltrow and the octogenarian Christopher Lee.

2. Ewan McGregor
3. George Clooney
4. Julia Roberts
5. Nicole Kidman
6. Tom Cruise
7. Jackie Chan
8. Sacha Baron Cohen
9. Russell Crowe
10. Eddie Murphy

Releases of the Year

This section contains details of all the films released in Great Britain from 1 July 2001 to the end of June 2002 – the period covered by all the reference features in this book.

Leading actors are generally credited with the roles they played, followed by a summary of supporting players. Where an actor further down a cast list is of special interest then his/her role is generally credited as well.

For technical credits the normal abbreviations operate, and are as follows: Dir – for Director; Pro – for Producer; Ex Pro – for Executive Producer; Co-Pro – for Co-Producer; Assoc Pro – for Associate Producer; Line Pro – for Line Producer; Ph – for Cinematographer; Ed – for Editor; Pro Des – for Production Designer; and M – for composer.

Abbreviations for the names of film companies are also obvious when used, such as Fox for Twentieth Century Fox, and UIP for Universal International Pictures. The production company (or companies) is given first, the distribution company last.

Information at the foot of each entry is presented in the following order: running time/country of origin/year of production/date of British release/British certification.

All films reviewed by James Cameron-Wilson unless otherwise specified. Additional contributors: Charles Bacon, Ewen Brownrigg, Eva Marie Bryer, Graham Clayton, Adam Keen, Scot Woodward Myers and Mansel Stimpson.

Star ratings

★★★★★ **Wonderful**
★★★★   **Very good**
★★★   **Good**
★★   **Mediocre**
★   **Insulting**

À l'Attaque! ★★★★

As with his warm and atmospheric *Marius et Jeannette* (1997), writer-director Robert Guédiguian presents a credible world of lived-in, endearing characters born from the clay of his native Estaque, Marseilles. Here, though, he frames them in a story of their own creation, as two contrary scriptwriters struggle to compose a political scenario built around the common man. As Yvan attempts to inject the film with some carnality and vulgar colloquialisms ('Only two things count in life – the class struggle and sex'), his partner, Xavier, strives for a more accessible, mainstream approach. Meanwhile, the emerging characters – a colourful bunch trying to save the future of their garage – get to have their authors' gateau and eat it as they act out various drafts of the plot. It is to the credit of Guédiguian that while his fictitious authors struggle with the outcome of their own story, the characters therein jump to life with an immediacy and credibility of their own. The third entry in his 'Tales of l'Estaque,' *À l'Attaque!* is an earthy, sharply original and utterly charming slice of whimsy.

• *Lola* Ariane Ascaride, *Mr Moreau* Pierre Banderet, *Marthe, Gigi's wife* Frédérique Bonnal, *Henri Manade, the layabout* Patrick Bonnel, *Jean-Do* Jean-Pierre Darroussin, *Neils, the banker* Alain Lenglet, *Gigi* Gerard Meylan, *Mouloud* Miloud Nacer, *Xavier* Jacques Pieiller, *Vanessa* Laetitia Pesenti, *Yvan* Denis Podalydes, Jacques Boudet, Christine Brucher, Francis Caviglia.
• *Dir* Robert Guédiguian, *Pro* Guédiguian, Gilles Sandoz and Michel Saint-Jean, *Ex Pro* Malek Hamzaoui, *Screenplay* Guédiguian and Jean-Louis Milesi, *Ph* Bernard Cavalié, *Pro Des* Michel Vandestien, *Ed* Bernard Sasia, *M* Jacques Menichetti; J S Bach, Johann Strauss, *Costumes* Catherine Keller, *Choreography* Laurence Roussarie.

Agat Films/Cie/Diaphana/TFI Films/Canal Plus-Gala. 90 mins. France. 2000. Rel: 20 July 2001. Cert 15.

À ma soeur! ★★★½

On holiday in the south of France with their parents, Elena, 15, pretty and slim, and Anaïs, 12, plump and plain, are constantly at each other's throats. Elena is looking for a holiday romance, while Anaïs seems content to stuff her face. Then Elena meets an Italian student, Fernando, who sees in her a chance to satisfy his sexual needs... There are a number of dull patches in Catherine Breillat's extraordinary film, but they are as essential to the complete picture as the blue sky in a landscape jigsaw puzzle. This is a wholly naturalistic study of sisterhood, the loss of innocence and the contradictions in any close-knit family. At times, the film is so real that it takes the viewer aback: the red flush on Anaïs' cheek after her mother has slapped her, the girl's examination of her half-developed breasts, not to mention the sight of Fernando's erection. However, it is the spontaneous intimacy between the two sisters that is so revealing, a bond and rivalry seldom captured so intensely by the camera. Overall, then, this is a far more human and insightful work than Breillat's previous effort, the pretentious and controversial *Romance* (1998). English translation: *To My Sister!*; American title: *Fat Girl*.

Right: Love machine: Haley Joel Osment in Steven Spielberg's stunningly cinematic *A.I. Artificial Intelligence* (from Warner)

• *Anaïs* Anaïs Reboux, *Elena* Roxane Mesquida, *Fernando* Libero de Rienzo, *the mother* Arsinée Khanjian, *the father* Romain Goupil, *Fernando's mother* Laura Betti, *killer* Albert Goldberg.
• *Dir and Screenplay* Catherine Breillat, *Pro* Jean-François Lepetit, *Ph* Yorgos Arvanitis, *Pro Des* François Renaud Labarthe, *Ed* Pascale Chavance, *M* various, *Sound* Jean Minondo.

Flach Film/CB Films/Arte France Cinéma/Immagine & Cinema/Urania Pictures/Canal Plus-Metro Tartan. 93 mins. France/Italy. 2001. Rel: 7 December 2001. Cert 18.

A.I. Artificial Intelligence ★★★★

When her only son contracts a terminal illness (and is cryogenically preserved until a cure can be found), Monica Swinton is given an unusual gift by her husband. It is an android child, the first programmed to love. As God made Adam in his own image and taught him to love his maker, so the technology of mankind has evolved to such a degree that machines can be manipulated to 'feel' emotion. However, following a near fatal accident inadvertently precipitated by David, the android child, Monica abandons him in the woods. Desperate for his mother's love, David resolves to become a 'real' human boy... If anybody could pull

off a modern fairy tale, it is Steven Spielberg. Only this time's he's working in collaboration with Stanley Kubrick, following seven years of conversation and the consultation of around 1000 drawings, notes and notebooks left to him by Kubrick's widow, Christiane. Released at a time when most studios were processing join-the-digital-dot travesties, *A.I.* soars beyond all expectations. Tantalising the intellect and captivating the heart, it is a work that is thematically courageous and technically awe-inspiring. And, even as it filters the concept of *Pinocchio* through elements of *E.T.*, *Short Circuit* and *Close Encounters*, it is a stunning original that unleashes one breathtaking scene after another. This, surely, is what cinema is all about.

• *David* Haley Joel Osment, *Gigolo Joe* Jude Law, *Monica Swinton* Frances O'Connor, *Lord Johnson-Johnson* Brendan Gleeson, *Professor Hobby* William Hurt, *Henry Swinton* Sam Robards, *Martin Swinton* Jake Thomas, *Patricia* Paula Malcolmson, Ken Leung, April Grace, Matt Winston, Ashley Scott, John Prosky, Michael Berresse, Haley King, Kathryn Morris, Rena Owen, Michael Mantell, Matt Malloy, Adrian Grenier, Diane Fletcher; *the voice of Teddy* Jack Angel, *the voice of Dr Know* Robin Williams, *the voice of the specialist* Ben Kingsley, *the voice of blue Mecha* Meryl Streep, *the voice of the comedian* Chris Rock.
• *Dir* and *Screenplay* Steven Spielberg, based on the short story *Supertoys Last All Summer Long* by Brian Aldiss, *Pro* Spielberg, Kathleen Kennedy and Bonnie Curtis, *Ex Pro* Jan Harlan and Walter F Parkes, *Ph* Janusz Kaminski, *Pro Des* Rick Carter, *Ed* Michael

Kahn, *M* John Williams; Richard Strauss; songs performed by Ministry, Dick Powell, Stubby Kaye and Johnny Silver, and Fred Astaire, *Costumes* Bob Ringwood, *Sound* Gary Rydstrom, *Visual effects* Industrial Light & Magic, *Special effects* Michael Lantieri, *Robots* Stan Winston Studio.

Warner/DreamWorks/Amblin/Stanley Kubrick-Warner. 146 mins. USA. 2001. Rel: 21 September 2001. Cert 12.

About a Boy ★★★★¹⁄₂

London; today. Living off the royalties of a naff Christmas song penned by his father, Will Freeman has transformed the act of doing nothing into an art form. He's now had the bright idea of joining a single parents' group – SPAT, Single Parents Alone Together – so as to meet lonely, horny and available women. All he has to do is pretend that he has a son. He then meets Marcus, a 12-year-old in gruesome knitwear with the mother from Hell... It's not often that a film lives up to the book on which it is based, but *About a Boy* is the exception. Given a Hollywood polish by the brothers Paul and Chris Weitz (whose last collaboration was, astonishingly, the numbingly unfunny *Down to Earth*), the film hits its comic and profound notes with a deft touch that is totally disarming. As a feel-good British comedy, this is light years more convincing than *Bridget Jones's Diary*, while Hugh Grant buffs up his new screen persona as a cad (after his days as a buffoonish romantic) with an advanced comic skill. Indeed, the casting is perfect throughout, with

Above: The parent trap: Nicholas Hoult and Hugh Grant do some unconventional bonding in Chris and Paul Weitz's hilarious *About a Boy* (from UIP)

the miraculous Toni Collette tightrope-walking the narrow thread between absurdity and credibility and the 12-year-old Nicholas Hoult simply ideal as the doggedly honest, wise and nerdy Marcus. The script, too, is excellent, homing in on the essence of Nick Hornby's bestseller and making a number of expedient changes (for instance, it seems far more appropriate – and funny – that Marcus should sing The Carpenters and not Joni Mitchell at school).

• *Will Freeman* Hugh Grant, *Fiona* Toni Collette, *Rachel* Rachel Weisz, *Susie* Victoria Smurfit, *Marcus Brewer* Nicholas Hoult, *Angie* Isabel Brook, *Christine* Sharon Small, *Clive* Mark Drewry, *with* Ben Ridgeway, Jonathan Franklin, Joyce Henderson, Janine Duvitski, Sidney Livingstone, Joanne Petitt, Annabelle Apsion, Denise Stephenson, Rosalind Knight, Mark Heap.
• *Dir* Chris and Paul Weitz, *Pro* Jane Rosenthal, Robert De Niro, Brad Epstein, Tim Bevan and Eric Fellner, *Ex Pro* Nick Hornby and Lynn Harris, *Screenplay* Peter Hedges, Chris and Paul Weitz *Ph* Remi Adefarasin, *Pro Des* Jim Clay, *Ed* Nick Moore, *M* and songs written and performed by Badly Drawn Boy, *Costumes* Joanna Johnston.

Universal/Canal Plus/Working Title/Tribeca-UIP.
101 mins. UK/USA/France. 2002. Rel: 26 April 2002.
Cert 12.

The Affair of the Necklace ★★★¹/₂
Set in late 18th century France, this is the story of Jeanne de la Motte-Valois, a young woman who sets out to restore her family's name and fortune after having it stripped by a capricious French Crown. Her struggle embroils her in the various intrigues of the pre-Revolution court, with numerous flashbacks demonstrating the cruelty done to her family. Her efforts are hampered by her estranged husband (Adrien Brody), who realises too late the woman he allowed to get away… A lavish production, Charles Shyer's direction coupled with Ashley Rowe's brilliant cinematography makes this world truly come alive. Unfortunately, it's Hilary Swank's thoroughly modern performance as Jeanne that upsets the delicate balance of the period mise en scène. However, Jonathan Pryce is delicious as the corrupt Cardinal Rohan, while Jeanne's ex-gigolo boyfriend, played by Simon Baker, is also highly appealing. [*Scot Woodward Myers*]

• *Comtesse Jeanne de la Motte-Valois* Hilary Swank, *Cardinal de Rohan* Jonathan Pryce, *Retaux de Villette* Simon Baker, *Count Nicolas de la Motte* Adrien Brody, *Baron de Breteuil* Brian Cox, *Marie Antoinette* Joely Richardson, *Count Cagliostro* Christopher Walken, *with* Paul Brooke, Peter Eyre, Simon Kunz, Hayden Panettiere, Geoffrey Hutchings, Diana Quick, Miranda Pleasence, John Grillo, Christopher Logue.
• *Dir* Charles Shyer, *Pro* Broderick Johnson, Andrew

A. Kosove, Redmond Morris and Charles Shyer, *Ex Pro* Nancy Myers, *Screenplay* John Sweet, *Ph* Ashley Rowe, *Pro Des* Alex McDowell, *Ed* David Moritz, *M* David Newman, *Costumes* Milena Canonero.

Alcon Entertainment-Warner.
117 mins. USA. 2001. Rel: 11 January 2002. Cert 12.

Aimée & Jaguar ★★★★
Berlin, 1943. While working during the day as a tireless and indispensable assistant to the editor of a Nazi newspaper, Felice Schragenheim is actually a key member of the underground resistance. She is also a Jewish lesbian who thrives on danger. When she falls for Lilly Wurst, a young married mother of four, the seeds of a rash and tumultuous intrigue are sown. Now in her eighties, Lilly Wurst looks back on a time that changed her life for ever… With Britain and America rediscovering the fertile thematic ground of World War II, it is refreshing to encounter a German drama set entirely within the confines of war-torn Berlin. Played out on a rich chiaroscuro palette (lit by Britain's Tony Imi) and superbly acted by its female cast, *Aimée & Jaguar* is an evocative, compelling portrait of wartime Germany. At its most powerful in its quieter moments, the film boasts one of the most nakedly authentic love scenes (a 'contest of trembles') ever acted out between two women.

• *Felice Schragenheim* aka *Jaguar* Maria Schrader, *Lilly Wust* aka *Aimée* Juliane Köhler, *Ilse* Johanna Wokalek, *Klärchen* Heike Makatsch, *Lotte* Elisabeth Degen, *Günther Wust* Detlev Buck, *Lilly (today)* Inge Keller, *Ilse (today)* Kyra Mladeck, *Mrs Jäger* Margit Bendokat, *editor-in-chief Keller* Peter Weck, *Stefan Schmidt* H.C. Blumenberg, Jochen Stern, Klaus Manchen, Sarah Camp, Desirée Nick, Patrizia Moresco, Dani Levy, Lya Dulitzkaya.
• *Dir* Max Färberböck, *Pro* Günter Rohrbach and Hanno Huth, *Ex Pro* Stefaan Schieder, *Screenplay* Färberböck and Rona Munro, based on the novel by Erica Fischer, *Ph* Tony Imi, *Pro Des* Albrecht Konrad and Uli Hanisch, *Ed* Barbara Hennings, *M* Jan A P Kaczmarek, *Costumes* Barbara Baum, *Sound* Hubert Bartholomae and Friedrich M. Dosch.

Sentator Film/Filmboard Berlin-Brandenburg GmbH Nodrhein-Westfalen GmbH-Optimum Releasing.
126 mins. Germany. 1998. Rel: 6 July 2001. Cert 15.

Ali ★★★★
Between the years 1964 and 1974, the loud-mouthed upstart from Louisville, Kentucky snatched the World Heavyweight Boxing crown from Sonny Liston, converted to the Nation of Islam, changed his name from Cassius Clay to Muhammad Ali, and then, in 1967, refused to fight in Vietnam and was stripped of his

boxing licence. Forced to pay his own legal fees and unable to capitalise on his physical prime, Ali ended up destitute, divorced and disillusioned. He was then thrown out of Islam… Opening with an extended montage (set to a medley of Sam Cooke standards) that sums up the essence of its period, place and protagonist, *Ali* starts as it means to go on – for another two hours-plus. A hypnotic fusion of cinema, craft, art, performance, emotion, story, politics, history and music, the film is a tour de force in every department. Will Smith perfectly captures the vocal cadence, arrogance and determination of the champ (and bulked up from 185 to 220 pounds), Jon Voight is unrecognisable as the celebrated sports commentator Howard Cosell, and the extended boxing sequences are some of the most poetic and exciting ever committed to celluloid. While the film has been criticised in some quarters for whitewashing the image of Ali, it is still an affecting and well-rounded portrait of a man who overcame insurmountable odds to become the best-loved figure in sporting history.

FYI: Ali's ubiquitous photographer Howard Bingham (played by Jeffrey Wright) is also executive producer of the film; Nona Gaye, who plays Ali's second wife Belinda, is the daughter of Marvin Gaye; and David Elliott, who plays Sam Cooke, is the son of Dionne Warwick.

• *Cassius Clay Jr* aka *Muhammad Ali* Will Smith, *Drew 'Bundini' Brown* Jamie Foxx, *Howard Cosell* Jon Voight, *Malcolm X* Mario Van Peebles, *Angelo Dundee* Ron Silver, *Howard Bingham* Jeffrey Wright, *Don King* Mykelti Williamson, *Sonji Roi* Jada Pinkett Smith, *Belinda* Nona Gaye, *Veronica Porsche* Michael Michele, *Chauncy Eskridge* Joe Morton, *Dr Derdie Pacheco* Paul Rodriguez, *Bradley* Bruce McGilll, *Herbert Muhammad* Barry Shabaka Henley, *Cassius Clay Sr* Giancarlo Esposito, *Luis Sarria* Laurence Mason, *Martin Luther King Jr* LeVar Burton, *Elijah Muhammad* Albert Hall, *Odessa Clay* Candy Brown Houston, *Sam Cooke* David Elliott, *Sonny Liston* Michael Bentt, *Joe Frazier* James Toney, *George Foreman* Charles Shufford, David Cubitt, Al Cole, Robert Sale, David Haines, *Joseph Mobutu* Malick Bowens, Ted Levine, Shari Watson, Victoria Dillard, Brad Greenquist, Morgana Van Peebles, Maya Van Peebles, Gailard Sartain, Leonard Termo, Michael Dorn.
• *Dir* Michael Mann, *Pro* Mann, Jon Peters, Paul Ardaji and A. Kitman Ho, *Ex Pro* Howard Bingham and Graham King, *Screenplay* Mann, Stephen J Rivele, Christopher Wilkinson and Eric Roth, from a story by Gregory Allen Howard, *Ph* Emmanuel Lubezki, *Pro Des* John Myhre, *Ed* William Goldenberg, Stephen Rivkin and Lynzee Klingman, *M* Lisa Gerrard and Pieter Bourke; songs performed by David Elliott, Moby, Salif Keita, Truth Hurts, Martin Tillman, Al Green and Booker T and The MGs, Aretha Franklin, Mighty Joe Young, The

Watchtower Four, Lisa Gerrard and Pieter Bourke, Alicia Keys, R Kelly, The Pointer Sisters, etc, *Costumes* Marlene Stewart, *Make-up* Greg Cannom, *Boxing technical adviser* Angelo Dundee.

Initial Entertainment/Columbia Pictures/Peters Entertainment/Forward Pass Prods, etc-Entertainment. 159 mins. USA. 2001. Rel: 15 February 2002. Cert 15.

Ali G Indahouse ★★★¹/₂

The big screen incarnation of Britain's favourite pseudo-gangbanger (alter ego of Cambridge graduate Cohen) is a relentless expedition into bad taste. With the irreverence of Monty Python and the relative harmlessness of a Carry On caper (albeit one with prosthetic penises, drugs, bestiality and bouncing buttocks), *Ali G Indahouse* embarrasses by revealing the adolescent depravities we secretly find funny. Duped into the MP-ship of Staines to save his beloved Rec Centre from developers, Ali G demonstrates how the country would be run if a clueless hip-hop fanatic had the Prime Minister's ear. Nothing is sacred as Ali G bungles from sketch to sketch, inadvertently solving the problems of the world in true Clouseau fashion. [*Adam Keen*]

• *Ali G* Sacha Baron Cohen, *Me Julie* Kellie Bright, *Prime Minister* Michael Gambon, *David Carlton* Charles Dance, *Kate Hedges* Rhona Mitra, *Ricky C* Martin Freeman, *Nan* Barbara New, *Hassan B* Ray Panthaki, *The Queen* Jeanette Vane, *with* Tony Way, Nabil Elouahabi, Anna Keaveney, Naomi Campbell, Carolyn Pickles, David Henry, Jeffrey Wickham, John Humphries, Jon Snow, Rudolph Walker, Colin Stinton, Martin Wimbush, Richard Madeley, Judy Finnigan.
• *Dir* Mark Mylod, *Pro* Tim Bevan, Eric Fellner and Dan Mazer, *Ex Pro* Natascha Wharton, Sacha Baron Cohen and Peter Fincham, *Screenplay* Sacha Baron Cohen and Dan Mazer, *Ph* Ashley Rowe, *Pro Des* Grenville Horner, *Ed* Paul Knight, *M* Adam F; J S Bach, Mozart, Handel; songs performed by NWA, So Solid Crew, Lil' Kim, Backyard Dog, Foxy Brown, Chaka Demus, The Commodores, Ali G and Shaggy, Ms Dynamite, Mis-teeq, Montell Jordan, etc, *Costumes* Annie Hardinge.

Universal/Canal Plus/Working Title/TalkBack Prods, etc-UIP. 88 mins. UK/USA/France/Germany. 2002. Rel: 22 March 2002. Cert 15.

Ali Zaoua ★★

Casablanca today reveals a street scene in which kids, surviving by any means possible, live a harsh life. Indeed, the eponymous character meets an early death as a victim of gang rivalry, and the tale revolves

around the attempts of his friends to give him a burial fit for a prince. Nabal Ayouch's approach to this material is sincere but misguided since he provides too much fictional gloss, extending even to a sentimental upbeat ending which features animation. By adding fable to raw reality in order not to leave the audience too despondent, he not only creates a most uneasy blend but forgets that a comparable film made with no compromise at all, Mira Nair's *Salaam Bombay!* of 1987, reached a wide audience and achieved far greater impact. Original title: *Prince de la rue*. [*Mansel Stimpson*]

• *Kwita* Maunim Kbab, *Omar* Mustapha Hansali, *Boubker* Hicham Moussoune, *Ali Zaoua* Abdelnak Zhayra, *Dib* Saïd Taghmaoui.
• *Dir* and *Ex Pro* Nabil Ayouch, *Pro* Etienne Comar, Antoine Voituriez and Jean Cottin, *Screenplay* Nabil Ayouch and Nathalie Saugeon, *Ph* Vincent Mathias, *Art Dir* Saïd Rais, *Ed* Jean-Robert Thomann, *M* Krishna Levy, *Costumes* Nezha Dakil.

Playtime/Canal Plus, etc-Millennium.
95 mins. France/Morocco/Belgium. 2001. Rel: 22 March 2002. Cert 12.

Amélie ★★★★★

Tracing the singular life of Amélie Poulain from her conception to adulthood, Jean-Pierre Jeunet's first film since *Alien Resurrection* is a triumph of joie de vivre. With more originality in any given five minutes than most films have in their entire running time, the film paints a magical universe in contemporary Paris as Amélie struggles with her shyness and purpose in life. The daughter of an emotionally aloof doctor, Amélie is diagnosed as having a heart condition when, during her monthly check-ups, her little heart races at the only physical contact with her father. Thus, kept out of school, Amélie develops an inclination for solitude and enters adulthood with a timorous predisposition. As Jeunet expands his narrative canvas to include neighbours and work colleagues (Amélie ends up waitressing at The Two Windmills café), his heroine is forced to interact with society, albeit on a limited scale. However, it is the Glass Man – an elderly recluse who paints exact replicas of Renoir's *The Luncheon of the Boating Party* over and over again – who has the greatest impact on Amélie's soul. Amélie, who has devoted her life to anonymously helping others, must seek and find her own happiness in another. Packed with wild detail and anecdotage (each character's likes and dislikes are detailed in on-screen captions), Jeunet's human masterpiece leaps off the screen. With his painter's eye, musician's ear and optimist's heart, he has fashioned a unique entertainment that changes the rules of cinema as it recharges the soul. Oh, and Audrey Tautou as Amélie is a dream.

FYI: The title was derived from the fact that Jeunet and Guillaume Laurant wrote the script with Emily Watson in mind to star. Also known as *Le Fabuleux destin d'Amélie Poulain* and *Amelie from Montmartre*.

• *Amélie Poulain* Audrey Tautou, *Nino Quicampoix* Mathieu Kassovitz, *Raphael Poulain, Amélie's father* Rufus, *Madeleine Wallace, the concierge* Yolande Moreau, *Hipolito, the writer* Arthus de Penguern, *Collignon, the grocer* Urbain Cancellier, *Joseph* Dominique Pinon, *Bretodeau, the box man* Maurice Benichou, *Gina* Clotilde Mollet, *Dufayel* Serge Merlin, *Lucien* Jamel Debbouze, *Amandine Poulain* Lorella Cravotta, *Amélie, eight years old* Flora Guiet, *the photo booth man* Ticky Holgado, Claude Perron, Michel Robin, Claire Maurier, Armelle, Jean Darie, Valérie Zarrouk, Isis Peyrade, with the voice of André Dussolier.
• *Dir* Jean-Pierre Jeunet, *Pro* Claudie Ossard, *Line Pro* Jean-Marc Deschamps, *Screenplay* Jean-Pierre Jeunet and Guillaume Laurant, *Ph* Bruno Delbonnel, *Pro Des* Aline Bonetto, *Ed* Hervé Schneid, *M* Yann Tiersen; Samuel Barber, Georges Delerue, Johann Strauss, *Costumes* Madeline Fontaine, *First assistant dir* Mathieu Jeunet.

UGC/Victoires/Tapioca Films/France 3 Cinéma/Canal Plus, etc-Momentum.
123 mins. France/Germany. 2001. Rel: 5 October 2001. Cert 15.

American Outlaws ★★¹⁄₂

A vapid fantasy, *American Outlaws* recasts the legend of the Jesse James Gang as a Robin Hood fairy tale, whipped extra frothy by the conventions of an American teen movie. As gun-toting quarterback we have Colin Farrell (who barely bothers to lose his Irish accent). He plays Jesse James, charming his way through a series of bank robberies with the Younger brothers in tow as part of a war against the rapacious plans of railway baron Thaddeus Rains. Eventually the gang becomes too successful for its own good and the mercenary lawman Allan Pinkerton (played with embarrassingly manic intensity by Timothy Dalton) is called in to terrorise them into submission. Meanwhile, there is dissension in the ranks as the James and Younger brothers succumb to their own rivalries. Since historical accuracy never mattered to begin with, you can guess how the duel between smalltown heroes and big industry ends. [Adam Keen]

• *Jesse James* Colin Farrell, *Cole Younger* Scott Caan, *Zee Mimms* Ali Larter, *Frank James* Gabriel Macht, *Jim Younger* Gregory Smith, *Thaddeus Rains* Harris Yulin, *Bob Younger* Will McCormack, *Ma James* Kathy Bates, *Allan Pinkerton* Timothy Dalton, *with* Ronny Cox, Terry O'Quinn, Nathaniel Arcand, Ty O'Neal, Barry Tubb, Muse Watson.
• *Dir* Les Mayfield, *Pro* Bill Gerber and James G. Robinson, *Ex Pro* Jonathan A. Zimbert, *Screenplay* Roderick Taylor and John Rogers, *Ph* Russell Boyd, *Pro Des* John Frick and Cary White, *Ed* Michael Tronick, *M* Trevor Rabin, *Costumes* Luke Reichle, *Historical consultant* Jack Lilley.

Morgan Creek Productions-Warner.
94 mins. USA. 2001. Rel: 14 December 2001. Cert 12.

American Pie 2 ★★★¹⁄₂

Despite booming careers for virtually every member of *American Pie*'s original cast, each one of them returns in *American Pie 2*. However, things don't quite click for everyone after a year away at college, so the boys rent a beach house and devote their energies to hosting the ultimate summer's end party. Along the way, we're treated to some of the sexual tomfoolery we've come to expect from this franchise. Originally pigeonholed as a *Porky's* for a new generation of sexually frustrated adolescents, *American Pie 2* leaps out of the teen-sex genre to become something quite special and unique. At first, the awkwardness of the characters is unsettling, as even the audience feels that something has changed between these friends. The realities of life, the nature of relationships, the fragility of friendships have all affected their interaction. But growing up doesn't mean the loss of youthful pleasures as our young friends set out to remind themselves, and us, that relationships don't have to end when they change, but can often grow in to something far more meaningful. An excellent script, genuine characters, and heartfelt performances make *American Pie 2* a surprising treat. [Scot Woodward Myers]

• *Jim Levinstein* Jason Biggs, *Nadia* Shannon Elizabeth, *Michelle Flaherty* Alyson Hannigan, *Chris 'Oz' Ostreicher* Chris Klein, *Jessica* Natasha Lyonne, *Kevin Myers* Thomas Ian Nicholas, *Vicky* Tara Reid, *Stifler* Seann William Scott, *Heather* Mena Suvari, *Finch* Eddie Kaye Thomas, *Mr Levinstein* Eugene Levy, *with* Chris Owen, Molly Cheek, Eli Marienthal, Casey Affleck, George Wyner, Larry Drake, Lee Garlington, Ernie Lively, Jack Wallace, J B Rogers, and (uncredited) Jennifer Coolidge.
• *Dir* James B Rogers, *Pro* Chris Moore, Craig Perry and Warren Zide, *Ex Pro* Adam Herz, Chris Weitz and Paul Weitz, *Screenplay* Adam Herz, *Ph* Mark Irwin, *Pro Des* Richard Toyon, *Ed* Larry Madaras and Stuart H. Pappe, *M* David Nessim Lawrence,

Billie Joe Armstrong, Tre Cool and Mike Dirnt; songs performed by Libra presents Taylor, Transmatic, American Hi-Fi, Hoi Polloi, Michelle Branch, Alien Ant Farm, Toilet Boys, Lit, Sum 41, Oleander, Lemonheads, Green Day, Lucia, etc, *Costumes* Alexandra Welker.

Liveplanet/Universal/Zilde/Perry Productions-UIP.
105 mins. USA. 2001. Rel: 12 October 2001. Cert 15.

America's Sweethearts ★★★¹/₂

Los Angeles/Nevada; the present. Eddie Thomas and Gwen Harrison are the hottest couple in Hollywood. Their joint vehicles *Autumn with Greg and Peg*, *Requiem for an Outfielder* and *Sasha and the Optometrist* have captured the hearts of America. However, since shooting their last movie together, the $86m *Time Over Time*, Gwen has fallen in love with a Spanish Lothario and Eddie has checked into a New Age 'wellness' clinic. Meanwhile, the eccentric, reclusive director of *Time Over Time* has taken 18 months to complete his picture and refuses to let the studio see it. So it's up to veteran publicist Lee Phillips to persuade Gwen and Eddie to attend the press junket and for studio boss Dave Kingman to make sure the film turns up… The funniest inside take on mainstream Hollywood since Albert Brooks' *The Muse*, *America's Sweethearts* may appeal more to film buffs than mainstream audiences but has enough good gags to please everybody. As producer, co-scenarist and co-star, Billy Crystal is on splendid form, raiding Hollywood's past with gleeful abandon (Alan Arkin's non sequitur-spouting guru recalls Peter Sellers in *Being There*). It's a shame that the characters never really come alive, although there's enough recognisable flotsam to give Tom Cruise and Nicole Kidman sleepless nights. Favourite line, spouted by John Cusack's Eddie Thomas: 'I'm a paranoid schizophrenic – I am my own entourage.'

• *Kiki Harrison* Julia Roberts, *Lee Phillips* Billy Crystal, *Gwen Harrison* Catherine Zeta-Jones, *Eddie Thomas* John Cusack, *Hector* Hank Azaria, *Dave Kingman* Stanley Tucci, *Hal Weidmann* Christopher Walken, *'wellness' guide* Alan Arkin, *Danny Wax* Seth Green, *Davis* Scot Zeller, *himself* Larry King, Steve Pink, Rainn Wilson, Keri Lynn Pratt, Maria Canals.
• *Dir* Joe Roth. *Pro* Billy Crystal, Donna Roth and Susan Arnold, *Ex Pro* Charles Newirth and Peter Tolan, *Screenplay* Billy Crystal and Peter Tolan, *Ph* Phedon Papamichael, *Pro Des* Garreth Stover, *Ed* Stephen A. Rotter, *M* James Newton Howard; songs performed by Kelly Levesque, Clara's Star, The Corrs, Mark Knopfler, Anoushka Shankar, The Eagles, Bekka Bramlett, Anika Moa, Geri Halliwell, and Hank Azaria, *Costumes* Ellen Mirojnick and (Ms Roberts' costumes) Jeffrey Kurland.

Revolution Studios/Face Prods/Roth/Arnold-Columbia TriStar.
103 mins. USA. 2001. Rel: 19 October 2001. Cert 12.

And Your Mother Too
See *Y Tu Mamá Tambien*

Angel Eyes ★★¹/₂

South Side Chicago; the present. Sharon Pogue (Jennifer Lopez) is a tough cop who buries herself in the violence of her job so as to avoid dealing with her unsatisfying personal life and rejection from her family. Catch Lambert is a local Good Samaritan who deals with his own 'issues' by helping people in the neighbourhood. When Catch rescues Sharon from a nearly fatal assault, the two connect and begin an unlikely romance. Director Luis Mandoki previously worked with writer Gerald Di Pego on *Message in a Bottle*. Though opting for the ultra-real violence of *Angel Eyes'* urban setting, the same tender issues are being explored here as in the 1999 film. Can people who've been broken by life and love manage to overcome their pain to build something meaningful in today's world? Sonia Braga seethes as Sharon's mother Josephine and sets an acting standard to which J-Lo can only aspire. [*Scot Woodward Myers*]

• *Sharon Pogue* Jennifer Lopez, *Catch Lambert* Jim Caviezel, *Larry Pogue Sr* Jeremy Sisto, *Robby* Terrence Howard, *Josephine Pogue* Sonia Braga, *Carl Pogue* Victor Argo, *Kathy Pogue* Monet Mazur, *with* Shirley Knight, Daniel Magder, Michael Cameron, Grant Nickalls, Eric Coates.
• *Dir* Luis Mandoki, *Pro* Bruce Berman, Mark Canton, Bernie Goldmann and Elie Samaha, *Ex Pro* Neil Canton, Don Carmody and Andrew Stevens, *Screenplay* Gerald Di Pego, *Ph* Piotr Sobocinski, *Pro Des* Dean Tavoularis, *Ed* Gerald B Greenberg, *M* Marco Beltrami and Julius Robinson, *Costumes* Marie-Sylvie Deveau, *Sound* Tim Walston.

Warner/Franchise Pictures/Morgan Creek/The Canton Company-Warner
103 mins. USA. 2001. Rel: 31 August 2001. Cert 15.

L'Anglaise et le duc
See *The Lady & the Duke*.

The Animal ★★¹/₂

After a nearly fatal car crash in the mountains, inept police file clerk Marvin (Rob Schneider) is saved through a series of transplants. Unfortunately, all the donor organs are from various animals. The replacement parts give him amazing abilities and he quickly becomes a local hero and paramour to innocent young Rianna (American *Survivor* star Colleen Haskell). Schneider's comedic versatility is the only thing that holds this simplistic, albeit charming, story together, although Haskell delivers an unexpectedly sweet performance.

FYI: Fellow *SNL* alum and lowbrow humour aficionado Adam Sandler (who was also behind Schneider's *Deuce Bigalow: Male Gigolo*) serves as executive producer.
[*Scot Woodward Myers*]

• *Marvin Mange* Rob Schneider, *Rianna* Colleen Haskell, *Sgt Doug Sisk* John C. McGinley, *Chief Wilson* Edward Asner, *Dr Wilder* Michael Caton, *Fatty* Louis Lombardi, *Miles* Guy Torry, *Bob Harris* Bob Rubin, *townie* Adam Sandler, *with* Pilar Schneider, Scott Wilson, Michael Papajohn, Sandy Gimpel, Norm MacDonald.
• *Dir* Luke Greenfield, *Pro* Barry Bernadi, Carr D'Angelo and Todd Garner, *Ex Pro* Adam Sandler and Jack Giarraputo, *Screenplay* Tom Brady and Rob Schneider, *Ph* Peter Lyons Collister, *Pro Des* Alan Au, *Ed* Jeff Gourson and Peck Prior, *M* Teddy Castellucci, *Costumes* James Lapidus.

Happy Madison/Revolution Studios-Columbia Tristar
83 mins. USA. 2001. Rel: 2 November 2001. Cert 12.

Animal Attraction ★★¹/₂

New York; the present. A talent booker for a popular TV talk show, Jane Goodale is swept off her feet by the show's dashing new executive producer. While the latter is in the middle of a three-year courtship with another woman, he breaks it off to commit to Jane. But he then gets cold feet and so, to exorcise her misery, Jane writes up her complaints in a glossy men's magazine. The column, written under the pseudonym of the septuagenarian 'Dr Marie Charles', becomes an unexpected success... It's interesting that a romantic comedy set in today's media could just as easily have been made 50 or even 60 years ago. Then, the wise-cracking best friend would have been played by Eve Arden, the debonair, vacillating cad by George Sanders and the romantic heroine by any number of emoting leading ladies. *Animal Attraction* certainly has the polish of those battle-of-the-sexes comedies of yore. Ashley Judd is, as always, eminently watchable and many of the lines are fab (Marisa Tomei: 'We must learn to be attracted to the men we are not attracted to'). Yet, in spite of the film's effortless affability, it now all seems rather irrelevant. Previously known as *Animal Husbandry* and, in the US, *Someone Like You*.

• *Jane Goodale* Ashley Judd, *Ray Brown* Greg Kinnear, *Eddie Alden* Hugh Jackman, *Liz* Marisa Tomei, *Diane Roberts* Ellen Barkin, *Evelyn* Laura Regan, *Alice* Catherine Dent, *Stephen* Peter Friedman, *Mary Lou Corkle* Donna Hanover, *Isabel*

Murielle Arden, *Rebecca* LeAnna Croom, *with* Matthew Coyle, Colleen Camp, Sabine Singh, Veronica Webb, Naomi Judd.
• *Dir* Tony Goldwyn, *Pro* Lynda Obst, *Ex Pro* Jim Chory, *Screenplay* Elizabeth Chandler, *Ph* Anthony B. Richmond, *Pro Des* Dan Leigh, *Ed* Dana Congdon, *M* Rolfe Kent; songs performed by Shelby Lynne, Madness, Annie Lennox, Taj Mahal, London Bus Stop, Van Morrison, Tom Jones and The Cardigans, and Wynnona Judd, *Costumes* Ann Roth and Michelle Maitlin.

Fox 2000 Pictures-Fox.
97 mins. USA. 2001. Rel: 20 July 2001. Cert 12.

Asoka ★★★★¹/₂

Internationally hailed as India's own *Gladiator*, this spectacular retelling of an ancient Hindu legend may actually be a better film. (Did Ridley's pic have a bouncy singalong Hindi soundtrack? I don't think so.) Director Santosh Sivan brings 20 years' experience as India's premier cinematographer to only his second feature film and delivers perhaps the most arresting images to come out of Bollywood all year. An epic romance based on the legend of an emperor-warrior from the 3rd century BC, the film follows Asoka on a journey to rediscover an inner harmony lost in the conquering bloodlust of his brutal campaigns. He meets and falls in love with an exiled princess and her little brother fleeing the intrigues of usurpers, becoming their saviour while hiding his true identity. Just before he can tell her the truth about himself he is called home to find he cannot so easily escape the darkness in his own soul. Sivan's fluid camerawork cools the fevered Bollywood dramatics, tempering what may otherwise have been a bloated sword-slasher wrapped around a syrupy tragi-romance. The narrative is usefully lightened by interludes from either a Greek chorus of buffoons or platoons of energetic dancers in musical routines Baz Luhrmann would kill for, helping it feel much shorter than its 180 minutes. [*Adam Keen*]

• *Asoka* Shahrukh Khan, *Kaurwaki* Kareena Kapoor, *Virat* Danny Denzongpa, *Susima* Ajit Kumar, *Bheema* Rahul Dev, *Devi* Hrishitaa Bhatt, *Emperor Chadragupta* Umesh Mehra.
• *Dir* Santosh Sivan, *Pro* Shahrukh Khan, *Ex Pro* Mark Burton, Sanjiv Chawla and Francis Thomas, *Screenplay* Saket Chaudhary, Santosh Sivan and Abbas Tyrewala, *Ph* Santosh Sivan, *Pro Des* Sabu Cyril, *Ed* A Sreekar Prasad, *M* Sandeep Chowta and Anu Malik, *Costumes* Manish Malhotra, Naresh Rohira and Anu Vardhan.

Arclightz and Filmz India-Enzo Pictures/Miracle Communications.
180 mins (full-length version). India. 2001. Rel: 26 October 2001. Cert 12.

At the Height of Summer ★★★¹⁄₂

Matrimonial infidelities, a secret double life and a rapport close to incest are among the problems confronted by the siblings – three sisters and a brother – in this family tale set in Hanoi. Since the writer/director is Tran Anh Hung, who made the visually ravishing *The Scent of Green Papaya*, it's not surprising that, as photographed by Mark Lee, this is the most sheerly beautiful film of recent times. In contrast, the plotting although acceptable, seems somewhat contrived and quite lacks the subtlety of the visuals. The scenes shared by the youngest sister and the brother work best, but as soap opera this is less telling by far than *A One and a Two*. Nevertheless, if art galleries give you pleasure this film will provide enchantment. Original title: *Mua he chieu thang dung*. [*Mansel Stimpson*]

• *Lien* Tran Nu Yen-Khe, *Suong* Nhu Quynh Nguyen, *Khanh* Le Khanh, *Hai* Quang Hai Ngo, *Quoc* Chu Hung, *Kien* Manh Cuong Tran, *Tuan* Le Tuan Anh.
• *Dir* and *Screenplay* Anh Hung Tran, *Pro* Christophe Rossignon, *Ph* Pin Bing Lee, *Pro Des* Benoit Barouh, *Ed* Mario Battistel, *M* Ton That Tiet, *Costumes* Susan Lu.

Hàng Phim Truyên/Lazennec Films/Canal Plus/Arte France Cinéma-Artificial Eye.
112 mins. Vietnam/France/Germany. 2000. Rel: 24 August 2001. Cert PG.

Atanarjuat: The Fast Runner ★★★★

This epic work echoes Robert Flaherty by showing a remote, unfamiliar environment through material which is partly anthropological documentary and partly a story enacted by non-professionals. Here the setting is a region close to the Arctic Circle and the film retells an Inuit legend. This involves not only a community seeking to cast out shamanistic evil spirits but a personal drama of rivalry over a woman leading to jealousy and revenge. Some have called this a masterpiece, but the narrative could sometimes be clearer, and some of the ritual and folklore go unexplained. Nevertheless, the film offers a remarkable experience and, making us share the lifestyle depicted, it proves special, being more than the sum of its parts. The film was shot on video but has been transferred to 35mm. [*Mansel Stimpson*]

• *Atanarjuat* Natar Ungalaaq, *Atuat* Sylvia Ivalu, *Oki* Peter-Henry Arnatsiaq, *Puja* Lucy Tulugarjuk, *Panikpak* Madeline Ivalu, *Qulitalik* Paul Qulitalik, *Sauri, the chief* Eugene Ipkarnak.
• *Dir* Zacharias Kunuk, *Pro* Paul Apak Angilirq, Norman Cohn and Zacharias Kunuk, *Screenplay* Paul Apak Angilirq, *Ph* Norman Cohn, *Pro Des* James Ungalaaq, *Ed* Norman Cohn, Zacharias Kunuk and Marie-Christine Sarda, *M* Chris Crilly.

Aboriginal Peoples Television Network/CTF License Fee Program/Canadian Film and Video Production Tax Credit/Canadian Government/Canadian Television (CTV)/Channel 24 Iglooik/Iglooik Isuma/National Film Board of Canada (NFB)/Telefilms Equity Investment Program/Vision Television-ICA Projects.
172 mins. Canada. 2000. Rel: 1 February 2002. Cert 15.

Atlantis: The Lost Empire ★★★¹⁄₂

Washington DC/North Atlantic; 1914. Repeatedly refused funding for his quest to find the lost city of Atlantis, linguist and cartographer Milo Thatch hands in his notice at the museum where he works. Just then he's contacted by a mysterious old man who has set up an expedition to explore the ocean around Iceland... Jettisoning such traditional Disney ingredients as talking animals and musical songs, *Atlantis* is a surprisingly straightforward cartoon that might have worked even better as a live-action spectacle. With the script's vivid characters and intriguing premise, it could've been *The Abyss* revisited by Ivan Reitman (now there's an intriguing thought), but ends up as a cross between *The Road to El Dorado* and *Titan A.E.* It seems odd that as animation becomes increasingly photo-realistic, Disney insists on producing such badly drawn characters and framing them with awe-inspiring backdrops. Here, though, the story is the thing, with heaps of good jokes and a number of memorable protagonists, not least James Garner's deliciously unscrupulous villain, Don Novello's sardonic explosives expert and Florence Stanley's world-weary Mrs Packard (whose catchphrase is 'We're all gonna die'). The high excitement factor is unusual for a summer Disney cartoon, although the death of the heroine's mother (before the story even starts) now seems to be a staple component.

• Voices: *Moliere* Corey Burton, *Helga* Claudia Christian, *Milo* Michael J Fox, *Rourke* James Garner, *Preston Whitmore* John Mahoney, *Dr Sweet* Phil Morris, *Atlantean king* Leonard Nimoy, *Vinny* Don Novello, *Audrey* Jacqueline Obradors, *Mrs. Packard* Florence Stanley, *Mr Harcourt* David Ogden Stiers, *young Kida* Natalie Strom, *Princess Kida* Cree Summer, *Cookie* Jim Varney; additional voices: Jim Cummings, Pat Pinney, Steve Barr.
• *Dir* Kirk Wise and Gary Trousdale, *Pro* Don Hahn, *Assoc Pro* Kendra Haaland, *Screenplay* Tab Murphy, *M* James Newton Howard, *Sound* Gary Rydstrom, *Artistic Coordination* Chris Jenkins, *Computer graphics* Kiran Joshi, *Linguistics* Marc Okrand.

Walt Disney Pictures-Buena Vista.
96 mins. USA. 2001. Rel: 19 October 2001. Cert U.

B

Baby Boy ★★¹/₂

Ten years on it seems that John Singleton is destined never to repeat the success of his feature debut *Boyz N the Hood*. His latest attempt is again set in South Central LA. It deals with an irresponsible 20-year-old (he has already fathered children by two women) and his relationship with his mother. She has a new man in her life, a one-time gangster, who is resented by her son. The broader themes of immaturity and responsibility take the film out of the self-created ghetto world of most recent black cinema but, disappointingly, its tone degenerates into melodrama; the script quality is variable and the ending schmaltzy. But the acting, with Ving Rhames taking the honours, is good enough, and the pace does not slacken. [*Mansel Stimpson*]

• *Jody* Tyrese Gibson, *Yvette* Taraji P Henson, *Sweetpea* Omar Gooding, *Peanut* Tamara LaSeon Bass, *Ms Herron* Candy Ann Brown, *Melvin* Ving Rhames, *Rodney* Snoop Doggy Dogg.
• *Dir, Pro* and *Screenplay* John Singleton, *Ex Pro* Dwight Williams, *Ph* Charles Mills, *Pro Des* Keith Brian Burns, *Ed* Bruce Cannon, *M* David Arnold, *Costumes* Ruth E Carter.

New Deal Productions/Columbia-Tristar
129 mins. USA. 2001. Rel: 23 November 2001. Cert 15.

Baise-moi ★¹/₂

After Nadine sees her only friend shot dead and Manu barely survives a brutal gang rape, the girls decide to exploit their mutual hatred of men. And so, empowered by their will to kill, the girls go on a rampage of sex, alcohol, cocaine and murder. For only in death can they experience the joy of living… A delirious, visually unprepossessing film shot on video and fuelled by hatred, *Baise-moi* is one of the most notorious works of its time. Featuring a pair of bona-fide porn actresses performing a series of real sex acts, the film does have an authentic edge, not to mention a sense of 'anything can happen next' spontaneity. It is also morally irresponsible, revelling in its sex, violence and ruthless misanthropy, gleefully painting all men as bastards, faggots and rapists. A really ugly experience.
English title: *Rape Me.*

• *Manu* Raffaëla Anderson, *Nadine* Karen Bach, *Severine* Delphine McCarty, *Karla* Lisa Marshall, *Alice* Estelle Isaac, *Martin* HPG, *architect* Marc Rioufol, *rapist* Philippe Houillez, *lady at cashpoint* Elodie Chérie, *Arsehole* Jean-Louis Costes.
• *Dir* and *Screenplay* Virginie Despentes and Coralie Trinh Thi, *Pro* Philippe Godeau and Alain Sarde, *Ph* Benoit Chamaillard and Julian Pamart, *Pro Des* Baudoin Capet, *Ed* Alio Auguste, Francine Lemaitre and Veronique Rosa, *M* Varou Jean, *Costumes* Isabelle Fraysse and Magali Baret.

Toute Première Fois/Canal Plus-Feature Film Company.
77 mins. France. 2000. Rel: 3 May 2002. Cert 18.

Bandits ★★★¹/₂

As bank robbers go, Terry Collins and Joe Blake are an unlikely double-act. Terry is a neurotic, lactose-intolerant, multi-phobic obsessive-compulsive intellectual with an irregular heart beat, tinnitus and a dread of antique furniture, Charles Laughton and black-and-white movies. In the words of Kate Wheeler, he is also 'smart and sweet'. Joe Blake is undergoing anger management and, in the words of Kate Wheeler, is 'handsome and assertive'. Together, they are the perfect man and as bandits they have become national celebrities, bypassing the mess of daylight robbery by taking the bank manager hostage the night before… Chemistry counts for a lot in the cinema and Bruce Willis, Billy Bob Thornton and Cate Blanchett provide it by the bucketload in this most engaging of crime comedies. With their appalling dress sense and polite demands on their victims, Blake and Collins are the stuff of celluloid iconolatry, but it is Ms Blanchett (an undervalued comic genius) who provides the spark in this three-way character caper.
FYI: The daughter of the first kidnapped bank manager (who reveals a noteworthy talent for belching at the dinner table) is played by Scout LaRue Willis, the real-life daughter of Bruce.

• *Joe Blake* Bruce Willis, *Terry Collins* Billy Bob Thornton, *Kate Wheeler* Cate Blanchett, *Harvey Pollard* Troy Garity, *Darill Miller* Brian F O'Byrne, *Cloe Miller* Stacey Travis, *Darren Head* Bobby Slayton, *Claire* January Jones, *Cheri* Azura Skye, *Mildred Kronenberg* Peggy Miley, *Charles Wheeler* William Converse-Roberts, *Lawrence Fife* Richard Riehle, *Sarah Fife* Micole Mercurio, *Phil* Anthony Burch, *Monica Miller* Scout LaRue Willis, *Erika Miller* Tallulah Belle Willis, Scott Burkholder, Sam Levinson, John Evans, Michael Birnbaum.
• *Dir* Barry Levinson, *Pro* Levinson, Michael Birnbaum, Michele Berk, Paul Weinstein, Ashok Amritraj, David Hoberman and Arnold Rifkin, *Ex Pro* Patrick McCormick, Harley Peyton and David Willis, *Screenplay* Harley Peyton, *Ph* Dante Spinotti, *Pro Des* Victor Kempster, *Ed* Stu Linder, *M* Christopher Young; songs performed by Bob Dylan, Jimmy Page and Robert Plant, Mindless Self Indulgence, Bonnie Tyler, In Bloom, Tanita Tikaram, Lucas Shine, Mark Knopfler, U2, Five For Fighting, Pete Yorn, Grover Washington Jr and Bill Withers, *Costumes* Gloria Gresham, *Sound* Chris Scarabosio.

MGM/Hyde Park Entertainment/Empire Pictures/Spring Creek Pictures/Cheyenne Enterprises-Fox.
122 mins. USA. 2001. Rel: 30 November 2001. Cert 12.

Right: A figure of fun: Russell Crowe as the ridiculed mathematician John Forbes Nash in Ron Howard's Oscar-winning *A Beautiful Mind* (from UIP)

Bangkok: Dangerous ★★★★

The Pang brothers bring sufficient style and assurance to their work to ensure that this thriller about a hit-man plays like a collaboration between John Woo and Wong Kar-Wei. Despite a plot which makes the hit-man a mute who comes to realise that he should turn his back on his trade, this is not to be taken seriously as a moral tale. Instead it's a tough thriller, well played, well photographed and well directed. If you don't like the genre, you won't be won over, but of its kind this is very good indeed. [*Mansel Stimpson*]

• *Kong* Pawalit Mongkolpisit, *Fon* Premsinee Ratanasopha, *Aom* Patharawarin Timkul, *Jo* Pisek Intrakanchit, *with* Korkiate Limpapat, Piya Boonak.
• *Dir, Screenplay* and *Ed* Oxide Pang Chun and Danny Pang, *Pro* Nonzee Nimibutr, *Ex Pro* Pracha Maleenont, Brian L Marcar and Adirek Wattaleela, *Ph* Decha Srimantra, *Pro Des* Wut Chaosilp, *M* Orange Music, *Costumes* Ekasith Meeprasertsakul.

Film Bangkok/Pang Brothers-Metro Tartan.
106 mins. Thailand. 2000. Rel: 22 February 2002. Cert 18.

Battle Royale ★★★

In the near future Japan is in a state of chaos, with ten million out of work and teenage delinquency at an all-time high. In an effort to curb the growing revolt against authority, the government initiates a very public deterrent: Battle Royale. Until teenagers get their act together, the state will take a randomly selected class of school children, deposit them on a deserted island and submit them to an assault course in which only one can survive. With an explosive monitor locked to their throats, the children have three days to kill each other – or be killed... Sometimes, it seems, a director will make a film purely to test the moral fibre of his critics. Banned outright in the US, this brutal shotgun marriage of *Lord of the Flies* and *Series 7* seems to take sadistic delight in showing pretty 15-year-old schoolgirls shot to pieces – or just stabbed, gutted and sliced. In one scene a schoolboy is saved by his bullet-proof vest, only to be summarily decapitated and then, with a grenade lodged in his mouth, his head used as a human bomb. You get the drift. As a work of visceral power, the film has few equals, but its morality is highly questionable, even if it is intended as an allegorical fable.

• *Shuya Nanahara* Tatsuya Fujiwara, *Noriko Nakagawa* Aki Maeda, *Shogo Kawada* Taro Yamamoto, *Kitano* Beat Takashi, *Kazuo Kiriyama* Masanobu Ando, *Hiroki Sugimura* Sosuke Takaoka.
• *Dir* and *Screenplay* Kinji Fukasaku, based on the novel by Koshun Takami, *Pro* Masao Sato, Masumi Okada, Teruo Kamaya and Tetsu Kayama, *Ex Pro* Ikuro Takano, *Ph* Katsumi Yanagijima, *Pro Des* Kyoko Heya, *Ed* Hirohide Abe, *M* Masamichi Amano, *Original paintings* Takeshi Kitano.

Toei Co.-Metro Tartan.
113 mins. Japan. 2000. Rel: 14 September 2001. Cert 18.

A Beautiful Mind ★★★★

John Forbes Nash Jr, one of the most influential mathematicians of the 20th century, was not like other men. Obsessed by the concept of equilibrium, he distanced himself from his fellow students at Princeton, yet could not find an application for his genius. Then he had the temerity to propose a new game theory that threatened to demolish the accepted wisdom of 150 years... Eccentric, wayward geniuses are always good fodder for a movie, whether it's Dustin Hoffman playing an autistic savant in *Rain Man* or Matt Damon a mathematical prodigy in *Good Will Hunting*. Here, Russell Crowe's Nash is a little bit of both, a man whose directness and honesty, if not his social graces, are both disarming and commendable. Crowe has a field day as the shuffling, confused wunderkind and is well matched by Jennifer Connelly as the strong, outspoken love interest (she is an actress who just gets better and better). Indeed, this is really an actors' film, with several of the cast members

required to age into layers of latex. The script, by veteran scenarist Akiva Goldsman (*The Client*, *A Time to Kill*), is equally accomplished, bringing a potent humanity to the rarefied world of mathematics. If only it hadn't gone on for so long.

• *John Forbes Nash Jr* Russell Crowe, *William Parcher* Ed Harris, *Alicia Larde* Jennifer Connelly, *Charles Herman* Paul Bettany, *Sol* Adam Goldberg, *Helinger* Judd Hirsch, *Hansen* Josh Lucas, *Bender* Anthony Rapp, *Dr Rosen* Christopher Plummer, *Marcee* Vivien Cardone, *Governor* Roy Thinnes, Jason Gray-Stanford, Austin Pendleton, Cheryl Howard, Rance Howard, Josh Pais.
• *Dir* Ron Howard, *Pro* Howard and Brian Grazer, *Ex Pro* Karen Kehela and Todd Hallowell, *Screenplay* Akiva Goldsman, *Ph* Roger Deakins, *Pro Des* Wynn Thomas, *Ed* Mike Hill and Dan Hanley, *M* James Horner; 'All Love Can Be' sung by Charlotte Church, *Costumes* Rita Ryack, *Dialect coach* Judi Dickerson.

DreamWorks/Universal/Imagine Entertainment-UIP.
135 mins. USA. 2001. Rel: 22 February 2002. Cert 12.

Before You Go ★★★½

Following the death of their mother, three sisters convene for the impending funeral and confront the ghosts of their childhood. However, each sibling has her own interpretation of the past and deals with her grief in her own way. The eldest, Teresa, does the hoovering and chants a mantra of recipes, Mary embarks on a dialogue with her mother's ghost and Catherine smokes her way through a small harvest of marijuana... A dramatic comedy that explores the four stages of grief – disbelief, anger, denial and acceptance – *Before You Go* is a faintly old-fashioned but insightful and frequently hilarious diversion. Adapted by Shelagh Stephenson from her own stage play, *The Memory of Water*, the film is enlivened by another peerless performance from Julie Walters, supplemented by a wry one from Tom Wilkinson as her world-weary husband (drawing on an eloquent 'repertoire of silences'). Here, the family skeletons don't so much drop out of the cupboard as jump out screaming, but they do so with a vivid wealth of human truth.
FYI: Lewis Gilbert, who also brought *Alfie*, *Educating Rita* and *Shirley Valentine* to the big screen, was 81 years old when he directed this.

• *Teresa* Julie Walters, *Mike* John Hannah, *Mary* Joanne Whalley, *Catherine* Victoria Hamilton, *Violet* Patricia Hodge, *Frank* Tom Wilkinson, *Father Cunningham* Dermot Crowley, *with* Hugh Ross, Theo Fraser Steel, John Biggins, Eoin O'Callaghan, Raquel Cassidy, Malcolm Rogers.
• *Dir* Lewis Gilbert, *Pro* Eoin O'Callaghan, *Ex Pro* Clive Brill, Tom Treadwell, Steve Christian and Nigel Green, *Screenplay* Shelagh Stephenson, *Ph* Nic

Above : John Hannah and Tom Wilkinson ponder the skeletons in the family cupboard in *Before You Go* (Entertainment)

Baines, *Ed* Alistair Waterson, *M* Shriek Music, *Costumes* B Marx and Chas, *Choreography* Sean Fernandez.

Late Night Pictures/Angel Eye Films-Guerilla Films. 84 mins. UK. 2001. Rel: 7 June 2002. Cert 15.

Behind Enemy Lines ★★★¹/₂

Seven years in the US Navy and aviator Lt Chris Burnett has never seen a single day of active combat. Then, while on a routine reconnoitre over Bosnia-Herzegovina, his F-18 is shot down by a rebel Serbian outfit. Now his admiral has his hands tied by international red tape and Chris Burnett is left to fight his own war – on his own… *Behind Enemy Lines* is so damned exciting and so superbly shot that you can't help but forgive its many failings. Working from a formulaic and corny script welded onto a topical canvas, ex-cameraman and commercials director John Moore exhibits a genuine flair for action, owing an obvious debt to *Saving Private Ryan*. With its muted colours and rugged terrain (Slovakia standing in for Bosnia-Herzegovina), the film does look terrific, although it would have been even better had the producer put a restraining order on Moore's more acrobatic camerawork. As for the acting, Hackman turns in another sterling performance as the old school admiral neutered by protocol, while Owen Wilson is refreshingly human as the soldier forced into heroism.
NB. This is not to be confused with either the Hal Holbrook or David Carradine films of the same name.

• *Lt Chris Burnett* Owen Wilson, *Admiral Reigart* Gene Hackman, *Admiral Piquet* Joaquim De Almeida, *O'Malley* David Keith, *Lokar* Olek Krupa, *Jeremy Stackhouse* Gabriel Macht, *Rodway* Charles Malik Whitfield, *Sasha, the tracker* Vladimir Mashkov, Marko Igonda, Eyal Podell, Geoff Pierson, Kamil Kollárik, Salaudin Bilal, Leon Russom, Vladimir Oktavec, Lucia Srncova, Daniel Margolius.
• *Dir* John Moore, *Pro* John Davis, *Ex Pro* Stephanie Austin and Wyck Godfrey, *Co-Pro* T Alex Blum, *Screenplay* David Veloz and Zak Penn, from a story by James Thomas and John Thomas, *Ph* Brendan Galvin, *Pro Des* Nathan Crawley, *Ed* Paul Martin Smith, *M* Don Davis; songs performed by Compufonic, Ray Charles, Johnny Reno, Feeder, Dion, Orion, Fluke, and Ryan Adams, *Costumes* George L Little, *Sound* Craig Berkey.

Twentieth Century Fox/Davis Entertainment-Twentieth Century Fox.
105 mins. USA. 2001. Rel: 4 January 2002. Cert 12.

Behind the Sun ★★¹/₂

In 1998, the documentary filmmaker Walter Salles directed the poetic, haunting and uncompromising *Central Station*, a picture that went on to win two Oscar

Morrisa, *Pro Des* Jon Bunker, *Ed* John Wilson, *M* Debbie Wiseman, *Costumes* Candy Paterson.

Entertainment/Capitol Films/Arkangel Prods/Isle of Man Film Commission/Pacificus/Big Fish Films-Entertainment. 95 mins. UK. 2002. Rel: 21 June 2002. Cert 15.

Beginner's Luck ★★

London/Edinburgh/Paris; the 1980s. Resolved to take an experimental version of *The Tempest* on tour, aspiring impresario Mark Feinman forms the Vagabond Theatre Company – with disastrous results… An inconsistent, shambolic and almost hallucinogenic homage to bad theatre (shot on a camcorder), *Beginner's Luck* is woefully short of the good fortune it needs. Brave, yes, and even occasionally witty, the film ultimately falls foul of its perversely personal agenda. [*Ewen Brownrigg*]

• *Anya* Julie Delpy, *Bob* Steven Berkoff, *Andrew Fontaine* Christopher Cazenove, *Aunt Emily* Fenella Fielding, *Javaad* Jean Yves Bertolot, *Mark Feinman* James Callis, *Jason Keritos* Tom Redhill, *with* Rosanna Lowe, Sarah Belcher, Amelia Lowdell, Debbie Chazen, Alexander Armstrong, Chris Smith, Ralph Spall, Sam Callis, Harriet Evans-Lombe, Martin Jarvis, John Bennett, Mike Shannon, Nick Cohen, David Cohen.
• *Dir* and *Screenplay* Nick Cohen and James Callis, *Pro* Harriet Evans-Lombe, *Co-Pro* Richard Osborne and James Harding, *Ph* Chris Preston, *Art Dir* Tracey Ann

Left: Antsy Semitism: Ryan Gosling as a Jew in conflict in Henry Bean's difficult, thought-provoking *The Believer* (from Pathé)

nominations and countless international trophies (including the best film award at Berlin). For his follow-up, Salles steps back in time and narrows his focus to a stretch of parched countryside in the Brazilian badlands. Here, a sugarcane farmer, his wife and two sons toil in the broiling heat to eke out a spartan living. It was not always thus: in the old days they had slaves and a large family, but a bloody, generations-old feud with a rival family has taken its toll. In spite of its potentially grim subject matter, *Behind the Sun* is little more than a lyrical vignette, an inconsequential celluloid poem that is a constant pleasure to the eye, although somewhat underwhelming in its emotional impact. Definitely a step down from *Central Station*, then.
Original title: *Abril despedaçado.*

• *Father* José Dumont, *Tonio* Rodrigo Santoro, *Mother* Rita Assemany, *Salustiano* Luiz Carlos Vasconcelos, *Pacu* Ravi Ramos Lacerda, *Clara* Flavia Marco Antonio, *old blind man* Everaldo Pontes, *Ferreira boy* Vinícius de Oliveira.
• *Dir* Walter Salles, *Pro* Arthur Cohn, *Screenplay* Salles, Sérgio Machado and Karim Aïnouz, inspired by the novel *Broken April* by Ismail Kadaré, *Ph* Walter Carvalho, *Pro Des* Cassio Amarante, *Ed* Isabelle Rathery, *M* Antonio Pinto, Ed Côrtes and Beto Villares, *Costumes* Cao Albuquerque.

Videofilmes/Haut et Court/Bac Films/Dan Valley-Buena Vista. 92 mins. Brazil/Switzerland/France. 2001. Rel: 8 March 2002. Cert 12.

Beijing Bicycle ★★¹/₂
Beijing, today. A country boy seeks employment in the city but is deprived by theft of the bicycle necessary for

his work, a fact which leads him into a feud with street kids including the youngster who has purchased the stolen bike… There's great location shooting and the film has won awards, but the first third is quite overshadowed by the masterpiece it resembles, *Bicycle Thieves.* Later developments echo a more recent movie, the Iranian *Children of Heaven,* and the film's intended comment on the divide between rich and poor gets lost in the escalating feud which renders the characters unappealing. Improbabilities in the storyline add to the sense of disappointment, despite the efforts of the cast.
Original title: *Shi qi sui de dan che.*
[*Mansel Stimpson*]

• *Guei* Cui Lin, *Jian* Li Bin, *Qin* Zhou Xun, *Xiao* Gao Yuanyuan, *Da Huan* Li Shuang, *father* Zhao Yiwei, *mother* Pang Yan.
• *Dir* Wang Xiaoshuai, *Pro* Peggy Chiao and Hsu Hsaio-Ming, *Screenplay* Wang Xiaoshuai, Tang Danian, Peggy Chiao and Hsu Hsaio-Ming, *Ph* Liu Jie, *Art Dir* Tsai Chao-Yi and Cao Anjun, *Ed* Liao Ching-Song, *Costumes* Pang Yan, *Sound* Tu Duu-Chih.

Arc Light Films/Pyramide Prods/Beijing Film Studio, etc-Metro Tartan.
113 mins. Taiwan/France/China. 2001. Rel: 28 June 2002. Cert PG.

The Believer ★★★¹/₂
There are some truths in the human condition that are a given. A man loves his children, fears death and hates Jews. It just is. So says Danny Balint, a well-read, enraged 22-year-old who opens this disturbing examination of the nature of Judaism by kicking the shit out of a timid Jewish student on a New York

street. Sporting a swastika T-shirt and shaven head, Danny preaches anti-Semitism with his fists and aspires to encourage the killing of Jews by airing his views at right-wing soirées and a neo-Nazi boot camp. But Danny harbours a terrible secret – he is himself a Jew… Condemned by the Simon Wiesenthal Centre as 'a primer for anti-Semitism', *The Believer* was denied a theatrical release in the US in spite of winning the Grand Jury prize at Sundance. Yet the film is a ferociously intelligent, deeply personal exploration of the contradictions of the Jewish faith, is written and directed by a Jew and demands to be seen – and extensively discussed. Both the scenes of physical brutality and the desecration of a synagogue pull no punches, but the director, Henry Bean, backs up his portrayal of anti-Semitism with some valid soul-searching. Much like his protagonist – who is based on a real person, a Jewish member of the Ku Klux Klan – Bean displays a deep-seated, passionate ambiguity towards his faith.

• *Danny Balint* Ryan Gosling, *Carla Moebius* Summer Phoenix, *Drake* Glenn Fitzgerald, *Billings* Garret Dillahunt, *Carleton* Kris Eivers, *Lina Moebius* Theresa Russell, *Curtis Zampf* Billy Zane, Joel Garland, Joshua Harto, Tommy Nohilly, Ronald Guttman, Heather Goldenhersh, Elizabeth Reaser, *Ilio Manzetti* Henry Bean.
• *Dir* and *Screenplay* Henry Bean, from a story by Bean and Mark Jacobson, *Pro* Christopher Roberts and Susan Hoffman, *Ex Pro* Jay Firestone, Adam Haight, Daniel Diamond and Eric Sandys, *Line Pro* Kimberly Fajen, *Ph* Jim Denault, *Pro Des* Susan Block, *Ed* Mayin Lo and Lee Percy, *M* Joel Diamond, *Costumes* Alex Alvarez and Jennifer Newman, *Yom Kippur Davener/Jonah* Sasha Weiss.

Fireworks Pictures/Peter Hoffman/Fuller Films-Pathé. 98 mins. USA. 2001. Rel: 7 December 2001. Cert 15.

Bend it Like Beckham ★★★¹/₂

Southall, West London; today. Jess Bhamra not only worships David Beckham and loves playing football, she is an extremely talented player. But Jess comes from a traditional Indian family, where appearance and honour is far more important than the pursuit of one's own selfish dreams. Besides, football is a man's sport, innit? … A sort of *East is East* meets *Billy Elliot* via *Gregory's Girl*, this is about as feelgood as contemporary films about Britain can get. Applying more gloss than on her previous pictures, *Bhaji on the Beach* and *What's Cooking?*, the Kenyan-born, Southall-raised Gurinder Chadha has concocted a breezy, delightful and charming comedy that juggles its many elements with some aplomb. True, there is an element of predictability in the story arc and the accent of the lovely Keira Knightley fluctuates from Cheltenham to Chigwell, but this film is not pretending to provide

anything other than a great time. Good, too, to see Juliet Stevenson turning in such a finely honed comic performance, while the soundtrack of Western pop standards given an Indian twist is a real bonus.

• *Jess Bhamra* Parminder Nagra, *Jules Paxton* Keira Knightley, *Joe* Jonathan Rhys Meyers, *Mr Bhamra* Anupam Kher, *Pinky Bhamra* Archie Panjabi, *Mel* Shaznay Lewis, *Alan Paxton* Frank Harper, *Paula Paxton* Juliet Stevenson, *Mrs Bhamra* Shaheen Khan, *Tony* Ameet Chana, *with* Poojah Shah, Paven Virk, Preeya Kalidas, Trey Farley, Saraj Chaudry, Imran Ali, Kulvinder Ghir, Gary Lineker, Alan Hansen, John Barnes, Adlyn Ross, Shobu Kapoor, Zohra Segal, Balwant Kaur Chadha, Sheran Chadha.
• *Dir* Gurinder Chadha, *Pro* Chadha and Deepak Nayar, *Ex Pro* Ulrich Felsberg, Russel Fischer, Simon Franks, Zygi Kamasa and Haneet Vaswani, *Screenplay* Chadha, Guljit Bindra and Paul Mayeda Berges, *Ph* Jong Lin, *Pro Des* Nick Ellis, *Ed* Justin Krish, *M* Craig Pruess; songs performed by Gunjan, B21, Nusrat Fateh Ali Khan, Backyard Dog, Basement Jaxx, Curtis Mayfield, Amar, Melanie C, Blondie, Victoria Beckham, Shaznay Lewis, Bally Sagoo, Texas; Bina Mistry, Parminder Nagra, Keira Knightley, Archie Panjabi, Ameet Chana, Gurinder Chadha, Paul Berges and Craig Pruess, etc, *Costumes* Ralph Holes.

Kintop Pictures/Film Council/Filmfoerderung Hamburg/BskyB/British Screen/HelkonSK/The Works/Future Film Financing/Roc Media/Road Movies/National Lottery-Helkon SK. 112 mins. UK. 2001. Rel: 12 April 2002. Cert 12.

Betty Fisher and Other Stories ★★

The story of Betty Fisher, previously explored in the 1988 British film *Tree of Hands* (also adapted from the Ruth Rendell novel), is a compelling one. Betty Fisher, a successful first-time novelist, lives on her own with her young son, Joseph, in the Paris suburbs. When her mother comes to stay, childhood wounds are opened up and allowed to haemorrhage when tragedy strikes. Then new stories are drawn into the equation, throwing the film off course. Had Claude Miller had the courage of a Robert Altman or Paul Thomas Anderson to build up a dramatic mosaic from the start, then *Betty Fisher* may have had something to work with. As it is, the film lacks style and pace, not to mention a single sympathetic character. Deprived of suspense and humour, it wanders off into a variety of different directions, losing momentum as it goes.
Original title: *Betty Fisher et autres histoires.*

• *Betty Fisher* Sandrine Kiberlain, *Margot Fisher* Nicole Garcia, *Carole Novacki* Mathilde Seigner, *François Diembélé* Luck Mervil, *Alex Basato* Éduoard Baer, *Edouard* Stephane Freiss, *René the Canadian* Yves Jacques, *Dr Jérôme Castang* Roschdy Zem, *José*

Left: Movie mendacity: Frankie Muniz tries to get a credit in Shawn Levy's breezy, lowbrow *Big Fat Liar* (from UIP)

Novacki Alexis Chatrian, *with* Michael Abiteboul, Arthur Setbon, Yves Verhoeven.
• *Dir* and *Screenplay* Claude Miller, *Pro* Annie Miller and Yves Marmion, *Ex Pro* Annie Miller and Claire Barrau, *Ph* Christophe Pollock, *Pro Des* Jean-Pierre Kohut Svelko, *Ed* Véronique Lange, *M* François Dompierre; J S Bach, Chopin, *Costumes* Jacqueline Bouchard.

UGCYM/Les Films de la Boissière/Go Films/France 2 Cinéma/Canal Plus, etc-Optimum Releasing.
103 mins. France/Canada. 2001. Rel: 14 June 2002. Cert 15.

Big Fat Liar ★★

A compulsive liar and under-achiever, 14-year-old Jason Shepherd is ordered to knock out a creative writing assignment if he doesn't want to repeat his academic year. On the way to school with his paper, titled *Big Fat Liar*, he is knocked down by a limousine, given a lift and then leaves his paper behind in the car. Some time later, Jason sees his story up on the big screen… Aimed squarely at kids weaned on American TV, this lowbrow, OTT and predictable take on Hollywood corruption is both satirically blunt and curiously old-fashioned. Nevertheless, it is halfway redeemed by a performance of malodorous amorality by Paul Giamatti (as a predatory producer) and is steered along at an agreeable clip by first-time director Shawn Levy. [*Ewen Brownrigg*]

• *Jason Shepherd* Frankie Muniz, *Marty Wolf* Paul Giamatti, *Kaylee* Amanda Bynes, *Monty Kirkham* Amanda Detmer, *Frank Jackson/Kenny Trooper*

Donald Faison, *Vince* Lee Majors, *Mrs Caldwell* Sandra Oh, *with* Russell Hornsby, Michael Bryan French, Christine Tucci, John Gatins, Pat O'Brien, Sandy Gimpel, Shawn Levy.
• *Dir* Shawn Levy, *Pro* Michael Tollin and Brian Robbins, *Ex Pro* Michael Goldman, *Co-Pro* Marie Cantin, *Screenplay* Dan Schneider, from a story by Schneider and Robbins, *Ph* Jonathan Brown, *Pro Des* Nina Ruscio, *Ed* Stuart Pappe and Kimberly Ray, *M* Christopher Beck, *Costumes* Sanja Milkovic Hays.

Universal/Mediastream Film-UIP.
88 mins. USA. 2002. Rel: 28 June 2002. Cert PG.

Biggie and Tupac ★★★★★

Nick Broomfield's latest documentary feature is fascinating. It's a model of lucidity in its presentation of complex facts as Broomfield, an on-screen presence and narrator, investigates two murders, the killings of the actor-rapper Tupac Shakur and the rap-singer Biggie Smalls (aka Christopher Wallace and The Notorious B.I.G.) in 1996 and 1997 respectively. The film not only suggests that these unsolved cases involved police corruption but points to the man who could have been responsible for their deaths. In portraying the victims without whitewash and by assembling so clearly and convincingly a case to answer, Broomfield has created an important document and it's surely his best work to date. Furthermore, despite the serious nature of the project, the behaviour of those interviewed provides some memorably amusing episodes. [*Mansel Stimpson*]

Right: Gang related: The Notorious B.I.G. and Tupac Shakur pose for the camera in Nick Broomfield's cogent social document, *Biggie and Tupac* (from Optimum Releasing)

• *Dir* Nick Broomfield, *Pro* Michele D'Acosta, *Ex Pro* Georgea Blakey and Barney Bloomfield, *Ph* Joan Churchill, *Ed* Mark Atkins and Jaime Estrada, *M* Christian Henson, *Sound* Mark Rozett.

Lafayette Film/Channel 4-Optimum Releasing. 108 mins. UK. 2001. Rel: 24 May 2002. Cert 15.

Birthday Girl ★★¹/₂

John Buckingham, a mild-mannered bank clerk, is having trouble with ants, his car and his love life. As a solution to his last predicament, he advertises for a bride on the Internet and ends up with another problem: Nadia. She is not the girl he expected: she chain-smokes, throws up and appears to know only one word of English: 'Yes.' Then, on her birthday, her two vodka-swigging cousins turn up to stay… Of course, any film starring Nicole Kidman as a Russian cannot be taken too seriously. Yet any film starring Nicole Kidman is bound to have its pleasures. Even so, the leggy, scrubbed-down siren looks oddly out of place in English suburbia, like a purebred Palomino roped into a fourth-rate circus. The problem, though, is not Nicole – she looks and acts fabulous, all staring eyes and thick, guttural indignation; it's the script. The story is seriously under-developed, while John Buckingham, the put-upon Everyman we are meant to root for, is a one-dimensional cliché. By attempting to dazzle us with its surprise twists and madcap humour, the film forgets to provide its characters with any rooting in reality. The result is not so much silly as just plain sketchy.

• *Nadia* Nicole Kidman, *John Buckingham* Ben Chaplin, *Alexei* Vincent Cassel, *Yuri* Mathieu Kassovitz, *Clare* Kate Evans, *Karen* Sally Phillips,

with Stephen Mangan, Xander Armstrong, Jo McInnes, Ben Miller, Rebecca Clarke, Mark Gatiss.
• *Dir* Jez Butterworth, *Pro* Steve Butterworth and Diana Phillips, *Ex Pro* Paul Webster, Julie Goldstein, Colin Leventhal and Sydney Pollack, *Line Pro* Donna Grey and Vicki Popplewell, *Screenplay* Tom Butterworth and Jez Butterworth, *Ph* Oliver Stapleton, *Pro Des* Hugo Luczyc-Wyhowski, *Ed* Christopher Tellefsen, *M* Stephen Warbeck, *Costumes* Phoebe De Gaye.

FilmFour/HAL Films/Mirage Enterprises-FilmFour. 93 mins. UK/Australia. Rel: 28 June 2002. Cert 15.

Black Hawk Down ★★★¹/₂

Mogadishu, Somalia; 2-3 October 1993. As General Mohammed Aidid, the rebel leader of Somalia, turns the hunger of his people into a weapon to fuel his power, US Rangers and a Delta commando unit join forces to root out two of Aidid's lieutenants in the Somalian capital. However, what starts off as a routine assignment is immeasurably complicated when a US Black Hawk helicopter is shot down in the centre of the city. What follows is a horrendously bloody conflict as thousands of committed, heavily armed supporters of Aidid launch a bombardment on their foreign aggressors... In the tradition of *Saving Private Ryan*, *Black Hawk Down* dramatises a moment of military history with the accent on flesh-shattering, eardrum-blowing realism. As a history lesson and yet another vision of the unconscionable brutality of war, it is second to none. Furthermore, it captures the chaos and total confusion of warfare, albeit producing the unfortunate side-effect of distancing the viewer from the substantial number of faceless cast members. Yet, while the story may lack a human dimension and most of the characters are hard

Left: Naughty but Nyssa: Leonar Varela provides some sex appeal in Guillermo del Toro's occasionally exciting if pre-dictable *Blade II* (from Entertainment)

to tell apart, this is a superb piece of filmmaking that keeps the heart pounding for two-and-a-quarter hours.

• *Ranger Staff Sergeant Matt Eversmann* Josh Hartnett, *'Hoot' Gibson* Eric Bana, *Grimes* Ewan McGregor, *McKnight* Tom Sizemore, *Sanderson* William Fichtner, *Major General Garrison* Sam Shepard, *Nelson* Ewen Bremner, *Kurth* Gabriel Casseus, *Wex* Kim Coates, *Schmid* Hugh Dancy, *Durant* Ron Eldard, *Blackburn* Orlando Bloom, *Yurek* Thomas Guiry, *Busch* Richard Tyson, *Steele* Jason Isaacs, *Beales* Ioan Gruffud, *Struecker* Brian Van Holt, *Atto* George Harris, Danny Hoch, Charlie Hofheimer, Zeljko Ivanek, Matthew Marsden, Glenn Morshower, Jeremy Piven, Enrique Murciano, Brendan Sexton, Johnny Strong, Nikolaj Coster-Waldau, Ian Virgo, Thomas Hardy, Chris Beetem, Razaaq Adoti, Treva Etienne, Boyd Kestner.
• *Dir* Ridley Scott, *Pro* Scott and Jerry Bruckheimer, *Ex Pro* Simon West, Mike Stenson, Chad Oman and Branko Lustig, *Assoc Pro* Terry Needham and Harry Humphries, *Screenplay* Ken Nolan, based on the book by Mark Bowden, *Ph* Slawomir Idziak, *Pro Des* Arthur Max, *Ed* Pietro Scalia, *M* Hans Zimmer; songs performed by Badawi, Omar Sharif, Elvis Presley, Rachid Taha, Alice in Chains, Days of the New, Denez Prigent and Lisa Gerrard, House of Pain, Stone Temple Pilots, Faith No More, Stevie Ray Vaughan, Joe Strummer and the Mescaleros, and BHD Band, *Costumes* Sammy Howarth-Sheldon and David Murphy, *Military Adviser* Harry Humphries.

Revolution Studios/Jerry Bruckheimer Films/Scott Free-Columbia TriStar.
135 mins. USA. 2001. Rel: 18 January 2002. Cert 15.

Blade II ★★¹/₂

Half-man, half-vampire, Blade is a 'day-walker' who continues his quest to rid the world of full-blooded bloodsuckers. He is then offered a truce by Nyssa, daughter of his arch enemy, the vampiric overlord Damaskinos. It transpires that a new strain of vampire has emerged – the 'Reaper' – that preys on fellow vampires. So, reluctantly it has to be said, Blade joins the formerly hostile Blood Pack and heads for the Czech Republic… An exercise in frenetic action and posturing cool, *Blade II* gamely struggles to pump new blood into this limited franchise. With the aid of Hong Kong choreographer Donnie Yen, the film certainly has exciting moments, although its basic recycling of the original's template is more than a tad tiresome. [*Charles Bacon*]

• *Blade* Wesley Snipes, *Abraham Whistler* Kris Kristofferson, *Reinhardt* Ron Perlman, *Nyssa* Leonar Varela, *Scud* Norman Reedus, *Damaskinos* Thomas Kretschmann, *with* Luke Goss, Matthew Schulze, Danny John Jules, Tony Curran, Pete Lee Wilson.
• *Dir* Guillermo del Toro, *Pro* Peter Frankfurt, Wesley Snipes and Patrick Palmer, *Ex Pro* Lynn Harris, Michael De Luca, David S Goyer, Toby Emmerich, Stan Lee and Avi Arad, *Screenplay* Goyer, *Ph* Gabriel Beristain, *Pro Des* Carol Spier, *Ed* Peter Amundson, *M* Marco Beltrami and Danny Saber, *Costumes* Wendy Partridge, *Visual effects* Nicholas Brooks, *Fight choreographer* Donnie Yen.

New Line Cinema/Amen Ra/Imaginary Forces-Entertainment.
117 mins. USA. 2002. Rel: 29 March 2002. Cert 18.

The Body ★

When a Palestinian discovers a tomb beneath his hardware store, the 2000-year-old occupant appears to have been crucified. Sent by the Vatican to make sure that the body is not that of Christ, Jesuit priest Matt Gutierrez clashes with Israeli archaeologist Sharon Golban. Then both he and she come under fire from Palestinian gunmen, Orthodox Jews and the corrupt hand of the Vatican itself… After a promising beginning, *The Body* quickly succumbs to the clichés of the international thriller as innumerable opportunities to confront its serious issues are thrown out the window. While poorly cast and thematically shallow, the film's greatest crime is its implausibility and exploitative irreverence. [*Charles Bacon*]

• *Father Matt Gutierrez* Antonio Banderas, *Sharon Golban* Olivia Williams, *Moshe Cohen* John Shrapnel, *Father Pierre Lavelle* Derek Jacobi, *Father Walter Winstead* Jason Flemyng, *Cardinal Pesci* John Wood, *Nasir Hamid* Makhram J Khoury, *with* Vernon Dobtcheff, Ian McNeice, Muhamed Bakri.
• *Dir* and *Screenplay* Jonas McCord, from the novel by Richard Ben Sapir, *Pro* Rudy Cohen, *Ex Pro* Diane Sillan Isaacs, Werner Koenig, Mark Damon

and Moshe Diamant, *Ph* Vilmos Zsigmond, *Pro Des* Allan Starski, *Ed* Alain Jakubowicz, *M* Serge Colbert, *Costumes* Caroline Harris.

MDP Worldwide Entertainment/Helkon Media AG/Green Moon Prods-Metrodome.
108 mins. USA/Germany. 2000. Rel: 9 November 2001. Cert 12.

Brotherhood of the Wolf ★★¹/₂

France; 1766. Following the savage killings of countless women and children by an unseen wolf-like creature, King Louis XV dispatches Grégoire de Fronsac to the remote, densely wooded area. A naturalist, artist and all-round Renaissance man, Fronsac is accompanied by a Mohawk Iroquois Indian, Mani, whom he befriended while in 'New France'. Together, the unconventional duo resolve to unravel the mystery of the pre-Revolutionary terror... A hybrid of genres vacuum-packed into one indigestible mass, this really is a welter of missed opportunities. From the opening homage to *Jaws* (nubile beauty thrust across the screen by an unseen force), the film gallops with panache into territory already well mapped by Hammer, Made in Hong Kong, *Eyes Wide Shut*, a number of historical French epics and, finally, *The Wizard of Oz*. Over-produced, over-baked, over-wrought but seemingly never over (it stretches to almost two-and-a-half hours), *Brotherhood of the Wolf* is as visually accomplished as it is silly.
FYI: Between the years 1765-1768, the region of Gèvaudan in south-central France really was subjected to the indiscriminate attacks of an unidentified 'beast', which was apparently responsible for the deaths of over 100 locals.
Original title: *Le Pacte des loups*.

• *Grégoire de Fronsac* Samuel Le Bihan, *Jean François de Morangias* Vincent Cassel, *Marianne de Morangias* Emilie Dequenne, *Sylvia* Monica Bellucci, *Marquis Thomas d'Apcher* Jérémie Renier, *Mani* Marc Dacascos, *Thomas Agé* Jacques Perrin, *Henri Sardis* Jean-François Stévenin, *Mme de Morangias* Edith Scob, *Count de Morangias* Jean Yanne, Bernard Farcy, Johan Leysen, Hans Meyer, Virginie Darmon, Jean-Loup Wolff [!], Bernard Fresson, Karin Kriström, Virginie Arnaud, Franckie Pain.
• *Dir* Christophe Gans, *Pro* Samuel Hadida and Richard Grandpierre, *Line Pro* Claude Albouze, *Screenplay* Stephane Cabel, *Ph* Dan Lautsen, *Pro Des* Guy Claude François, *Ed* Sébastien Prangère, David Wu and Xavier Loutreuil, *M* Joseph Lo Duca and Robby Gall, *Costumes* Dominique Borg, *Stunts* Philip Kwok, *Creature* Jim Henson's Creature Shop.

Davis Film/Eskwad/Canal Plus/TF1 Films/Studio Images, etc-Pathé.
134 mins. France. 2001. Rel: 19 October 2001. Cert 15.

The Brothers ★★★

Four charming and highly successful African-American men try to balance their careers, love lives and inexorable journey towards maturity amidst vengeful exes, marital ennui and the seemingly never-ending search for 'Miss Right'… Former TV scribe Gary Hardwick dubbed this movie *Refusing to Exhale* and it shows in several of the more contrived scenes. Exposing his roots in what could easily have been an entire season of a television sitcom, the film-maker makes his expertise work to his advantage. And so we get 22 episodes' worth of material lovingly abbreviated to just under two hours. [*Scot Woodward Myers*]

• *Jackson Smith* Morris Chestnut, *Derrick West* D L Hughley, *Brian Palmer* Bill Bellamy, *Terry White* Shemar Moore, *Denise Johnson* Gabrielle Union, *Cherie Smith* Tatyana Ali, *Louise Smith* Jenifer Lewis, *with* Clifton Powell, Marla Gibbs, Vanessa Bell Calloway, Kimberly Scott, *T-Boy* Gary Hardwick.
• *Dir* and *Screenplay* Gary Hardwick, *Pro* Paddy Cullen and Darin Scott, *Ex Pro* Doug McHenry, *Ph* Alexander Gruszynski, *Pro Des* Amy B Ancona, *Ed* Earl Watson, *M* Eric Benet, *Costumes* DeBrae Little.

Reachfar Films, Inc/Screen Gems, Inc-Columbia TriStar.
102 mins. USA. 2001. Rel: 28 September 2001. Cert 15.

Bully ★★★

Broward County, South Florida; the present. With unparalleled access to drugs, alcohol, pornography, casual sex, rap music and violent video games, a group of teenagers hang out and routinely pollute their minds and morals. However, Bobby Kent, the product of a strict middle-class family, is worse than the rest, subjecting his lifelong best friend, Marty, to unprovoked abuse and regularly raping his female acquaintances. So Bobby's friends plot to kill him… Exploring the nihilistic lifestyle of a circle of aimless teenagers, Larry Clark, the director of *Kids* and *Another Day in Paradise*, once again plumbs the lower depths of a society that obviously fascinates him. Here, he pushes his restless camera even deeper into the crevices of his acne-dappled protagonists, as if such physical proximity can expose an even greater truth. But, while co-scenarist David McKenna observes that Jim Schutze's source novel, *Bully: A True Story of High School Revenge*, explains how such repugnant and irrational acts of violence can arise, Clark fails to convey this in cinematic terms. Instead, the director switches to a dystopian black comedy that actually cloaks the real frustration and misery that informs the lives of these desperate people. All the same, *Bully* is disturbing and thought-provoking stuff. Based on real events.

• *Mario 'Marty' Puccio* Brad Renfro, *Alice 'Ali' Willis* Bijou Phillips, *Lisa Connelly* Rachel Miner, *Donny Semenec* Michael Pitt, *Heather Swallers* Kelli Garner, *Derek Kaufman, the hitman* Leo Fitzpatrick, *Bobby Kent* Nick Stahl, *Claudia* Nathalie Paulding, *Derek Dzvirko* Daniel Franzese, *with* Jessica Sutta, Edward Amatrudo, Steven Raulerson, *Derek Kaufman's father* Larry Clark.
• *Dir* Larry Clark, *Pro* Chris Hanley, Fernando Sulichin and Don Murphy, *Ex Pro* Jordan Gertner, Mark Mower, Manuel Cheche, Arnaud Duteuil, Vincent Maraval and David McKenna, *Assoc Pro* Brad Renfro, *Screenplay* Zachary Long (aka David McKenna) and Roger Pullis, *Ph* Steve Gainer, *Pro Des* Linda Burton, *Ed* Andrew Hafitz, *M* Howard Paar; songs performed by J T Money and Sole, Dillinger & Young Gotti, Tricky, Dr Dre and Eninem, Smut Peddlers, Cypress Hill, Fatboy Slim, Zoë Poledouros, etc, *Costumes* Carleen Ileana Rosado.

Canal Plus/Lions Gate/Muse/Blacklist Films/Gravity Entertainment-FilmFour.
112 mins. USA. 2001. Rel: 1 March 2002. Cert 18.

The Business of Strangers ★★½

In the impersonal landscape of an airport terminal, Julie Styron, a middle-aged businesswoman, conducts a crucial meeting in the absence of her new assistant, Paula, who is late. Firing Paula on the spot, Julie then discovers that she has been promoted to chief executive officer. On her next encounter with Paula, Julie takes a more conciliatory approach to the girl, then finds herself drawn into an extraordinary night of psychological powerplay… Stockard Channing and Julia Stiles are both fantastic actresses and it's great to see them firing off each other. However, it's a shame that Patrick Stettner's directorial debut amounts to nothing more than an actors' showcase. Stagey and stilted, the film never once drifts into anything resembling real life and even ends on a highly predictable note. Nonetheless, it is beautifully shot and at times exudes an almost surreal hypnotism.

• *Julie Styron* Stockard Channing, *Paula Murphy* Julia Stiles, *Nick Harris* Frederick Weller, *Robert* Marcus Giamatti, *with* Mary Testa, Jack Hallett, Buddy Fitzpatrick.
• *Dir* and *Screenplay* Patrick Stettner, *Pro* Susan A Stover and Robert H Nathan, *Ex Pro* Scott McGehee and David Siegel, *Assoc Pro* Ramsey Fong, *Ph* Teo Maniaci, *Pro Des* Dina Goldman, *Ed* Keiko Deguchi, *M* Alexander Lasarenko, *Costumes* Kasia Walicka Maimone and Dawn Weisberg.

i5 Films/Headquarters/Sundance-Momentum Pictures.
83 mins. USA. 2001. Rel: 3 May 2002. Cert 15.

C

Cats & Dogs ★★★

As absent-minded Professor Brody attempts to create a vaccine that counteracts man's allergy to dogs, cats around the world conspire to stop him. Armed with hi-tech surveillance systems and state-of-the-art weaponry, the feisty felines declare open war on caninekind... *Cats & Dogs* would make a great trailer. Actually, *Cats & Dogs* did make a good trailer – and that's largely the problem with this entertaining, facile and cynical film. Playing on the audience's affection for our four-legged friends, it takes a great concept and runs with it. There are some fine tackles along the way, even a few good goals, but this is not a championship match. As the homo sapiens, Jeff Goldblum and Elizabeth Perkins make a believable married couple, although, as human beings, they are mere ciphers. The cats, though, are wonderful, particularly a heavily armed Ninja from Russia and the pampered white Persian Mr Tinkles, whose cute, puffy features belie the megalomaniac evil lurking within. A concept movie with great effects and some genuine laughs, *Cats & Dogs* forgets to engage on a more essential, even human level.

• *Professor Brody* Jeff Goldblum, *Mrs Brody* Elizabeth Perkins, *Sophie* Miriam Margolyes, *Scott Brody* Alexander Pollock, *Mr Mason* Myron Natwick, *Mrs Calvert* Doris Chillcott.
Voices: *Lou* Tobey Maguire, *Butch* Alec Baldwin, *Mr Tinkles* Sean Hayes, *Ivy* Susan Sarandon, *Peek* Joe Pantoliano, *Sam* Michael Clarke Duncan, *Calico* Jon Lovitz, *mastiff* Charlton Heston, *Russian Kitty* Glenn Ficarra, Victor Wilson, Salome Jens, Paul Pape.
• *Dir* Lawrence Guterman, *Pro* Andrew Lazar, Christopher DeFaria, Warren Zide and Craig Perry, *Ex Pro* Bruce Berman, Chris Bender and J C Spink, *Co-Pro* and *Screenplay* John Requa and Glenn Ficarra, *Ph* Julio Macat, *Pro Des* James Bissell, *Ed* Michael A Stevenson and Rick W Finney, *M* John Debney, *Visual effects* Ed Jones.

Warner/Village Roadshow/NPV Entertainment/Mad Chance-Warner.
87 mins. USA/Australia. 2001. Rel: 3 August 2001. Cert PG.

The Centre of the World ★★½

In spite of his virtual isolation from the human race, computer engineer Richard Longman feels that he is at the centre of the world. Already a multi-millionaire in his early twenties, he can access the stock exchange, order pizza or browse the net for live porn at the flick of a mouse. However, Richard craves real human contact and offers a stripper $10,000 to join him on a three-day break in Las Vegas. Agreeing to the latter's terms of no kissing or penetration, he looks forward to an instant relationship replete with sex... Motivated by movies like *I Am Curious Yellow* and *Last Tango in Paris*, Wayne Wang wanted to bring the sex film into the computer age. Confronting such issues as fantasy and role-playing, the director rips the comfortable sheen off the air-brushed sexuality promoted by *Playboy* and its ilk and presents a very real scenario of carnal immediacy, complete with all its illusions and frustrations. Shooting on digital video and coaxing extraordinarily honest performances from his stars, Wang does create an aura of queasy spontaneity. However, the conclusions he draws are terribly simplistic, while Richard, for all his sweet intentions, is a most unsympathetic dolt.

• *Florence* Molly Parker, *Richard Longman* Peter Sarsgaard, *Jerri* Carla Gugino, *taxi driver* Pat Morita, *Brian Pivano* Balthazar Getty, Shane Edelman, Alisha Klass, Mel Gorham, Jason McCabe Calacanis.
• *Dir* Wayne Wang, *Pro* Wang and Peter Newman, *Ex Pro* Greg Johnson and Ira Deutchman, *Co-Pro* Francey Grace, Heidi Levitt and Andrew Loo, *Screenplay* Ellen Benjamin Wong, from a story by Wang, Miranda July and Siri Hustvedt, *Ph* Mauro Fiore, *Pro Des* Donald Graham Burt, *Ed* Lee Percy, *M* songs performed by Laika, Robbie Robertson, Joe Henry, Nicky Love, Euphoria, Bob Holroyd, Suba, etc, *Costumes* Sophie de Rakoff Carbonell.

Artisan Entertainment/Redeemable Features-Momentum.
88 mins. USA. 2001. Rel: 21 September 2001. Cert 18.

Charlotte Gray ★★★

England/France; 1943-45. Determined to make a difference in the war effort, Charlotte Gray signs up with the government's Special Operations Executive. Secretly, she hopes to find her lover, an RAF pilot lost in France. But when she joins the French Resistance herself, she finds her emotional priorities dramatically adjusted... In the tradition of such wartime romances as *The English Patient* and *Captain Corelli's Mandolin*, *Charlotte Gray* is a sumptuously filmed, impeccably crafted and largely articulate contemplation of the currency of emotion under fire. Adapted from the best-selling novel by Sebastian Faulks, it does, though, lack cinematic thrust – in spite of spectacular scenery and Dion Beebe's fluid camerawork. The drama is also undercut by irregularity in the accents – the Australian Cate Blanchett plays a Scotswoman, the American Billy Crudup and English Michael Gambon are Frenchmen – creating a certain distance from reality. In the end, *Charlotte Gray* falls down because it fails to convince – or to move – even though it is replete with small, telling moments.

Left: 'Allo, 'Allo: Cate Blanchett brings considerable class to Gillian Armstrong's chocolate boxy look at the French Resistance in *Charlotte Gray* (from FilmFour)

• *Charlotte Gray* Cate Blanchett, *Julien Levade* Billy Crudup, *Levade* Michael Gambon, *Peter Gregory* Rupert Penry-Jones, *Renech* Anton Lesser, *Mirabel* Ron Cook, *Richard Cannerly* James Fleet, *Daisy* Abigail Cruttenden, *Sophie, the telephonist* Rosanna Lavelle, *Pichon* Jack Shepherd, *with* Charlotte McDougall, Tom Goodman-Hill, Hugh Ross, Nicholas Farrell, Miranda Bell, Lewis Crutch, Matthew Plato, Victoria Scarborough, David Birkin, Gillian Barge, Helen McCrory, John Benfield, John Bennett, Wolf Kahler.
• *Dir* Gillian Armstrong, *Pro* Sarah Curtis and Douglas Rae, *Ex Pro* Paul Webster, Robert Bernstein and Hanno Hutch, *Co-Pro* Elinor Day and Catherine Kerr, *Assoc Pro* Cathy Lord, *Screenplay* Jeremy Brock, *Ph* Dion Beebe, *Pro Des* Joseph

Right: 'God bless us, every one!' A scene from Jimmy T Murakami's work-manlike, uninspired *Christmas Carol The Movie* (from Pathé)

Bennett, *Ed* Nicholas Beauman, *M* Stephen Warbeck, *Costumes* Janty Yates, *Dialogue coach* Joan Washington.

FilmFour/Senator Film/Ecosse Film/Pod Films-Film Four. 121 mins. UK/Australia. 2001. Rel: 22 February 2002. Cert 15.

Christmas Carol The Movie ★★¹/₂

Boston, Massachusetts; 1867. In America on a lecture tour, Charles Dickens regales a New England audience with his story of a hard-hearted moneylender called Ebenezer Scrooge... There is just one sequence that recalls the lyrical resonance of the director's award winning short *The Snowman* (1982). Set to the song 'Quis est Deus', performed with technical expertise by Charlotte Church, the scene eschews the slick draughtsmanship of Disney & co, resembling an animated painting by Chagall, complete with pastel shading. Sadly, the rest of the film is nowhere near as distinctive, its drawings being rudimentary caricatures, apparently modelled on the work of Daumier and Gustave Doré. Only the power of the original story remains, although even this has been tampered with.

• Voices: *Scrooge/Charles Dickens* Simon Callow, *Belle* Kate Winslet, *Ghost of Christmas Past* Jane Horrocks, *Ghost of Christmas Present* Michael Gambon, *Bob Cratchit* Rhys Ifans, *Mrs Cratchit/Mother Gimlet* Juliet Stevenson, *Jacob Marley* Nicolas Cage, *Old Joe* Robert Llewellyn, *Fred*

Iain Jones, *Fezziwig* Colin McFarlane, *Fan* Beth Winslet, *Dr Lambert* Arthur Cox.
• *Dir* Jimmy T Murakami, *Pro* Iain Harvey, *Ex Pro* Nik Powell and Rainer Mockert, *Screenplay* Robert Llewellyn and Piet Kroon, *Ed* Taylor Grant, *M* Julian Nott; songs performed by Kate Winslet, Charlotte Church, etc.

Pathé/The Film Consortium/Illuminated Films/Scala/MBP/Film Council/FilmFour-Pathé. 80 mins. UK/Germany. 2001. Rel: 7 December 2001. Cert U.

La Ciénaga ★★

The 35-year-old filmmaker Lucrecia Martel spent much of her teens filming her large family. Here, in her feature debut, she creates a tapestry of dissolute family life, as various cousins, siblings and nieces and nephews hang out at a rundown estate in rural Argentina. With the constant rumble of thunder on the soundtrack and gloating close-ups of sweat-daubed flesh, Martel rustles up an almost palpable atmosphere of humidity and apprehension, but seems content to provide little else. *La Ciénaga* is certainly a moody and picturesque portrait of contemporary Argentina, but a more disciplined narrative would have made it more accessible. Amazingly, Martel took five years to realise this project, not that you'd think it. US title: *The Swamp*.

• *Tali* Mercedes Moran, *Mecha* Graciela Borges, *Gregorio* Martin Adjemian, *Joaquin* Diego Baenas,

Momi Sofia Bertolotto, *José* Juan Cruz Bordeu, *Isabel* Andrea Lopez.
• *Dir* and *Screenplay* Lucrecia Martel, *Pro* Lita Stantic, *Line Pro* Marta Parga, *Ph* Hugo Colace, *Pro Des* Graciela Oderigo, *Ed* Santiago Ricci.

Lita Stantic/4K Films/Cuatro Cabezas Films-ICA Projects.
100 mins. Argentina/Spain. 2000. Rel: 5 October 2001. No Cert.

The Circle ★★★★¹/₂

This remarkable Iranian film finds Jafar Panahi, director of *The White Balloon*, portraying in the most vivid way imaginable the position of women in that country.

Linked episodes rather than fully-fledged stories show us this patriarchal society where giving birth to a female child is tantamount to disgrace. It's done through the eyes of women, including three recently detained in prison. But the film doesn't offer special pleading for special cases; it's about the experience of being a woman in Iran today. Using hand-held cameras and a skilled application of natural sounds to convey atmosphere, Panahi makes viewers of both sexes identify with his central female characters and share their world. It's a minor flaw that a late sequence involving the arrest of a prostitute is less telling than what precedes it, but, for the rest, this is great filmmaking allied to pertinent social comment, the importance of which is self-evident.
Original title: *Dayereh*.
[*Mansel Stimpson*]

• *Nargess* Nargess Mamizadeh, *Arezou* Maryiam Palvin Almani, *Prostitute* Mojgan Faramarzi, *Nurse* Elham Saboktakin, *Ticket Seller* Monir Arab, *Solmaz* Solmaz Panahi, *Pari* Fereshteh Sadr Orfani.
• *Dir* and *Pro* Jafar Panahi, *Screenplay* Kambuzia Partovi, based on an idea by Panahi, *Ph* Bahram Badakshani, *Art Dir* Iraj Raminfar, *Ed* Jafar Panahi.

Jafar Panahi Film Productions/Lumiere & Company/Mikado-Artificial Eye.
90 mins. Iran/Italy/Switzerland. 2000. Rel: 21 September 2001. Cert PG.

The Closet ★★★¹/₂

François Pignon is divorced from the woman he loves, his 17-year-old son is avoiding him and now he's been fired from his accountancy job of 20 years. Then, in an act of flamboyant genius, François' new neighbour anonymously sends his company some compromising photographs, manipulated images which leave no doubt that François is gay. The ruse works a treat – how can a company whose main product is condoms fire its only homosexual employee? However, François

suddenly has a lot to live up to… As a contemplation of homosexuality in contemporary society, *The Closet* is surprisingly naïve, if not provincial, and often feels like it was made 20 years ago. Nevertheless, that doesn't prevent it from being very funny, with heterosexual attitudes towards homosexuality being satirised rather than gayness itself. And as farce it is everything it should be: tight, nimble and ingeniously contrived, buoyed by some splendid comic playing from Gérard Depardieu, Jean Rochefort and, of course, the peerless Daniel Auteuil.
Original title: *La Placard*.

• *François Pignon* Daniel Auteuil, *Félix Santini* Gérard Depardieu, *Guillaume* Thierry Lhermitte, *Mlle Bertrand* Michèle Laroque, *Belone* Michel Aumont, *Kopel, Company Director* Jean Rochefort, *Christine* Alexandra Vandernoot, *Franck* Stanislas Crevillén, *Ariane* Armelle Deutsch, *Madame Santini* Michèle Garcia, *with* Edgar Givry, Thierry Ashanti, Laurent Gamelon, Vincent Moscato, Irina Ninova, Marianne Groves, Philippe Vieux.
• *Dir* and *Screenplay* Francis Veber, *Pro* Alain Poiré, *Ph* Luciano Tovoli, *Art Dir* Hugues Tissander, *Ed* Georges Klotz, *M* Vladimir Cosma, *Costumes* Jacqueline Bouchard.

Gaumont/EFVE Films/TF1 Films/Canal Plus-Optimum Releasing.
85 mins. France. 2001. Rel: 17 May 2002. Cert 15.

Collateral Damage ★★

When his wife and young son are killed in a terrorist bomb attack on the Colombian consulate in Los Angeles, fireman Gordon Brewer decides to take the law into his own hands. Discovering the identity of the anarchist responsible, Brewer slips into the Colombian jungle to mete out justice… The problem with *Collateral Damage* is that it takes itself so seriously. If you're going to cast Arnold Schwarzenegger as an avenging fireman, you must feed your audience some token crumbs of self-parody. After all, it was Arnie, in *Commando*, who took on a South American army of rebels single-handedly (and won). Here, 16 years on, he stumbles into the Colombian jungle like a bull elephant in a Wedgwood store and is neither convincing as an Everyman nor as an all-American. And there are some dreadful inconsistencies. At various points the rebels bark out dialogue in Spanish, accompanied by subtitles, at other times the Spanish is left unlabelled, and at others the protagonists revert to English and then back again to Spanish. It is this complete disregard for logic that disarms the film at very turn, and which the undistinguished direction of Andrew Davis fails to overcome. Incidentally, the original release of *Collateral Damage* was suspended 'indefinitely' after the events of 11 September 2001.

• *Gordon Brewer* Arnold Schwarzenegger, *Brandt* Elias Koteas, *Selena* Francesca Neri, *Claudio aka 'The Wolf'* Cliff Curtis, *Felix* John Leguizamo, *Armstrong* John Turturro, *Phipps* Miguel Sandoval, *Anne Brewer* Lindsay Frost, *Matt Brewer* Ethan Dampf, *with* Harry Lennix, Raymond Cruz, Jack Conley, Todd Allen, Bruce Ramsay, Nicholas Pryor, J Kenneth Campbell, Pedro Damian, Jay Acovone.
• *Dir* Andrew Davis, *Pro* Steven Reuther and David Foster, *Ex Pro* Hawk Koch and Nicholas Meyer, *Screenplay* David Griffiths and Peter Griffiths, from a story by Ronald Roose, David Griffiths and Peter Griffiths, *Ph* Adam Greenberg, *Pro Des* Philip Rosenberg, *Ed* Dennis Virkler and Dov Hoenig, *M* Graeme Revell, *Sound* Tim Walston, *Military adviser* Stan Goff.

Warner/Bel-Air Entertainment-Warner.
109 mins. USA. 2001. Rel: 5 April 2002.
Cert 15.

The Colour of Lies ★★★★

Less elegant than *Merci pour le chocolat* but with much more compelling characters, this is the best of recent Chabrol. Sandrine Bonnaire plays the wife of a painter (Jacques Gamblin) whose career is in decline. Despite a brief adulterous encounter with a TV personality (Antoine de Caunes), she stands by her husband when, as an outsider in a Breton community, he is suspected of strangling a child. Although the police investigation propels the narrative, the film is also a clever study of various forms of lying (the TV star's bogus persona, lying through what is not said, lying to oneself). In addition it supplies an unexpectedly subtle answer to a big question (do we really know the person we live with?). Not enough impact for a masterpiece, but highly satisfying nevertheless.
Original title: *Au coeur du mensonge.*
[*Mansel Stimpson*]

• *Viviane Sterne* Sandrine Bonnaire, *René Sterne* Jacques Gamblin, *Germain-Roland Desmot* Antoine de Caunes, *Frederique Lesage* Valeria Bruni Tedeschi, *Inspecteur Loudin* Bernard Verley, *Yvelyne Bordier* Bulle Ogier, *Regis Marchal* Pierre Martot.
• *Dir* Claude Chabrol, *Pro* Marin Karmitz, *Screenplay* Claude Chabrol and Odile Barski, *Ph* Eduardo Serra, *Pro Des* Françoise Benoit-Fresco, *Ed* Monique Fardoulis, *M* Matthieu Chabrol, *Costumes* Corinne Jorry.

France 3 Cinéma/Canal Plus/MK2 Productions-Cinéfrance.
113 mins. France. 1998. Rel: 13 July 2001.
Cert 15.

Comédie de l'innocence ★★

Paris; today. On his ninth birthday Camille reveals his suspicions that Ariane is not his mother. Disturbed by her son's behaviour, Ariane agrees to take him to the house where, he believes, his real mother lives. There, a retired violin teacher, Isabella, embraces Camille as if he was hers... With an intriguing premise if ever there was one, *Comédie de l'innocence* is a handsomely crafted, well-acted mystery that becomes mired in its own improbabilities. Nobody behaves as they would in real life, yet the film is nothing if not naturalistic. Meanwhile, Jorge Arriagada's discordant music alerts the viewer to a more sinister agenda, which seems hardly necessary. An element of humour would have reaped dividends and might have wiped the pretentiousness off the face of this silly, self-important indulgence.
Aka *The Son of Two Mothers.* **English title:** *Comedy of Innocence.*

• *Ariane d'Orville* Isabelle Huppert, *Isabella Stirner* Jeanne Balibar, *Serge* Charles Berling, *Camille d'Orville* Nils Hugon, *Laurence* Edith Scob, *Pierre d'Orville* Denis Podalydes, *Hélène* Laure de Clermont-Tonnerre, *Martine* Chantal Bronner.
• *Dir* Raoul Ruiz, *Pro* Martin de Clermont-Tonnerre, *Screenplay* Ruiz and Françoise Dumas, from the novel *Il Figlio di due Madri* (*The Boy With Two Mothers*) by Massimo Bontempelli, *Ph* Jacques Bouquin, *Pro Des* Bruno Beaugé, *Ed* Mireille Hannon, *M* Jorge Arriagada, *Costumes* Nathalie Raoul.

MACT Prods/TFI International/Les Films du Camelia/Canal Plus/CNC/Procirep-Artificial Eye.
98 mins. France. 2000. Rel: 8 March 2002. Cert PG.

Comment j'ai tué mon père ★★★

A great cast – Bouquet, Berling, Natacha Régnier from *The Dream Life of Angels* – raises the highest hopes for this French tale of a father/son relationship (the title indicates not a thriller but a Freudian view of a child's need to break free of a father's influence). Unfortunately, writer-director Fontaine adopts an oblique approach as the successful but materialistic Jean-Luc is confronted by the father who, although an idealist, deserted his family. The latter may be a ghost or a figure of fantasy – it's up to us. Good performances and a satirical take on the bourgeoisie hardly compensate for the lack of involvement and the absence of any clear viewpoint: it gets by, but it's never memorable.
US title: *The Way I Killed My Father.*
[*Mansel Stimpson*]

• *Maurice* Michel Bouquet, *Jean-Luc* Charles Berling, *Isa* Natacha Regnier, *Myriem* Amira Casar, *Patrick* Stephane Guillon, *Jean-*

Toussaint Hubert Kounde, *with* François Berleand, Karole Rocher, Marie Micla, Jean-Christophe Lemberton.

• *Dir* Anne Fontaine, *Pro* Philippe Carcassonne, *Screenplay* Fontaine and Jacques Fieschi, *Ph* Jean-Marc Fabre, *Pro Des* Sylvain Chauvelot, *Ed* Guy Lecorne, *M* Jocelyn Pook; Andrzej Panufnik, *Costumes* Corinne Jorry.

Ciné B/Cinéa/France 2 Cinéma/Canal Plus-Pathé. 98 mins. France/Spain. 2001. Rel: 28 June 2002. Cert 15.

Cool and Crazy ★★★¹/₂

For two thirds of its length this is a highly engaging documentary which, recording the success of a male-voice choir in a remote coastal community, emerges with a distinctively Norwegian tone. Pleasant though the music is, it's the frank comments of those involved, many of them elderly, which make this a memorable human document often marked by humour. But, if singing becomes something that gives life value, much as stripping did for the men in *The Full Monty*, you feel that a full-length feature ought to find time to ask what the women think of

being left out of it. A trip by the singers to Murmansk extends the film, but doesn't help to justify its length by providing further insights.
Original title: *Heftig og begeistret.*
[*Mansel Stimpson*]

• *Dir* Knut Erik Jensen, *Pro* Tom Remlov and Jan-Erik Gammleng, *Ph* Aslaug Holm and Svein Krøvel, *Ed* Aslaug Holm.

Barentsfilm AS/Giraff Film/Norsk Film-Artificial Eye. 105 mins. Norway/Sweden/Finland. 2000. Rel: 8 February 2002. Cert 15.

The Count of Monte Cristo ★★¹/₂

No sooner has he been promoted to captain than the French sailor Edmond Dantes is accused of treason and imprisoned in the formidable Chateau d'If. It transpires that his best friend, Fernand Mondego, jealous of his beautiful fiancée and of his promotion, has betrayed him to the unscrupulous magistrate of Marseilles. So Dantes, with plenty of time on his hands, plots his revenge… To do Alexandre Dumas' story justice you really need a good three hours and Kevin Reynolds, who brought us the overblown *Robin Hood: Prince of Thieves*, does the material few favours

Above: Papa was a rolling stone: Natacha Régnier and Charles Berling contemplate parental indifference in Anne Fontaine's dull and uninvolving *Comment j'ai tué mon père* (from Pathé)

Right: Sex, lies and haute couture: Guy Pearce asks Dagmara Dominczyk where he can purchase a bonnet like hers, in Kevin Reynolds' stodgy *The Count of Monte Cristo* (from Buena Vista)

with his clunky, uninspired direction. He is not helped by Edward Shearmur's mundane, intrusive score, nor by Jim Caviezel's bland interpretation of Dantes, the latter robbing the film of a sympathetic – or credible – hero for whom to root. Still, this is a ripping good yarn and after the halfway mark the story kicks in, with the sweet lubricant of revenge oiling the final hour. The tongue-in-cheek dialogue ('God isn't in France at this time of year') also helps. Filmed in Ireland and Malta.

FYI: Edmond Dantes has previously been played on screen by James O'Neill (1913), John Gilbert (1922), Robert Donat (1934), Louis Hayward (1940 and 1946), Jean Marais (1954), Louis Jourdan (1961) and Richard Chamberlain (1975).

• *Edmond Dantes* Jim Caviezel, *Fernand Mondego* Guy Pearce, *Abbe Faria* Richard Harris, *Mercedes* Dagmara Dominczyk, *Jacopo* Luis Guzman, *Villefort* James Frain, *Albert* Henry Cavill, *Danglar* Albie Woodington, *Dorleac* Michael Wincott, *Napoleon Bonaparte* Alex Norton, *with* Christopher Adamson, Patrick Godfrey, Katherine Holme, Freddie Jones, Helen McCrory.
• *Dir* Kevin Reynolds, *Pro* Roger Birnbaum, Gary Barber and Jonathan Glickman, *Ex Pro* Chris Brigham, *Screenplay* Jay Wolpert, *Ph* Andrew Dunn,

Pro Des Mark Geraghty, *Ed* Stephen Semel and Chris Womack, *M* Edward Shearmur, *Costumes* Tom Rand, *Dialect coach* Lilene Mansell.

Touchstone Pictures/Spyglass Entertainment/Birnbaum/ Barber/Irish Film Industry-Buena Vista. 131 mins. USA/UK/Ireland. 2001. Rel: 19 April 2002. Cert PG.

crazy/beautiful ★★★¹/₂

Los Angeles; the present. The 17-year-old daughter of a US congressman, Nicole Oakley has been materially blessed but is emotionally deprived. With her mother long dead, Nicole has evolved into a rebellious teenager with a predisposition for junk food, alcohol and drugs. On the opposite scale of the social spectrum, Carlos Nuñez lives in the Hispanic neighbourhood of East LA and travels two hours to school each day. Dedicated to becoming a Navy pilot, he has transformed himself into a straight-A student. Mutually attracted to each other, Nicole and Carlos embark on a relationship that, inevitably, can only lead to trouble... Tackling as familiar territory as ever there was, director John Stockwell has fashioned a good-looking love story for the MTV generation without the inherent ticks of the genre.

Armed with some distinctive photography and another outstanding performance from Kirsten Dunst (who here ditches her persona as the cheery cheerleader-next-door), the film is appealing, relevant and touching. There's also an excellent turn from Bruce Davison as Nicole's tortured father and an exceptionally strong soundtrack. Previously known as *At 17*.

• *Nicole Oakley* Kirsten Dunst, *Carlos Nuñez* Jay Hernandez, *Tom Oakley* Bruce Davison, *Courtney Oakley* Lucinda Jenney, *Maddy* Taryn Manning, *Luis* Herman Osorio, *Eddie* Miguel Castro, *Victor* Tommy De La Cruz, *Hector* Rolando Molina, *Mrs Nuñez* Soledad St Hilaire, *Coach Bauer* Richard Steinmetz.
• *Dir* John Stockwell, *Pro* Mary Jane Ufland, Harry J Ufland and Rachel Pfeffer, *Ex Pro* Guy Riedel, *Screenplay* Phil Hay and Matt Manfredi, *Ph* Shane Hurlbut, *Pro Des* Maia Javan, *Ed* Melissa Kent, *M* Paul Haslinger; songs performed by Mellow Man Ace, Lily Frost, David Snell, Emiliana Torrini, Cypress Hill, Urban Dance Squad, The Pimps, Delinquent Habits, Nydia Rojas, Viktor Serralde, Fastball, The Getaway People, Collective Soul, David Gray, Gipsyland, Revolution Tropical, The Dandy Warhols, La Ley,

Osker, Remy Zero, Seven Mary Three, Maren Ord, etc, *Costumes* Susan Matheson.

Touchstone Pictures-Buena Vista.
99 mins. USA. 2001. Rel: 21 September 2001. Cert 12.

Crocodile Dundee in Los Angeles ★★

Walkabout Creek, Australia/Los Angeles; the present. 13 years after he braved the streets of New York, Mick 'Crocodile' Dundee finds himself accompanying his partner Sue and their son Mikey to Hollywood. As naïve as ever, Dundee encounters a variety of local types, including a flirtatious roller-blader, a gang of muggers and Mike Tyson. Meanwhile, his sheila finds that the business she's been called in to tidy up might be a cover for a major smuggling operation... Having made just six films in 15 years, Paul Hogan is something of an anomaly. However, at 61 he still exudes an ineffable, laid-back charm that even makes something as mediocre as this seem inoffensive. It makes one wonder, though, how much more rewarding the film could have been if it had had some sort of structure, edge or decent dialogue.

• *Mick 'Crocodile' Dundee* Paul Hogan, *Sue*

Above: Driving Miss Britney: Zoë Saldana, Taryn Manning and Britney Spears in Tamra Davis's wickedly mundane *Crossroads* (from Momentum Pictures)

Charleton Linda Kozlowski, *Diego* Paul Rodriguez, *Arnon Rothman* Jere Burns, *Milos Drubnik* Jonathan Banks, *Mikey Dundee* Serge Cockburn, *Jean Ferraro* Aida Turturro, *Jacko* Alec Wilson, *with* Gerry Skilton, Steve Rackman, Jay Acovone, Steven Grives, Nicholas Hammond, George Hamilton, Mike Tyson.
• *Dir* Simon Wincer, *Pro* Lance Hool and Paul Hogan, *Ex Pro* Kathy Morgan, Steve Robbins and Jim Reeve, *Co-Pro* Conrad Hool and Perry Katz, *Screenplay* Matthew Berry and Eric Abrams, *Ph* David Burr, *Pro Des* Leslie Binns, *Ed* Terry Blythe, *M* Basil Poledouris, *Costumes* Marion Boyce, *Sound* Tim Chau.

Universal/Silver Lion/Bangalow Films/Paramount-UIP. 95 mins. USA/Australia. 2001. Rel: 24 August 2001. Cert PG.

Crossroads ★★

As described by Kit, her erstwhile playmate and confidante, Lucy is a 'perfect, sweet, proper, nerdy, virginal daddy's girl'. Having sacrificed her partying youth for a diploma towards a medical career, Lucy suddenly decides to join Kit and Mimi on a cross-country trip from Georgia to California. You see, she has decided to track down her mother, who walked out on her when she was just three years old. However, on the way, Lucy discovers that there's more to life than upholding her father's staid and suffocating standards… As a gift to the starry-eyed, undemanding devotees of pop's No 1 princess, *Crossroads* fulfils its mandate efficiently enough. The characters are easy on the eye, the story moves at a comprehensible pace and there are a sprinkling of faux musical numbers. For anybody not infatuated with Britney, though, on the Roquefort scale of cheesiness, the film rates a bland Edam. Of course, as an actress, Britney is no Madonna, a fact that is underlined by the spunky playing of her female co-stars, Zoë Saldana and Taryn Manning. Stranger still is her screen persona. Even as she espouses the virtues of virginal wholesomeness, Britney's sexuality seems aimed at the masturbatory fantasies of middle-aged men. Talk about a sexual oxymoron (with the accent on moron). Previously known as *Not a Girl* and *What Friends Are For*.

• *Lucy* Britney Spears, *Ben* Anson Mount, *Kit* Zoë Saldana, *Mimi* Taryn Manning, *Caroline, Lucy's mom* Kim Cattrall, *Pete, Lucy's dad* Dan Aykroyd, *Henry* Justin Long, *Kit's mom* Beverly Johnson, *with* Bahni Turpin, Kool Mo Dee, Richard Voll.
• *Dir* Tamra Davis, *Pro* Ann Carli, *Ex Pro* Clive Calder, Larry Rudolph, David Gale, Van Toffler and Johnny Wright, *Screenplay* Shonda Rhimes, *Ph* Eric Edwards, *Pro Des* Waldemar Kalinowski, *Ed* Melissa Kent, *M* Trevor Jones; songs performed by

Madonna, Bowling For Soup, Marvin Gaye, Lit, The Cult, *Nsync, Anti Matter, Matthew Sweet, New Birth Brass Band, Britney Spears, Mystikal, Shania Twain, Travis, Jars of Clay, Sheryl Crow, Beastie Boys, etc, *Costumes* Wendy Schecter.

Paramount/Zomba Films/MTV Films-Momentum Pictures.
93 mins. USA. 2001. Rel: 29 March 2002. Cert PG.

Crush ★★

Chipping Camden and its environs, Gloucestershire; today. A headmistress, a police superintendent and a doctor meet up regularly to drink, smoke and swap stories about their romantically barren lives. The winner of the saddest story wins a box of Tunnock's caramel wafer biscuits. Then Kate, the teacher, starts to fall for the local 25-year-old organist, a former pupil… The setting is picturesque, the phrases nicely turned and the performances of the highest order. Yet John McKay's script merely scratches the surface of his intriguing world, where three top professional women from different fields happen to be best friends. Frankly, it's all so unlikely, with the men merely one-dimensional tokens for the women to poke fun at or swoon over. Jed, the movie's dramatic lynchpin, is given no background shading, emotional detail or romantic motive, while the fact that Kate is an American lording it over the Cotswolds is never really explained. Here was a wonderful opportunity for Anglo-American satire, but Kate's nationality doesn't seem to be an issue. On a superficial level, some women may embrace the film, but its brazen manipulation of the tear ducts smacks more of Mills & Boon than Jeanette Winterson.

• *Katherine Isabelle Scales* Andie MacDowell, *Janine* Imelda Staunton, *Molly* Anna Chancellor, *Jeffrey Adam Willis aka 'Jed'* Kenny Doughty, *Gerald Farque Marsten* Bill Paterson, *with* Caroline Holdaway, Joe Roberts, Josh Cole, Christian Burgess, Morris Perry, Richenda Carey, Roger Booth, Lauren Stone.
• *Dir* and *Screenplay* John McKay, *Pro* Lee Thomas, *Ex Pro* Paul Webster, Hanno Huth and Julia Chasman, *Co-Pro* Elinor Day, *Line Pro* Fiona Morham, *Ph* Henry Braham, *Pro Des* Amanda MacArthur, *Ed* Anne Sopel, *M* Kevin Sargent; Igor Stravinsky, Delius, Elgar, Mendelssohn, Chopin, J S Bach, Richard Wagner, *Costumes* Jill Taylor.

FilmFour/Film Council/Senator Film and Industry Entertainment/Pipedream Pictures/National Lottery-Film Four.
112 mins. UK/Germany/USA. 2001. Rel: 7 June 2002. Cert 15.

D

Dancing at the Blue Iguana ★★★

The Blue Iguana is a strip club in the heart of Los
Angeles' San Fernando Valley and the dancers there
are not a happy bunch… Jennifer Tilly supplies the
laughs, Sandra Oh provides the pathos and Daryl
Hannah – well, she's the dumb blonde. This product of an improvisational workshop at first looks
like a rather obvious 'it takes all types' melodrama.
However, as the layers are stripped off these
inevitably sad individuals a genuine profundity
emerges. The club's owner, uncompromisingly
etched by W Earl Brown, gradually evolves into a
flesh-and-blood hustler, thankfully sidestepping the
clichés of the streetwise, gold-medallioned poser. In
fact, the film's strength is its constant reversal of
expectation, including the abandonment of a trite-
looking subplot involving a Russian agent, while the
marvellous Sandra Oh anchors the story's credibility with a performance that is both very funny and
terribly affecting.

• *Becky Willow aka Angel* Daryl Hannah, *Ellen
Taylor aka Jo* Jennifer Tilly, *Cathy aka Jasmine*
Sandra Oh, *Jessie* Charlotte Ayanna, *Marie Hughes
aka Stormy* Sheila Kelley, *Eddie Hazel* Robert
Wisdom, *Sully* Elias Koteas, *Sacha* Vladmir
Mashkov, *Nico* Kristin Bauer, *Bobby* W Earl Brown,
Dennis Chris Hogan, *Officer Pete Foster* Jack Conley,
Sarah Peggy Jo Jacobs, *with* Rodney Rowland, Jessie
Bradford, Isabelle Pasco.
• *Dir* Michael Radford, *Pro* Radford, Ernst 'Etchie'
Stroh, Ram Bergman, Graham Broadbent,
Damian Jones, Sheila Kelley and Dana Lustig,
Ex Pro Samuel Hadida, Leslie Jean Porter and
Willi Baer, *Screenplay* Radford and David Litner,
Ph Ericson Core, *Pro Des* Martina Buckley, *Ed*
Roberto Perpignani, *M* Tal Bergman and Renato
Neto; songs performed by Charlotte Ayanna,
Franka Potente and Thomas Düerr, Sloan,
Anoushka Fisz and Dave Stewart, Marianne
Faithfull, The Newlydeads, Mother Superior,
Leonard Cohen, Pigeonhed, Moby, Echo & The
Bunnymen, Eric Clapton, Robbie Robertson,
etc, *Costumes* Louise Frogley, *Character development
coach* Dominique Sire.

Moonstone Entertainment/Dragon/Gallery-Miracle
Communications.
123 mins. USA/UK. 2000. Rel: 21 June 2002. Cert 18.

Dark Blue World ★★★

Following their collaboration on the Oscar-winning
Czech film *Kolya*, the director Jan Sverák and his
scriptwriter father Zdenek Sverák focus on the little-
known exploits of Czech pilots during the Second

Above: Strip molls:
Sandra Oh, Sheila
Kelley, Daryl
Hannah, Daryl
Hannah and Sheila
Kelley in Michael
Radford's periodi-
cally absorbing
*Dancing at the
Blue Iguana*
(from Miracle
Communications)

World War. Again applying a painterly eye and a humanistic approach to his subject, Jan Sverák has created a poignant, detailed and frequently amusing film that addresses a fascinating episode of Czech history. Following the Nazi occupation in 1939, around 3500 Czech pilots escaped to England to help the war effort and found themselves struggling with a foreign language and culture in between fearfully dangerous missions over France. Then, once the war was won, the pilots were imprisoned in their homeland by the new Communist regime and subjected to torture and forced labour. To alleviate such a depressing theme, the Sveráks have introduced a triangular romance (just like the one in *Pearl Harbor*) and have presented the film in flashback. Unfortunately, the romance comes off as contrived and hackneyed while the flashback structure is frequently jarring. And the Sveráks were this close to creating something really, really special.
Original title: *Tmavomodry svet.*

• *Frantisek Slama* Ondrej Vetchy, *Karel Vojtisek* Krystof Hadek, *Susan* Tara Fitzgerald, *Wing-Commander Bentley* Charles Dance, *Machaty* Oldrich Kaiser, *Mrtvy* David Novotny, *Hanicka* Linda Rybova, *English teacher* Anna Massey, *with* Jaromir Dulava, Lukas Kantor, Radim Fiala, Jeremy Swift, Jan Dvorak.
• *Dir* Jan Sverák, *Pro* Jan Sverák and Eric Abraham, *Screenplay* Zdenek Sverák, *Ph* Vladimir Smutny, *Pro Des* Jan Vlasak, *Ed* Alois Fisarek, *M* Ondrej Soukup, *Costumes* Vera Mirova, *Sound* Zbynek Mikulik.

Biograf Jan Sverak & Portobello Pictures/Helkon Media/Phoenix Film/Fandango, etc-Columbia TriStar. 112 mins. Czech Republic/UK/Germany/Denmark/Italy. 2001. Rel: 10 May 2002. Cert 12.

The Day I Became a Woman ★★★

On the day of her ninth birthday, little Hava is told that she cannot go and play with her friend, a boy. Today she has become a woman and can no longer be allowed out of the house... When Ahoo competes in a bicycle race, her husband is incensed. Galloping alongside her on a horse, he declares that her participation in such an event is grounds for divorce... Arriving in the city in a wheelchair, an old woman hires a young black boy to take her shopping. Now that she has the money, she is determined to buy everything that she has never been able to afford in her life, even though she now has no need for it... A film about women made by a woman is hardly a novelty. However, in the male-dominated society of Iran, it is something of a revelation. Marziyeh Meshkini, wife of the filmmaker Mohsen Makhmalbaf, makes her debut here with a keen eye for the absurd and the lyrical. The film's deathly pace

may put off many viewers, but those with the patience could glean a lot from this simple tale of Islamic inequality.
Original title: *Roozi Keh Zan Shodam.*

• *Hava* Fatemeh Cheragh Akhar, *Ahoo, the cyclist* Shabnam Toloui, *Hoora, the elderly woman* Azizeh Sedighi.
• *Dir* Marziyeh Meshkini, *Pro* Mohsen Makhmalbaf, *Screenplay* Meshkini and Makhmalbaf, *Ph* Ebrahim Ghafouri and Mohammad Ahmadi, *Pro Des* Akbar Meshkini, *Ed* Shahrzad Poya and Maysam Makhmalbaf, *M* Mohammad-Reza Darvishi.
Makhmalbaf/Film House-Artificial Eye. 77 mins. Iran. 2000. Rel: 28 December 2001. Cert U.

The Deep End ★★¹/₂

With her husband away at sea for most of the year, Margaret Hall has found her place in the world catering for her three children and her dependent father-in-law. Then something terrible happens and Margaret does the only thing she knows how in order to protect her 17-year-old son. But as she struggles to hold her life together, a strange man turns up demanding $50,000 in return for the destruction of a compromising videotape. Juggling her existing priorities, Margaret attempts to raise the money, while her domestic commitments repeatedly get in the way... By weaving a generic thriller around the pegs of a domestic drama, *The Deep End* promises to be a work of unusual distinction. Unfortunately, the Scottish-born Tilda Swinton fails to convince as the all-American mother forced into extraordinary circumstances (Joan Allen or Michelle Pfeiffer would have been perfect). Furthermore, the deliberate pacing of the film is such that the viewer never feels part of a real family or situation. With its stylised, almost austere setting, *The Deep End* is wonderful to look at yet fails to engage on an emotional level.

• *Margaret Hall* Tilda Swinton, *Alek Spera* Goran Visnjic, *Beau Hall* Jonathan Tucker, *Jack Hall* Peter Donat, *Darby Reese* Josh Lucas, *Carlie Nagle* Raymond J Barry, *Paige Hall* Tamara Hope, Jordan Dorrance, Heather Mathieson, Richard Gross, F W McGehee.
• *Dir, Pro* and *Screenplay* Scott McGehee and David Siegel, based on the novel *The Blank Wall* by Elisabeth Sanxay Holding, *Ex Pro* Robert H Nathan, *Co-Pro* Laura Greenlee, *Ph* Giles Nuttgens, *Pro Des* Kelly McGehee and Christopher Tandon, *Ed* Lauren Zuckerman, *M* Peter Nashel, *Costumes* Sabrina Rosen; Ravel, Tchaikovsky, *Dialect coach* Julie Adams.

i5-Fox.
101 mins. USA. 2001. Rel: 14 December 2001. Cert 15.

The Devil's Backbone ★★

A day's walk from the nearest town, the Santa Lucia orphanage stands alone in a hot, barren wilderness. It is there that young Carlos arrives one day, unaware that his father has been killed in the Spanish Civil War. As he stands up to the teasing and baiting of the other orphans, Carlos begins to notice another presence, a boy who looks on quietly from the shadows... Had Guillermo Del Toro lavished as much attention on his script as the opulent production values of this handsome slice of Grand Guignol, then the viewer's nerves might have tingled more. As it is, Del Toro's characters are strictly one-dimensional and the fear factor rather dissipated. A major problem is Javier Navarrete's lush, insistent score, which from the very start casts a blanket over the credibility of the story. Del Toro could well take a lesson from fellow South American Alejandro Amenábar, who wrote the music to his spectral *The Others* himself, using it only when he needed to.
Original title: *El espinazo del diablo*.

• *Jacinto* Eduardo Noriega, *Carmen* Marisa Paredes, *Casares* Federico Luppi, *Jaime* Iñigo Garces, *Carlos* Fernando Tielve, *Conchita* Irene Visedo, *Alma* Berta Ojea.
• *Dir* Guillermo Del Toro, *Pro* Agustin Almodovar and Berta Navarro, *Co-Pro* Rosa Bosch, *Screenplay* Del Toro, Antonio Trashorras and David Muñoz, *Ph* Guillermo Navarro, *Pro Des* Cesar Macarron,

Ed Luis De La Madrid, *M* Javier Navarrete, *Costumes* Jose Vico.

El Deseo SA/Tequila Gang/Canal Plus-Optimum Releasing.
107 mins. Spain/Mexico. 2001. Rel: 30 November 2001. Cert 15.

Dinner Rush ★★★★★

With its blend of operatic arias and mouth-watering close-ups of Italian cuisine, *Dinner Rush* is a film that stokes the senses. Sensuously photographed, elegantly edited and superlatively played by an eclectic cast, the film, without ever losing its step, threads comedy and drama through one chaotic evening in a New York trattoria. Filmed in the 25-year-old director's own TriBeCa eatery (Gigino's), *Dinner Rush* demonstrates its authenticity from the word go, revealing, in slow motion, the frenetic skill that goes into the orchestration of multiple haute cuisine. Dispensing with captions, voice-over and exposition, the story kicks in immediately, establishing the character of Louis Cropa (Danny Aiello, marvellous), who runs a restaurant as a cover for his book-keeping activities. Actually, it's his son, master chef Udo, who really runs the restaurant and is pressuring his father for a partnership in the thriving business. But then a couple of rival hoods also want a share, as recompense for the debt of $13,000 owed to them by

Above: Table matters: Summer Phoenix and Mike McGlone in Bob Giraldi's poetically palatable *Dinner Rush* (from Pathé)

the trattoria's sous-chef. As it happens, a senior cop has booked a table on the same night, as has one of New York's most influential restaurant critics (an acidic Sandra Bernhard). Throw in a customer-from-Hell (a dyspeptic Mark Margolis) and a power cut and you have the stamp of a farce that would make the Marx Brothers proud. It is to Bob Giraldi's credit, then, that he manages to keep a restraining order on any melodrama and brings a narrative poetry to the proceedings. Every character, every dish and every nuance has its place, creating a platter of suspense, comedy and good company that is a small cinematic miracle.

• *Louis Cropa* Danny Aiello, *Udo Cropa* Edoardo Ballerini, *Nicole* Vivian Wu, *Carmen* Mike McGlone, *Duncan* Kirk Acevedo, *Jennifer* Freeley Sandra Bernhard, *Ken* John Corbett, *Marti* Summer Phoenix, *Natalie Clemente* Polly Draper, *Sean* Jamie Harris, *Fitzgerald* Mark Margolis, *Paolo* Alex Corrado, *Piper* Tessa Ghylin, *Gary* John Rothman, *Det. Drury* Walt MacPherson, *Ademir* Ajay Naidu, *Enrico* Frank Bongiorno, *Joseph* Juan Hernandez, *with* Manny Perez, Joe Gatti Jr, Lexie Sperduto, Zainab Jah, Ted Koch, Minnie Giraldi.
• *Dir* Bob Giraldi, *Pro* Louis DiGiaimo and Patti Greaney, *Ex Pro* Phil Suarez, Robert Cheren, Robert Steuer and Michael Baumohl, *Screenplay* Rick Shaughnessy and Brian Kalata, *Ph* Tim Ives, *Pro Des* Andrew Bernard, *Ed* Allyson C Johnson, *M* Alexander Lasarenko, *Costumes* Constance Pavlounis.

Giraldi Suarez DiGiaimo-Pathé.
98 mins. USA. 2000. Rel: 29 March 2002. Cert 15.

Disco Pigs ★★★

Almost simultaneously, Darren (aka Pig) and Sinead (aka Runt) are born next door to each other in hospital. From that day forward, they remain inseparable, living next door, attending the same school and inhabiting their own closeted, secret world. Then their elders decide that their friendship is unhealthy and decide to separate them… *Disco Pigs*, marking the directorial debut of the 25-year-old Kirsten Sheridan, is adapted by Enda Walsh from her own play, yet is a singularly cinematic experience. Sheridan obviously has a fertile eye for her medium, combining magical imagery with a poetic simplicity. But she is not experienced enough to know when to draw back and overloads the second half of her film with increasingly banal visual concepts. It's a shame, too, that Pig and Runt are such perversely unsympathetic characters. Nonetheless, this is a startlingly original work.
[*Charles Bacon*]

• *Runt* aka *Sinead* Elaine Cassidy, *Pig* aka *Darren*

Cillian Murphy, *Gerry, Runt's dad* Brian O'Byrne, *Bernie, Pig's mam* Eleanor Methven, *Eileen, Runt's mam* Geraldine O'Rawe, *Marky* Darren Healy, *young Runt* Sarah Gallagher, *young Pig* Charles Bank-Frisby, *with* Tara Lynne O'Neill, Michael Rawley, Gavin Friday, Enda Walsh.
• *Dir* Kirsten Sheridan, *Pro* Ed Guiney, *Ex Pro* Stephen Evans, Angus Finney and Ron Stoneman, *Line Pro* Noëlette Buckley, *Assoc Pro* Sophie Janson, *Screenplay* Enda Walsh, from her play, *Ph* Igor Jadue-Lillo, *Pro Des* Zoë MacLeod, *Ed* Ben Yeates, *M* Gavin Friday and Maurice Seezer, *Costumes* Lorna Marie Mugan.

Temple Films/Renaissance Films-Entertainment.
93 mins. UK/Ireland. 2000. Rel: 16 November 2001.
Cert 15.

Divided We Fall ★★★

Echoing the 1965 Oscar-winner from Czechoslovakia *The Shop on Main Street*, this is a tale of World War II that looks at the plight of Jews needing protection from Czech neighbours. It's very well cast and undoubtedly sincere, but your response depends on how readily you can take the stylistic mix. To eschew out-and-out drama for a lighter tone while recognising the serious centre is fine, but when farce is allowed in it destroys belief. Subsequently, prior to a climax which seeks too obviously to manipulate the audience's emotions and a final touch of symbolism which strives too hard, an impotent husband's need to allow his beloved wife to be made pregnant by another is more poignant than the film acknowledges. But if, for me, the second half misfires, I recognise that this is a matter of taste. It's worth seeking out the film to check your own reaction.
Original title: *Musime Si Pomahat.*
[*Mansel Stimpson*]

• *Josef Cízek* Boleslav Polivka, *David Wiener* Csongor Kassai, *Horst Prohazka* Jaroslav Dusek, *Marie Cízek* Anna Siskova, *Frantisek Simácková* Jiri Pecha, *with* Martin Huba, Simona Stasova, Vladimir Marek.
• *Dir* Jan Hrebejk, *Pro* Ondrej Trojan, *Ex Pro* Ondrej Trojan, *Screenplay* Petr Jarchovsky, based on his novel, *Ph* Jan Malir, *Pro Des* Milan Myceck, *Ed* Vladimir Barak, *M* Ales Brezina; JS Bach, Beethoven, *Costumes* Katarina Holla.

Total HelpArt THA Film and Television Company/Czech Television-Metrodome.
122 mins. Czech Republic. 2000. Rel: 31 May 2002. Cert PG.

Dog Eat Dog ★★¹/₂

West London; the present. It's a dog-eat-dog world out there and don't Rooster, CJ, Jess and Chang know

Left: Barking orders: Kevin McKidd (left), Emma Cleasby and Liam Cunningham (middle background) face the brotherhood of the wolf in Neil Marshall's overblown and very silly *Dog Soldiers* (from Pathé)

it. Rooster is in trouble with the local crime lord; CJ has discovered that his girlfriend is cheating on him (with her ex); Jess loses his hot new conquest when she overhears him bragging about her; and Chang can only secure custody of his daughter if he can find £5000. Then the aspiring DJs' gig is cancelled at the last moment and their records are stolen... Proudly promoted as the new film from the makers of *Kevin and Perry Go Large* (in fact, the production company: Tiger Aspect Films), this sketchy jumble wears its TV roots on its sleeve (the director and co-writer worked together on the BBC's *Uncut Funk*). However, its ethnic compass (the cast is Asian, Caucasian, Jamaican and Nigerian) is refreshingly non-judgmental and there is style and charm to spare.
[*Ewen Brownrigg*]

• *Rooster* Mark Tonderai, *Jess* Nathan Constance, *CJ* David Oyelowo, *Changarcy* Crunski, *Phil* Alan Davies, *Kelly, ex-girlfriend* Melanie Blatt, *Jesus* Gary Kemp, *Darcy* Steve Toussaint, *Mina* Rebecca Hazlewood, *with* Ricky Gervais, Geff Francis, Anna Wing, Dilys Laye, Jonah Russell, Stewart Wright, John Thomson, Trevor Peacock.
• *Dir* Moody Shoaibi, *Pro* Amanda Davis, *Ex Pro* Peter Bennet-Jones, Hanno Huth and Paul Webster, *Screenplay* Shoaibi and Mark Tonderai, *Ph* John Daly, *Pro Des* Greg Shaw, *Ed* Luke Dunkley, *M* Mark Hinton Stewart, *Costumes* Ffion Elinor.

FilmFour/Shona Productions/Tiger Aspect-Film Four. 93 mins. UK/Germany. 2000. Rel: 7 December 2001. Cert 15.

Dog Soldiers ★¹⁄₂

On a routine training exercise in the Scottish highlands, a squad of six British soldiers find themselves up against an indestructible enemy. Something vicious, omnipresent and invisible is stalking them. And soon it will be full moon… Taking the werewolf genre and ploughing it into the fertile furrow of *Assault on Precinct 13*, *Dog Soldiers* is an overblown mess that thinks disembowelment is funny. From the condescending approach to its cheeky chappie commandos to the overblown score, the film fires off in all the wrong directions. Riddled with clichés and disabled by distorted logic, it does achieve a kind of gross-out high, albeit one that subjugates boredom in favour of nausea and a pounding headache.

• *Wells* Sean Pertwee, *Cooper* Kevin McKidd, *Ryan* Liam Cunningham, *Megan* Emma Cleasby, *Spoon* Darren Morfitt, *Joe* Chris Robson, *Terry* Leslie Simpson.
• *Dir, Screenplay* and *Ed* Neil Marshall, *Pro* Christopher Figg, Tom Reeve and David E Allen, *Ex Pro* Harmon Kaslow, Romain Schroeder and Vic Bateman, *Assoc Pro* Caroline Waldron, *Ph* Sam McCurdy, *Pro Des* Simon Bowles, *M* Mark Thomas; Debussy, *Creature effects* Bob Keen.

Kismet Entertainment/Noel Gay Motion Picture Company/ Victor Film/Carousel/Luxembourg Film Fund-Pathé.
105 mins. UK/Luxembourg. 2001. Rel: 10 May 2002. Cert 15.

Domestic Disturbance ★★★¹⁄₂

Southport, Maryland; today. 12-year-old Danny Morrison has never lied to his father but now that his mom is marrying the handsome, rich and all-round nice guy Rick Barnes, he is starting to act up. Against his better instincts, Frank Morrison attempts to steer his son closer to the lad's new stepfather, arguing that it is just as hard on Barnes as it is on Danny. Then Danny tells Frank something that a father just can't ignore… Taking into account that a big-budget, mainstream thriller is inevitably bound by formula, *Domestic Disturbance* is way ahead of the game, serving up some genuine suspense and surprises. Skilfully set up, the scenario quickly becomes almost unbearable as the bond between Frank and his son is tested by the cruel machinations of the plot. Of course, it helps that Travolta is such an ineffably likeable guy and that Vince Vaughn never overplays his villainy to the camera. Thrillers this clean, slick and tight are a rare commodity in Hollywood.

• *Frank Morrison* John Travolta, *Rick Barnes* Vince Vaughn, *Susan* Teri Polo, *Danny Morrison* Matt O'Leary, *Ray Coleman* Steve Buscemi, *Diane* Susan Floyd, *Sgt. Edgar Stevens* Ruben Santiago-Hudson, *Patty* Angelica Torn.
• *Dir* Harold Becker, *Pro* Donald De Line and Jonathan Krane, *Screenplay* Lewis Colick, from a story by Colick, William S Comanor and Gary Drucker, *Ph* Michael Seresin, *Pro Des* Clay A Griffith, *Ed* Peter Honess, *M* Mark Mancina, *Costumes* Bobbie Read.

Paramount/De Line Pictures-UIP.
88 mins. USA. 2001. Rel: 11 January 2002. Cert 12.

Don't Say a Word ★★★

Dr Nathan Conrad is a top-flight psychiatrist who specialises in troubled, affluent teenagers. With a beautiful, loving wife, a sweet, precocious, eight-year-old daughter and a luxurious New York apartment, he has everything to live for. Then his daughter is kidnapped and, if he wants to see her alive again, he has just one day to extract a six-digit number from the mind of a traumatised 18-year-old girl… *Don't Say a Word* is an efficient thriller, but it's almost too efficient. The Iranian-born cinematographer Amir Mokri gives Manhattan a handsome, gritty sheen, there is an effective score from Isham and the standard of acting is high, particularly from the female cast members, including Brittany Murphy, Famke Janssen, Jennifer Esposito (who recalls a ballsy Jennifer Aniston) and, as the Conrads' resourceful daughter, Skye McCole Bartusiak. However, one never suspects for a moment that there won't be a happy ending (what do you expect with an English villain?), so the suspense is never unbearable. An accomplished night's entertainment, *Don't Say a Word* keeps one engaged, if not overly concerned. Sad, but true: although the film is set over the Thanksgiving weekend of 2001, the World Trade Center is clearly visible in two shots.

• *Dr Nathan Conrad* Michael Douglas, *Patrick Barry Koster* Sean Bean, *Elisabeth Burrows* Brittany Murphy, *Det Sandra Cassidy* Jennifer Esposito, *Aggie Conrad* Famke Janssen, *Dr Louis Sachs* Oliver Platt, *Jessie Conrad* Skye McCole Bartusiak, *Martin J Dolen* Guy Torry, *Russel Maddox* Shawn Doyle, *Max J Dunlevy* Conrad Goode, Victor Argo, Paul Schulze, Lance Reddick, Larry Block.
• *Dir* Gary Fleder, *Pro* Arnon Milchan, Arnold Kopelson and Anne Kopelson, *Ex Pro* Jeffrey Downer and Bruce Berman, *Screenplay* Anthony Peckham and Patrick Smith Kelly, based on the novel by Andrew Klavan, *Ph* Amir Mokri, *Pro Des* Nelson Coates, *Ed* William Steinkamp and Armen Minasian, *M* Mark Isham; songs performed by Tone-Loc, Nat King Cole, Ray Charles, James Brown, and The Mamas & The Papas, *Costumes* Ellen Mirojnick.

Regency Enterprises/Village Roadshow Pictures/NPV Entertainment/Furthur Films/Epsilon Motion-Pictures-

Twentieth Century Fox.
113 mins. USA. 2001. Rel: 22 February 2002. Cert 15.

Down From the Mountain ★★★★

This documentary about bluegrass music may be less memorable than Wim Wenders' *Buena Vista Social Club*, but it is never less than attractive. Once again there are some oldies on parade, including Dr Ralph Stanley, he who coined the term 'bluegrass', and the dryly humorous, laid-back MC, John Hartford, who has since died. The first half is free-style (rehearsals for a benefit concert in Nashville, some old footage, comments by the performers), while the second part is a well-shot and well-edited concert movie. This is really a spin-off from the successful use of similar music in the film *O Brother, Where Art Thou?*, but there's much variety in what is performed here. An affectionate document, this will please those drawn to it.
[*Mansel Stimpson*]

• with Evelyn Cox, Sidney Cox, Suzanne Cox, Willard Cox, Nathan Best, Isaac Freeman, Robert Hamlett, John Hartford, Emmylou Harris, Chris Thomas King, Alison Krauss and Union Station, Colin Linden, The Nashville Bluegrass Band, The Peasall Sisters, Gillian Welch, Mike Compton, T-Bone Burnett, Ethan Coen, Joel Coen, Holly Hunter, Tim Blake Nelson, etc.
• *Dir* Nick Doob, Chris Hegedus and D A Pennebaker, *Pro* Bob Neuwirth and Frazer Pennebaker, *Ex Pro* T-Bone Burnett, Ethan Coen and Joel Coen, *Ph* Joan Churchill, Jim Desmond, Nick Doob, Chris Hegedus, Bob Neuwirth, Jehane Noujaim, D A Pennebaker and John Paul Pennebaker, *Ed* Doob and D A Pennebaker, *M Director* T-Bone Burnett.

Mike Zoss Productions/Pennebaker Hegedus Films-Momentum Pictures
98 mins. USA. 2000. Rel: 26 October 2001. Cert U.

Dr Dolittle 2 ★★

San Francisco; today. Returning from a working trip in France and Mexico (don't ask), John Dolittle promises his family more quality time and in a moment of rare temerity suggests a family outing to Europe. Then, on the day of their departure, a

Above: Race against the clock: Michael Douglas looks for the time in Gary Fleder's handsome if predictable *Don't Say a Word* (from Fox)

Mafioso beaver (don't ask) begs Dolittle to help save a nearby forest which is to be cut down by a corporate profiteer. Failing to convince a judge of the forest's environmental importance, Dolittle can only save the wilderness if, in just three weeks, he can get a circus bear to successfully breed in the wild (don't ask)... While the animals stole the show the first time round, on this occasion they seem both less convincing and less funny. Murphy, however, is on better form – *just* – but the big ecological message and the odd inside joke (the kids' TV presenter Steve Irwin losing his arm to a crocodile) are not enough to overcome the tired mediocrity of it all.

• *Dr John Dolittle* Eddie Murphy, *Lisa Dolittle* Kristen Wilson, *Joseph Potter* Jeffrey Jones, *Jack Riley* Kevin Pollak, *Charisse Dolittle* Raven-Symoné, *Maya Dolittle* Kyla Pratt, *Eric* Lil' Zane, *crocodile hunter* Steve Irwin, *with* Denise Dowse, James L Avery, Elayn J Taylor, Andy Richter, Victor Raider-Wexler, Ken Campbell, Googy Gress, Tank the Bear.
Voices: *Archie* Steve Zahn, *Pepito* Jacob Vargas, *Ava* Lisa Kudrow, *Sonny* Mike Epps, *Joey the Racoon* Michael Rapaport, *God Beaver* Richard C Sarafian, *Lennie the Weasel* Andy Dick, *Crocodile* Kevin Pollak, *Squirrel* Joey Lauren Adams, *Boy Bear Cub* Frankie Muniz, Jamie Kennedy, Renée Taylor, Phil Proctor, Isaac Hayes, Reni Santoni, Cedric the Entertainer, John Witherspoon, Mandy Moore, David Cross, David DeLuise, John DiMaggio, Clyde Kusatso, Michael McKean, Kenny Campbell, Georgia Engel, Tara Mercurio, Bob Odenkirk and (uncredited) *Lucky* Norm MacDonald.
• *Dir* Steve Carr, *Pro* John Davis, *Ex Pro* Neil Machlis and Joe Singer, *Co-Pro* Michele Imperato-Stabile and Heidi Santelli, *Screenplay* Larry Levin, *Ph* Daryn Okada, *Pro Des* William Sandell, *Ed* Craig P Herring, *M* David Newman; G F Handel; songs performed by Alicia Keyes, Flipmode Squad and Busta Rhymes, Luther Vandross, R L Snoop Dog and Lil' Kim, Medeiros, Lil' Zane, The Product G&B and Wyclef, Andrew Dorfman, Morcheeba, Lionel Richie, Jimmy Cozier, etc, *Costumes* Ruth Carter, *Visual effects* Rhythm & Hues.

Fox/Davis Entertainment-Fox.
87 mins. USA. 2001. Rel: 27 July 2001. Cert PG.

Dr T & The Women ★★★¹⁄₂

Dallas, Texas; today. 'Sully' Travis adores women in every shape and form and declares that they should be treated as saints. Which is just as well as he is married to one, has two daughters and, as a gynaecologist, spends his waking hours attending to child birth, the menopause and yeast infections. Then he meets Bree Davis, a self-confident, independent golf pro who doesn't play by the rules of the Country Club... A loose update of the Biblical story of Job, Robert Altman's latest ensemble comedy is both a savage satire on a certain class of female dilettante and a portrait of a man who dedicates his life to pleasing women. In the end, the love that Sully lavishes on his wife sends her off the rails and into a sanatorium. There, she is diagnosed as suffering from 'Hestia complex', a rare condition in which high-bred, advantaged women retreat into a child-like state when their motivation for improvement is stifled. Suffused with Altman's characteristic use of irony (a rare ingredient in mainstream American cinema), *Dr T* is actually an extremely tragic film, lightly dressed as comedy.

• *Dr Sullivan 'Sully' Travis* Richard Gere, *Bree Davis* Helen Hunt, *Kate Travis* Farrah Fawcett, *Peggy* Laura Dern, *Carolyn* Shelley Long, *Connie Travis* Tara Reid, *Dee Dee Travis* Kate Hudson, *Marilyn* Liv Tyler, *Harlan* Robert Hays, *Bill* Matt Malloy, *Eli* Andy Richter, *Dr Harper* Lee Grant, *Dorothy* Janine Turner, Holly Pellham-Davis, Jeanne Evans, Ramsey Williams, Dorothy Deavers, Cameron Cobb, Mike Scott, Irene Cortez, Kelli Finglass, Wren Arthur, *birth baby* Eric Ryan.
• *Dir* Robert Altman, *Pro* Robert Altman and James McLindon, *Co-Pro* David Levy, Tommy Thompson, and Graham King and David A Jones, *Ex Pro* Cindy Cowan, *Screenplay* Anne Rapp, *Ph* Jan Kiesser, *Pro Des* Stephen Altman, *Ed* Geraldine Peroni, *M* Lyle Lovett, *Costumes* Dona Granata.

Initial Entertainment/Sandcastle 5-Columbia TriStar.
122 mins. USA. 2000. Rel: 6 July 2001. Cert 12.

Dragonfly ★★

When his wife is killed on a mercy mission in Venezuela, ER doctor Joe Darrow struggles to hold on to his reason. The strain begins to show when, working 20-hour shifts seven days a week, he starts to put two and two together to make five. Why does Joe start to see dragonflies and wiggly crucifixes everywhere? Is his late wife trying to communicate with him or is he losing his mind? ... Neither frightening enough to be an effective thriller nor believable enough to engage the emotions on a tenable level, *Dragonfly* coagulates into a sluggish, soporific and rather dull 'thriller'. Much like *The Sixth Sense*, the film relies too heavily on a single idea and is in dire need of fleshing out. Still, for a suspenser from the director of *The Nutty Professor* and *Patch Adams*, one should hardly expect miracles.

• *Joe Darrow* Kevin Costner, *Hugh Campbell* Joe Morton, *Charlie Dickinson* Ron Rifkin, *Sister Madeline* Linda Hunt, *Emily Darrow*

Susanna Thompson, *pilot* Jacob Vargas, *Mrs Belmont* Kathy Bates, *Jeffrey Reardon* Robert Bailey Jr, *Ben* Jacob Smith, *with* Jay Thomas, Lisa Banes, Matt Craven, Casey Biggs, Leslie Hope, Peter Hansen, Liza Weil, Deirdre O'Connell, Ana Garcia.
• *Dir* Tom Shadyac, *Pro* Shadyac, Mark Johnson, Roger Birnbaum and Gary Barber, *Ex Pro* James D Brubaker and Michael Bostick, *Screenplay* David Seltzer, Brandon Camp and Mike Thompson, *Ph* Dean Semler, *Pro Des* Linda DeScenna, *Ed* Don Zimmerman, *M* John Debney, *Costumes* Judy Ruskin Howell.

Universal/Spyglass Entertainment/Gran Via/Shady Acres-Buena Vista.
104 mins. USA. 2002. Rel: 7 June 2002. Cert 12.

Driven ★★

As the new boy wonder of championship racing starts to lose his touch, veteran car owner Carl Henry calls in his secret weapon: Joe Tanto. Tanto, a former god of the track himself, has to swallow his pride as he takes on the role of coach and tries to cut through the new boy's defences. On the world's most dangerous circuits there is no room for doubt, fear or pride, a lesson Tanto himself has had to learn at some cost... The problem with this chrome-plated, assembly-line vehicle is that it is driving in two gears at once. Sylvester Stallone, the producer, star and writer, seems to be telling a story of forgiveness, regret, competition, redemption and achieving the top of one's form. Renny Harlin, the producer, director and co-story writer, would appear to be aiming for an MTV-style, turbo-charged adrenaline rush. As it happens, the racing sequences, the spectacular, digitally enhanced crashes and the whole glorification of 'open-wheel' racing is what really keeps the movie moving. Then, when the sermonising and soul-searching starts, the film brakes to an abrupt stop. Furthermore, Kip Pardue (previously seen in *Remember the Titans*) appears about as tortured as a freshly ironed cheesecloth, while Burt Reynolds acts on one piston.

• *Joe Tanto* Sylvester Stallone, *Carl Henry* Burt Reynolds, *Jimmy Bly* Kip Pardue, *Beau Brandenburg* Til Schweiger, *Cathy* Gina Gershon, *Sophia Simone* Estella Warren, *Memo Heguy* Cristián de la Fuente, *Lucretia Clan* Stacy Edwards, *Crusher* Brent Briscoe, *Demille Bly* Robert Sean Leonard, *replacement driver* Renny Harlin, Verona Feldbusch, Jasmine Wagner, Chip Ganassi, John Della Penna, Dan Duran, Rob Smith, Luukas Harlin.
• *Dir* Renny Harlin, *Pro* Elie Samaha, Sylvester Stallone and Renny Harlin, *Ex Pro* Andrew Stevens, Don Carmody and Kevin King, *Co-Ex Pro* Rebecca Spikings and Tracee Stanley, *Assoc Pro*

Leeza-Maria el Khazen and Michelle Davis, *Screenplay* Stallone, from a story by Stallone and Harlin, *Ph* Mauro Fiore, *Pro Des* Charles Wood, *Ed* Stuart Levy and Steve Gilson, *M* BT; songs performed by Leroy, Rob Dougan, The Crystal Method, Tamara Walker, Pigeonhed, Tim McGraw, Rare Blend, Insolence, Jo Dee Messina, Ohio Players, Doyle Bramhall II & Smokestack, LeAnn Rimes, Hank III, BT, The Chemical Brothers, Tantric, Filter, Apollo 440, Grand Theft Auto, Aphrodite, ERA, Fat Boy Slim, Mary Griffin, Leroy, etc, *Costumes* Mary McLeod.

Franchise Pictures-Warner.
117 mins. USA. 2001. Rel: 5 October 2001. Cert PG.

D-Tox ★

Following the sadistic murder of his fiancée, FBI agent Jake Malloy has taken to the bottle in a big way. Now his colleague and 'other half', Charlie Hendricks, has checked him into a cops' detox clinic situated in a former military silo in the heart of Wyoming. But a blizzard blows up, communications are down, the boiler has broken, the temperature is plummeting below zero, the cops have the DTs and there's a deranged psychopath on the loose... Sometimes you can tell a film is going to be bad just by the name of the lead protagonist – and the combination of actors in the cast. Sadly, a cop called Jake Malloy and the combined forces of Stallone, Berenger and Kristofferson does not bode well. Yet even such low expectations cannot prepare one for the astonishing ineptitude of this bargain-bin aberration. A jumble sale of clichés plucked from the twin stables of the serial killer/Ten Little Indians format, *D-Tox* only offers value in the number of star names dispatched in the shortest amount of time.

• *Jake Malloy* Sylvester Stallone, *Hank* Tom Berenger, *Charlie Hendricks* Charles S Dutton, *John 'Doc' Mitchell* Kris Kristofferson, *Jenny Munroe* Polly Walker, *Connor* Sean Patrick Flanery, *Frank Slater* Christopher Fulford, *Jack* Stephen Lang, *Mary Donahue* Dina Meyer, *Pete Noah* Robert Patrick, *McKenzie* Robert Prosky, *Willie Jones* Courtney B Vance, *Lenny Jaworski* Jeffrey Wright, *Lopez* Angela Alvarado Rosa, *with* Rance Howard, MIF, Alan C Peterson, Frank Pellegrino.
• *Dir* Jim Gillespie, *Pro* Ric Kidney, *Assoc Pro* Kevin King, *Screenplay* Ron L Brinkerhoff and Patrick Kelly, *Ph* Dean Semler, *Pro Des* Gary Wissner, *Ed* Steve Mirkovich and Tim Alverson, *M* John Powell, *Costumes* Catherine Adair.

Universal/KC Medien/Capella-Warner.
96 mins. USA/Canada. 2001. Rel: 1 February 2002. Cert 18.

Above: Brothers in arms: Joseph Fiennes and David Wenham go East in Milcho Manchevski's grandly misconceived *Dust* (from Pathé)

Dust ★¹/₂

The American West/Paris/Macedonia/New York; 1900-2000. A pair of gun-slinging brothers, Luke and Elijah, fall foul of one another when they both fall for the same prostitute. Disgruntled and disillusioned, Luke heads to Europe (with his custom-made pistol in tow) and ends up heading a bloodthirsty gang of brigands in Macedonia. Elijah follows, bent on revenge for Luke's betrayal. At least, that's what a dying old woman in New York tells her burglar… Well, here's one for the history books: a British-German-Italian-Macedonian-Spanish-Swiss-American movie set in the Old West, Macedonia and contemporary New York with two Englishmen and an Australian playing the main American parts. And if that sounds like a recipe for disaster, it is. Gratuitously violent (the action scenes are incredibly heavy-handed), the film resolutely refuses to make sense, sacrificing plausibility for effect, while the characters' motives remain consistently incomprehensible. Indeed, this is one of those films where nothing rings true, from the likelihood of Joseph Fiennes and David Wenham being brothers, to their frequent encounters in the Balkans.

• *Elijah* Joseph Fiennes, *Luke* David Wenham, *Edge* Adrian Lester, *Lilith* Anne Brochet, *Neda* Nikolina Kujaca, *Angela* Rosemary Murphy, *teacher* Vlado Jovanovski, *mayor* Salaetin Bilal, *Amy* Vera Farmiga, *Stitch* Matthew Ross, *Sigmund Freud* Jon Ivanovski, *with* Meg Gibson, Tamer Ibrahim, Louise Goodall, Saundra McClain.

• *Dir* and *Screenplay* Milcho Manchevski, *Pro* Chris Auty, Vesna Jovanoska and Domenico Procacci, *Ph* Barry Ackroyd, *Pro Des* David Munns, *Ed* Nic Gaster, *M* Kiril Dzajkovski, *Costumes* Anne Jendritzko, Ane Crabtree and Meta Sever.

Film Consortium/History Dreams/ena Film/Fandango Prods/South Fork Pictures/Film Council/BskyB/British Screen, etc-Pathé.
124 mins. UK/Germany/Italy/Macedonia/USA/Spain/Switzerland. 2001. Rel: 3 May 2002. Cert 18.

E

Left: The Spy Who Came in for the Code: Dougray Scott and Kate Winslet talk business in Michael Apted and Mick Jagger's glossy wartime thriller, *Enigma* (from Buena Vista)

Ed Gein ★★

Plainfield, Wisconsin; the late 1950s. Still under the influence of his late, Bible-bashing mother (who inculcated in her sons an abomination of sex), Ed Gein now lives by himself in the family farmhouse. Having abandoned the upkeep of the homestead for more personal pursuits, Gein is considered an oddball by the locals. If only they knew *how* odd... Though he was the inspiration for *Psycho*, *The Texas Chain Saw Massacre*, *Deranged* and *The Silence of the Lambs*, Ed Gein was a fairly unprepossessing man. And, by attempting to strip away the myth surrounding the monster, writer-director Chuck Parello has produced a very ordinary movie. Executive producer Steve Railsback, who gave an electric impersonation of Charles Manson in *Helter Skelter* 25 years ago, fails to bring Gein alive, creating a puppet-like caricature of a simple, misguided little man. The story of Ed Gein, America's most perverted serial killer, should, at the very least, chill or nauseate. However, it seems that in staking out the banality of his subject's 'social' persona, Parello has fashioned a biography that is itself banal.

• *Ed Gein* Steve Railsback, *Augusta Gein* Carrie Snodgress, *Collette Marshall* Carol Mansell, *Mary Hogan* Sally Champlin, *Brian* Steve Blackwood, *Pete Anderson* Craig Zimmerman, *Sheriff Jim Stillwell* Pat Skipper, *Eleanor Adams* Nancy Linehan Charles, *George Gein* Bill Cross.
• *Dir* Chuck Parello, *Pro* Hamish McAlpine and Michael Muscal, *Ex Pro* Karen Nicholls and Steve Railsback, *Screenplay* Stephen Johnston, *Ph* Vanja Cernjul, *Ed* Elena Maganini, *M* Robert McNaughton, *Costumes* Niklas J Palm, *Make-up* Dan Striepeke.

Tartan Films-Metro Tartan.
88 mins. USA. 2000. Rel: 20 July 2001. Cert 15.

Éloge de l'amour ★★★★★

Godard's latest film is in two parts and features an artist (Putzulu) who is first seen casting for a project about love and then, in the second half set three years earlier, is found researching the French Resistance in World War II and meeting a couple involved in it who have sold their stories to Hollywood. But the film is really an essay in which plot-lines exist mainly to enable Godard to express his own ideas on life, memory, politics, society, art and commercial movies. As befits a man who first triumphed in the sixties, cinema's most intellectual decade, it's thought-provoking, idiosyncratic, experimental (the wonderful black-and-white photography of the first part yields to colour-saturated digital shooting in the second) and witty. A Proustian reflection, the film also concerns itself with the changing phases of love between youth and old age. Those not attuned to Godard are liable to be bored stiff, but his admirers will be stimulated by a work likely to be regarded as epitomising everything for which he stands.
[*Mansel Stimpson*]

• *Edgar* Bruno Putzulu, *Berthe* Cécile Camp, *Mr Rosenthal* Claude Baignères, *Mayor Forlani* Remo Forlani, *grandfather* Jean Davy, *grandmother* Françoise Verny, *Eglantine* Audrey Klebaner, *waiter* Philippe Lyrette, *Perceval* Jeremy Lippmann.
• *Dir* and *Screenplay* Jean-Luc Godard, *Pro* Alain Sarde and Ruth Waldburger, *Ph* Julien Hirsch and Christophe Pollock, *Ed* Raphaële Urtin, *M* Ketil Bjornstad, David Darling, Karl Amadeus Hartmann, Maurice Jaubert, Arvo Pärt and Georges Van Parys, *Costumes* Marina Thibaut.

Avventura Films/Canal Plus/Les Films Alain Sarde/Peripheria/Television Suisse-Romande/Vega Film/arte France Cinema-Optimum Releasing.
98 mins. France/Switzerland. 2001. Rel: 23 November 2001. Cert PG.

L' emploi du temps ★★

Vincent Renault is a happily married father of three who seems to relish his job. But his endless journeys away from home, in which he spends most of his time in his car and in cafés, seem to have nothing to do with the busy schedule he talks of. Vincent is in fact just keeping up appearances – he has been fired and can't bring himself to face the truth… Inspired by the true story of a killer who led a double-life – but with the homicides removed – *L' emploi du temps* is a murder mystery without the murder. While beautifully made and often intriguing at times, the film is just too long and too slow to support the thinness of its conceit. With most of the plot played out on the gentle face of Aurélien Recoing (a blend of younger versions of Dan Aykroyd, Klaus Maria Brandauer and Tommy Lee Jones), the film goes nowhere but in.
English title: *Time Out.*

• *Vincent Renault* Aurélien Recoing, *Muriel Renault* Karin Viard, *Jean-Michel* Serge Livrozet, *Vincent's father* Jean-Pierre Mangeot, *Vincent's mother* Monique Mangeot, *Julien* Nicolas Kalsch, *Alice* Marie Cantet, *Félix* Félix Cantet, *Jeffrey* Nigel Palmer.
• *Dir* Laurent Cantet, *Pro* Caroline Benjo, *Ex Pro* Barbara Letellier, *Assoc Pro* Carole Scotta and Simon Arnal, *Screenplay* Cantet and Robin Campillo, *Ph* Pierre Milon, *Art Dir* Romain Denis, *Ed* Campillo, *M* Jocelyn Pook, *Costumes* Elizabeth Mehu.

Haut et Court/Arte France Cinéma/Canal Plus-Artificial Eye.
134 mins. France. 2001. Rel: 5 April 2002. Cert PG.

Enigma ★★★¹/₂

What is or *who* is the 'enigma'? The Enigma was a signalling machine invented by the Germans to encode strategic military messages prior to and during the Second World War. At Bletchley Park, 60 miles north of London, a team of mathematicians, linguists, electrical engineers and crossword enthusiasts work around the clock to break the code. Meanwhile, the largest shipment of merchandise ever launched by the Americans across the North Atlantic is under threat from a U-boat division. And Bletchley's leading code breaker, Tom Jericho, has lost his marbles over a woman. She has gone missing – and with her the secret to her mysterious identity… As a colourful look at a top-secret operation that remained classified until 1974 (up until the publication of Frederick William Winterbotham's *The Ultra Secret*), *Enigma* succeeds with knobs on. However, as a romantic wartime thriller – based on Robert Harris' 1995 bestseller – it is less successful. While the pieces of the narrative puzzle are artfully shuffled into place around the factual reconstruction of Bletchley, the film deteriorates into far-fetched melodrama as the fictitious story takes over. Still, there is much to enjoy, not least Jeremy Northam's cut-glass portrayal of the tenacious, silver-tongued secret service agent Wigram, John Barry's distinctive, luxurious score and some attractive location work.

• *Tom Jericho* Dougray Scott, *Hester Wallace* Kate Winslet, *Wigram* Jeremy Northam, *Claire Romilly* Saffron Burrows, *Puck* Nikolaj Coster Waldau, *Logie* Tom Hollander, *Leveret* Donald Sumpter, *Cave* Matthew MacFadyen, *Baxter* Richard Leaf, *Skynner* Robert Pugh, *Admiral Trowbridge* Corin Redgrave, *Mermagen* Michael Troughton, *Heaviside* Edward

Hardwicke, Ian Felce, Bohdan Poraj, Paul Rattray, Richard Katz, Tom Fisher, Nicholas Rowe, Angus MacInnes, Mary MacLeod, Anne-Marie Duff, Tim Bentinck, Mick Jagger.
• *Dir* Michael Apted, *Pro* Lorne Michaels and Mick Jagger, *Ex Pro* Victoria Pearman, Guy East and Nigel Sinclair, Hanno Huth and Michael White, *Co-Pro* David Brown, *Assoc Pro* Ate de Jong, Julian Plunkett-Dillon and Jeanney Kim, *Screenplay* Tom Stoppard, *Ph* Seamus McGarvey, *Pro Des* John Beard, *Ed* Rick Shaine, *M* John Barry; Ralph Vaughan Williams, J S Bach, *Costumes* Shirley Russell, *Historical adviser* Tony Sale.

Miramax/Intermedia Films/Senator Entertainment/MeesPierson/Jagged Films/Broadway Video-Buena Vista.
119 mins. UK/USA/Netherlands/Germany. 2001. Rel: 28 September 2001. Cert 15.

Eureka ★★★

For some two hours this epic film deals brilliantly with the theme of readjustment after a traumatic experience. We follow the lives of three people from a small town in Japan who have survived the hijacking of a bus when many died. Two of the three are teenage passengers, a brother and sister, and the third, who subsequently looks after the children when they are orphaned, is the driver who feels guilty for having survived. Sadly, the second half of this mammoth work (217 minutes) is less convincing, over-extended and ultimately both banal and sentimental (colour replaces black-and-white for an affirmative ending). No rating system can really make sense of a film which becomes so boring but which also contains so much of quality. The acting is excellent throughout. [*Mansel Stimpson*]

• *Makoto Sawai* Koji Yakusho, *Kozue Tamura* Aoi Miyazaki, *Naoki Tamura* Masaru Miyazaki, *Akihiko* Yoichiro Saito, *Yumiko* Sayuri Kokusho, *Shigeo* Ken Mitsuishi, *Busjack Man* Go Riju.
• *Dir* Shinji Aoyama, *Pro* Takenori Sento, *Screenplay* Shinji Aoyama, *Ph* Masaki Tamura, *Pro Des* Takeshi Shimizu, *Ed* Shinji Aoyama, *M* Shinji Aoyama, Albert Ayler, Jim O'Rourke and Isao Yamada.

Dentsu/Imagica Corp/J Works/Les Films de L'Observatoire/Suncent Cinema Works/Tokyo Theaters Co.
217 mins. Japan/France. 2000. Rel: 26 October 2001. Cert 15.

Everything Put Together ★★★★

Made prior to his acclaimed *Monster's Ball*, this is Marc Forster's study of three friends brought closer by shared pregnancies but then pulled apart when one of them, Angie, unexpectedly loses her child following the birth. The sense of immediacy attained by shooting on digital video has rarely been better used to capture the illusion of authenticity and the film strongly recalls Ingmar Bergman's *So Close to Life*. Add the fact that the women are as individually characterised as those in Eric Rohmer's films and it's clear why the first half, aided by superb acting, is masterly. The later scenes dealing with Angie's extreme grief and the reactions of husband and friends are not always quite so convincing, either in the writing or the direction. Despite this reservation, the film demands to be seen. [*Mansel Stimpson*]

• *Angie* Radha Mitchell, *Barbie* Megan Mullally, *Russ* Justin Louis, *Judith* Catherine Lloyd Burns, *Kessel* Alan Ruck, *April* Michele Hicks, *Dr Reiner* Matt Malloy, *Bill* Mark Boone Junior, *Angie's mother* Judy Geeson, *with* Tom McCleister, Jacqueline Heinze, Courtney Watkins.
• *Dir* Marc Forster, *Pro* Sean Furst, *Ex Pro* Adam Forgash, *Co-Pro* Jill Silversthorne, *Assoc Pro* Radha Mitchell, *Screenplay* Forster, Forgash and Catherine Lloyd Burns, *Ph* Roberto Schaefer, *Pro Des* Paul Jackson, *Ed* Matt Chessé, *M* Thomas Koppel, *Costumes* Judi Jordan, *Sound* Victor Iorillo.

Furst Films-ICA Projects.
85 mins. USA. 2000. Rel: 14 June 2002. No cert.

Evil Woman ★★★¹/₂

Wayne, JD and Darren Silverman have been friends since the fifth grade, united in their mutual obsession with Neil Diamond. When sexy but coldly manipulative Judith sets her sights on Darren, it's up to his loving, though inept, friends to 'save' him from marrying the wrong woman and reuniting Darren with his one, true love. Their psychotic former coach lends a hand and Neil Diamond himself helps bring this comedy home to its surprisingly satisfying conclusion… Director Dennis Dugan usually runs about 50/50 when it comes to delivering solid comedy. He's almost on target here, but it really comes down to the first-rate cast to deliver the laughs. Fortunately, Steve Zahn, Jack Black and Jason Biggs are at their hysterical best.
Original US title: *Saving Silverman.*
[*Scot Woodward Myers*]

• *Wayne Lefessier* Steve Zahn, *J D McNugent* Jack Black, *Darren Silverman* Jason Biggs, *Judith Snodgrass-Fessbeggler* Amanda Peet, *Sandy Perkus* Amanda Detmer, *Coach Norton* R Lee Ermey, *himself* Neil Diamond
• *Dir* Dennis Dugan, *Pro* Neal H Moritz, *Ex Pro* Bruce Berman, Bernie Goldmann, Brad Luff and Peter Ziegler, *Screenplay* Hank Nelken and Greg DePaul, *Ph* Arthur Albert, *Pro Des* Michael S Bolton, *Ed* Patrick J Don Vito and Debra Neil-

F

Fisher, *M* Mike Simpson; songs performed by Neil Diamond, Red Hot Chilli Peppers, Groove Armada, Apollo Four Forty, Everclear, Stereo MC's, Moby, Backstreet Boys, Mile, The Vandals, etc, *Costumes* Melissa Toth.

Columbia/NPV Entertainment/Original Film/Village Roadshow Prods-Columbia TriStar.
96 mins. USA/Australia/Canada. 2001. Rel: 11 January 2002. Cert 15.

The Experiment ★★★★

Cologne, Germany; the present. The ad in the newspaper is straightforward enough: 'Test participants needed. 4000 DM for 14 days. Experiment in mock prison.' Taxi driver Tarek Fahd could do with the money and when he's told that the experiment will involve no pain or any medicines or drugs, he cannot see the harm in it. He just has to play the part of a prisoner for two weeks. Of course, intimidation, humiliation and dehumanisation can have some unsettling side-effects… In August 1971 an experiment was carried out at Stanford University in order to evaluate the psychological effects of prison conditions. However, after just six days the experiment was cancelled. The volunteers randomly picked to 'play' the guards had resorted to extreme sadism, while the other volunteers, playing the prisoners, were breaking down under the stress. Taking this exercise as its starting point, Oliver Hirschbiegel's disturbing film is both a gripping and suspenseful thriller and, in the tradition of *Lord of the Flies*, a harrowing insight into the fragile balance of human nature. Expertly crafted and slickly realised, the film provides powerful and disconcerting food for thought.

• *Tarek Fahd* Moritz Bleibtreu, *Steinhoff, Prisoner #38* Christian Berkel, *Schütte, Prisoner #82* Oliver Stokowski, *Joe, Prisoner #69* Wotan Wilke Möhring, *Berus* Justus Von Dohnànyi, *Kamps* Nicki Von Tempelhoff, *Eckert* Timo Dierkes, *Professor Dr Klaus Thon* Edgar Selge, *Dr Jutta Grimm* Andrea Sawatzki, *Dora* Maren Eggert, *with* Stephan Szasz, Polat Dal, Danny Richter, Antoine Monot Jr, Philipp Hochmair.
• *Dir* Oliver Hirschbiegel, *Pro* Norbert Preuss, Marc Conrad and Fritz Wildfeuer, *Ex Pro* Philip Evenkamp, *Screenplay* Mario Giordano, Christoph Darnstädt and Don Bohlinger, based on the book *Black Box* by Giordano, *Ph* Rainer Klausmann, *Art Dir* Andrea Kessler, *Ed* Hans Funck, *M* Alexander Van Bubenheim; Vivaldi; songs performed by Linkin Park, The Beach Boys, Mohammed Abdu, and Marianne & Michael, *Costumes* Claudia Bobsin, *Sound* Magda Habernickel, *Prison design* Uli Hanisch.

Typhoon Film/Fanes Film-Metrodome.
114 mins. Germany. 2000. Rel: 22 March 2002. Cert 18.

The Farewell ★★★

That sensitive director Jan Schütte turns to history with this portrayal of one day in the life of the playwright and poet Bertolt Brecht just before his death. Well cast, well played and persuasive as a portrait of a writer, it spotlights the women, including his wife, who slaved for Brecht. It shows, too, how, at a time of political menace in the 1950s, the once radical artist compromised to retain his lifestyle, while justifying everything by placing above all else the need to continue his work for posterity. It's certainly a worthy film, but so sober that to kindle any dramatic fire here you have to be a Brecht enthusiast bringing your interest with you.
Original title: *Abschied*.
[*Mansel Stimpson*]

• *Bertolt Brecht* Josef Bierbichler, *Helene Weigel* Monica Bleibtreu, *Elisabeth Hauptmann* Elfriede Irrall, Margit Rogall, Jeannette Hain, Samuel Fintzi.
• *Dir* Jan Schütte, *Pro* Gesche Carstens, Henryk Romanowski and Jan Schütte, *Screenplay* Klaus Pohl, *Ph* Edward Klosinski, *Pro Des* Katharine Wöppermann, *Ed* Renate Merck, *M* John Cale.

Novoskop Film/WDR/ORB/SWR/ARTE, etc-Artificial Eye.
91 mins. Germany. 2000. Rel: 10 August 2001. Cert PG.

The Fast and the Furious ★★★★

Addicted to speed and illegal racing in the back streets of Los Angeles, Dominic Toretto is the emperor of his own underground world. But there's a new kid in town, the hungry, equally possessed Brian Earl Spilner, who is determined to usurp Toretto's crown. However, Brian is an outsider and is viewed with suspicion by Toretto's cohorts, a distrust that may even prove to be valid... Leaving such notions as credibility and character development aside, this turbo-charged, fuel-injected adrenaline rush is a modern classic of B-movie cinema. With its ear-piercing soundtrack, roaring engines, screaming tyres, knee-weakening stunts and hot babes – not to mention a refreshingly streamlined plot – this is a film that delivers. Of course, how the Earth Summit will view such gas-guzzling is another question entirely. Formerly known as *Redline*.

• *Brian Earl Spilner/Brian O'Connor* Paul Walker, *Dominic Toretto* Vin Diesel, *Letty* Michelle Rodriguez, *Mia Toretto* Jordana Brewster, *Johnny Tran* Rick Yune, *Jesse* Chad Lindberg, *Leon* Johnny Strong, *Vince* Matt Schulze, *Edwin* Ja Rule, *Sgt Tanner* Ted Levine, *Agent Bilkins* Thom Barry, *Hector* Noel Guglielmi, *Ferrari driver* Neal H Moritz, Vyto Ruginis, Stanton Rutledge, R J de Vera, Beau Holden, Reggie Lee.
• *Dir* Rob Cohen, *Pro* Neal H Moritz, *Ex Pro* Doug Claybourne and John Pogue, *Screenplay* Gary Scott Thompson and Erik Bergquist and David Ayer, *Ph* Ericson Core, *Pro Des* Waldemar Kalinowski, *Ed* Peter Honess, *M* BT; songs performed by Live, Benny

Cassette, Shawna, Limp Bizkit, DMX, Redman and Method Man, Ja Rule, Caddillac Tah, Digital Assassins, Organic Audio, Ludacris, Tank, Santana, Molotov, Say Yes, Dope, Saliva, Faith Evans, BT, Brian Tyler, etc, *Costumes* Sanja Milkovic Hays, *Sound* Tim Walston and Charles Deenen, *Firearms consultant* Paul Walker III.

Universal/Mediastream-UIP.
107 mins. USA. 2001. Rel: 14 September 2001. Cert 15.

Fat Girl

See *A Ma Soeur!*

The 51st State ★★★¹/₂

Master chemist Elmo McElroy has invented the ultimate designer drug, a 'personal visit from God' that is 51 times stronger than cocaine and 51 times more hallucinogenic than LSD. And the beauty of it is that it's fashioned entirely from legal, over-the-counter ingredients. Elmo is asking $20m for the formula and, having made himself unwelcome in LA, reckons that Liverpool is as good a place as any to launch his party favour... The very idea of Samuel L Jackson in Merseyside, wearing a bad attitude and a kilt, is an appealing one. LJ surrounded by a menagerie of hard-arsed grotesques, each of whom thinks he's tougher than the next guy, is also an attractive scenario. Add some stylish directorial flourishes from Hong Kong-born Ronny Yu, an avalanche of colourful expletives from first-time scripter Stel Pavlou and a concept that is just this side of tenable, and you have an entertainment that delivers. The film could have done with a bit more edge (Ronny Yu is no Guy Ritchie), but the breathless exuberance of it all glosses over most complaints.

• *Elmo McElroy* Samuel L Jackson, *Felix DeSouza* Robert Carlyle, *Dakota Phillips* Emily Mortimer, *Iki* Rhys Ifans, *Leopold Durant* Ricky Tomlinson, *Virgil Kane* Sean Pertwee, *The Lizard* Meat Loaf, *Arthur* Michael Stark, *Frederick* Paul Barber, *Shirley DeSouza* Anna Keaveney, Steven Walters, Nigel Whitmey, Michael J Reynolds, Nick Bartlett, Angus MacInnes, Joan Campion, Terry O'Neill, Robert Fyfe.
• *Dir* Ronny Yu, *Pro* Andras Hamori, Samuel L Jackson, Seaton McLean, Jonathan Debin, David Pupkewitz and Malcolm Kohll, *Ex Pro* Julie Yorn, Eli Selden and Stephanie Davis, *Co-Pro* Mark Aldridge, *Screenplay* Stel Pavlou and (uncredited) David Leland, *Ph* Poon Hang-sang, *Pro Des* Alan MacDonald, *Ed* David Wu, *M* Casper Kedros and Darius Kedros; songs performed by Buddy Miles, House of Pain, Run DMC, P J Harvey, Nelly, Saliva, Warrior, Robby Real, Headrillaz and Ricky Barrow, *Costumes* Kate Carin, *Sound* Garrett Kerr.

Alliance Atlantis/The Film Consortium/Film Council/
Focus Films/Fifty First Films/National Lottery-

Momentum Pictures.
92 mins. UK/Canada. 2001. Rel: 7 December 2001. Cert 18.

Final Fantasy: The Spirits Within ★★★¹/₂

Earth; 2065. By far the best film based on a video game to date, *Final Fantasy* is a post-apocalyptic, New Age story of alien invasion. More significantly, it is a computer-animated adventure that presents its human protagonists as photo-realistic beings the like of which the cinema has never seen. Indeed, the story's heroine, Dr Aki Ross, is a far more human creation than the sinewy, cartoonish Lara Croft, even though the latter was played by a real actress. For the record, Aki has been invaded by an alien entity that appears to travel through her body of its own free will, impervious to the boundaries of cavity walls and membranes. Nonetheless, Aki is able to function normally in her conscious state, although her subconscious is haunted by horrific nightmares. Meanwhile, larger aliens, which have arrived on the back of a meteor, have depleted the earth's population. And so it's a race against time as Aki's mentor searches for the eight spirits that, combined, can dissipate the foreign menace – before the military blows the Earth to smithereens. Amazingly, in spite of its groundbreaking visuals (facilitated by a $100 million budget), *Final Fantasy* was a major disappointment at the US box-office. Maybe *Final Fantasy* enthusiasts were unwilling to watch a film where the moves are predetermined, when they could play the game on a video console at home…

• *Voices*: *Dr Aki Ross* Ming-Na, *Captain Gray Edwards* Alec Baldwin, *Ryan* Ving Rhames, *Neil* Steve Buscemi, *Jane* Peri Gilpin, *Dr Sid* Donald Sutherland, *General Hein* James Woods, *council members* Keith David, Jean Simmons, *Major Elliot* Matt McKenzie, John DiMaggio, Dwight Schultz, Vicki Davis.
• *Dir* Hironobu Sakaguchi and Motonori Skakibara, *Pro* Sakaguchi, Jun Aida and Chris Lee, *Line Pro* Deirdre Morrison, *Screenplay* Al Reinert and Jeff Vintar, from a story by Sakaguchi, *Ed* Christopher S Capp, *M* Elliot Goldenthal, *Animation* Andy Jones, *Sound* Randy Thom.

Columbia Pictures/Square Pictures/Final Fantasy/Amuse Inc/
Bandai Co Ltd/Dentsu Inc/Digicube, etc-Columbia TriStar.
106 mins. USA. 2001. Rel: 3 August 2001. Cert PG.

The Fluffer ★★

Aspiring cameraman Sean McGinnnis checks out *Citizen Kane* from his local video store only to find that he has rented *Citizen Cum*. Intrigued by what he sees, he applies for a job with the video's production company and falls for its star player, gay icon Johnny Rebel. However, Johnny – aka Mikey – is really into women and has just got his girlfriend pregnant… With a bare minimum of nudity, *The Fluffer* is a tame look at a sensational subject: ie, the gay porn industry. Indeed, a

Right: Roadkill: Brendan Fehr, Izabelle Miko and Kerr Smith drive into trouble in J S Cardone's unpleasant and occasionally inventive *The Forsaken* (from Columbia TriStar)

'fluffer' is actually somebody employed to keep the male performer 'ready for action'. Some of the writing is sharp ('The only thing worse than being gay is being straight – but at least you don't have to worship Cher'), the performances less so, while the dramatic climax fails to deliver.

• *Michael 'Mikey' Rossini aka Johnny Rebel* Scott Gurney, *Sean McGinnis* Michael Cunio, *Babylon* Roxanne Day, *Tony Brooks* Taylor Negron, *Sam Martins* Richard Riehle, *Alan Diesler* Tim Bagley, *Silver* Adina Porter, *Chad Cox* Robert Walden, Ruben Madera, Josh Holland, Mickey Cottrell, Guinevere Turner, *Marcella* Deborah Harry, and *as themselves* Chad 10" Donovan, Thomas Lloyd, Chi Chi LaRue, Karen Dior, Bradley Picklesheimer, Ron Jeremy, etc.
• *Dir* Richard Glazier and Wash West, *Pro* John R Sylla and Victoria Robinson, *Ex Pro* Rose Kuo, *Line Pro* Pat Scanlon, *Screenplay* West, *Ph* Mark Putnam, *Pro Des* Devorah Herbert, *Ed* John Binninger, *M* The Bowling Green and John Vaughn; songs performed by The Bowling Green, John Vaughn, The Supreme Beings of Leisure, The Inner Thumb, The Dandy Warhols, The Johnny Depp Clones, Tricky, The Buzzcocks, etc, *Costumes* Gitte Meldgaard.

Fluff and Fold LLC-Metrodome.
94 mins. USA. 2000. Rel: 1 February 2002. Cert 18.

The Forsaken ★★¹/₂

It all started a long time ago. However, to cut a long story short, eight French knights were condemned to roam eternity lusting for blood. Now there's one in Texas and he's set his sights on the beauteous Megan, to whom he's telegenetically linked. Meanwhile, 'coming attractions' editor Sean is driving a flash Mercedes from LA to Miami to attend his sister's wedding. On the way he picks up a hitchhiker who, in turn, rescues Megan

from the side of the road, thus attracting the destructive attention of the Texan Forsaken... You have to give writer-director J S Cardone some credit for trying. Even so, in spite of Cardone's makeover of the vampiric myth (here there are no fangs, stakes or garlic), *The Forsaken* feels nowhere near as fresh as either *Near Dark* or *From Dusk Till Dawn*. There are some photogenic locations (filmed in and around Yuma, Arizona), a handsome, unforgivable villain (who mocks his victims' abject fear before killing them) and credible turns from the young leads. But besides some inventive (and unpleasant) slaughter, *The Forsaken* lacks tension, style and humour.

• *Sean* Kerr Smith, *Nick* Brendan Fehr, *Megan* Izabella Miko, *Cym* Phina Oruche, *Pen* Simon Rex, *Ina Hamm* Carrie Snodgress, *Kit* Johnathon Schaech, *Teddy* Alexis Thorpe, Ed Anders, A J Buckley, Sara Downing, Bert Emmett.
• *Dir* and *Screenplay* J S Cardone, *Pro* Carol Kottenbrook and Scott Einbinder, *Ph* Steven Bernstein, *Pro Des* Martina Buckley, *Ed* Norman Buckley, *M* Johnny Lee Schell and Tim Jones.

Sandstorm Films-Columbia TriStar.
94 mins. USA. 2001. Rel: 7 September 2001. Cert 18.

40 Days and 40 Nights ★★¹/₂

Unable to exorcise the romantic demons of his last serious relationship (six months ago), web designer Matt Sullivan is an emotional mess. So, in order to overcome his sexual dysfunction, he decides to give up sex for Lent. That means no penetration, kissing, fondling, biting or even self-gratification for 40 days and 40 nights. Then Matt meets the incredibly sexy Erica… In an age that bombards us with sexual imagery from every available angle, abstinence does seem tricky – at least, the act of trying not to *think* about sex. For a hormonally normal 22-year-old web designer living in San Francisco, it must be especially hard, er, difficult. In real life a 40-day vow of celibacy would hardly be insurmountable, so it's up to the filmmakers to concoct a universe in which every girl is a babe and most of the imagery is suggestive. This is achieved with some skill, resulting in a slick fantasy where every guy's a wise-cracker and every woman's a nympho. It's kind of amusing in a romanticised smutty way, but it's not very convincing. And Josh Hartnett is no John Cusack.

• *Matt Sullivan* Josh Hartnett, *Erica Sutton* Shannyn Sossamon, *Nicole* Vinessa Shaw, *Ryan* Paulo Costanzo, *Jerry* Griffin Dunne, *John* Adam Trese, *Chris* Glenn Fitzgerald, *Candy* Monet Mazur, *Bagel Guy* Michael Maronna, *Matt's father* Barry Newman, *Matt's mother* Mary Gross, *Sam* Maggie Gyllenhaal, *David Broker* Dylan Neal, *with* Emmanuelle Vaugier, Lorin Heath, Christine Chatelain, Keegan Connor Tracy, Stanley Anderson, Jarrad Paul, Terry Chen, Kai Lennox, Christopher Gauthier, Nicole Wilder, Lina Teal.
• *Dir* Michael Lehmann, *Pro* Tim Bevan, Eric Fellner and Michael London, *Ex Pro* Liza Chasin and Debra Hayward, *Screenplay* Robert Perez, *Ph* Elliot Davis, *Pro Des* Sharon Seymour, *Ed* Nicholas C Smith, *M* Rolfe Kent; songs performed by Bob Schneider, Lords of Acid, INXS, Sugarbabes, Semisonic, Pete Yorn, Teddy Pendergrass, Fatboy Slim, Moby, Scapegoat Wax, Everclear, Prozzak, Sophie B Hawkins, Sgt Rock, etc, *Costumes* Jill Ohanneson.

Universal/Canal Plus/Miramax/Working Title/MiLo Prods-UIP.
95 mins. USA/France/UK/Canada. 2001. Rel: 31 May 2002. Cert 15.

Freddy Got Fingered ★

Big brother Gordy (Tom Green) wants to be an animator but can't seem to escape the tedium of working with cheese sandwiches. Younger brother Freddie makes it on his own and (along with the audience) is incredulous at the support his parents lavish on Gordy. After indulging in a variety of manic stunts, Gordy successfully pursues his own dream after meeting the inspirational and orally fixated Betty. Along the way, Gordy destroys the life of his increasingly exasperated father Jim (the always excellent Rip Torn). There are one or two laughs to be found amid Tom Green's surprisingly uninspired antics but nothing that justifies the time and money wasted here.
[*Scot Woodward Myers*]

• *Gordy Brody* Tom Green, *Jim Brody* Rip Torn, *Betty* Marisa Coughlan, *Freddy Brody* Eddie Kaye Thomas, *Darren* Harland Williams, *Mr Dave Davidson* Anthony Michael Hall, *Julie Brody* Julie Hagerty, *with* Jackson Davies, Conor Widdows, Drew Barrymore, Shaquille O'Neal

• *Dir* Tom Green, *Pro* Larry Brezner, Howard Lapides and Lauren Lloyd, *Ex Pro* Arnon Milchan, *Screenplay* Tom Green and Derek Harvie, *Ph* Mark Irwin, *Pro Des* Bob Ziembicki, *Ed* Jacqueline Cambas, *M* Mike Simpson; Wagner; songs performed by The Sex Pistols, Gary Numan, Sammy Davis Jr, Iggy Pop, The Ramones, The New Seekers, The New York Dolls, Moby, Green Day, The Dead Kennedys, Percy Sledge, Eminem, The Adolescents, etc, *Costumes* Glenne E Campbell.

Epsilon Motion Pictures/MBST/Regency Enterprises-Fox.
87 mins. USA. 2001. Rel: 19 October 2001. Cert 18.

From Hell ★★'/₂

Whitechapel, East London; 1888. Having witnessed the marriage of her friend Ann Crook to Queen Victoria's grandson Prince Albert, Mary Kelly and four of her closest associates have become a threat to the security of the monarchy. So the five 'unfortunates' are routinely and gruesomely dispatched by a shadowy figure, creating a panic among the working women of the East End. Meanwhile, Inspector Frederick Abberline calls on his powers of clairvoyance to help solve the murders…

If one is going to revisit the Jack the Ripper case (after all, this is at least the 26th film to feature the killer in one guise or another), then one might at least bring to it an iota of reality. With American stars, Prague locations and production design that sits up and begs for an Oscar, *From Hell* is a strange amalgam of artifice, fact, fantasy and theory. Like a lush nightmare conjured up through the doses of laudanum imbibed by Inspector Abberline, the film never registers as anything other than an operatic gore-fest.

• *Frederick Abberline* Johnny Depp, *Mary Kelly* Heather Graham, *Sir William Gull* Ian Holm, *Peter Godley* Robbie Coltrane, *Netley* Jason Flemyng, *Liz Stride* Susan Lynch, *Annie Chapman* Katrin Cartlidge, *Sir Charles Warren* Ian Richardson, *Kate Eddowes* Lesley Sharp, *Ben Kidney* Terence Harvey, *Ada* Estelle Skornik, *Dr Ferral* Paul Rhys, *Ann Crook* Joanna Page, *Prince Albert, The Duke of Clarence* Mark Dexter, *Lord Hallsham* Peter Eyre, *Queen Victoria* Liz Moscrop, *John Merrick* Anthony Parker, Nicholas McGaughey, Annabelle Apsion, Danny Midwinter, David Schofield, John Owens, Roger Frost, Ian McNeice, Melanie Hill.
• *Dir* Allen and Albert Hughes, *Pro* Don Murphy and Jane Hamsher, *Ex Pro* Allen and Albert Hughes Amy Robinson and Thomas M Hammel, *Screenplay* Terry Hayes and Rafael Yglesias, based on the graphic novel by Alan Moore and Eddie Campbell, *Ph* Peter Deming, *Pro Des* Martin Childs, *Ed* Dan Lebental and George Bowers, *M* Trevor Jones, *Costumes* Kym Barrett, *Sound* Tim Gedemer and Steve Boeddeker.

Fox/Underworld Pictures-Fox.
122 mins. USA. 2001. Rel: 8 February 2002. Cert 18.

Right: There must be an angel: Sean Landless tries on his feathers in Udayan Prasad's brave but pedestrian *Gabriel & Me* (from Pathé)

Gabriel & Me ★★

Newcastle, England; the present. Jimmy Spud is an 11-year-old boy whose father, an unemployed welder, is suffering from depression and a debilitating cough. Denied an outlet for his musical interests and his thirst for knowledge, Jimmy turns to the Archangel Gabriel to help him overcome his miserable domestic circumstances. Furthermore, if Jimmy can become an angel, then maybe he could save his father... Lee Hall has a thing about imaginative young lads from the north of England with narrow-minded, iron-fisted fathers. After he wrote *I Luv You Jimmy Spud* – the radio play on which this film is based – he went on to pen his first screenplay, *Billy Elliot* (which secured him an Oscar nomination). Unfortunately, *Gabriel & Me* doesn't really work. It's not because one can understand little of what newcomer Sean Landless says, it's because the film presents stock stereotypes with little shading, humour or nuance. As for the fantasy elements, they could have been imbued with a little more magic, even if they are a figment of Jimmy's imagination.

• *Dad, Peter Spud* Iain Glen, *Grandad* David Bradley, *Jimmy Spud* Sean Landless, *Mam* Rosie Rowell, *Gabriel* Billy Connolly, *Ridley* Ian Cullen, *Scout* Jordan Routledge, Sean Foley, Trevor Fox, Bridie Hales, Nicky Hayer, Jacqueline King, Dominic McHale.
• *Dir* Udayan Prasad, *Pro* Marc Samuelson and Peter Samuelson, *Ex Pro* Chris Bould, Ellen Bronfman and Andrew Hauptman, *Assoc Pro* Rachel Cuperman, *Line Pro* Miara Martell, *Screenplay* Lee Hall, *Ph* Alan Almond, *Pro Des* Andy Harris, *Ed* Barrie Vince, *M* Stephen Warbeck; Handel; 'Swing Low Sweet Chariot' performed by Ladysmith Black Mambazo, *Costumes* Mary-Jane Reyner.

Film Consortium/Film Council/FilmFour/Isle of Man Film Commission/British Screen/National Lottery-Pathé. 87 mins. 2001. UK. Rel: 2 November 2001. Cert 15.

George Washington ★★★★

Set in rural North Carolina, *George Washington* recounts one life-altering summer in the lives of a group of adolescents. They spend their time together dreaming of a better future and indulging the simpler pleasures of youth. When one of the friends is killed during an innocent game, they choose to cover it up with a lie. The literal tragedy of a child's death takes a back seat to the larger tragedy that is the loss of innocence. NC School of the Arts alumnus David Gordon Green has written and directed a poignant tale of children facing the very real consequences of their actions while taking their first steps into adulthood. [*Scot Woodward Myers*]

• *Nasia* Candace Evanofski, *George* Donald Holden, *Vernon* Damian Jewan Lee, *Buddy* Curtis Cotton III, *Sonya* Rachael Handy, *Rico Rice* Paul Schneider, *Damascus* Eddie Rouse, *Euless* Jonathan Davidson, *Ruth* Janet Taylor.
• *Dir* and *Screenplay* David Gordon Green, *Pro* Green, Sacha W Mueller and Lisa Muskat, *Ex Pro* Sam Froelich, *Ph* Tim Orr, Adam Stone, Steve Pedulla and Karey Williams, *Pro Des* Richard Wright, *Ed* Zene Baker and Steven Gonzales, *M* Michael Linnen, David Wingo, Andrew Gillis, Brian McBride and Mazinga Phaser, *Costumes* Michael Tully.

Blue Moon Filmed Prods/Code Red/Down Home Entertainment/Youandwhatarmy Filmed Challenges-BFI. 89 mins. USA. 2000. Rel: 28 September 2001. Cert 12.

Ghost World ★★★★¹/₂

Overweight and bespectacled, Enid is an outsider who takes some comfort from mocking those even weirder than her. Following graduation, she resists the conventional routes out of her small-town prison, dyes her hair green and half-heartedly looks for an apartment with her equally sarcastic friend, Rebecca. She then plays a practical joke on a middle-aged loser and finds herself inexplicably drawn to him... The first adaptation of a graphic novel to forge credible, flesh-and-blood characters, *Ghost World* is a haunting, funny and sardonic twist on the teen flick. Marking the fictional debut of the idiosyncratic documentarian Terry Zwigoff (*Louie Bluie*, *Crumb*), the film deftly exposes the underbelly of its milieu from the start, while taking sidelong swipes at corporate sponsorship and squeaky-clean over-achievers. Indeed, this is a perverse hymn to the underdog as well as a cautionary tale of the cruelty that lies in us all, whether it be dormant or hurtfully manifest. As the aimless, impatient misfit Enid, Thora Birch demolishes memories of her earlier career as a cute child star, while Steve Buscemi is painfully affecting and disarming as the loser who, to quote Enid, 'is such a clueless dork he is almost cool.'

FYI: The drawings in Enid's sketchbook are supplied by Sophie Crumb, the daughter of Robert Crumb, the subject of Terry Zwigoff's last film.

• *Enid* Thora Birch, *Rebecca* Scarlett Johansson, *Josh* Brad Renfro, *Roberta* Illeana Douglas, *Seymour* Steve Buscemi, *Enid's dad* Bob Balaban, *Joe* Tom McGowan, *Gerrold, pushy guy* David Cross, *Dana* Stacey Travis, *John Ellis* Pat Healy, *Norman* Charles C Stevenson Jr, *Doug* Dave Sheridan, *Melorra* Debra Azar, *with* Brian George, Rini Bell, T J Thyne, Ezra Buzzington, Lindsey Girardot, Joy Bisco, Venus DeMilo Thomas, Ashley Peldon, Marc Vann, Charles Schneider, Diane Salinger, Anna Berger, Bruce Glover, and (uncredited) *Maxine* Teri Garr.
• *Dir* Terry Zwigoff, *Pro* Lianne Halfon, John Malkovich and Russell Smith, *Ex Pro* Pippa Cross and Janette Day, *Line Pro* Barbara A Hall, *Screenplay* Zwigoff and Daniel Clowes, from the comic book by Clowes, *Ph* Affonso Beato, *Pro Des* Edward T McAvoy, *Ed* Carole Kravetz-Aykanian and Michael R Miller, *M* David Kitay; songs performed by Mohammed Rafi, Orange Colored Sky, The Unknowns, The Shadowmen, Sirens, The Buzzcocks, Mr Freddie, Rachid, Tom Anderson, Paul Cafaro, Skip James, Vince Giordano and The Nighthawks, Craig Ventresco, Blueshammer, Lionel Belasco, Joel Evans, Ashford and Simpson, ADZ, Gene Harris, Patience & Prudence, etc, *Costumes* Mary Zophres.

Granada Film/United Artsists/Jersey Shore/Advanced Medien/Mr Mudd-Icon.
111 mins. USA. 2001. Rel: 16 November 2001. Cert 15.

The Glass House ★★¹/₂

The comfortable and happy world of Ruby, 16, and Rhett Baker, 11, is shattered when their mother and father are killed in a car accident. However, their parents had invested well and the children have a handsome allowance to see them through the years. They are also lucky to be taken in by Erin and Terry Glass, an apparently wealthy middle-aged couple who live in a spacious, modern pile on the edge of the Pacific. Yet in spite of the new wealth (Rhett is given his own TV set with the latest in video game accessories, Ruby is plied with a designer wardrobe), there is something decidedly sinister about the new set-up... Seasoned scenarist Wesley Strick (*Arachnophobia*, *Cape Fear*, *Wolf*) has developed a nightmarish scenario here in which the true vulnerability of childhood is exploited to the full. But *The Glass House* has a major problem: because the eponymous residence is so sterile and open, it offers little threat to the viewer, while the film's glossy sheen negates any foreboding atmosphere. Even as the mounting evidence backs up Ruby's worst fears, the house and the children's predicament never feels entirely real. It's a shame, too, that the villain of the piece develops into such a one-dimensional monster, tipping the final act into the sort of formulaic horror that the film lampoons in its opening scene.

• *Ruby Baker* Leelee Sobieski, *Dr Erin Glass* Diane Lane, *Terry Glass* Stellan Skarsgård, *Alvin Begleiter* Bruce Dern, *Nancy Ryan* Kathy Baker, *Rhett Baker* Trevor Morgan, *Uncle Jack* Chris Noth, *Dave Baker* Michael O'Keefe, *Grace Baker* Rita Wilson, *Don Whitworth* Gavin O'Connor, *Whitey* Vyto Ruginis, Carly Pope, Chind Shavers, Agnes Bruckner, Michael Paul Chan, Rachel Wilson, Rutanya Alda, Maya Danziger, Leslie Sackheim, Drew Snyder.
• *Dir* Daniel Sackheim, *Pro* Neal H Moritz, *Ex Pro* Michael Rachmil, *Screenplay* Wesley Strick, *Ph* Alar Kivilo, *Pro Des* Jon Gary Steele, *Ed* Howard E Smith, *M* Christopher Young; songs performed by Superchick, BT, Powerman 5000, and Sukpatch, *Costumes* Chrisi Karvonides Dushenko.

Columbia Pictures/Original Film-Columbia TriStar.
106 mins. USA. 2000. Rel: 25 January 2002. Cert 15.

Glitter ★

Years after Billie Frank (Mariah Carey) is put into foster care by her alcoholic mother, she forms a musical group with her best friends. When DJ Julian Dice singles the gifted Billie out, it's not long before she lands a big recording contract, concert gigs and stardom. She also gains a manager, producer and boyfriend in Julian. But fame has its pitfalls and Julian spirals out of control, threatening to take Billie with him... Even Mariah Carey fans will cringe at the tedium of this

Above: Down the Up Staircase: Helen Mirren in her award-winning performance as Mrs Wilson in Robert Altman's ambitious and well-acted *Gosford Park* (from Entertainment)

Gohatto ★★★¹/₂

Returning to the cinema with a samurai tale of 1865, Japan's veteran director Nagisa Oshima proves that his cinematic sense is as potent as ever (superb visuals, intelligent use of sound). The well-staged action scenes do not predominate, however, because, once past an opening episode in which two teenagers demonstrate their fitness to become samurai through their swordsmanship, the film turns to its main theme: the extent to which such an all-male environment encourages homosexual feelings, acknowledged or repressed. What is described as a 'certain leaning' proves to be so widespread that some will feel the film overplays its hand, especially towards the close. But the cast, including famed actor-director Takeshi Kitano, is able, and the film is far from negligible. [*Mansel Stimpson*]

• *Captain Toshizo Hijikata* Beat Takeshi (aka Takeshi Kitano), *Lt. Soji Okita* Shinji Takeda, *Hyozo Tashiro* Tadanobu Asano, *Sozaburo Kano, young samurai* Ryuhei Matsuda, *Isami Kondo* Yoichi Sai, *Heibei Sugano* Koji Matoba.
• *Dir* and *Screenplay* Nagisa Oshima, based on the novel *Shinsengumi Keppuroku* by Ryotaro Shiba, *Pro* Eiko Oshima, Shigehiro Nakagawa and Kazuo Shimizu, *Ex Pro* Nobuyoshi Otani, *Ph* Toyomichi Kurita, *Pro Des* Yoshinobu Nishioka, *Ed* Tomoyo Oshima, *M* Ryuichi Sakamoto, *Costumes* Emi Wada, *Swordplay instructor* Hidenobu Togo.

Shôchiku Co Ltd/BS Asahi/Bac Films/Eisei Gekijo/ Imagica Corp/Kadokawa Shoten Publishing/Canal Plus/Oshima Prods/Recorded Picture Co-Momentum. 100 mins. Japan. 1999. Rel: 3 August 2001. Cert 15.

Gosford Park ★★★¹/₂

Gosford Park, the English countryside; November 1932. As a variety of aristocratic ne'er-do-wells and an American producer descend on Gosford Park for a weekend of shooting and gossip, the stage is set for scandal and revelation... Continuing his consummate return to form, Robert Altman turns his eye on the British class system and the traditional corpse in the library. After his now standard introduction to a menagerie of eccentric characters (seemingly embodied by half the British film industry), Altman then dissects the minutiae of England's social infrastructure. All this is fascinating stuff, like *Upstairs Downstairs* with a Merchant Ivory veneer and an Agatha Christie twist. Unfortunately, it is the Christie element that introduces a pat note of triteness to the proceedings, reducing an ambitious, masterly project to the level of a calculated whodunit. That doesn't mean we can't enjoy the wonderful performances (Maggie Smith has become the past mistress of the withering gaze) or the delicious dialogue supplied by Julian Fellowes' script. Filmed at Wrotham Park in Hertfordshire.

hackneyed story with its cookie-cutter lines and pathetic tugs at our heartstrings. It's positively eerie to watch the never-changing expression on Carey's face regardless of the emotional content of any given scene. [*Scot Woodward Myers*]

• *Billie Frank* Mariah Carey, *Julian Dice* Max Beesley, *Louise* Da Brat, *Roxanne* Tia Texada, *Lillian Frank* Valarie Pettiford, *Kelly* Ann Magnuson, *Timothy Walker* Terrence Howard, *with* Dorian Harewood, Grant Nickalls, Eric Benét, Bill Sage, Kate McNeil.
• *Dir* Vondie Curtis-Hall, *Pro* Laurence Mark, *Co-Pro* E Bennett Walsh, *Screenplay* Kate Lanier, from a story by Cheryl L West, *Ph* Geoffrey Simpson, *Pro Des* Dan Bishop, *Ed* Jeff Freeman, *M* Terence Blanchard, *Costumes* Joseph G Aulisi.

Twentieth Century Fox/Columbia/Glitter Productions/ Laurence Mark Productions/Maroon Entertainment-Columbia TriStar. 104 mins. USA/Canada. 2001. Rel: 23 November 2001. Cert PG.

• *Mrs Croft* Eileen Atkins, *Morris Weissman* Bob Balaban, *Jennings* Alan Bates, *Raymond, Lord Stockbridge* Charles Dance, *Inspector Thompson* Stephen Fry, *Sir William McCordle* Michael Gambon, *George* Richard E Grant, *Probert* Derek Jacobi, *Mary Maceachran* Kelly Macdonald, *Mrs Wilson* Helen Mirren, *Ivor Novello* Jeremy Northam, *Robert Parks* Clive Owen, *Henry Denton* Ryan Phillippe, *Constance, Countess of Trentham* Maggie Smith, *Lady Sylvia McCordle* Kristin Scott Thomas, *Elsie* Emily Watson, *Lieutenant Commander Anthony Meredith* Tom Hollander, *Louisa, Lady Stockbridge* Geraldine Somerville, *Dorothy* Sophie Thompson, *The Hon Freddie Nesbitt* James Wilby, *Mabel Nesbitt* Claudie Blakley, *Isobel McCordle* Camilla Rutherford, *Lady Lavinia Meredith* Natasha Wightman, Laurence Fox, Trent Ford, Ron Webster, Jeremy Swift, Meg Wynn Owen, Adrian Scarborough, Frances Low, Joanna Maude, Teresa Churcher, Finty Williams, Emma Buckley, Laura Harling, Frank Thornton, *Pip* Widget.
• *Dir* Robert Altman, *Pro* Altman and Bob Balaban, *Ex Pro* Jane Barclay, Sharon Harel, Robert Jones and Hannah Leader, *Co-Pro* Jane Frazer and Joshua Astrachan, *Screenplay* Julian Fellowes, from an idea by Altman and Balaban, *Ph* Andrew Dunn, *Pro Des* Stephen Altman, *Ed* Tim Squyres, *M* Patrick Doyle; songs performed by Jeremy Northam, Abigail Doyle, *Costumes* Jenny Beavan, *Home economist* Debbie Brodie.

Capitol Films/Film Council/USA Films/Sandcastle 5/Chicagofilms/Medusa Film-Entertainment.
137 mins. UK/USA. 2001. Rel: 1 February 2002. Cert 15.

Greenfingers ★★★★¹/₂

Near the tail end of his sentence, the antisocial Colin Briggs is 'reclassified to category D' and is transferred to Edgefield, an open prison in the Cotswolds. There, he is free to roam the grounds at will and shares a room with a wizened old inmate with a surprisingly sunny outlook. However, Colin resolves to keep himself to himself and is nonplussed when the old man gives him a packet of violet seeds as a Christmas present. When, against the odds, the violets flower the following spring, Colin is put in charge of a horticultural project initiated by the warder... Amazingly inspired by real events, this orchid in a weed patch of British comedy exploits a facet of the British character – and, indeed, of its wonderful countryside – seldom touched on in contemporary cinema. While sharing certain elements with *The Full Monty*, *Saving Grace* and *Lucky Break*, the film emits its own distinctive scent as it sows the seeds of hope and heart into the fabric of England's criminal underclass. As always, Clive Owen exhibits a central presence of unforced integrity, although it is the supporting cast that brings the full colour of this film alive. David Kelly, who played Michael O'Sullivan in *Waking Ned*, deserves a medal for his portrayal of grounded wisdom, while

the Brooklyn-born writer-director Joel Hershman should receive an honorary citizenship of Britain.

• *Colin Briggs* Clive Owen, *Georgina Woodhouse* Helen Mirren, *Fergus Wilks* David Kelly, *Primrose Woodhouse* Natasha Little, *Governor Hodge* Warren Clarke, *Tony* Danny Dyer, *Raw* Adam Fogerty, *Jimmy* Paterson Joseph, *Dudley* Peter Guinness, *Holly* Lucy Punch, *Susan Hodge* Sally Edwards, *Nigel* Donald Douglas, Kevin McMonagle, Julie Saunders, Jorden Maxwell, David Lyon, Jan Chappell, Timothy Carlton, Brenda Cowling, Charles De'Ath, Trevor Bowen.
• *Dir* and *Screenplay* Joel Hershman, *Pro* Travis Swords, Daniel J Victor and Trudie Styler, *Ex Pro* Daniel J Victor, *Ph* John Daly, *Pro Des* Tim Hutchinson, *Ed* Justin Krish and Tariq Anwar, *M* Guy Dagul; songs performed by Stereophonics, Dave King, Capricorn, Tears for Fears, Sting, U2, Bruce Springsteen, Capella Istropolitania, Elton John and Little Richard, *Costumes* Frances Tempest.

Boneyard Entertainment/Xingu Films/Travis Swords Prods-Winchester Film Distributors.
91 mins. UK/USA. 2000. Rel: 14 September 2001. Cert 15.

Grégoire Moulin ★★¹/₂

With the titular hero being born on Friday the 13th in the Franz Kafka clinic, this French farce opens promisingly but soon becomes predictable, episodic and even unpleasant (Grégoire's ardent pursuit by a bisexual man is meant to be side-splittingly comic). As star, writer and director, Artus De Penguern would clearly like to be considered another Jacques Tati, but he lacks personality. As for the plot, it centres on the unending misfortunes which dog Grégoire on a day when, with Paris given over to football fever, he tries to keep an appointment with the girl he dotes on (charming Pascale Arbillot). Some may be won over by the film's energy, but, when compared to a great farce replete with surprises like *Le Dîner de cons*, it's a case of chalk and cheese.
Original title: *Grégoire Moulin contre l'humanité*.
[*Mansel Stimpson*]

• *Grégoire Moulin* Artus De Penguern, *Odile Bonheur/Emma in 'Madame Bovary'* Pascale Arbillot, *Jean-François* Didier Benureau, *Jacky* Clovis Cornillac, *Emmanuel Lacarrière* Antoine Dulery, *with* Serge Riaboukine, Elisabeth Vitali, Philippe Magnan.
• *Dir* Artus De Penguern, *Pro* Cyrile Colbeau-Justin, *Ex Pro* Patrick Aumigny, *Screenplay* De Penguern and Jerome L'Hotsky, *Ph* Vincent Mathias, *Art Dir* Sylvie Olive, *Ed* Corinne Cahour, Claude-France Husson and Christophe Marthoud, *M* Benoit Pimont; Brahms, *Costumes* Marie-Laure Lasson.

LGM/M6 Films/Litswa/SFP Cinéma, etc-Millennium Films.
91 mins. France. 2001. Rel: 7 June 2002. Cert 15.

H

Right: Field day: Yep, *Hardball* (from UIP) is another film about disadvantaged kids who manage to overcome impossible odds to make it on the field

Happy Man ★★

If there's any irony in this terrible tale, then it's pretty abstruse. The story of an unemployed, unattached no-hoper coming to terms with his mother's terminal cancer, *Happy Man* is a grim, humourless and virtually immobile piece of cinema. From the opening shots of unsmiling faces to the open-ended conclusion, this is one miserable experience crying out for a single good joke.
Original title: *Szczesliwy Czlowiek*.

• *Maria* Jadwiga Jankowska-Cieslak, *Jas* Piotr Jankowski, *Marta* Malgorzata Hajewska-Krzysztofik, *with* Roman Gancarczyk, Mieczyslaw Grabka.

• *Dir* and *Screenplay* Malgorzata Szumowska, *Pro* Wojciech J Has, *Ph* Marek Gajczak and Michal Englert, *Pro Des* Marek Zawjerucha, *Ed* Jacek Drosio, *M* Zygmunt Konieczny.

Indeks Film Studio-NFT.
84 mins. Poland. 2000. Rel: 17 May 2002. No cert.

Hardball ★¹/₂

Inveterate gambler Conor O'Neill owes $12,000 in ill-placed bets and can see no way out of his dilemma. He is then offered $500 a week to coach a team of African-American children from the housing projects

of Chicago. Conor hates kids but it appears to be his only option to keep his head above water… It's hardly reassuring to know that *Hardball* is 'inspired' by real events (chronicled in Daniel Coyle's book *Hardball: A Season in the Projects*). Keanu Reeves still acts like an automaton with a cog missing, while the schmaltz is laid on with a JCB. Worse, though, is the familiarity of a story about a deadbeat baseball team overcoming impossible odds to find their self-confidence. To be fair, there is a remarkable performance from fifth grader DeWayne Warren, although it's a shame that much of his dialogue is unintelligible.

• *Conor O'Neill* Keanu Reeves, *Elizabeth Wilkes* Diane Lane, *Ticky Tobin* John Hawkes, *Matt Hyland* D B Sweeney, *Jimmy Fleming* Mike McGlone, *Sterling* Sterling Elijah Brim, *Duffy* Graham Beckel, *Jefferson Albert Tibbs* Julian Griffith, *G-Baby* DeWayne Warren, *with* Bryan Hearne, Michael B Jordan, Kristopher Lofton, Michael Perkins, Brian Reed, Alexander Telles.
• *Dir* Brian Robbins, *Pro* Robbins, Mike Tollin and Tina Nides, *Ex Pro* Kevin McCormick, Herbert W Gains and Erwin Stoff, *Screenplay* John Gatins, *Ph* Tom Richmond, *Pro Des* Jaymes Hinkle, *Ed* Ned Bastille, *M* Mark Isham; songs performed by RL, Fundisha, Lil Bow Wow, Lil' Wayne, Lil' Zane and Sammie, Jagged Edge, The Notorious B.I.G., The Isley Brothers, DMX, R

Kelly, etc, *Costumes* Francine Jamison-Tanchuck, *Baseball guru* Mark Ellis.

Paramount/Fireworks Pictures/MFP Munich Film Partners-UIP.
106 mins. USA/Germany. 2001. Rel: 21 June 2002. Cert 12.

Harry Potter and the Philosopher's Stone ★★★

By turns ignored and mistreated, Harry Potter is brought up at No 4 Privet Drive by his aunt and uncle in tandem with their spoiled, obnoxious son, Dudley. Then one day Harry receives a visit from Hagrid the giant, who tells him that it's time to attend Hogwarts School of Witchcraft and Wizardry… The problem with a property as successful as the Harry Potter franchise is that everyone is terrified of spoiling the magic formula. So, inevitably, the film is long and starry and loyal to the book to a fault. It's easy to see why Chris Columbus (*Home Alone*, *Mrs Doubtfire*) was chosen to helm this particular ship: he's hard-working, conventional and great working with kids. Indeed, the film's real magic is between Radcliffe, Grint and Watson, all of whom are wonderful and hint at successful showbiz careers well into adulthood. The grown-ups aren't half-bad either, although Ian Hart is terribly miscast as Professor Quirrell. Be that as it may, the matte shots

Above: Judgement at Augsburg: Colin Farrell battles with ingrained racism in Gregory Hoblit's dull and implausible *Hart's War* (from Fox)

aren't perfect, John Williams' score is intrusive and leaden and the film never comes close to realising the excitement of the book. If *Harry Potter* hadn't been such a protected species – and had somebody with the creative ingenuity of, say, Jean-Pierre Jeunet (*The City of Lost Children, Amélie*) been given free rein with the material – then HP could have been as wizard on celluloid as on the written page.

US title: *Harry Potter and the Sorcerer's Stone.*

• *Harry Potter* Daniel Radcliffe, *Ronald 'Ron' Weasley* Rupert Grint, *Hermione Granger* Emma Watson, *Nearly Headless Nick* John Cleese, *Gamekeeper Rubeus Hagrid* Robbie Coltrane, *Professor Flitwick* Warwick Davis, *Uncle Vernon Dursley* Richard Griffiths, *Professor Albus Dumbledore* Richard Harris, *Professor Quirrell/Voldemort* Ian Hart, *Mr Ollivander* John Hurt, *Professor Severus Snape* Alan Rickman, *Aunt Petunia Dursley* Fiona Shaw, *Professor Minerva McGonagall* Maggie Smith, *Mrs Molly Weasley* Julie Walters, *Madam Hooch* Zoë Wanamaker, *Neville Longbottom* Matthew Lewis, *Draco Malfoy* Tom Felton, *Mr Filch* David Bradley, *Dudley Dursley* Harry Melling, *Oliver Wood* Sean Biggerstaff, *Griphook* Vern Troyer, *Fat Lady* Elizabeth Spriggs, *Angelina Johnson* Danielle Taylor, *Alicia Spinnet* Leilah Sutherland, *Katie Bell* Emily Dale, *Adrian Pucey* David Holmes, *Marcus Flint* Will Theakston, *The Sorting Hat* Leslie Phillips, *the Bloody Baron* Terence Bayler, *Lily Potter* Geraldine Somerville, *James Potter* Adrian Rawlins.
• *Dir* Chris Columbus, *Pro* David Heyman, *Ex Pro* Columbus, Mark Radcliffe, Michael Barnathan and Duncan Henderson, *Co-Pro* Tanya Seghatchian, *Ass Pro* Paula Dupre Pesmen and Todd Arnow, *Screenplay* Steve Kloves, from the novel by Joanne Kathleen Rowling, *Ph* John Seale, *Pro Des* Stuart Craig, *Ed* Richard Francis-Bruce, *M* John Williams, *Costumes* Judianna Makovsky, *Visual Effects* Robert Legato.

Warner/Heyday Films/1492 Pictures-Warner.
152 mins. USA. 2001. Rel: 16 November 2001. Cert PG.

Hart's War ★★

Stalag VI A, Augsburg, Germany; December 1944. Following a brutal interrogation in which he is forced to reveal the whereabouts of Allied positions, Lt Thomas Hart is consigned to the barracks of a German POW camp. Having been a second-year law student at Yale before the war, Hart ends up defending a black officer accused of murder. Even in war, it seems, racism is rife and Hart can accrue little evidence to combat the ingrained prejudice of his fellow inmates… Lacking the directorial authority to bring this literary material alive, Gregory Hoblit has produced a film strong on visual accomplishment but weak on excitement or credibility. With Rachel Portman's downbeat and intrusive score casting a shadow over the proceedings from the outset, the film struggles to find its feet, helped little by the off-putting presence of Bruce Willis in an ambiguous part that he is ill qualified to fill. This is really Colin Farrell's movie, but he's given precious little to chew on. More expedient casting might have been Brad Pitt in the lead, with Billy Bob Thornton supplying the weight of ambiguity.

• *Colonel William A McNamara* Bruce Willis, *Lt Thomas Hart* Colin Farrell, *Lt Lincoln A Scott* Terrence Howard, *Staff Sgt Vic W Bedford* Cole Hauser, *Colonel Werner Visser* Marcel Iures, *Captain Peter A Ross* Linus Roache, *Lt Lamar T Archer* Vicellous Reon Shannon, *Sgt Carl S Webb* Rory Cochrane, *with* Maury Sterling, Sam Jaegar, Scott Michael Campbell, Adrian Grenier, Jonathan Brandis, Joe Spano, Ruaidhri Conroy, Tony Devlin.
• *Dir* Gregory Hoblit, *Pro* Hoblit, David Ladd, David Foster and Arnold Rifkin, *Ex Pro* Wolfgang Glattes, *Assoc Pro* Patricia Graf, *Screenplay* Billy Ray and Terry George, based on the novel by John Katzenbach, *Ph* Alar Kivilo, *Pro Des* Lilly Kilvert, *Ed* David Rosenbloom, *M* Rachel Portman, *Costumes* Elisabetta Beraldo.

MGM/David Ladd Films/David Foster Prods/Cheyenne Enterprises-Fox.
125 mins. USA. 2002. Rel: 24 May 2002. Cert 15.

Heartbreakers ★★¹/₂

When the spoils of their latest con goes to the IRS, mother-and-daughter team Max and Page Connors decide to stake out the ageing and horny millionaires of Palm Beach, Florida. But as Max homes in on a decrepit, chain-smoking billionaire, Page falls for the sweet charms of a potentially wealthy bartender… With their dark hair and tall, willowy figures, Sigourney Weaver and Jennifer Love Hewitt do make a convincing mother and daughter. But quite how anybody could fall for their burlesque act is another matter. Had these characters – or the farcical situations that they find themselves in – had an iota of credibility, then this over-long comedy could have been a real winner. As it is, *Heartbreakers* is a pretty naff film, albeit one perked up with a number of good moments. It's also nice to see such heavyweights as Gene Hackman and Ray Liotta try their hand at comedy. Of course, the best film about con artists is still David Mamet's *House of Games* (1987). Previously known as *Breakers*.

• *Maxine Connors/Angela Nardino/Ulga Yevanova* Sigourney Weaver, *Page Connors/Wendy/Jane Helstrom* Jennifer Love Hewitt, *Dean Cumanno/Vinny Staggliano* Ray Liotta, *Jack Withrowe*

Left: Life is a cabaret: Writer-director John Cameron Mitchell gives one of the year's most remarkable performances in his daring and exuberant *Hedwig and the Angry Inch* (from Entertainment)

Jason Lee, *William B Tensy* Gene Hackman, *Mr Appel* Jeffrey Jones, *Gloria Vogal/Barbara* Anne Bancroft, *Miss Madress* Nora Dunn, *Leo* Julio Oscar Mechoso, *auctioneer* Ricky Jay, *Linda* Sarah Silverman, *female minister* Shawn Colvin, Zach Galifianakis, Michael Hitchcock, Michael Andrew, Andy Brewster, Carrie Fisher, Jack Shearer, Elya Baskin, *Jack's lawyer* David Mirkin.
• *Dir* David Mirkin, *Pro* John Davis and Irving Ong,

Ex Pro Clayton Townsend, Gary Smith and Hadeel Reda, *Screenplay* Robert Dunn, Paul Guay and Steve Mazur, *Ph* Dean Semler, *Pro Des* Lilly Kilvert, *Ed* William Steinkamp, *M* John Debney; Mozart; theme by Danny Elfman; songs performed by Michael Andrew and Swingerhead, Sarah Vaughan, Beck, Alison Krauss, The Red Elvises, Sigourney Weaver, Shawn Colvin, John Lennon, etc, *Costumes* Gary Jones, *Ms Weaver's nutritionist* Brian Kula Fong.

Winchester Films/MGM/Davis Entertainment/Irving Ong-Icon.
124 mins. USA. 2001. Rel: 24 August 2001. Cert 15.

Hearts in Atlantis ★★★¹/₂

Broad Street, Harwich, Connecticut; 1960. 'Sometimes when you're young, you have moments of such happiness, you think you're living in someplace magical, like Atlantis must have been... Then we grow up and our hearts break into two.' So says Ted Brautigan, the enigmatic old man who has moved into the upstairs apartment of the house where Bobby Garfield, 11, and his mother live. For Bobby, it is a time of intense happiness and of continuing resentment, a time when friendship counts for more than family. It is also a period when the outside world intrudes on Bobby's sense of innocence... Although an adaptation of a Stephen King story, this is King in reflective, nostalgic mood, more *Stand by Me* than *The Shining*. And director Scott Hicks, who previously brought David Guterson's novel *Snow Falling on Cedars* to the screen, has really established a visual nuance to match the novella's simple, poetic prose, allowing events to unfold at a gentle, economic pace. And there are some wonderful performances here: Hope Davis' brittle, vulnerable Liz Garfield, Mika Boorem's self-assured Carol and, indeed, Anton Yelchin's wide-eyed yet wise-beyond-his-years Bobby Garfield. True, the overly familiar pop songs, the golden hues of summer and the general evocation of childhood is a bit heavy-handed, but the film ultimately casts a spell that is quite affecting.

• *Ted Brautigan* Anthony Hopkins, *Bobby Garfield* Anton Yelchin, *Liz Garfield* Hope Davis, *Carol Gerber* Mika Boorem, *adult Bobby Garfield* David Morse, *Monte Man* Alan Tudyk, *Len Files* Tom Bower, *Donald Biderman* Adam LeFevre, *with* Celia Weston, Will Rothhaar, Deirdre O'Connell, Timmy Reifsnyder.
• *Dir* Scott Hicks, *Pro* Kerry Heysen, *Ex Pro* Bruce Berman and Michael Flynn, *Screenplay* William Goldman, from the Stephen King story 'Low Men in Yellow Coats' (included in the book *Hearts in Atlantis*), *Ph* Piotr Sobocinski, *Pro Des* Barbara C Ling, *Ed* Pip Karmel, *M* Mychael Danna; songs performed by Fats Domino, Chubby Checker, The Platters, James Darren, Chuck Berry, Otis Rush, Paul Gayten, etc, *Costumes* Julie Weiss.

Castle Rock/Village Roadshow/NPV Entertainment-Warner.
101 mins. USA. 2001. Rel: 8 March 2002. Cert 12.

Hedwig and the Angry Inch ★★★★¹/₂

A drag queen, failed transsexual and 'internationally ignored' rock performer, Hedwig Robinson draws on his tragic past to fuel his bizarre cabaret act. Born Hansel Schmidt to an American GI and German housewife in East Berlin, Hedwig spent much of his youth listening to American Forces radio in his mother's oven. Then he's given the chance for freedom when a black American soldier offers him marriage in exchange for a sex change operation... What started as a drag act and ended as a hit off-Broadway show, *Hedwig* now reaches the screen as a startlingly original and touching tribute to the enormous talent of its creator, the writer-director-drag queen John Cameron Mitchell. Himself the son of an American soldier once stationed in Berlin, Mitchell opens his guts in an extraordinary performance that preaches tolerance and the power of love. A compulsive melange of rock performance, narrative flashback and animation, the film sucks the viewer into Hedwig's singular, strange and tragic world with a force that is completely disarming.
FYI: The role of Yitzhak, Hedwig's husband, is played by the actress Miriam Shor, who originated the role in New York.

• *Hedwig Robinson/Hansel Schmidt* John Cameron Mitchell, *Yitzhak* Miriam Shor, *Skszp* Stephen Trask, *Jacek* Theodore Liscinski, *Krzystof* Rob Campbell, *Schlatko* Michael Aronov, *Phyllis Stein* Andrea Martin, *Hansel's mother* Alberta Watson, *Tommy Gnosis* Michael Pitt, *Sgt Luther Robinson* Maurice Dean Wint, Gene Pyrz, Karen Hines, Renate Options.
• *Dir* and *Screenplay* John Cameron Mitchell, *Pro* Christine Vachon, Katie Roumel and Pamela Koffler, *Ex Pro* Michael De Luca, Amy Henkels and Mark Tusk, *Ph* Frank G DeMarco, *Pro Des* Thérése DePrez, *Ed* Andrew Marcus, *M* and *lyrics* Stephen Trask; songs performed by John Cameron Mitchell, Stephen Trask, Girls Against Boys, Dar Williams, Miriam Shor, Maggie Moore, Alexander Lasarenko, and Traci Reynolds, *Costumes* Arianne Phillips, *Animation* Emily Hubley.

New Line Cinema/Killer Films/Sundance Institute-Entertainment.
92 mins. USA. 2001. Rel: 31 August 2001. Cert 15.

Heist ★★¹/₂

When veteran thief Joe Moore is identified by a clerk during the robbery of a jewellery store, he decides to call it a day. However, his grasping fence Mickey Bergman insists he do one last job, the robbery of a shipment of Swiss gold bullion. Mickey also stipulates that his arrogant nephew, Jimmy, goes along for the ride... As technology has advanced, so heist films have become increasingly complex. David Mamet, who started his filmmaking career as something of a double feinter (cf *House of Cards*, *Homicide*, *The Spanish Prisoner*) moved on to make more universal films, such as his affecting, understated version of *The Winslow Boy* and the hilarious, madcap *State and Main*. Here, Mamet returns to his love of intrigue, adding a few ingenious twists to the old double/triple-cross thriller but ultimately twisting himself into a corner. As the actors sound off like characters from one of Mamet's early plays, spiking their conversation with profane, stylised non-sequiturs, so the film lurches into a state of stilted realism, undone by several scams too many. This being David Mamet territory, there are some great lines ('Everybody needs money – that's why they call it money') but it's not enough.

• *Joe Moore* Gene Hackman, *Mickey Bergman* Danny DeVito, *Bobby Blane* Delroy Lindo, *Jimmy Silk* Sam Rockwell, *Fran* Rebecca Pidgeon, *Don 'Pinky' Pincus* Ricky Jay, *Betty Croft* Patti LuPone, Jim Frangione, Emilie Cassini, Marlyne Affleck.
• *Dir* and *Screenplay* David Mamet, *Pro* Art Linson, Elie Samaha and Andrew Stevens, *Ex Pro* Don Carmody, Tracee Stanley and James Holt, *Line Pro* Josette Perrotta, *Ph* Robert Elswit, *Pro Des* David Wasco, *Ed* Barbara Tulliver, *M* Theodore Shapiro, *Costumes* Renée April.

Warner/Morgan Creek/Franchise Pictures/Indelible Pictures-Warner.
109 mins. USA/Canada. 2001. Rel: 23 November 2001. Cert 15.

Help! I'm a Fish ★★★
When Fly, his little sister Stella and their cousin Chuck go on a covert fishing trip, they stumble across an eccentric professor. Holed up in an underground marine-biology lab, the latter has concocted a potion that can turn humans into fish – in the event of widespread flooding produced by global warming. Mistaking the brew for lemonade, Stella takes a swig and is transformed into a starfish. To save her, Fly and Chuck also imbibe the liquid and embark on a miraculous oceanic adventure... It's nice to know that in the age of *Shrek* and *Final Fantasy*, there are still cartoons out there that can get by on charm and storytelling alone. Actually, for traditional cel animation, the underwater scenes are quite beguiling, with the aquatic effects and spectacular carpets of fish a constant delight to the eye. The English-language version is also treated to a delightfully sardonic reading from Alan Rickman as a power-hungry pilot fish.
Original title: *Hjælp, jegeren fisk*.

• *Voices*: *Joe* Alan Rickman, *Professor H O Mac Krill* Terry Jones, *Chuck* Aaron Poul, *Fly* Jeff Pace, *Stella* Michelle Westerson, *Sasha* Louise Fribo, *Aunt Anna* Pauline Newstone, David Bateson, Teryl Rothery, John Payne.

• *Dir* Michael Hegner and Stefan Fjeldmark, *Pro* Anders Mastrup, Eberhard Junkersdorf and Russell Boland, *Ex Pro* Christoph Sieciechowwicz, Harro von Have and Gerry Shirren, *Screenplay* Fjeldmark, Karsten Kiilerich and John Stefan Olsen, *Art* Matthias Lechner, *Ed* Per Risager, *M* Søren Hyldgaard; songs performed by Eddi Reader, Terry Jones, Solveig, Creamy, Alan Rickman, and Molly Jay.

A. Film ApS/Egmont Imagination/Munich Animation, etc-Metrodome.
80 mins. Denmark/Germany/Ireland. 2000. Rel: 10 August 2001. Cert U.

High Heels and Low Lifes ★★★
Shannon is an overworked nurse at a London hospital (St Catherine's), Frances is an American actress struggling to make ends meet and Mr Mason is a vicious ex-army thug without a sense of humour. When Shannon and Frances accidentally eavesdrop on Mason's successful robbery of a nearby bank, they decide to blackmail him for a token $300,000. So he decides to kill them... Taken in the right spirit, *High Heels and Low Lifes* is a goofily endearing, high-spirited and unpredictable comedy in which Minnie Driver and Mary McCormack appear to be enjoying themselves enormously. Giving the British gangster genre an irreverent spin (imagine Thelma and Louise in *Lock, Stock* territory), Kim Fuller's witty script juggles its various worlds – nursing, acting, crime – with unabashed glee. There's also some colourful location work of little-seen corners of London and a priceless turn from Michael Gambon as an exasperated (and homosexual) Mr Big.

• *Shannon* Minnie Driver, *Frances* Mary McCormack, *Mr Mason* Kevin McNally, *Kerrigan* Michael Gambon, *Danny* Danny Dyer, *Tremaine* Mark Williams, *McGill* Kevin Eldon, *Barry Tarson* Len Collin, *Chief Inspector Rogers* Julian Wadham, *Ray* Darren Boyd, *Mickey* Junior Simpson, *farmer* Hugh Bonneville, Ranjit Krishnamma, John Sessions, Paul Bown.
• *Dir* Mel Smith, *Pro* Uri Fruchtmann and Barnaby Thompson, *Co-Pro* Nicky Kentish-Barnes, *Screenplay* and *Assoc Pro* Kim Fuller, from a story by Fuller and Georgia Pritchett, *Ph* Steven Chivers, *Pro Des* Michael Pickwoad, *Ed* Christopher Blunden, *M* Charlie Mole; Elgar; numbers performed by The Trammps, Edwin Starr, Groove Armada, The Meters, Chris Montez, Faithless, Mr Natural, Bert Kaempfert, Sugarbabes, Eurythmics and Aretha Franklin, and Mica Paris, *Costumes* Jany Temime.

Fragile Films-Buena Vista.
86 mins. UK. 2001. Rel: 20 July 2001. Cert 15.

Right: Grand Sam: Sean Penn proves that he's in touch with his inner child in Jessie Nelson's skilfully manipulative *I Am Sam* (from Entertainment)

I Am Sam ★★★★

Los Angeles; the present. On her seventh birthday, Lucy Diamond is taken into care by the authorities. Brought up solely by her autistic father, Lucy has been unable to keep up with the academic standards expected of her. Yet Lucy and her father cannot live without one another… On one level, *I Am Sam* is a pornographically sentimental, tricksily photographed and brutally manipulative cross between *Rain Man* and *Kramer vs Kramer*. In short, it is the sort of endeavour that critics live to crucify. On another level, the film hits so many recognisable truths, and does so with such a raw intensity, that it elevates the weepy to a higher art form. The notion of a gorgeous seven-year-old (played with uncanny precocity by the junior veteran Dakota Fanning) unable to live without her father (who has the intellectual capacity of a seven-year-old) is dramatic manna. Throw in Michelle Pfeiffer as the superficial ideal of a professional success story (with an unsettling resemblance to Ally McBeal, the TV heroine created by Ms Pfeiffer's husband David A Kelly), and one has the makings of a gut-twisting melodrama. Check your cynicism at the door and you should sob buckets.

• *Sam Dawson* Sean Penn, *Rita Harrison* Michelle Pfeiffer, *Annie Cassell* Dianne Wiest, *Lucy Diamond Dawson* Dakota Fanning, *Turner* Richard Schiff, *Margaret Calgrove* Loretta Devine, *Ifty* Doug Hutchison, *Randy Carpenter* Laura Dern, *Robert* Stanley DeSantis, *Brad* Brad Allan Silverman, *Joe* Joseph Rosenberg, *George* Bobby Cooper, *Dr Blake* Mary Steenburgen, *with* Rosalind Chao, Marin Hinkle, Ken Jenkins, Wendy Phillips, Scott Paulin, Kimberly Scott, Caroline Keenan, Eileen Ryan, Pamela Dunlap, Brent Spiner, Kathleen Robertson, Dennis Fanning, R D Call.
• *Dir* Jessie Nelson, *Pro* Nelson, Marshall Herskovitz, Edward Zwick and Richard Solomon, *Ex Pro* Claire Rudnick Polstein, Michael De Luca and David Scott Rubin, *Co-Pro* Barbara A Hall, *Screenplay* Nelson and

Kristine Johnson, *Ph* Elliot Davis, *Pro Des* Aaron Osborne, *Ed* Richard Chew, *M* John Powell; songs performed by The Black Crowes, Aimee Mann and Michael Penn, Rufus Wainwright, The Wallflowers, Ben Harper, Ben Folds, Eddie Vedder, Sarah McLachlan, and Sheryl Crow, *Costumes* Susie DeSanto.

New Line Cinema/Bedford Falls/Red Fish, Blue Fish Films-Entertainment.
125 mins. USA. 2001. Rel: 10 May 2002. Cert 12.

Ice Age ★★★

Against their better judgement, a woolly mammoth and a dim-witted sloth team up with a sabre-toothed tiger to help return a human baby to its family… With its vivid characters and spectacular backdrops of ice and snow, *Ice Age* promised to be the cartoon that put Twentieth Century Fox animation on the map. Yet while the film is constantly entertaining and frequently amusing, not to mention technically accomplished, it lacks the artistic ingenuity of Disney's better films, not to mention the savvy irreverence of DreamWorks' rival cartoons. In addition, Sid is a most annoying creation, while the 'adorable' baby at the heart of the story is too ugly to gain our empathy. In fact, the one-dimensional depiction of the humans is strangely at odds with the detailed, three-dimensional creation of the animals, producing a jarring inconsistency. Indeed, while much effort has gone into bringing the physical textures of the animals to life, the humans come off as merely plastic. But then in the wake of *Shrek* and *Monsters, Inc.*, expectations were unduly high. Had *Ice Age* arrived two years earlier, its simple pleasures may have been appreciated more.

• Voices: *Manfred* Ray Romano, *Sid* John Leguizamo, *Diego* Denis Leary, *Soto* Goran Visnjic, *Zeke* Jack Black, *Roshan* Tara Strong, *Rhinos* Cedric 'The Entertainer' and Stephen Root, *with* Diedrich

Left: The big chill: Sid and Manny look for the jerk who threw the snowball in Chris Wedge and Carlos Saldanha's enormously popular *Ice Age* (from Fox)

Bader, Alan Tudyk, Jane Krakowski, Josh Hamilton, and as *Scrat* Chris Wedge.
• *Dir* Chris Wedge and Carlos Saldanha, *Pro* Lori Forte, *Ex Pro* Christopher Meledandri, *Screenplay* Michael Berg, Michael J Wilson and Peter Ackerman, *Pro Des* Brian McEntee, *Ed* John Carnochan, *M* David Newman, *Sound* Sean Garnhart.

Twentieth Century Animation/Blue Sky-Fox.
81 mins. USA. 2002. Rel: 22 March 2002. Cert U.

I'm Going Home ★★★★★

Now in his nineties, the Portuguese writer-director Manoel de Oliveira brings a minimalist style to a film which haunts the mind but won't be to all tastes. Michel Piccoli, himself 76, plays a noted Parisian actor who, with good roles increasingly hard to find, recognises that it's time to end his career. Extracts from *The Tempest* and Ionesco's play *Exit the King* confirm that this, too, is about approaching death, and the actor's situation is contrasted with that of his grandson starting out in life. Humour is present in John Malkovich's portrayal of a quirky film director and in the film's wonderfully comic observation of human foibles. Piccoli illustrates perfectly the art of 'being' without seeming to act, and in this subtle, understated movie all human life exists. Wonderful. Original title: *Je rentre à la maison.*
[*Mansel Stimpson*]

• *Gilbert Valence* Michel Piccoli, *George* Antoine Chappey, *Marguerite* Catherine Deneuve, *John Crawford, the director* John Malkovich, *Sylvia* Leonor Baldaque, *Marie* Leonor Silveira, *with* Adrien de Van, Ricardo Trepa.
• *Dir* and *Screenplay* Manoel de Oliveira, *Pro* Paulo Branco, *Ph* Sabine Lancelin, *Pro Des* Yves Fournier, *Ed* Valerie Loiseleux, *M* Richard Wagner, Chopin,

Léo Ferré, *Costumes* Isabel Branco.
Madragoa Filmes/Gemini Films/France 2 Cinéma/Canal Plus-Artificial Eye.
89 mins. Portugal/France. 2000. Rel: 17 May 2002. Cert PG.

Impostor ★★★★

Planet Earth; 2079. Spencer Olham has grown up in a world without democracy, without a sky and without a concept of peace. The earth is at war with the genetically superior alien race of Centauri and Spencer has dedicated his adult years to developing new weapons to defeat the enemy. But then he is plunged into a nightmarish plot when he finds that he is a hunted man: the government believes that he is a replicant of his former self, with a bomb planted in his ribcage… Like *Blade Runner* and *Minority Report, Impostor* is based on a short story by the late Philip K Dick and shares much of the vivid imagination and dystopian scenario of the other films. Here, then, is a future foreseeably in our grasp, a world where voice activation has become the norm and where the advances of science already have a shabby look. As the hero-on-the-run, Gary Sinise is a refreshingly down-to-earth presence, with his passion for his wife providing the film's emotional core. The look of the film is also excellent and the story a superior blend of psychological thriller and detective mystery. Amazingly, Dick penned this tale back in 1953.

• *Spencer John Olham* Gary Sinise, *Dr Maya Olham* Madeleine Stowe, *Hathaway* Vincent D'Onofrio, *Nelson Gittes* Tony Shalhoub, *Dr Carone* Tim Guinee, *Cale* Mekhi Phifer, *Captain Burke* Gary Dourdan, *Chancellor* Lindsay Crouse, *midwife* Elizabeth Peña, *with* Shane Brolly, Golden Brooks, Scott Burkholder, Una Damon, John Gatins, Erica Gimpel, Kimberly Scott, Mac Sinise, Tracey Walter, and (uncredited) Rosalind Chao and Phil Hawn.
• *Dir* Gary Fleder, *Pro* Fleder, Gary Sinise, Marty Katz

and Daniel Lupi, *Ex Pro* Michael Phillips, *Co-Ex Pro* Bob Weinstein and Harvey Weinstein, *Screenplay* Caroline Case, Ehren Kruger and David Twohy, from an adaptation by Scott Rosenberg, *Ph* Robert Elswit, *Pro Des* Nelson Coates, *Ed* Armen Minasian and Bob Ducsay, *M* Mark Isham, *Costumes* Abigail Murray, *Visual effects* George Murphy and Joseph Grossberg.

Dimension Films/Mojo Films-Metrodome.
86 mins. USA. 2001. Rel: 14 June 2002. Cert 15.

In the Bedroom ★★★★¹/₂

Camden, Maine; the present. Matt and Ruth Fowler are a happily married, middle-aged couple leading comfortable lives, he as a local doctor, she as a choral music teacher. Meanwhile, their only son, a talented architectural student, has taken up with an older woman, with two children of her own and an estranged husband... Focusing on the minutiae of everyday life and coaxing exemplary performances from his outstanding cast, the actor Todd Field has fashioned an extraordinarily resonant, insightful and affecting film for his directorial debut. A hugely intelligent meditation on the various ramifications of grief, *In the Bedroom* may prove too slow for some viewers, but its deliberate pace and attention to domestic detail builds up a very real and credible scenario for the action to unfold upon. Far from the histrionics of Tennessee Williams and his ilk, the terrible drama at the film's core hits all the harder for its understatement. The scene, following the funeral, in which Dr Fowler and his wife are unable to express their heartache is simply numbing in its refusal to succumb to melodrama. And what a pleasure to see actors of the calibre of Wilkinson, Spacek and Tomei – not to mention the supporting players – being given room to exercise their considerable powers. Only the very end, which seems to drift into the conventional arena of film noir, fails to ring entirely true.

• *Ruth Fowler* Sissy Spacek, *Matt Fowler* Tom Wilkinson, *Frank Fowler* Nick Stahl, *Natalie Strout* Marisa Tomei, *Richard Strout* William Mapother, *Willis Grinnel* William Wise, *Katie Grinnel* Celia Weston, *Marla Keyes* Karen Allen, *Father McCasslin* Jonathan Walsh, *young Frank Fowler* Henry Field, Frank T Wells, W Clapham Murray, Justin Ashforth, Terry A Burgess, Camden Munson, Deborah Derecktor, Harriet Dawkins, Bill Dawkins, The Honorable Joseph Field, Alida P Field, Veronica Cartwright.
• *Dir* Todd Field, *Pro* Field, Graham Leader and Ross Katz, *Ex Pro* Ted Hope and John Penotti, *Co-Pro* Tim Williams, *Screenplay* Field and Rob Festinger, from a story by Andre Dubus, *Ph* Antonio Calvache, *Pro Des* Shannon Hart, *Ed* Frank Reynolds, *M* Thomas Newman; 'Baby I Love Your Way' sung by Peter Frampton, *Costumes* Melissa Economy.

Miramax International/Greenstreet Films/Good Machine-Buena Vista.
131 mins. USA. 2001. Rel: 25 January 2002. Cert 15.

Intimacy ★★

Having left his wife and children for no apparent reason, Jay now lives on his own in an empty house. During the evenings he tends a bar and on Wednesdays he indulges in some passionate, wordless sex with a woman he knows little about. Then, one day, he follows his lover through the streets of London to uncover her identity... Recalling *Last Tango in Paris* in its sexual frankness and sparse settings, *Intimacy* courts some controversy but is likely to turn anybody off sex for weeks. But then neither Jay nor Claire seem to know why they're involved with each other and are even less convincing when they open their mouths. No doubt much was lost in the translation (the screenplay is by the French-speaking Patrice Chéreau and Anne-Louise Trividic), but no amount of grainy photography and hand-held camerawork can make the material credible. A real turn-off, despite the fact that this controversial film notoriously claimed to depict real, not simulated, scenes of sexual intercourse.
FYI: The last film shot in London by a French director was Michel Blanc's *The Escort*, also from a story by Hanif Kureishi and also about a man who suddenly leaves his family, ends up working in a bar and embarks on a sexual marathon. Hmm…

• *Jay* Mark Rylance, *Claire Nicholls* Kerry Fox, *Andy Nicholls* Timothy Spall, *Betty* Marianne Faithfull, *Victor* Alastair Galbraith, *Ian* Philippe Calvario, *Susan* Susannah Harker, *Pam* Rebecca Palmer, Frazer Ayres, Robert Addie, Paola Dionisotti.
• *Dir* Patrice Chéreau, *Pro* Patrick Cassavetti and Jacques Hinstin, *Ex Pro* Charles Gassot, *Screenplay* Chéreau, Anne-Louise Trividic and Nigel Gearing, *Ph* Eric Gautier, *Pro Des* Hayden Griffin, *Ed* Francois Gédigier, *M* Eric Neveux; Shostakovich; songs performed by David Bowie, The Clash, Clinic, Dream City, Stooges, The Chemical Brothers, Eyeless in Gaza, Boney M, Nick Cave, etc, *Costumes* Caroline De Vivaise.

Telema Prods/Canal Plus/Arte France Cinéma/Mikado Film/Greenpoint Films, etc-Pathé.
120 mins. France/UK. 2000. Rel: 27 July 2001. Cert 18.

Invincible ★★¹/₂

Werner Herzog's old mastery is present in the visual quality and atmospheric potency of this thirties tale about a Jewish strongman (Ahola) and his Jewish mentor, the charlatan clairvoyant Hanussen (Roth). The former is made to conceal his nationality on attaining fame in Berlin, while the latter hides his in the hope of obtaining a powerful position in Hitler's

Germany. Comparable themes were better handled in two Istvan Szabo films, *Sunshine* and *Hanussen*, for here the promising arthouse fare of the start yields to schmaltz and mawkish melodrama. The fact that Ahola and pianist Anna Gourari as the romantic lead are not actors is all too obvious. The film was made in English and some of the dialogue is distinctly weak. [*Mansel Stimpson*]

• *Erik Jan Hanussen* Tim Roth, *Zishe Breitbart* Jouko Ahola, *Marta Farra* Anna Gourari, *Master of Ceremonies* Max Raabe, *Benjamin Breitbart* Jacob Wein, *Count Helldorf* Udo Kier, *Himmler* Alexander Duda, *Goebbels* Klaus Haindl, *with* Herbert Golder, Gustav Peter Wohler, Tina Bordhin, Gary Bart, Rebecca Wein, Raphael Wein, Daniel Wein, Chana Wein, Rudolph Herzog, Hark Bohm.
• *Dir* and *Screenplay* Werner Herzog, *Pro* Herzog, Gary Bart and Christine Ruppert, *Ex Pro* James Mitchell and Lucki Stipetic, *Ph* Peter Zeitlinger, *Pro Des* Ulrich Bergfelder, *Ed* Joe Bini, *M* Hans Zimmer and Klaus Badelt; Beethoven, Handel, *Costumes* Jany Temime.

FilmFour/Werner Herzog Filmproduktion/Tatfilm/Little Bird/Fine Line, etc-Film Four.
133 mins. Germany/Ireland/UK/USA. 2001. Rel: 29 March 2002. Cert 12.

Iris ★★★

Translating the lives of the great and famous into filmic terms has always been a formidable task. Knowing this, scenarists Richard Eyre and Charles Wood have focused on the love affair between the writer Iris Murdoch and her long-suffering husband, the academic John Bayley, jumping back and forth from the couple's courting days at Oxford to Murdoch's last days dying from Alzheimer's. While this pares away the fat of most celluloid biographies, it does preclude a more rounded picture of the novelist. So, this works best as a snapshot of the bond between an idiosyncratic couple and of the tragedy of that love fractured by old age. A terribly sad film, *Iris* is redeemed by superlative production values and exemplary performances from the four leads, who play the couple in youth and old age. Indeed, seldom have four actors been so symbiotically matched on screen.

• *Iris Murdoch* Judi Dench, *John Bayley* Jim Broadbent, *young Iris Murdoch* Kate Winslet, *young John Bayley* Hugh Bonneville, *Principal of Somerville College* Eleanor Bron, *Janet Stone* Penelope Wilton, *young Janet Stone* Juliet Aubrey, *Dr Gudgeon* Kris Marshall, *neurologist* Tom Mannion, *young Maurice* Samuel West, *Phillida Stone* Saira Todd, *older Maurice* Timothy West, Angela Morant, Joan Bakewell, Derek Hutchinson, Juliet Howland, Charlotte Arkwright, Harriet Arkwright, Emma Handy, Stephen Marcus.
• *Dir* Richard Eyre, *Pro* Scott Rudin and Robert Fox, *Ex Pro* Anthony Minghella, Sydney Pollack, Tom

Above: Danish patsies: Peter Gantzler and Lars Kaalund in Lone Scherfig's delightfully eccentric *Italian for Beginners* (from Pathé)

Hedley, Guy East and David M. Thompson, *Screenplay* Eyre and Charles Wood, *Ph* Roger Pratt, *Pro Des* Gemma Jackson, *Ed* Martin Walsh, *M* James Horner; *solo violin* Joshua Bell; songs performed by The Inkspots, Charles Trénet, *Costumes* Ruth Myers.

Intermedia Films/BBC Films/Miramax/Mirage Enterprises-Buena Vista.
90 mins. UK/USA. 2001. Rel: 18 January 2002. Cert 15.

Italian for Beginners ★★★¹/₂

Filmbyen, Denmark; today. Various characters who have lost their way in life find their fortunes changing when they join a poorly attended Italian evening class… The very creed of the Dogme tradition (the jettisoning of props, music and any technical artifice) seems to reject the notion of romantic comedy, yet the director Lone Scherfig has used the concept's limitations to create a naturalistic spontaneity that serves her material well. Recalling a low-key Scandinavian Mike Leigh farce without the bite (and polish), *Italian for Beginners* does often feel naked, deprived of the emotional buttons of packaged entertainment. However, its generous humanity creeps up on one, its ludicrous excesses being all the funnier for being underplayed. The film's pleasures are slow-burning but they glow with the fuel of genuine compassion. Original title: *Italiensk for begyndere.*

• *Andreas* Anders W Berthelsen, *Jørgen Mortensen* Peter Gantzler, *Hal-Finn* Lars Kaalund, *Karen* Ann Eleonora Jørgensen, *Olympia* Anette Støvelbæk, *Giulia* Sara Indrio Jensen, *Olympia's father* Jesper Christensen, *Karen's mother* Lene Tiemroth, *with* Elisebeth Steenhtoft, Rikke Walck, Karen Lise Mynster.
• *Dir* and *Screenplay* Lone Scherfig, *Pro* Ib Tardini, *Ph* Jørgen Johansson, *Ed* Gerd Tjur, *M* Puccini, Anette Støvelbæk.

Zentropa Entertainments6/DOGME XII/Danish Film Institute-Pathé.
112 mins. Denmark. 2000. Rel: 26 April 2002. Cert 15.

Right: A shot in the dark: Eileen Brennan aims below the belt in Victor Salva's disappointing *Jeepers Creepers* (from Helkon SK)

Jay and Silent Bob Strike Back ★★

Having taken on the Catholic faith in his provocative and articulate *Dogma*, writer-director Kevin Smith decided to let his hair down and have some fun with his ubiquitous commentators Jay and Silent Bob. A kind of doped-out Greek chorus, Jay and Silent Bob have appeared in all of Smith's films to date – *Clerks*, *Mallrats*, *Chasing Amy* and *Dogma* – dismantling any sense of pretentiousness his films may have aspired to. Like Bill and Ted and Beavis and Butt-Head before them, they set the tone in *Clerks* when, in his very first line on film, Jay shouted, 'We need some tits and ass! Yeah!' Since then, the dumb and dumber duo have been transformed into the comic strip anti-heroes Bluntman and Chronic, who are about to be turned into a Miramax movie. Wanting a slice of the action, the duo takes to the road, hitching from New Jersey to Hollywood. Along the way, they encounter various characters from Smith's previous movies, while Jay falls for comely criminal Justice (whom he nicknames 'Boo-Boo Kiddie-Fuck'). For Smith aficionados there are some genuine belly laughs (particularly at the expense of Miramax and Ben Affleck's less creditable movies), but for the most part the director's rampant profanity and adolescent self-indulgence borders on public masturbation.

• *Holden/himself* Ben Affleck, *Justice* Shannon Elizabeth, *Willenholly* Will Ferrell, *Brodie/Banky* Jason Lee, *Jay* Jason Mewes, *Chaka* Chris Rock, *Silent Bob* Kevin Smith, *Randal* Jeff Anderson, *Sissy* Eliza Dushku, *Cockknocker* Mark Hamill, *Chrissy* Ali Larter, *Dante Hicks* Brian Christopher O'Halloran, *Brent* Seann William Scott, Diedrich Bader, Jules Asner, Marc Blucas, George Carlin, Shannen Doherty, Carrie Fisher, Jamie Kennedy, Steve Kmetko, Tracy Morgan, Judd Nelson, Jennifer Schwalbach, Jon Stewart, *Will Hunting* Matt Damon, Gus Van Sant, *himself/Bluntman* Jason Biggs, *himself/Chronic* James Van Der Beek, Morris E Day, *baby Silent Bob* Harley Quinn Smith, Ever Carradine, Wes Craven, Renée Humphrey, Joey Lauren Adams, Dwight Ewell, *that woman* Alanis Morissette.
• *Dir* and *Screenplay* Kevin Smith, *Pro* Scott Mosier, *Ex Pro* Bob Weinstein, Harvey Weinstein and Jonathan Gordon, *Co-Pro* Laura Greenlee, *Ph* Jamie Anderson, *Pro Des* Robert 'Ratface' Holtzman, *Ed* Smith and Scott Mosier, *M* James L Venable; songs performed by Joe Walsh, David Pirner, Run DMC and Davy D, The Bee Gees, Jason Mewes, Marcy Playground, Steppenwolf, Bon Jovi, P J Harvey, The New Pornographers, The Dandy Warhols, Morris Day and The Time, etc, *Costumes* Isis Mussenden.

Miramax/Dimension Films/View Askew-Buena Vista. 104 mins. USA. 2001. Rel: 30 November 2001. Cert 18.

Jeepers Creepers ★ 1/2

A cross-country drive home for siblings Darry (*Galaxy Quest*'s Justin Long) and Trish (Gina Phillips) goes terribly wrong after an encounter with an old truck and its maniacal driver. When they witness the man dumping several bodies down a pipe, they decide to see if they can help the victims. Entering the lair of a supernatural serial killer, they find themselves his next targets. The man is The Creeper, an ancient gargoyle that dines on the human parts it needs to regenerate its own body. Local psychic Jezelle provides all the exposition necessary and, sadly, a lone old woman (Eileen Brennan) puts up a better fight against the monster than a stationhouse full of cops… Some genuine eeriness is generated early on, but watching our young heroes do nothing more than gape and grind car gears saps it away right up to the movie's wholly unsatisfying denouement.
[*Scot Woodward Myers*]

• *Patricia Jenner* Gina Philips, *Darius Jenner* Justin Long, *The Creeper* Jonathan Breck, *Jezelle Gay Hartman* Patricia Belcher, *the cat lady* Eileen Brennan, *Sgt Davis Tubbes* Brandon Smith, *waitress Beverly* Peggy Sheffield.
• *Dir* Victor Salva, *Pro* Tom Luse and Barry Opper, *Ex Pro* Willi Baer, Francis Ford Coppola, Eberhard Kayser, Mario Ohoven and Linda Reisman, *Screenplay* Victor Salva, *Ph* Don E Fauntleroy, *Pro Des* Steven Legler, *Ed* Ed Marx, *M* Bennett Salvay, *Costumes* Emae Villalobos.

United Artists/American Zoetrope/Cinerenta Medien-beteiligungs/VCL Communications GmbH-Helkon SK. 90 mins. USA/Germany. 2001. Rel: 19 October 2001. Cert 15.

Jimmy Neutron – Boy Genius ★★★

Retroville, USA; the present. In spite of his astonishing gift for concocting state-of-the-art technology from household objects, Jimmy is largely unappreciated by his parents and classmates. Then, when all the grown-ups of Retroville are abducted by egg-like aliens (the race of Yokians), it's up to Jimmy to save the day… Blending many familiar elements (from *Independence Day* and *Inspector Gadget* via *Recess: School's Out* and *Spy Kids*), *Jimmy Neutron* makes up for its narrative familiarity with a vibrant visual style (3D computer animation with a retro-futurist spin) and a slew of vivid characters. It's also surprisingly funny, with plenty of asides for adult viewers (Nick's campfire narrative of *The Blair Witch Project* is a hoot), while the broad physical comedy and obvious sentiments should appeal to younger kids. Incidentally, the animation was created entirely from over-the-counter technology, a first for a 3D cartoon feature.

• *Jimmy Neutron* Debi Derryberry, *King Goobot* Patrick Stewart, *Mom* Megan Cavanagh, *Dad* Mark DeCarlo, *Sheen* Jeff Garcia, *Cindy* Carolyn Lawrence, *Nick* Candi Milo, *Carl* Rob Paulsen, *Libby* Crystal Scales, *with* Frank Welker, Jim Cummings
• *Dir* John A Davis, *Pro* Davis, Steve Oedekerk and Albie Hecht, *Ex Pro* Julia Pistor and Keith Alcorn, *Co-Pro* Gina Shay, *Screenplay* Davis, Oedekerk, David N Weiss and J David Stem, *Pro Des* Fred Cline, *Ed* Jon Michael Price and Gregory Perler, *M* John Debney; songs performed by Bowling for Soup, Aaron Carter, *NSYNC, Britney Spears, No Secrets, The Backstreet Boys, Stupid, True Vibe, Go-Go's, The Ramones, etc, *Sound* Michael Jonascu and Paul Ottosson.

Paramount/Nickelodeon Movies/O Entertainment-UIP. 81 mins. USA. 2001. Rel: 22 March 2002. Cert U.

John Carpenter's Ghosts of Mars ★★

Mars; 2176. The sole survivor of a ghost train, Lt Melanie Ballard is called up to testify at a 'discovery hearing' in front of a matriarchal council. It transpires that Ballard and a squad of fellow police officers were recruited to pick up feared killer James 'Desolation' Williams from the mining camp of Shining Canyon. However, when they got there, the camp was deserted, save for a lot of headless corpses strung up from the ceiling… Of course, with a cast like this, what do you expect? Still, it's sad to see John Carpenter, director of such gems as *Assault on Precinct 13*, *Halloween* and *Starman*, reduced to this. Part of the problem is that Carpenter fails to mine the high camp that the film calls out for (there is no sense of self-parody whatsoever), while anther major snag is the film's lazy and cumbersome structure. As Lt Ballard relates the horrendous events of the past few hours to a po-faced Rosemary Forsyth, flashbacks-within-flashbacks unravel like a savaged cardigan. Recalling *Assault on Precinct 13* in tone – but with none of that film's economy or intensity – this could equally be called *The Ghosts of John Carpenter*. Still, the stunning Natasha Henstridge must be commended for keeping a straight face throughout.

• *James 'Desolation' Williams* Ice Cube, *Lt Melanie Ballard* Natasha Henstridge, *Jericho Butler* Jason Statham, *Helena Braddock* Pam Grier, *Bashira Kincaid* Clea DuVall, *Whitlock* Joanna Cassidy, *Michael Descanso* Liam White, *Akooshay* Wanda DeJesus, Duane Davis, Rodney A Grant, Lobo Sebastian, Robert Carradine, Rosemary Forsyth, Doug McGrath, Rex Linn, *narrator* Charlotte Cornwall.
• *Dir* and *M* John Carpenter, *Pro* Sandy King, *Screenplay* Carpenter and Larry Sulkis, *Ph* Gary B Kibbe, *Pro Des* William Elliott, *Ed* Paul C Warschilka, *Costumes* Robin Michel Bush, *Make-up* Robert Kurtzman, Greg Nicotero and Howard Berger, *Visual effects* Lance Wilhoite, *Physiotherapist* Flora Brickner.

Screen Gems/Storm King-Columbia TriStar. 98 mins. USA. 2001. Rel: 30 November 2001. Cert 15.

John Q ★★★¹/₂

Chicago; today. When nine-year-old Mike Archibald suffers a massive heart attack, his father, factory worker John Q Archibald, is told that his insurance no longer covers the operation that will save his son's life. So, unable to raise the $75,000 down-payment to put his son on a donor list, John Q takes the emergency room hostage and demands an operation… Like John Travolta in *Mad City* and Samuel L Jackson in *The Negotiator*, Denzel Washington takes hostages for all the 'right' reasons in this emotive if manipulative social drama. Indeed, in spite of their financial pressures, Denzel's family is a little too perfect for comfort, the sort of blissfully happy unit that plays word games on the school run and spends sunny weekends at the baseball park. Had there been any emotional cracks in this domestic fold, then the payoff at the end

may have wielded an even greater punch. Still, Denzel's dilemma is an engrossing one and is skilfully if formulaically established, followed by an act of valiant folly that is the stuff of popcorn heroics. Unfortunately, there are just too many stereotypes clamouring for attention (sympathetic cop vs gung-ho police chief), but at least the state of American health care, not Denzel's colour, is the issue here.
FYI: The director's own daughter has a congenital heart condition.

• *John Quincy Archibald* Denzel Washington, *Lt Frank Grimes* Robert Duvall, *Dr Turner* James Woods, *Rebecca Payne* Anne Heche, *Denise Archibald* Kimberly Elise, *Chief Monroe* Ray Liotta, *Lester* Eddie Griffin, *Mitch* Shawn Hatosy, *Jimmy Palumbo* David Thornton, *Max* Ethan Suplee, *Tuck Lampley* Paul Johansson, *Sgt Moody* Obba Babatunde, *beautiful woman* Gabriela Oltean, *Mike Archibald* Daniel E Smith, *Gina Palumbo* Laura Harring, *with* Troy Winbush, Larissa Laskin, Dina Waters, Martha Chaves, Kevin Connolly, Heather Wahlquist, Troy Beyer, Noam Jenkins, Kirsta Teague, Simon Sinn, Frank Cassavetes, Colin Evans, Jay Leno, Gloria Allred, Larry King, Ted Demme, Bill Maher.
• *Dir* Nick Cassavetes, *Pro* Mark Burg and Oren Koules, *Ex Pro* Michael De Luca, Richard Saperstein and Avram Butch Kaplan, *Co-Pro* Hillary Sherman, *Screenplay* James Kearns, *Ph* Rogier Stoffers, *Pro Des* Stefania Cella, *Ed* Dede Allen, *M* Aaron Zigman; songs performed by Ana Maria Martinez, Pete Yorn, Stevie Wonder, and Patti LaBelle, *Costumes* Beatrix Aruna Pazstor.

New Line Cinema-Entertainment.
117 mins. USA. 2002. Rel: 26 April 2002. Cert 15.

Josie and the Pussycats ★★★
In cahoots with the government, Mega Records are taking over the US economy by subliminally selling brand-name products through the music of pre-fab bands. When the boy-group DuJour (a thinly veiled piss-take of 'N Sync) suspect foul play, they are immediately sacrificed in a plane crash. So music manager Wyatt Frame turns his attention to the garage band Josie and the Pussycats, promising the girls instant wealth and stardom... Swerving precariously between the astute satire of *This is Spinal Tap* and the crass mediocrity of *Spiceworld The Movie*, *Josie and the Pussycats* is an energetic piece of fluff with a valid message. Yet, with its deluge of product placement (Josie, Mel and Val's hotel rooms are, respectively, the Revlon Suite, the McDonald's Suite and the Red Bull Suite), the film feels like it's trying to have its cake and gorge on it. Still, there are some moments of genuine humour and a number of pleasing songs, while the film's up-to-the-minute stance ('Heath Ledger is the new Matt Damon') is in itself a pop cul-

tural education. Amazingly, this was based on a 1970 cartoon TV series, itself inspired by a 1963 *Archie* comic book.
FYI: MTV's Carson Daly – real-life fiancé of co-star Tara Reid – plays himself as a corporate pawn and assassin!

• *Josie McCoy* Rachael Leigh Cook, *Melody Valentine* Tara Reid, *Valerie Brown* Rosario Dawson, *Wyatt Frame* Alan Cumming, *Alan M* Gabriel Mann, *Alexander Cabot* Paulo Costanzo, *Alexandra Cabot* Missi Pyle, *Fiona* Parker Posey, *agent Kelly* Tom Butler, *Les* Alex Martin, *Carson Daly* Carson Daly, *the other Carson Daly* Aries Spears, Serena Altschul, Mark Seliger, Sally Hershberger, Jann T Carl, and (uncredited) Seth Green, Breckin Meyer.
• *Dir* and *Screenplay* Deborah Kaplan and Harry Elfont, *Pro* Marc Platt, Tracey E Edmonds, Chuck Grimes and Tony DeRosa-Grund, *Ex Pro* Kenneth Edmonds, *Co-Pro* Grace Gilroy, *Ph* Matthew Libatique, *Pro Des* Jasna Stefanovich, *Ed* Peter Teschner, *M* John Frizzell; songs performed by Presidential Campaign, DuJour, Josie and the Pussycats (lead singer: Kay Hanley, backing singers: Rachael Leigh Cook, Tara Reid, Rosario Dawson, Bif Naked, Ninette Terhart), Pink Martini, and Captain & Tennille, *Costumes* Leesa Evans, *Sound* Paul N J Ottoson, *Choreographer* Viktoria Langton, *Second unit dir* Betty Thomas.

MGM/Universal/Riverdale/Marc Platt/Harry Elfont/Deborah Kaplan-Fox.
98 mins. USA. 2001. Rel: 24 August 2001. Cert PG.

Joy Ride
See *Roadkill*

Jump Tomorrow ★★★¹⁄₂
New York/Niagara; today. When George Abiola, a shy, straight-laced ex-pat Nigerian, turns up at the airport to greet his arranged bride-to-be, he finds that he has arrived a day late. Instead, he bumps into a friendly, pretty Latino girl called Alicia who invites him to her party that night. He also encounters Gérard, a mercurial Frenchman beside himself with grief after his girlfriend has turned down his proposal of marriage. Inviting Gérard to Alicia's party, George finds himself falling for Alicia and talking Gérard down from the roof of the building, from which the Frenchman was intending to jump. 'Jump tomorrow,' George reasons, advice that he himself is beginning to warm to... Expanded from his prize-winning short *Jorge*, Joel Hopkins' debut feature is a delight from the word go. With its bright look and fanciful plot, the film glides along effortlessly as its cast of multi-cultural characters (from Nigeria, Spain, France and England) seek out love in the romantic melting pot of North America.
• *George Archer Abiola* Tunde Adebimpe, *Gérard*

Hippolyte Girardot, *Alicia* Natalia Verbeke, *Nathan* James Wilby, *Consuelo* Patricia Mauceri, *George's uncle* Isiah Whitlock Jr, *Heather Leather* Kaili Vernoff, *Alicia's uncle* Gene Ruffini, *Sophie Okenado* Abiola Wendy Abrams, *Maria* Cherie Jimenez, *with* Murielle Arden, Deen Badarou, Anthony Genco.
• *Dir* and *Screenplay* Joel Hopkins, *Pro* Nicola Usborne, *Ex Pro* Tim Perell and Paul Webster, *Co-Pro* Jake Myers, *Assoc Pro* Howard Gertler and Gill Holland, *Ph* Patrick Cady, *Pro Des* John Paino, *Ed* Susan Littenberg, *M* John Kimbrough; Frederic Handel; songs performed by William Parker & The Little Huey Creative Music Orchestra, the James Taylor Quartet, Vanity Fare, The Eels, Maita Vende Cá, John Lennon, etc, *Costumes* Sarah J Holden, *Physical Production* Tracey Josephs.

FilmFour/Eureka Pictures/Jorge Prods-Film Four.
96 mins. UK/USA. 2000. Rel: 9 November 2001. Cert PG.

Jurassic Park III ★★★★

Bravely sidestepping self parody (besides the jokey logos of Universal and Amblin, which quiver at the rumble of an approaching T-rex), *Jurassic Park III* plays it as straight as it can under the circumstances. Sam Neill returns as Dr Alan Grant, with a new respect for kids and a healthy dread of 'genetically engineered theme park monsters', and there are new dinos to add to the calamity – namely, the 44-foot amphibious Spinosaurus and the ferocious, flying Pteronadon. Setting itself up nicely – Grant announces that 'No force on earth or in Heaven could get me on that island,' while mercenary-cum-tour operator Udesky reassures his employer that 'It's going to be a walk in the park' – the film gets down to basics pretty fast. Promised funding for his research into the unique intelligence of Velociraptors, palaeontologist Grant agrees to accompany wealthy businessman Paul Kirby and his wife Amanda on an aerial tour of Isla Sorna, the location of *The Lost World*. As it happens, Isla Sorna is new to Grant (he barely escaped with his life from Isla Nublar, the decimated site of the original *Jurassic Park*), and the Kirbys are really in search of their missing son. Michael Crichton's original concept was great in 1993 and it still works a treat. Under the guidance of executive producer Steven Spielberg, director Joe Johnston (*Jumanji*) pulls off some marvellous sequences, including the surprise attack of a T-rex with a satellite phone ringing in its gut and a Spinosaurus onslaught intercut with a famous kids' character singing 'Barney is a Dinosaur' on TV. As threequels go, this is of a pretty high order.

• *Dr Alan Grant* Sam Neill, *Paul Kirby* William H Macy, *Amanda Kirby* Téa Leoni, *Billy Brennan* Alessandro Nivola, *Eric Kirby* Trevor Morgan, *Udesky* Michael Jeter, *Cooper* John Diehl, *Nash* Bruce A Young, *Ben Hildebrand* Mark Harelik, *Ellie Sattler* Laura Dern, *Mark* Taylor Nichols, *Enrique Cardoso*

Julio Oscar Mechoso.
• *Dir* Joe Johnston, *Pro* Kathleen Kennedy and Larry Franco, *Ex Pro* Steven Spielberg, *Screenplay* Peter Buchman, Alexander Payne and Jim Taylor, based on characters created by Michael Crichton, *Ph* Shelly Johnson, *Pro Des* Ed Verreaux, *Ed* Robert Salva, *M* Don Davis; theme by John Williams, *Costumes* Betsy Cox, *Visual effects* Jim Mitchell, *Live action dinosaurs* Stan Winston, *Animation* Dan Taylor, *Palaeontology consultant* Jack Horner.

Universal/Amblin Entertainment-UIP.
92 mins. USA. 2001. Rel: 20 July 2001. Cert PG.

Just Visiting ★★

England, 12th century/Chicago, 2000. On the eve of his wedding to the beautiful English Lady Rosalind, the noble French knight Thibault, Count of Malfete, is tricked – by witchcraft – into killing her. Only by stepping back in time can he repair the damage, but the wizard he enlists to help him sends him and his ill-smelling vassal to present-day Chicago! Not that *Les Visiteurs* (1993) was much cop, but this American remake is scuppered by sloppy logic, second-rate special effects and an undistinguished visual style. Furthermore, opportunities for a satiric swipe at Anglo-Franco-American relations are largely wasted, while the rampant slapstick is allowed to run unchecked. By now, the niceties of previous generations experiencing the wonders and terrors of the new world is old hat, and here the clichés are given little finesse or any sense of awe. Younger kids will lap it up but their guardians should steer a wide berth.
FYI: Jean Reno and co-star/co-scenarist Christian Clavier appeared in the French original and its sequel, *Les Couloirs du temps: Les visiteurs 2*.

• *Thibault, Count of Malfete* Jean Reno, *André le Pate* Christian Clavier, *Princess Rosalind/Julia Malfete* Christina Applegate, *Angelique* Tara Reid, *Wizard* Malcolm McDowell, *Hunter* Matthew Ross, *Amber* Bridgette Wilson-Sampras, *Byron* John Alyward, *Dr Brady* George Plimpton, *with* Sarah Badel, Oliver Ford Davies, Matyelock Gibbs, Richard Bremmer, Robert Glenister, Donna Palmer, Molly Price, Matthew Sussman.
• *Dir* Jean-Marie Gaubert (aka Jean-Marie Poiré), *Pro* Patrice Ledoux and Ricardo Mestres, *Ex Pro* Richard Hashimoto, *Screenplay* Christian Clavier, Jean-Marie Poiré and John Hughes, *Ph* Ueli Steigler, *Pro Des* Doug Kraner, *Ed* Michael A Stevenson, *M* John Powell; songs performed by Texas, Ray Greene, Basement Jaxx, Locksmith, The Jayhawks, BTK, Sonny and Cher, Kudisan Kai, etc, *Costumes* Penny Rose, *Special effects* Igor Sekulic, *Second unit dir* Peter Macdonald.

Gaumont/Hollywood Pictures-Momentum Pictures.
88 mins. USA/France. 2001. Rel: 8 February 2002. Cert PG.

Kandahar ★★★★¹/₂

Twelve years after leaving Afghanistan for Canada, Nafas receives a letter from her sister in Kandahar. The latter reveals that she is so depressed by the oppressive regime, that she intends to take her own life during the last eclipse of the 20th century. Desperate to reach her sister before then, Nafas returns to Afghanistan to find a country in the stranglehold of fear, famine and irrational rules of conduct... A recreation of real events acted out by the characters involved, *Kandahar* arrived at a time of extraordinary pertinence. As an insight into life under the Taliban in Afghanistan, the film exerts a devastating power by presenting its scenes of 'everyday' life with a matter-of-fact, almost documentary realism. A doctor examines a woman via a hole in a curtain, while directing his questions to the patient's child. Recent amputees haggle for spare limbs from the Red Cross before hobbling off towards a pair of prosthetic legs floating through the sky on a parachute. A woman, enshrouded in a *burqa*, attempts to apply lipstick to her hidden face... The cumulative power of such scenes, depicting the lunacy of life in Afghanistan, simply takes the breath away.
FYI: The Muslim actor David Belfield, who plays the American doctor, is reportedly wanted for the murder of an Iranian diplomat, whom he allegedly shot dead in Maryland 22 years ago.
Original title: *Safar é Ghandehar.*

• *Nafas* Nelofer Pazira, *Tabib Sahid* Hassan Tantaï, *Khak* Sadou Teymouri, *Hayat* Hayatalah Hakimi, David Belfield, etc.
• *Dir, Screenplay* and *Ed* Mohsen Makhmalbaf, *Ph* Ebraham Ghafouri, *M* Mohamad Reza Darvishi.

Makhmalbaf Film House/Bac Films-ICA Projects.
85 mins. Iran/France. 2001. Rel: 16 November 2001. Cert PG.

Kate & Leopold ★★★¹/₂

When amateur scientist Stuart Bessler discovers 'a crack in the fabric of time' and visits the year 1873, he inadvertently drags Leopold, the Duke of Albany, with him to contemporary New York. As the mismatched duo wait for the next temporal opening to transport the Duke back to his rightful period, Leopold and Stuart's ex-girlfriend, Kate, discover a mutual attachment that transcends the barriers of time itself... A seasoned theme is given a delightful facelift thanks to some sparkling dialogue and a highly charged display of charm from Hugh Jackman as the quintessentially courteous Englishman. Besides, the topic of the corruption of old-world values is always one worth revisiting, a sentiment encapsulated in Leopold's entreaty, 'What has happened to the world? You have every convenience, every comfort, yet no time for integrity.' There are also winning turns from the supporting cast, in particular Liev Schreiber as the put-upon Stuart and Breckin Meyer as Kate's romantically apprehensive brother.

• *Kate McKay* Meg Ryan, *Leopold, Duke of Albany* Hugh Jackman, *Stuart Bessler* Liev Schreiber, *Charlie McKay* Breckin Meyer, *Darci* Natasha Lyonne, *J J Camden* Bradley Whitford, *Otis* Philip Bosco, *Uncle Millard* Paxton Whitehead, *Dr Geisler* Spalding Gray, *Bob* Josh Stamberg, *Roebling* Andrew Jack, *Gretchen* Stephanie Sanditz, *with* Matthew Sussman, Charlotte Ayanna, Cole Hawkins.
• *Dir* James Mangold, *Pro* Cathy Konrad, *Ex Pro* Bob Weinstein, Harvey Weinstein, Meryl Poster and Kerry Orent, *Screenplay* Mangold and Steven Rogers, *Ph* Stuart Dryburgh, *Pro Des* Mark Friedberg, *Ed* David Brenner, *M* Rolfe Kent; Johann Strauss Sr, Lalo Schifrin, Henry Mancini; songs performed by University of Michigan Band, Django Reinhardt, Vanessa Williams; 'Until' written and sung by Sting, *Costumes* Donna Zakowska, *Visual effects* Robert Stromberg, *Dialect coach* Andrew Jack.

Miramax/Konrad Pictures-Buena Vista.
118 mins. USA. 2001. Rel: 5 April 2002. Cert 12.

Killing Me Softly ★¹/₂

In London for one-and-a-half years, Indiana native Alice Loudon seems to have found her place in life. She has a well-paid job, a nice flat and a boyfriend who allows her to be herself. Then she meets a stranger on the street and sacrifices everything to become his sex slave... Chen Kaige made his international reputation with the visually sumptuous *Farewell My Concubine, Temptress Moon* and epic *The Emperor and the Assassin* but seems less confident working outside his native Mandarin. He was partly drawn to the subject of Sean French and Nicci Gerrard's novel by its sexual frankness, explaining that 'I would never have been allowed to film this in China. [But] sex is an important part of human nature, and if you can't deal with sex, you can't deal with anything in life.' However, there is little sexual frisson in this 'erotic' thriller, regardless of how many times Heather Graham takes her shirt off. In fact, Ms Graham's performance of wide-eyed gaucherie goes some way towards scuttling the film's credibility (a high-powered web designer? I don't think so), although it's not entirely her fault. The script is risible; on her wedding day Alice tells her new husband: 'I have a mother who doesn't talk to me and a father I don't know,' to which he replies, 'It doesn't matter'. The ending is also wildly melodramatic, not to mention illogical.

• *Alice Loudon* Heather Graham, *Adam Tallis* Joseph Fiennes, *Deborah Tallis* Natascha McElhone, *Klaus* Ulrich Thomsen, *Daniel* Ian Hart, *Jake* Jason Hughes, *Sylvie* Amy Robbins, *Joanna Noble* Yasmin

Left: Love From a Stranger: High-powered web designer Heather Graham (yeh, right) waits for her man in Chen Kaige's visually sumptuous but totally dotty *Killing Me Softly* (from Pathé)

Bannerman, *Mrs Blanchard* Kika Markham, *with* Helen Grace, Ronan Vibert, Ian Aspinal, Rebecca Palmer, Donald Gee.
• *Dir* Chen Kaige, *Pro* Joe Medjuck, Kara Lindstrom, Lynda Myles and Michael Chinich, *Ex Pro* Ivan Reitman and Tom Pollock, *Line Pro* Donna Grey, *Screenplay* Lindstrom, *Ph* Michael Coulter, *Pro Des* Gemma Jackson, *Ed* Jon Gregory, *M* Patrick Doyle, *Costumes* Phoebe De Gaye.

MGM/The Montecito Picturte Company-Pathé. 100 mins. UK/USA. 2001. Rel: 14 June 2002. Cert 18.

Kiss of the Dragon ★★★★

Paris; the present. Brought over from Beijing to help the French police with their investigations, top government agent Liu Jiuan quickly realises that he has been imported as a pawn. When he escapes a massacre precipitated by his formidable host, Liu hides out in the red-light district of Pigalle. There he befriends an American prostitute who, as it happens, has a major score to settle with the corrupt French cop... *Kiss of the Dragon* kicks some serious ass. I mean, look at the credentials: Luc Besson as producer and co-writer, Thierry Arbogast as DP, Paris as a backdrop and

Above: Sexual tourism: Heather Juergensen and Jennifer Westfeldt in their jointly scripted *Kissing Jessica Stein* (from Fox), an insightful, wonderfully entertaining and gutbustingly-funny comedy

Tchéky Karyo as the year's most unforgivable villain. But let's not forget Jet Li – Bruce Lee's most credible successor to date. Li not only supplies the film's story but, in the first breath-stopping action sequence, incapacitates a small army of corrupt cops with everything from an iron and a washing machine to a snooker ball. Li's best trick, though, is his nifty use of acupuncture needles, which, by being flicked into the pressure points of his prey, act as instant sedatives. Of its genre, this stylish, extremely violent and adrenaline-pumping martial arts spectacle is tops.

• *Liu Jiuan* Jet Li, *Jessica* Bridget Fonda, *Jean-Pierre Richard* Tchéky Karyo, *Aja* Laurence Ashley, *Uncle Tai* Burt Kwouk, *twin #1* Cyril Raffaelli, *twin #2* Didier Azoulay, *Max* John Forgeham, *Mister Big* Ric Young, *Minister Tang* Vincent Wong, *Isabel* Isabelle Duhauvelle.
• *Dir* Chris Nahon, *Pro* Luc Besson, Jet Li, Steven Chasman and Happy Walters, *Co-Pro* Bernard Grenet, *Screenplay* Besson and Robert Mark Kamen, *Ph* Thierry Arbogast, *Pro Des* Jacques Bufnoir, *Ed* Marco Cave, *M* Craig Armstrong; songs performed by The Congos, N.E.R.D, Lee Harvey and Vita, Lisa Barbuscia, Assia, Mystikal, and Daft Punk, *Sound* Vincent Tulli, *Action Dir* Cory Yuen.

Fox/Europa Corp/Quality Growth International/Current & Immortal Entertainment/Canal Plus-Fox.
98 mins. USA/France. 2001. Rel: 9 November 2001. Cert 18.

Kissing Jessica Stein ★★★★¹/₂

Jessica Stein, who works as a copy editor for *The New York Tribune*, is Jewish, neurotic and uptight. She is also obsessive about the use of the English language and can't find a man smart enough or linguistically refined enough to meet her high expectations. Then there is Helen Cooper, who works as assistant manager at a fashionable art gallery, who is sexy, open, linguistically refined and, er, bi-curious. The tragedy is that the two women are completely incompatible… Starting out as an off-off-

Broadway evening of sketches called *Lipschtick* (great title), *Kissing Jessica Stein* has finally evolved into a smart, poignant and very funny film with both a strong story and an elegant cinematic finish. With the show's creators, Jennifer Westfeldt and Heather Juergensen, playing the characters they know so well, the film is secure in the ambiguities, complexities and quirks of its wonderfully rich and engaging protagonists. Jessica Stein herself may be a little too insufferable at times (recalling an intellectual Phoebe from TV's *Friends*), but the film is grounded by a circle of colourful characters who expose a recognisable truth in the writers' mordant wit.

• *Jessica Stein* Jennifer Westfeldt, *Helen Cooper* Heather Juergensen, *Josh Meyers* Scott Cohen, *Judy Stein* Tovah Feldshuh, *Joan* Jackie Hoffman, *Charles* Jon Hamm, *Grandma Esther* Esther Wurmfeld, *Greg* Michael Ealy, with Michael Mastro, Carson Elrod, David Aaron Baker, Robert Ari, Kevin Sussman, Ilana Levine.
• *Dir* Charles Herman-Wurmfeld, *Pro* Eden Wurmfeld and Brad Zions, *Co-Pro* and *Screenplay* Jennifer Westfeldt and Heather Juergensen, *Ph* Lawrence Sher, *Pro Des* Charlotte Bourke, *Ed* Kristy Jacobs Maslin and Greg Tillman, *M* Marcelo Zarvos; Vivaldi; songs performed by Blossom Dearie, The Inner Thumb, The JeepJazzProject, Adriana Evans, Jill Phillips, Barry White, Dave's True Story, Ute Lemper, Matt Rollings and Lyle Lovett, Ella Fitzgerald, Diana Krall, etc, *Costumes* Melissa Bruning, *Jessica's paintings* Anthony Titus.

Fox Searchlight/Eden Wurmfeld Films/Zions Films/Cineric-Fox.
96 mins. USA. 2001. Rel: 21 June 2002. Cert 15.

A Knight's Tale ★★★¹/₂

France/England; 1320. In days of yore, the bloody sport of jousting was the preserve of the nobility alone. However, a humble thatcher's son is determined to smash the lordly monopoly. And so, with considerable nerve and a little skill – not to mention some parchments forged by his friend Geoff Chaucer – he sets out to challenge the knights of Europe… Taken in the right spirit, *A Knight's Tale* is a jolly enjoyable romp that brings history alive with a little contemporary tinkering. While nobles and peasants sing along to 'We Will Rock You' by Queen (the rock group, not their royal patron) and courtiers break into an impromptu dance to David Bowie's 'Golden Years', the film actually displays a visual authenticity. The contemporary feel (in one scene, Lady Jocelyn looks to have been dressed by Cecil Beaton) is refreshing, yet the attention to period detail – particularly the minutiae of jousting – is equally enthralling. It's just a shame that William Thatcher could not have been made a more sympathetic fellow (it's all about winning for him), while the chemistry between our hero and Lady Jocelyn seems entirely misplaced. The underdeveloped character of Kate (to whom William is so rude)

Opposite: He Will Rock You: Heath Ledger rides tall in Brian Helgeland's most agreeable romp, *A Knight's Tale* (from Columbia TriStar)

Right: One Flew Into the Cuckoo's Nest: Kevin Spacey keeps Dr Jeff Bridges on his toes in Iain Softley's stylish and enthralling *K-PAX* (from FilmFour)

would have made a far more suitable love match; besides, she is every bit as beautiful as Jocelyn.

• *William Thatcher aka Ulrich von Liechtenstein of Gelderland* Heath Ledger, *Roland* Mark Addy, *Count Adhemar* Rufus Sewell, *Geoff Chaucer* Paul Bettany, *Wat* Alan Tudyk, *Kate* Laura Fraser, *Lady Jocelyn* Shannyn Sossamon, *Christiana* Bérénice Bejo, *Colville/Edward, the Black Prince* James Purefoy, *John Thatcher* Christopher Cazenove, *Germaine* Scott Handy, *Sir Ector* Nick Brimble, Steven O'Donnell, Jonathan Slinger, Roger Ashton-Griffiths.
• *Dir* and *Screenplay* Brian Helgeland, *Pro* Helgeland, Tim Van Rellim and Todd Black, *Ph* Richard Greatrex, *Pro Des* Tony Burrough, *Ed* Kevin Stitt, *M* Carter Burwell; songs performed by Queen, War, Bachman Turner Overdrive, David Bowie, Train, Heart, Eric Clapton, Rare Earth, Sly & the Family Stone, Thin Lizzy, Robbie Williams, Dan Powell, and Third Eye Blind, *Costumes/armour* Caroline Harris.

Columbia Pictures/Escape Artists/Finestkind-Columbia TriStar.
132 mins. USA. 2001. Rel: 31 August 2001. Cert PG.

K-PAX ★★★★

New York City; the present. A dedicated doctor at the Psychiatric Institute of Manhattan, Mark Powell has met people who've thought they were Joan of Arc or Jesus Christ. But the enigmatic, strangely articulate 'Prot' is the first patient to claim he comes from K-PAX, a planet one thousand lightyears away from Earth. Yet the more Powell talks to this soft-spoken man, the less convinced he is that Prot is lying… Having initially been typecast as men with less than laudable instincts, Kevin Spacey follows up the life-affirming *Pay It Forward* with a film of equal generosity of spirit. Indeed, in this stylish blend of *One Flew Over the Cuckoo's Nest* and *Starman*, Spacey plays a saintly figure who has a beneficial effect on all those he meets. But *K-PAX* is a film of many parts and is as much about religion and belief as it is about social stereotyping, insanity, space travel and the very concept of reality. Scenarist Charles Leavitt (*The Mighty*) skilfully pulls together all these themes from Gene Brewers' 1995 novel, which, in turn, are handsomely orchestrated by director Iain Softley. An accomplished, soul-enhancing piece, *K-PAX* has enough emotional and intellectual breadth to satisfy both cynics and dreamers.

• *Prot* Kevin Spacey, *Dr Mark Powell* Jeff Bridges, *Claudia Villars* Alfre Woodard, *Rachel Powell* Mary McCormack, *Howie* David Patrick Kelly, *Ernie* Saul Williams, *Sal* Peter Gerety, *Mrs Archer* Celia Weston, *Dr Chakraborty* Ajay Naidu, *Maria* Tracy Vilar, *Maria* Melanee Murray, *Joyce Trexler* Kimberly Scott, *Steve* Brian Howe, *with* John Toles-Bey, Conchata Ferrell, Vincent Laresca, Mary Mara, Aaron Paul, William Lucking, Peter Maloney, Clarke Peters.
• *Dir* Iain Softley, *Pro* Lawrence Gordon, Lloyd Levin and Robert F Colesberry, *Ex Pro* Susan G Pollock, *Screenplay* Charles Leavitt, *Ph* John Mathieson, *Pro Des* John Beard, *Ed* Craig McKay, *M* Edward Shearmur; songs performed by Sheryl Crow, Elton John, *Costumes* Louise Mingenbach.

Intermedia Films/Universal/IMF-Film Four.
120 mins. USA. 2001. Rel: 12 April 2002. Cert 12.

L

Opposite: No argument, Angelina Jolie *is Lara Croft: Tomb Raider*

The Ladies Man ★

A Courvoisier-swigging, sodomy-fixated 'agony aunt' with a lisp, Leon Phelps is Chicago's most offensive DJ. Preaching casual sex in favour of real love, Leon routinely beds the wives of other men and is surprised when his radio station fires him. With a small army of cuckolded husbands on the warpath and only his loyal (and beautiful) producer by his side, Leon is heading for a major downfall... Originating as a recurring sketch on NBC's *Saturday Night Live*, *The Ladies Man* is a depressing excuse for a comedy. Predictable, over-baked and treacherously sentimental, it showcases the shortcomings of a comedian destined to go nowhere (at least, on film) and abuses the talent of the supporting cast (in particular Julianne Moore as a sexually deviant clown). A strong contender for the most dispiriting film experience of the new millennium.

• *Leon Phelps* Tim Meadows, *Julie Simmons* Karyn Parsons, *Lester* Billy Dee Williams, *Lance DeLune* Will Ferrell, *Barney* Lee Evans, *Honey DeLune* Tiffani Thiessen, *Cheryl* Sofia Milos, *Candy* Jill Talley, *Scrap Iron* John Witherspoon, *Al* Ken Campbell, *Cyrus Cunningham* Rocky Carroll, *Teresa* Tamala Jones, *Audrey* Julianne Moore, *Hugh Hefner* Sean Thibodeau, *with* Eugene Levy, Kevin McDonald, David Huband, Mark McKinney, Chris Parnell, Robin Ward, Robyn Palmer, *Aloysius* Reginald Hudlin.
• *Dir* Reginald Hudlin, *Pro* Lorne Michaels, *Ex Pro* Robert K Weiss, Erin Fraser and Thomas Levine, *Screenplay* Tim Meadows, Andrew Steele and Dennis McNicholas, *Ph* Johnny E Jensen, *Pro Des* Franco de Cotiis, *Ed* Earl Watson, *M* Marcus Miller; Handel; songs performed by Grover Washington Jr, Al Green, Stevie Wonder, The Isley Brothers, Roberta Flack and Donny Hathaway, Teddy Pendergrass, Rufus and Chaka Khan, Bobby Womack, Parliament, Willie Hutch, Johnny Gill, and Lalah Hathaway, *Costumes* Eydi Caines-Floyd.

Paramount/SNL Studios-UIP.
84 mins. USA. 2000. Rel: 13 July 2001. Cert 15.

The Lady & the Duke ★¹⁄₂

For the last 40 years, Eric Rohmer, now 81, has produced a series of deft contemporary fables exploring the human condition. In a surprising – and ill-advised – change of tack, he now turns his attention to an episode from the French Revolution, drawn from the memoirs of the Scottish royalist Grace Elliott. A former mistress of the Prince of Wales (the future George IV), by whom she bore a daughter, Grace moved to France to conduct an affair with Prince Philippe, the Duke of Orleans. By the time the film opens, the affair has ended, replaced by a mutual affection that

flourishes in spite of the couple's political differences. As the Revolution rages outside (against a series of painted backdrops), Grace and her duke talk at great length in a series of static tableaux that defy the essence of cinema. What next? Ridley Scott tackling romantic comedy? The French Revolution has provided the backdrop for some rousing cinematic spectacle, but here Rohmer jettisons all such drama for a precious, talky narrative that recalls a dated play. Original title: *L'Anglaise et le duc.*

• *Prince Philippe, Duke of Orleans* Jean-Claude Dreyfus, *Grace Elliott* Lucy Russell, *Duc de Biron* Alain Libolt, *Pulcherie, the cook* Charlotte Very, *Fanchette* Rosette, *Champcenetz* Léonard Cobiant, *Dumouriez* François Marthouret, *Nanon* Caroline Morin, *Madame Meyler* Helena Dubiel, *Robespierre* François-Marie Banier.
• *Dir* and *Screenplay* Eric Rohmer, *Pro* François Etchegaray, *Ex Pro* François Ivernel, Romain Le Grand and Léonard Glowinski, *Ph* Diane Baratier, *Pro Des* Antoine Fontaine, *Ed* Mary Stephen, *M* various, *Costumes* Pierre-Jean Larroque, *Painted backdrops* Jean-Baptiste Marot.

Pathé Image/CER/KC Medien/FR3/Cinéma/Canal Plus-Pathé.
129 mins. France/Germany. 2001. Rel: 15 February 2002. Cert PG.

Lara Croft: Tomb Raider ★¹⁄₂

Time is of the essence for bad egg Manfred Powell, who has to find the second half of an antique key to unlock the power of an ancient force. For, when the nine planets of our solar system align themselves for the first time in 5000 years, mankind has the potential to manipulate the properties of time travel. As it happens, the second key belongs to one Lara Croft... In spite of its success at the box-office, *Lara Croft: Tomb Raider* is no better a film than any other based on a video game (cf *Double Dragon, Mortal Kombat, Street Fighter, Super Mario Bros, Wing Commander*). While Angelina Jolie is physically breathtaking as the heiress-cum-adventuress (complete with convincing English accent), her corporeal bounty cannot overcome the movie's withering lack of wit, originality and excitement. With its wanton destruction of ancient artefacts and feeble one-liners (Lara's assistant on Siberia: 'This is not a country, it's an ice cube'), it feels no more exciting than an overblown video game, without the interaction. Even the much-trumpeted locations (the Angkor Wat ruins in Cambodia and a giant glacier in Iceland) lack a sense of spectacle, while the villains are strictly third-rate.

• *Lara Croft* Angelina Jolie, *Lord Croft* Jon Voight, *Manfred Powell* Iain Glen, *Bryce* Noah Taylor,

Alex West Daniel Craig, *Wilson* Leslie Phillips, *Pimms* Julian Rhind-Tutt, *Hillary* Chris Barrie, *Distinguished Gentleman* Richard Johnson, *young Lara* Rachel Appleton, *with* Robert Phillips, Ayla Amiral, Ozzie Yue, Wai-Keat Lau, Stephanie Burns.
• *Dir* Simon West, *Pro* Lawrence Gordon, Lloyd Levin and Colin Wilson, *Ex Pro* Jeremy Heath-Smith and Stuart Baird, *Co-Pro* Chris Kenny and Bobby Klein, *Screenplay* Patrick Massett and John Zinman, from a story by West, Sara B Cooper, Mike Webb and Michael Colleary, *Ph* Peter Menzies, *Pro Des* Kirk M Petruccelli, *Ed* Dallas S Puett and Glen Scantlebury, *M* Graeme Revell; J S Bach; songs performed by U2, Fluke, OutKast, Chanticleer, VAS, Bosco, Fatboy Slim, Missy Elliott and Nelly Furtado, Leftfield, Moby, Nine Inch Nails, Craig Armstrong, Groove Armada, Chemical Brothers, Basement Jaxx, etc, *Costumes* Lindy Hemming, *Sound* Steve Boeddeker, *Dialogue coach* Mel Churcher.

Paramount/Mutual Film Co./Eidos Interactive/BBC/ Tele-Munchen/Marubeni/Toho-Towa/KFP-UIP. 101 mins. USA/Germany/UK/Japan. 2001. Rel: 6 July 2001. Cert 12.

The Last Castle ★★★¹/₂

Running his penitentiary with an authoritarian hand, warden Colonel Winter never forgets what his inmates are capable of. Conversely, three-star general and all-round American hero Eugene R Irwin likes to win respect by looking for the good in his men. Sentenced to imprisonment for disobeying orders during a fateful mission in Burundi, Irwin expects to be treated like any other convict – he just wants to do his time and go home. However, he soon takes exception to Winter's brutal disciplinary measures and resolves to wage a war of nerves on his oppressor... Old-fashioned may be a dirty word these days, but there are few substitutes for a decent story, good structure and solid character delineation. *The Last Castle* isn't exactly *The Shawshank Redemption*, but it's got a wonderful premise eloquently realised by David Scarpa and Graham Yost's gripping script. There's also excellent value from James Gandolfini (now taking the roles Gene Hackman played 20 years back), who makes his unscrupulous warden all the more malevolent by pinning back his villainy behind a fixed smile and a penchant for classical music. Filmed at the former Tennessee State Penitentiary.

• *Lt General Eugene R Irwin* Robert Redford, *Colonel Winter* James Gandolfini, *Clifford Yates* Mark Ruffalo, *General James Wheeler* Delroy Lindo, *Corporal Ramón Aguilar* Clifton Collins Jr, *Captain Peretz* Steve Burton, *Beaupre* Brian

Goodman, *Sgt Major Dellwo* Paul Calderon, *Doc Lee* Frank Military, *Enriquez* Michael Irby, *Duffy* Samuel Ball, *Thumper* George W Scott, *Cutbush* Jeremy Childs, and (uncredited) *Rosalie* Robin Wright Penn.
• *Dir* Rod Lurie, *Pro* Robert Lawrence, *Ex Pro* Don Zepfel, *Screenplay* David Scarpa and Graham Yost, *Ph* Shelly Johnson, *Pro Des* Kirk M. Petruccelli, *Ed* Michael Jablow and Kevin Stitt, *M* Jerry Goldsmith; J S Bach, Salieri, Mozart, *Costumes* Ha Nguyen, *Trumpet solos* Malcolm McNab.

DreamWorks-UIP. 131 mins. USA. 2001. Rel: 4 January 2002. Cert 15.

Last Orders ★¹/₂

On a bleak winter's day in Bermondsey, southeast London, three old codgers and a middle-aged car salesman meet up at a pub. They are there to toast their late friend Jack Dodds – and to take his ashes to Margate so as to scatter them in the sea. Along the way their thoughts turn to the past... If ever there was an example of how not to translate a novel to the screen, this episodic and provincial drama is it. *Last Orders* obviously aims to be a warm and bittersweet contemplation on the nature of friendship but is really just a lot of flashbacks and acting. With no narrative motor and with lighting from the *Carry On* school of photography, the film is about as cinematic as a 1960s' postcard. Based on the Booker Prize-winning novel by Graham Swift.

• *Jack Dodds* Michael Caine, *Vic Tucker* Tom Courtenay, *Lenny Tate* David Hemmings, *Ray 'Lucky' Johnson* Bob Hoskins, *Amy Dodds* Helen Mirren, *Vince Dodds/Vincent Ian Pritchett* Ray Winstone, *young Jack* J J Field, *young Vic* Cameron Fitch, *young Lenny* Nolan Hemmings, *young Ray* Anatol Yusef, *young Amy* Kelly Reilly, *young Vince* Stephen McCole, *Bernie* George Innes, *June Dodds* Laura Morelli, Sally Hurst, Denise Black, Sue James, Meg Wynn Owen, Kitty Leigh, Alex Reid, Tracey Murphy, Claire Harman, John Baker, Simon Oats, Patricia Valentine, Lois Winstone, Aislinn Sands.
• *Dir* and *Screenplay* Fred Schepisi, *Pro* Schepisi and Elisabeth Robinson, *Ex Pro* Nik Powell, Rainer Mockert, Gary Smith and Chris Craib, *Ph* Brian Tufano, *Pro Des* Tim Harvey, *Ed* Kate Williams, *M* Paul Grabowsky; songs performed by Roy Orbison, Neil Ford and the Fanatics, and The Piccadilly Dance Orchestra, *Costumes* Jill Taylor.

MBP/Scala/Winchester Films-Metrodome. 110 mins. UK/Germany. 2001. Rel: 11 January 2002. Cert 15.

Lava ★★¹/₂

Notting Hill, London; the present. Staying at a B&B in central London, soldier-of-fortune 'Smiggy' takes pity on the simple-minded Phillip, who acts as nurse-maid to his brain-damaged brother, Stevie. It turns out that Stevie was reduced to his vegetative state following an unprovoked attack by a hooligan called Darrel. So Smiggy offers to help Phillip exact his revenge... If *Kevin and Perry* remade *Reservoir Dogs*, it could well have turned out like this. One of the most relentlessly unpleasant films to come out of Britain in some time, this molten cocktail of profanity, acne and flippant homicide panders to the lager-swilling mentality of a country addicted to reality TV and *The Sun*. Even so, as a writer, director and actor, Joe Tucker does display considerable flair for dialogue, some visual style and screen presence and sustains the passages of suspense for remarkable stretches. It's just a shame that he has to produce a work of such ugliness to get our attention.

• *Smiggy* Joe Tucker, *Phillip* James Holmes, *Julie* Nicola Stapleton, *Darrel* Grahame Fox, *Neville* Mark Leadbetter, *Maxine* Tameka Empson, *Mr Aladdin* Leslie Grantham, *Eric* Tom Bell, *Curtis* Johann Myers, *Claude* Dennis Titus, *Stevie* Harry Iggulden, *Jason* Tyler Garni, *Warden 643* Golda Rosheuvel, Stephen Callender-Ferrier, Andrew Tiernan.
• *Dir* and *Screenplay* Joe Tucker, *Pro* Michael Riley and Gregor Truter, *Co-Pro* Jim Reeve, *Ph* Ian Liggett and Roger Eaton, *Pro Des* Philip Robinson, *Ed* St John O'Rorke, *M* Simon Fisher-Turner; songs performed by Pelham Goddard and Choko, Ninja Tune, Laid Back, Pick and Mixed, Kenny J, English, New Flesh For Old, etc, *Costumes* Saffron Webb.

Feature Film Company/IAC Film & Television/Orangetop/Walking Point/Sterling Pictures/Visionview-Winchester Film Distribution.
99 mins. UK. 2001. Rel: 25 January 2002. Cert 18.

The Lawless Heart ★★¹/₂

Loosely united at a funeral, three very different men find their lives dramatically altered as they come to terms with new change in their lives... Opening as a profound and melancholy contemplation of loss, *The Lawless Heart* serves up some intriguing characters and pointed dialogue before resorting to a hackneyed and spurious structural conceit. As if to make up for the lack of a decent storyline, the film cuts back and forth in time, presenting three perspectives on the aftermath of Stuart's death. While the characters are nicely played by the three leads, only Tom Hollander's Nick is remotely sympathetic, leaving an emotional hole in a scenario that doesn't seem to know where it wants to go.

• *Tim* Douglas Henshall, *Nick* Tom Hollander, *Dan* Bill Nighy, *Corinne* Clementine Celarie, *Judy* Ellie Haddington, *Charlie* Sukie Smith, *Leah* Josephine Butler, *David* Stuart Laing, *Michelle* Sally Hurst, *Darren* Dominic Hall, *Chef* Jim McManus, *with* Howard Gossington, Richard Cant, Hari Dillon, Peter Symonds, June Barrie, Will Hunter.
• *Dir* and *Screenplay* Neil Hunter and Tom Hunsinger, *Pro* Martin Pope, *Ex Pro* Francesca Barra, Steve Christian, Jim Reeve and Roger Shannon, *Ph* Sean Bobbitt, *Pro Des* Lynne Whitehead, *Ed* Scott Thomas, *M* Adrian Johnston, *Costumes* Linda Alderson.

Isle of Man Film Commission/British Screen/Film Council/October Prods/National Lottery/BFI/BBC-Optimum Releasing.
100 mins. UK/USA. 2001. Rel: 28 June 2002. Cert 15.

Legally Blonde ★★★¹/₂

Raised in Bel-Air by affluent parents, Elle Woods is president of her sorority, Homecoming Queen, a major in 'fashion merchandising' and a genuine blonde. However, when the love of her life ditches her prior to enrolling at Harvard law school – because she doesn't present the right image – her world falls apart. So, in order to get her man back, Elle joins Harvard herself, aided by an admissions video directed by 'a Coppola'. But in the cashmere-and-pearls world of the Ivy League, Elle's Cosmo Girl image is a joke. Yet Elle is determined to succeed – and without too many sartorial compromises... A clarion call to all blondes, this feelgood, slickly packaged *Ally McBeal Jr* is a fantasy with a big smile. Reese Witherspoon, on a roll after her 1999 hat-trick of *Best Laid Plans*, *Cruel Intentions* and *Election*, is sensible enough to play her bright bimbo absolutely straight, without any awkward winks to the camera. True, the film's narrative arc is foreseeable after the first ten minutes, but it's enormous fun hitching along for the ride.

• *Elle Woods* Reese Witherspoon, *Emmett Richmond* Luke Wilson, *Vivian Kensington* Selma Blair, *Warner Huntington* Matthew Davis, *Professor Callahan* Victor Garber, *Paulette* Jennifer Coolidge, *Professor Stromwell* Holland Taylor, *Brooke Taylor-Windmark* Ali Larter, *Margot* Jessica Cauffiel, *Serena* Alanna Ubach, *Dorky David* Oz Perkins, *Chutney* Linda Cardellini, *Enid* Meredith Scott Lynn, *Mrs Windham Vandermark* Raquel Welch, *with* Bruce Thomas, Samantha Lemole, Ted Kairys, Kimberly McCullough, Allyce Beasley, James Read, Tane McClure.
• *Dir* Robert Luketic, *Pro* Marc Platt and Ric Kidney, *Screenplay* Karen McCullah Lutz and Kirsten Smith, from the book by Amanda Brown, *Ph* Anthony B Richmond, *Pro Des* Melissa Stewart,

Ed Anita Brandt Burgoyne and Garth Craven, *M* Rolfe Kent; songs performed by Hoku, Valeria, Ron Fair, Samantha Mumba, Fatboy Slim, Lisa Loeb, Lo-Ball, Krystal Harris, Kool & The Gang, Black Eyed Peas, Joanna Pacitti, KC & The Sunshine Band, Mya, James Brown, Hot Chocolate, and Superchi(k), *Costumes* Sophie de Rakoff Carbonell, *Sound* Frederick Howard, *Choreography* Toni Basil.

MGM/Twentieth Century Fox.
96 mins. USA. 2001. Rel: 26 October 2001. Cert 12.

Life as a House ★★★¹/₂

Orange County, California; the present. Divorced, estranged from his 16-year-old son and stuck in the same job for 20 years, George Monroe has let his dreams slip by. Then, on the same day, he is made redundant and told that he has just four months to live. Determined to make up for lost time, George decides to knock down the old structure he lives in and, with the unwilling aid of his alienated son, build the house he has always wanted... On paper this looks pretty schematic, but once the narrative guidelines have been laid down the scenario is never as predictable as one might think. Sure, the outcome is inevitable, but there are a few unexpected – and humorous – detours on the way. The film's strength is that the characters bring with them a very real sense of their own history and are brought vividly to life by a splendid cast. In the supporting role of a horny neighbour, Mary Steenburgen is a delightful surprise, while Hayden Christensen (now better known as Anakin Skywalker) promises a fruitful future. It's just a shame that with his glutinous score Mark Isham underlines so many of the film's more telling moments.

• *George Monroe* Kevin Kline, *Robin Kimball* Kristin Scott Thomas, *Sam* Hayden Christensen, *Alyssa Beck* Jena Malone, *Coleen Beck* Mary Steenburgen, *Peter Kimball* Jamey Sheridan, *David Dokos* Sam Robards, *Kurt Walker* Scott Bakula, *Bryan Burke* John Pankow, *Josh* Ian Somerhalder, *nurse* Sandra Nelson, *Bob Larson* Kim Delgado, *with* Mike Weinberg, Scotty Leavenworth, Barry Primus, Margo Winkler, Brandon Kessel, Art Chudabula.
• *Dir* Irwin Winkler, *Pro* Winkler and Rob Cowan, *Ex Pro* Brian Frankish, Lynn Harris and Michael DeLuca, *Screenplay* Mark Andrus, *Ph* Vilmos Zsigmond, *Pro Des* Dennis Washington, *Ed* Julie Monroe, *M* Mark Isham; songs performed by Guster, Gob, On, Default, Marilyn Manson, Limp Bizkit, Joni Mitchell, Radiohead, etc, *Costumes* Molly Maginnis, *Dialogue coach* Francie Brown.

New Line Cinema-Entertainment.
125 mins. USA. 2001. Rel: 15 March 2002. Cert 15.

Little Otik ★★★

As his barren wife yearns to have a child, Karel Horák starts to see babies, pregnant women and signs of procreation everywhere. A stall in the street hawks fresh babies wrapped in newspaper, a baby turns up in a pumpkin that Karel has just prised open and the old woman downstairs is planting fresh seeds in her plot. As a joke, Karel hands his wife a tree stump which, with a bit of imagination, could resemble an infant. Mistaking it for one, Mrs Horák brings it up as her own, her frustrated love transforming it into a very odd child indeed... Starting out as a surreal black comedy, *Little Otik* – based on an old folk tale – promises to be both an inventive and wry commentary on the whole industry of paediatrics and impending parenthood. Indeed, the veteran Czech animator and filmmaker Jan Svankmajer fills the screen with some wonderful imagery, intercut with both traditional and stopmotion animation. But, as the film shifts into darker territory, resembling an Eastern European *Little Shop of Horrors* (without the songs), it ultimately loses its way, succumbing to repetition, banality and unwieldy farce. At 131 minutes, it is also gratuitously indulgent.
Original title: *Otesánek.*

• *Bozena Horáková* Veronika Ilková, *Karel Horák* Jan Hartl, *Mrs Stádlerová* Jaroslava Kretschmerová, *Frantiöek Stádler* Pavel Nový, *Alzbetka* Kristina Adamcová, *Mrs Správcová, the caretaker* Dagmar St Íbrná, *Mr Zlábek* Zden Kozák.
• *Dir, Screenplay* and *Costumes* Jan Svankmajer, *Pro* Jaromír Kallista, *Co-Pro* Keith Griffiths, *Ph* Juraj Galvánek, *Pro Des* Eva Svankmajerová and Jan Svankmajer, *Ed* Marie Zemanová, *M* Carl Maria von Weber, *Computer effects* Martin Stejskal.

Athanor/Illuminations Films/Barrandov Biografia/FilmFour/ Czech Literary Fund Foundation, etc-FilmFour Dist.
131 mins. Czech Republic/UK/Japan. 2000.
Rel: 26 October 2001. Cert 15.

Long Time Dead ★★¹/₂

At a drunken party a bunch of college mates unleash deadly forces from the past while fooling around with a ouija board. As they begin to perish in 'accidents' that all seem to involve mysterious burns, fears arise that spirits of the non-alcoholic kind are involved... A writing and directing debut by Marcus Adams, *Long Time Dead* has its talented young things dropping like so many fireflies while exploiting generic conventions and confidently delivering the shocks on cue. However, the casting of US indie darling Lukas Haas in an insignificant role is a hollow marketing indulgence that compromises the film's artistic credentials.
[*Adam Keen*]

Above: The Ring Cycle: Elijah Wood (extreme right) leads the Hobbits on an incredible journey in Peter Jackson's giddy, visually breathtaking and phenomenally successful *The Lord of the Rings: The Fellowship of the Ring* (from Entertainment)

• *Rob* Joe Absolom, *Stella* Lara Belmont, *Annie* Melanie Gutteridge, *Webster* Lukas Haas, *Spencer* James Hillier, *Liam* Alec Newman, *Joe* Mel Raido, *Becker* Tom Bell, *with* Michael Feast, Cyril Nri, Nicholas Chagrin.
• *Dir* Marcus Adams, *Pro* James Gay-Rees, *Ex Pro* Tim Bevan and Eric Fellner, *Co-Pro* Jonathan Finn and Natascha Wharton, *Screenplay* Eitan Arrusi, Chris Baker, Daniel Bronzite and Andy Day, *Ph* Nic Morris, *Pro Des* Alison Riva, *Ed* Lucia Zucchetti, *M* Don Davis, *Costumes* Pamela Blundell.

Working Title Films/Canal Plus/Universal Focus-UIP. 94 mins. UK. 2001. Rel: 18 January 2002. Cert 15.

The Lord of the Rings: The Fellowship of the Ring ★★★★

Hobbiton/Bree/Rivendell/Moria/Rohan/Mordor/Gondor; at a time before history. In an idyllic corner of the world known as The Shire, a young Hobbit called Frodo Baggins discovers a ring. It is a ring that, forged many centuries ago, wields phenomenal power and could reinstate the full might of Sauron,

the dark Lord of Mordor, who intends to enslave the inhabitants of Middle-Earth. So it is up to Frodo, along with a Fellowship comprised of hobbits, men, a dwarf, an elf and the wizard Gandalf, to take the ring back to the Crack of Doom and have it destroyed once and for all… Bearing in mind that *The Lord of the Rings* is unfilmable, Peter Jackson has done a remarkable job. Conjuring up awe-inspiring landscapes and recreating the fabulous monsters of J R R Tolkien's seemingly limitless imagination, the New Zealand visionary has colluded in bringing to the screen the ultimate fairy tale for grown-ups. Even so, the viewer is subjected to so many extraordinary characters, so many astonishing sets and so many scenes of far-reaching magic that the cumulative effect is of celluloid fatigue. Far surpassing the first *Harry Potter* film visually, Jackson's epic fantasy is almost too much of a good thing, leaving the brain spinning yet the heart unengaged. A phenomenal achievement, then, but one resigned to cinematic mortality from the outset.

• *Frodo Baggins* Elijah Wood, *Gandalf* Ian McKellen, *Arwen* Liv Tyler, *Aragorn* aka *Strider* Viggo Mortensen, *Samwise Gamgee* Sean Astin, *Galadriel*

Cate Blanchett, *Gimli* John Rhys-Davies, *Pippin aka Peregrin Took* Billy Boyd, *Merry aka Meriadoc Brandybuck* Dominic Monaghan, *Legolas* Orlando Bloom, *Saruman* Christopher Lee, *Elrond* Hugo Weaving, *Boromir* Sean Bean, *Bilbo Baggins* Ian Holm, *Gollum/Smeagol* Andy Serkis, *Celeborn* Marton Csokas, *Haldir* Craig Parker, *Lurtz* Lawrence Makoare, *voice of the King* Alan Howard, *Everard Proudfoot* Noel Appleby.
• *Dir* Peter Jackson, *Pro* Jackson, Barrie M Osborne, Fran Walsh and Tim Sanders, *Ex Pro* Robert Shaye, Michael Lynne, Mark Ordesky, Bob Weinstein and Harvey Weinstein, *Assoc Pro* Ellen M Somers, *Screenplay* Walsh, Jackson and Philippa Boyens, *Ph* Andrew Lesnie, *Pro Des* Grant Major, *Ed* John Gilbert and Michael J. Norton, *M* Howard Shore, *Costumes* Ngila Dickson, *Creature/Armour/Make-up effects* Richard Taylor, *Visual effects* Jim Rygiel.

New Line Cinema/Wingnut Films-Entertainment. 178 mins. USA/New Zealand. 2001. Rel: 19 December 2001. Cert PG.

Lovely Rita ★★¹/₂

A suburb of Vienna, Austria; today. Another ironic title, another exploration of disenfranchised youth. Rita, while quite pretty (if a tad overweight), is far from lovely, being a compulsive liar, an inveterate truant, a grump, a grouch and a world unto herself. But then this is hardly surprising given the loveless family into which she was born... First-time director Jessica Hausner is good at conjuring up the cold, purely functional world of this domestic no-man's-land. Like her compatriot Michael Haneke, she is at pains to reveal through implication, so that what should be the film's most dramatic moments (Rita copulating with and masturbating a boy noticeably younger than her; an act of dispassionate, mortal violence) almost pass by undetected. Hausner has also coaxed some exemplary performances from her non-professional cast, particularly Barbara Osika as the eponymous teenager, although the director's fondness for the zoom lens betrays her technical inexperience. *Lovely Rita* is credible enough and the scenes between its heroine and the only boy she can relate to are a revelation. Nonetheless, the film is dramatically underwhelming and feels more like an unfinished sketch than a real movie.

• *Rita* Barbara Osika, *Fexi* Christoph Bauer, *bus driver* Peter Fiala, *Norbert, Rita's father* Wolfgang Kostal, *Inge, Rita's mother* Karina Brandlmayer, *Fexi's mother* Gabriele Wurm Bauer, *Fexi's father* Harald Urban.
• *Dir* and *Screenplay* Jessica Hausner, *Pro* Antonin Svoboda, Philippe Bober and Heinz Stussak, *Ex Pro* Barbara Albert and Susanne Marian, *Ph*

Martin Gschlacht, *Pro Des* Katharina Wöppermann, *Ed* Karin Hartusch, *M* Chopin; various; songs performed by Moby, Eiffel 65, Okado, Opus, Lido Brothers, and Matz Müller, *Costumes* Tanja Hausner.

Coop99 Filmproduktion/Essential/Prisma-ICA Projects. 79 mins. Austria/Germany. 2001. Rel: 28 December 2001. Cert 15.

Lucky Break ★★★

Sentenced to 12 years following a botched bank robbery, Jimmy Hands decides he has no interest in long-term imprisonment. Latching on to the governor's fondness for show tunes, Jimmy becomes instrumental in setting up a musical production as an elaborate cover for a breakout... A feelgood comedy with some rather heavy-handed manipulation, *Lucky Break* succeeds wonderfully in parts. With its roster of colourful characters and ingenious escape plan, the film at times even recalls the golden era of Ealing. James Nesbitt is spot-on as the hard-nosed con with a romantic heart, Bill Nighy (as ever) steals every scene he's in (as an effete, apologetic inmate) and Ron Cook is good value as the warder who thrives on the misery of his wards. The musical itself – *Nelson* – isn't bad, either (with priceless lyrics by Stephen Fry), and there's a buoyant score from Anne Dudley (*The Full Monty*) to grease along the dull bits. Still, there's a distinct whiff of by-the-numbers plotting and a few too many facile jokes at the expense of hardened cons taking to musical theatre ('Kiss me, Hardy' indeed!).

• *Jimmy Hands* James Nesbitt, *Annabel Sweep* Olivia Williams, *Cliff Gumball* Timothy Spall, *Roger Chamberlain* Bill Nighy, *Rudy Guscott* Lennie James, *Mr Perry* Ron Cook, *John Toombes* Frank Harper, *Governor Graham Mortimer* Christopher Plummer, *Darren* Raymond Waring, *Paul* Julian Barratt, *Officer George Barratt* Peter Wight, *Amy* Celia Imrie, *Old Bill* Ram John Holder, *Wayne* Ofo Uhiara, *Julie* Annette Bentley, Pete McNamara, Andy Linden, John Pierce Jones, Des McNamara, William Howe, Kenneth Thompson.
• *Dir* Peter Cattaneo, *Pro* Cattaneo and Barnaby Thompson, *Ex Pro* Paul Webster and Hanno Huth, *Co-Pro* Lesley Stewart and Elinor Day, *Screenplay* Ronan Bennett, *Ph* Alwin Kuchler, *Pro Des* Max Gottlieb, *Ed* David Gamble, *M* Anne Dudley; *Nelson: The Musical, book & lyrics* Stephen Fry, *music* Anne Dudley, *Costumes* Ffion Elinor, *Choreography* Nicky Hinkley.

FilmFour/Senator Film/Paramount/Miramax/Fragile Films-FilmFour. 108 mins. UK/USA/Germany. 2001. Rel: 24 August 2001. Cert 12.

Right: A matter of *Life* and death: Billy Bob Thornton exhibits an extraordinary command of understatement in the Coen brothers' stylish, articulate and terminally irregular *The Man Who Wasn't There* (see page 88)

Made ★★★

Los Angeles/New York; today. When aspiring boxer and part-time bodyguard Bobby loses his cool at a striptease joint owned by a mobster, he is put on a fresh assignment. All he has to do is stay sober, stay calm and make a routine delivery in New York. However, Bobby makes the mistake of inviting his childhood buddy along for the ride, an obnoxious jerk unable to appreciate the expediency of keeping his mouth shut at all times... Having written and starred in the low-budget *Swingers* with his friend Vince Vaughn, Jon Favreau now takes over the directorial reins as well with this stylish, wryly amusing, character-driven soufflé. Gently revving the comedy with some gritty, naturalistic dialogue and a series of spot-on cameos (Peter Falk's avuncular, plain-speaking mobster is a gem), Favreau has fashioned a smart vehicle for his talents that invites a smile at every turn. The story itself leaves something to be desired, although the final scene (prior to the epilogue) does have a surprisingly emotive sting.

• *Bobby* Jon Favreau, *Ricky* Vince Vaughn, *Jessica* Famke Janssen, *Ruiz* Sean Combs, *Max* Peter Falk, *Chloe* Makenzie Vega, *Horrace* Faizon Love, *Jimmy* Vincent Pastore, *Tom, the Welshman aka 'Red Dragon'* David O'Hara, Reanna Rossi, Jonathan Silverman, Kimberly Davies, Vernon Vaughn, Jason Delgado, Leonardo Cimino, Joan Favreau, Jamie Harris, and (uncredited) *bellhop* Sam Rockwell.
• *Dir* and *Screenplay* Jon Favreau, *Pro* Favreau and Vince Vaughn, *Ex Pro* John Starke, *Ph* Christopher Doyle, *Pro Des* Anne Stuhler, *Ed* Curtiss Clayton, *M* John O'Brien and Lyle Workman; songs performed by Dean Martin, Nightmares On Wax, De La Soul,

A Tribe Called Quest, Underdogs, Monster Magnet, Black Eyed Peas, DJ Quik, Stargunn, etc, *Costumes* Laura Jean Shannon, *Swing* Jimmy Williams.

Artisan Entertainment-Momentum Pictures.
94 mins. USA. 2001. Rel: 1 February 2002. Cert 15.

The Majestic ★★★

Hollywood/Lawson, California; 1951. Pete Appleton has never had it so good. A Hollywood screenwriter, he is living the American dream, has a high-profile girlfriend and is about to have his first A-feature go into production. He is then suspected of harbouring Communist connections, his film is pulled and his girlfriend leaves him. Taking to the road in a state of drunken despair, Appleton drives north, loses control of his car, crashes into a river and loses his memory… Not one to shy away from big, primal, all-American stories, Frank Darabont (*The Shawshank Redemption, The Green Mile*) now tackles identity, Communism, the McCarthy witch-hunt, Hollywood gamesmanship, smalltown American integrity, the politics of heroism, the magic of cinema and amnesia. Connecting all these big themes is a tremendous story, albeit one littered with the great ideas of other movies (*Mr Deeds Goes to Town, Hail the Conquering Hero!, It's a Wonderful Life, I Love You Again, The Front, The Smallest Show on Earth*, etc). While the film has its share of terrific moments (Luke Trimble discovering that he can play honky-tonk jazz, the town turning out to welcome its returning hero), it has just as many sequences of colossal ham (a cloying death scene takes the biscuit). Furthermore, Darabont directs with an extremely heavy hand, while the miscasting of Jim

Carrey as a latterday James Stewart/Gary Cooper is an error of Biblical proportions. Sadly, it is impossible to separate Carrey the comic superstar from the misunderstood innocent of smalltown Americana. Previously known as *Bijou*.

• *Peter Appleton/Luke Trimble* Jim Carrey, *Harry Trimble* Martin Landau, *Doc Stanton* David Ogden Stiers, *Stan Keller* James Whitmore, *Adele Stanton* Laurie Holden, *Kevin Bannerman* Ron Rifkin, *Leo Kubelsky* Allen Garfield, *Majority Counsel Elvin Clyde* Bob Balaban, *Ernie Cole* Jeffrey DeMunn, *Sheriff Cecil Coleman* Brent Briscoe, *Sandra Sinclair* Amanda Detmer, *Congressman Doyle* Hal Holbrook, *Carl Leffert* Brian Howe, *Bob Leffert* Karl Bury, *Irene Terwilliger* Susan Willis, *Emmett Smith* Gerry Black, *Mabel* Catherine Dent, *with* Chelcie Ross, Daniel Von Bargen, Shawn Doyle, Kevin DeMunn, Bruce Campbell, Cliff Curtis; *vocal cameos*: Garry Marshall, Paul Mazursky, Sydney Pollack, Carl Reiner, Rob Reiner, Brian Howe, and (reading Luke's letter) Matt Damon.
• *Dir* and *Pro* Frank Darabont, *Ex Pro* Jim Behnke, *Screenplay* Michael Sloane, *Ph* David Tattersall, *Pro Des* Gregory Melton, *Ed* Jim Page, *M* Mark Isham; Liszt, Bernard Herrmann; songs performed by Nat King Cole, Chet Baker, The Mills Brothers, etc, *Costumes* Karyn Wagner, *Jim Carrey's massage therapist* Lineia Light.

Castle Rock/Village Roadshow/NPV Entertainment/Darkwoods-Warner.
152 mins. USA. 2001. Rel: 24 May 2002. Cert PG.

The Man Who Wasn't There ★★★¹/₂

Santa Rosa, California; 1949. Ed Crane is a barber in a small town and he doesn't say much. Then, when he sees an opportunity to make some dough out of the future of dry cleaning, he decides to blackmail his wife's lover for a down-payment. Maybe that was a mistake... As an homage to the pulp fiction of James M Cain and 1940s film noir in general, *The Man Who Wasn't There* is faultless. With its beautifully evocative dialogue and striking black-and-white photography, the film could have been unearthed from a vault at the National Film Theatre. However, this being a Coen Brothers production, such icing merely acts as a starting point. At times, things do get a little *too* abstruse and surreal – even for Joel and Ethan – but the film's wry sense of the absurd and consummate craftsmanship is a constant joy. As an ordinary man stretched into extraordinary circumstances, Billy Bob Thornton gives a performance of formidable passivity – but then everybody is superbly in character, from Richard Jenkins as an ambiguous drunk to the second banana police officers. At times, the pace does slow to a virtual stand-still and the downbeat ending will put off many

viewers, but even a minor Coen feature is preferable to most brainless Hollywood fare. Previously known as *The Barber Movie*.

• *Ed Crane* Billy Bob Thornton, *Doris Crane* Frances McDormand, *Big Dave Nirdlinger* James Gandolfini, *Frank* Michael Badalucci, *Ann Nirdlinger* Katherine Borowitz, *Creighton Tolliver* Jon Polito, *Birdy Abundas* Scarlett Johansson, *Walter Abundas* Richard Jenkins, *Freddy Riedenschneider* Tony Shalhoub, *Persky* Christopher Kriesa, *Krebs* Brian Haley, *Burns* Jack McGee, *Carcanogues* Adam Alexi-Malle, Gregg Binkley, Alan Fudge, Lilyan Chauvin, Abraham Benrubi, Brooke Smith, Stanley DeSantis, Christopher McDonald.
• *Dir* Joel Coen, *Pro* Ethan Coen, *Ex Pro* Tim Bevan and Eric Fellner, *Co-Pro* John Cameron, *Screenplay* Joel Coen and Ethan Coen, *Ph* Roger Deakins, *Pro Des* Dennis Gassner, *Ed* Roderick Jaynes and Tricia Cooke, *M* Carter Burwell; Beethoven, Mozart, *Costumes* Mary Zophres, *Sound* Skip Lievsay, *Barber trainer* Richard Vanegas.

USA Films/Working Title/Mike Zoss Prods/Gramercy Pictures-Entertainment.
116 mins. USA/UK. 2001. Rel: 26 October 2001. Cert 15.

The Martins ★

Hatfield, Herts; today. The Martins are a sorry lot. Robert Martin lives off the dole and spends most of his time entering competitions that he never wins. Angie Martin, his wife, struggles to keep the family together but is unable to get her husband to face reality. Their daughter, Katie, is 14 and pregnant and their son, Little Bob, eight, is the class loser. Things can only get worse... Neither succeeding as social commentary nor as a black comedy, *The Martins* is a depressing, resoundingly unfunny film that wastes some very fine talent. With no discernible point – other than to gloat at the misery of its unpleasant characters – the film makes you ashamed to be British. Previously known as *The Tosspots*.

• *Robert Martin* Lee Evans, *Angie Martin* Kathy Burke, *Anthea* Linda Bassett, *Little Bob Martin* Eric Byrne, *Katie Martin* Terri Dumont, *Mr Heath* Frank Finlay, *PC Alex* Lennie James, *DI Tony Branch* Jack Shepherd, *Doug* Mark Strong, *Mo* Tameka Empson, *Mr Marvel* Ray Winstone, *Lil* Lorraine Ashbourne, *Mrs Heath* Barbara Leigh Hunt, Paddy Considine, Alison Egan, Owen Brenman, Nick Lamont.
• *Dir* and *Screenplay* Tony Grounds, *Pro* Greg Brenman, Dixie Linder and Bruce Davey, *Ex Pro* Peter Bennett-Jones, Paul Tucker, Ralph Kamp and Steve Christian, *Line Pro* Tori Parry, *Ph* David Johnson, *Pro Des* Michael Carlin, *Ed* Robin Sales, *M* Richard Hartley; Handel; songs performed by Morgan, Caroldene, Libbie Delainie, Kellee, Wayne

Fontana and The Mindbenders, and Martha Reeves and The Vandellas, *Costumes* Stewart Meachem.

Icon/Tiger Aspect Pictures/Isle of Man Film Commission-Icon.
86 mins. UK. 2001. Rel: 14 September 2001. Cert 15.

Me Without You ★★

London; 1973-2001. Friends since childhood, Marina and Holly are inseparable. Then, some time after puberty, Holly loses her virginity to Marina's brother Nat. And, as Marina's interest in fashion and experimental drugs conflicts with Holly's passion for difficult books, the girls would seem to be drifting apart... The problem with *Me Without You* is that the viewer is never made to care for either of these fascinating characters. With far too much attention paid to the ephemera of the passing years (Adam Ant's name is always good for a laugh), the film comes off as flat, long-winded and episodic. Yet, while Anna Friel turns in her now familiar performance as an irascible cow, Michelle Williams (the reprobate blonde in *Dawson's Creek*) is remarkable as the plain, bookish English girl. There are also good turns from Allan Corduner and Deborah Findlay as Holly's parents.

• *Marina* Anna Friel, *Holly* Michelle Williams, *Daniel* Kyle MacLachlan, *Nat* Oliver Milburn, *Linda* Trudie Styler, *Isabel* Marianne Denicourt, *Ray* Nicky Henson, *Max* Allan Corduner, *Judith* Deborah Findlay, *Carl* Steve John Shepherd, *Leo* Adrian Lucas, *young Holly* Ella Jones, *young Marina* Anna Popplewell, *Meredith* Annabel Mullion.
• *Dir* Sandra Goldbacher, *Pro* Finola Dwyer, *Ex Pro* Jonathan Olsberg, *Screenplay* Goldbacher and Laurence Coriat, *Ph* Denis Crossan, *Pro Des* Michael Carlin, *Ed* Michael Ellis, *M* Adrian Johnston; J S Bach, Mozart, Verdi; songs performed by Lucy Street, The Clash, The Only Ones, Dillinger, The Normal, Wreckless Eric, Echo & The Bunnymen, Scritti Politti, Adam Ant, Imagination, Charlene, Cowboy Junkies, Sonny and Cher, Depeche Mode, Barbara Dickson, Johnny Nash, Tim Buckley, and Super Furry Animals, *Costumes* Rosie Hackett, *Dialect coach to Ms Williams* Penny Dyer (UK) and Carla Meyer (US).

Momentum Pictures/Road Movies/Isle of Man Film Commission/British Screen/BskyB/Dakota Films/Wave Pictures-Momentum.
107 mins. UK/West Germany. 2001. Rel: 23 November 2001. Cert 15.

Me You Them ★★★

Darlene Lima is not what one would call a beauty, but she is voluptuous and hard-working and has a way with men. However, after she is stood up on her wedding day – while several months pregnant, at that – she moves on, leaving behind everything she held dear. She then accepts the offhand proposal of one Osias Linhares, an elderly man of property, and finds herself cooking for him, running his house and even working in the fields to pay the bills. And so, deprived of affection, Darlene takes Osias' cousin as her lover... Inspired by the true story of a Brazilian woman who lived with her three husbands under one roof, *Me You Them* is a gentle, poetic tale shot through with unconventional humour. Bathed in the rich light of Bahia, north-eastern Brazil, the film is remarkable in that it strips away all sentimentality and contrivance to focus on characters so real that they could have been hewn from the red earth around them. Maybe too slow and raw for most tastes – and a little slight – this is nonetheless a refreshing change from the slickly packaged comedies of Hollywood and Richard Curtis. **Original title:** *Eu Tu Eles.*

• *Darlene* Regina Casé, *Osias Linhares* Lima Duarte, *Zezinho* Stênio Garcia, *Ciro* Luiz Carlos Vanconcelos, *Raquel* Nilda Spencer, *Darlene's mother* Helena Araújo.
• *Dir* Andrucha Waddington, *Pro* Leonardo M de Barros, Pedro B de Hollanda, Andrucha Waddington and Fávio R Tambelinni, *Assoc Pro* Flora Gil, *Screenplay* Elena Soárez, *Ph* Breno Silveira, *Pro Des* Toni Vanzolini, *Ed* Vicente Kubrusly, *M* Gilberto Gil, *Costumes* Claudia Kopke.

Conspiração Films/Columbia TriStar Filmes do Brasil-Columbia TriStar.
106 mins. Brazil/USA/Portugal. 2000. Rel: 10 August 2001. Cert PG.

Mean Machine ★★¹/₂

Longmarsh Prison, England; the present. Danny Meehan had it all. As captain of England's football team, he had fame, wealth and the admiration of the nation. Then he fixed the outcome of an international match, lost his job and, in a drunken stupor, assaulted a police officer. Sentenced to three years in prison, he now has to live side by side with men who never had his opportunities in life. Danny is then given the chance to redeem himself: to train a team of hardened convicts for a football match against the guards... It's a good story and one that worked a treat in 1974's *The Longest Yard* (retitled *The Mean Machine* in the UK), in which Robert Aldrich directed Burt Reynolds as the disgraced football star. Today, though, the scenario looks a bit corny and shop-worn, while in the charisma stakes Vinnie Jones is no substitute for Reynolds. Furthermore, it doesn't help that the film's real villain (the prison governor) is played by David Hemmings, bearing an uncanny resemblance to former Prime Minister Harold Wilson. Still, once the film has groped its way past the stock characters and abundant clichés, it builds up a head of steam in the climactic match, ending on a note of hilarity with some priceless 'what became of' captions.

• *Danny Meehan* Vinnie Jones, *Doc* David Kelly, *The Governor* David Hemmings, *Burton* Ralph Brown, *Trojan* Robbie Gee, *Massive* Vas Blackwood, *Sykes* John Forgeham, *Tracey* Sally Phillips, *Billy the Limpet* Danny Dyer, *Monk* Jason Statham, *Ketch* Andrew Grainger, *Nitro* Stephen Walters, Jason Flemyng, Geoff Bell, Martin Wimbush, Omid Djalili, Wally Downes.
• *Dir* Barry Skolnick, *Pro* Matthew Vaughn, *Ex Pro* Guy Ritchie, Al Ruddy and Cynthia Pett-Dante, *Co-Pro* Georgia Masters, *Screenplay* Charlie Fletcher, Chris Baker and Andy Day, from a story by Al Ruddy, *Ph* Alex Barber, *Pro Des* Russell De Rozario, *Ed* Dayn Williams and Eddie Hamilton, *M* John Murphy, *Costumes* Stephanie Collie, *Soccer coordinator* Wally Downes.

Paramount/Ruddy/Morgan/Ska Films/Brad Grey Pictures-UIP.
UK/USA. 2001. Rel: 26 December 2001. Cert 15.

Mike Bassett: England Manager ★¹/₂

When England's football manager suffers a near-fatal heart attack, the FA is hard-pressed to find a suitable replacement. In desperation, they home in on Mike Bassett, the ebullient manager of, er, Norwich City. However, with his outmoded ideas and misplaced forbearance, Bassett seems ill-suited to lead England into the World Cup. A documentary crew records his progress... Football and the cinema have seldom been comfortable bedfellows and this provincial, unconvincing mockumentary is hardly going to improve matters. Picking on English football for cheap laughs is distinctly below the belt, while the depiction of British sportsmen as either morons or psychos is depressing in the extreme. The mockumentary format has also been worked to death, although the genre's humour has never been rendered quite so predictable. Virtually every gag is telegraphed in advance and only the larger-than-life buffoonery and pathos of Ricky Tomlinson can keep this sorry project from being a total calamity.

• *Mike Bassett* Ricky Tomlinson, *Karine Bassett* Amanda Redman, *Lonnie Urquart* Philip Jackson, *Tommo Thompson* Phill Jupitus, *Dave Dodds* Bradley Walsh, *Prof Shoegaarten* Ulrich Thomsen, *Jack Marshall* Robert Putt, *interviewer* Martin Bashir, *himself* Pelé, *Alan Massey* Chris McQuarry, *Wacko* Geoff Bell, *Tonka* Dean Lennox Kelly, *Jason Bassett* Danny Tennant, *himself* Keith Allen, *themselves* Atomic Kitten, *himself* Ronaldo, Scott Mean, Julian Ballantyne, Dean Holness, Robbie Gee, Malcolm Terris, Geoffrey Hutchings, Angela Curran, Paul

Rattray, Barry Venison, Natasha Kapinski.
• *Dir* Steve Barron, *Pro* Barron and Neil Peplow, *Ex Pro* Robert Halmi Snr, Robert Jones, Nigel Green, Luc Roeg and Charles Finch, *Line Pro* Miara Martell, *Screenplay* and *Assoc Pro* Rob Sprackling and J R N Smith, *Ph* Mike Eley, *Pro Des* John Reid, *Ed* Colin Green, *M* Antony Genn, Duncan Mackay and Mark Neary; songs performed by Artful Dodger Vs Dreem Teem, Backyard Dog, Richard Ashcroft, British Meat Scene, All Seeing I and Cerys Matthews, Help, Jarvis Cocker, Omar, Primal Scream, Robbie Williams, etc, *Costumes* Siobhan Barron, *Football consultant* Andy Ansah.

Film Council/Entertainment/Artist Independent Network/National Lottery-Entertainment.
90 mins. UK. 2001. Rel: 28 September 2001. Cert 15.

Monsoon Wedding ★★★

As Lalit and Pimmi Verma gear up for their daughter's arranged marriage to an engineer from Houston, Texas, they cannot begin to foresee the bedlam to come... Erupting with colour, noise, passion, humour and pathos, *Monsoon Wedding* is an uplifting, shambolic valentine to the city of Delhi, both old and new. As tradition clashes with the brazen new world of mobile telephones, e-mail and American slang, so the multitudinous strata of contemporary India unravel with varying degrees of success. It is unfortunate that the dramatic elements (Aditi's infidelity, Tej Puri's paedophilia) are introduced so far in, thus producing a belated logjam of melodrama, while the comic relief of the romance between the 'event manager' and the Vermas' maid doesn't really ring true. The film's greatest strengths, then, are its snapshots of Delhi life, intercut with the panoply of Punjabi aunts, uncles and cousins all attempting to have their definitive, calamitous say.

• *Lalit Verma* Naseeruddin Shah, *Pimmi Verma* Lillete Dubey, *Ria Verma* Shefali Shetty, *P K Dubey* Vijay Raaz, *Alice* Tilotama Shome, *Aditi Verma* Vasundhara Das, *C L Chadha* Kulbhushan Kharbanda, *Hemant Rai* Parvin Dabas, *Tej Puri* Rajat Kapoor, *Ayesha Verma* Neha Duney, *Rahul Chadha* Randeep Hooda, *Mohan Rai* Roshan Seth, *Vikram Mehta* Sameer Arya.
• *Dir* Mira Nair, *Pro* Nair and Caroline Baron, *Ex Pro* Jonathan Sehring and Caroline Kaplan, *Assoc Pro* Robyn Aronstam, *Screenplay* Sabrina Dhawan, *Ph* Declan Quinn, *Pro Des* Stephanie Carroll, *Ed* Allyson C Johnson, *M* Mychael Danna, *Costumes* Arjun Bhasin, *Choreography* Farah Khan.

IFC Prods/Key Films/Pandora Films/Paradis Films/Mirabai Films-Film Four.
113 mins. USA/Italy/Germany/France. 2001. Rel: 4 January 2002. Cert 15.

Above: Bereave in me: Halle Berry in her Oscar-winning performance in Marc Forster's *Monster's Ball* (from Entertainment), a superbly calibrated contemplation of lust and loss

Monster's Ball ★★★★¹/₂

Georgia; the present. According to 'corrections officer' Hank Grotowski, 'In England they used to give the condemned man a 'party' the night before … they called it the Monster's Ball.' Hank, both the father and son of correction officers, is proud of his legacy and of the professionalism he brings to the job. However, Hank's son, Sonny, is cut from a different cloth and when he vomits immediately prior to an execution, father and son fall out big time… Considering that *Monster's Ball* (yes, a terrible title, admittedly) touches so many incendiary buttons (race, capital punishment, miscegenation, cunnilingus), it is to be commended for never resorting to melodrama. Indeed, from the economic dialogue and muted central performance of Billy Bob Thornton (brilliant) to the subtle, virtually imperceptible score, the film impacts through implication, allowing its displays of tenderness to hit all the harder. While the scenes of violence pull no punches, it is the redemptive moments that are so emotionally effective, such as when Hank stops to ask the black boys' names, thus finally allowing them an identity. Only the Oscar-winning Halle Berry, who gives a performance of enormous commitment, passion and frailty, seems out of place, her physical breeding and sophistication at odds with the character as written.

• *Hank Grotowski* Billy Bob Thornton, *Sonny Grotowski* Heath Ledger, *Leticia Musgrove* Halle Berry, *Buck Grotowski* Peter Boyle, *Lawrence Musgrove* Sean Combs, *Ryrus Cooper* Mos Def, *Tyrell Musgrove* Coronji Calhoun, *with* Taylor Simpson, Gabrielle Witcher, Francine Segal, Marcus Lyle Brown, Milo Addica, Will Rokos.
• *Dir* Marc Forster, *Pro* Lee Daniels, *Co-Pro* Eric Kopeloff, *Ex Pro* Mark Urman, Michael Burns and Michael Paseornek, *Screenplay* Milo Addica and Will Rokos, *Ph* Roberto Schaefer, *Pro Des* Monroe Kelly, *Ed* Matt Chesse, *M* Asche and Spencer; songs performed by Red Meat, Lynn Anderson, Jimmie Dale Gilmore, Bob Dylan, Jean Wells, and The Jayhawks, *Costumes* Frank Fleming, *Dialect coach* Sam Chwat.

Lions Gate/Lee Daniels Entertainment-Entertainment. 111 mins. USA. 2001. Rel: 7 June 2002. Cert 15.

Monsters, Inc. ★★★★★

In the alternative realm of Monstropolis, the grotesque inhabitants take their work very seriously. For their very energy source is the collective screams of children drawn from the nocturnal seams of humanity. Then, one night, a little girl escapes into the hermetically sealed environs of Monstropolis and all Hell breaks loose. As the city's chief 'scarer', James P Sullivan, attempts to usher the girl home undetected, an unexpected bond forms between the hairy green giant and his fearless ward… Had *Shrek* not come along first, *Monsters, Inc.* would definitely have merited the label of most original, visually ground-breaking and narratively inventive cartoon. As it is, this Pixar-Disney collaboration has a number of things in common with its predecessor – the lovable monster/ogre at the centre of the story, the inversion of a mythical stereotype (in this case the monsters' fear of children) and the fast-talking comic sidekick (the Donkey vis-à-vis One-Eyed Mike). Drawing on the same gross-as-funny sensibility of *Shrek* (Sulley's cologne is called *Wet Dog*, his company's slogan is 'We scare because we care'), and filtering it through the basic precept of *Through the Wardrobe*, *Monsters, Inc.* transforms the demons of childhood into comedy targets. Highlights include the city of doors (very *Blade Runner*, very Sanderson) and Sulley's encounter with the pitiful Abominable Snowman. Family cinema has just taken another giant leap forward.

• Voices: *'One-Eyed' Mike Wazowski* Billy Crystal, *James P 'Sulley' Sullivan* John Goodman, *Boo* Mary Gibbs, *Randall Boggs* Steve Buscemi, *Henry J Waternoose* James Coburn, *Celia Mae* Jennifer Tilly, *Roz* Bob Peterson, *Yeti* John Ratzenberger, *Fungus* Frank Oz, Daniel Gerson, Steve Susskind, Bonnie Hunt, Jeff Pidgeon, Sam Black, *Rex* Wallace Shawn.
• *Dir* Pete Docter, and Lee Unkrich and David Silverman, *Pro* Darla K Anderson, *Ex Pro* John Lasseter and Andrew Stanton, *Assoc Pro* Kori Rae, *Screenplay* Stanton and Daniel Gerson, from a story by Docter, Jill Culton, Jeff Pidgeon and Ralph Eggleston, *Pro Des* Harley Jessup and Bob Pauley, *M* Randy Newman; 'If I Didn't Have You' performed by Billy Crystal and John Goodman, *Sound* Gary Rydstrom and Tom Myers.

Walt Disney Pictures/Pixar Animation Studios-Buena Vista. 95 mins. USA. 2001. Rel: 8 February 2002. Cert U.

The Mothman Prophecies ★★★

Why is it so many odd things happen just prior to a major disaster? From November 1966 to December 1967, a number of residents of Point Pleasant, West Virginia, described seeing a man-sized creature with giant wings and glowing red eyes. Updating this bizarre phenomenon to the present, scenarist Richard Hatem borrows generously from John A Keel's 1975 book *The Mothman Prophecies*, while introducing the central character of John Klein, a reporter for *The Washington Post*. Two years after losing his wife to a brain tumour, Klein finds himself inexplicably transported to Mount Pleasant where he becomes privy to a series of incomprehensible events… On an intellectual level, *The Mothman Prophecies* is a fascinating insight into the inexplicable, delving into parallel realities of our own that occasionally cross over. On an aesthetic level, the film is equally intriguing, eschewing special effects in favour of mind games, reinforced through the reality

of its characters. Even so, the film fails to kick-start the emotional motor of its story to make us care for these people, resulting in a drama that is as soporific as it is spooky. *Jacob's Ladder* it ain't.

• *John Klein* Richard Gere, *Connie Mills* Laura Linney, *Gordon Smallwood* Will Patton, *Mary Klein* Debra Messing, *Denise Smallwood* Lucinda Jenney, *Alexander Leek* Alan Bates, *Ed Fleischman* David Eigenberg, *Lucy Griffin* Ann McDonough, *Indrid Cold* Bill Laing, Bob Tracey, Ron Emanuel, Tom Stoviak, Yvonne Erickson, Scott Nunnally, Tom Tully, Billy Mott, Nat Griffin, Dan Callahan, Christin Frame, *bartender* Mark Pellington.
• *Dir* Mark Pellington, *Pro* Tom Rosenberg, Gary Lucchesi and Gary Goldstein, *Ex Pro* Ted Tannebaum, Richard S. Wright and Terry McKay, *Screenplay* and *Co-Pro* Richard Hatem, *Ph* Fred Murphy, *Pro Des* Richard Hoover, *Ed* Brian Berdan, *M* tomandandy; songs performed by Biosphere, Brian Berdan, Jeff Rona, tomandandy, etc, *Costumes* Susan Lyall, *Special effects* Peter Chesney.

Lakeshore Entertainment/Screen Gems-Helkon SK. 118 mins. USA. 2001. Rel: 1 March 2002. Cert 12.

Moulin Rouge! ★★★★

Paris; 1900. Due to a case of mistaken identity, Satine, the sexy star of the Moulin Rouge – and a ruthless courtesan – falls for aspiring writer Christian. But she has been promised to the wealthy Duke of Worcester, whose coffers are to finance Satine's debut as a leading actress in a show scripted by none other than Christian… At first, it's hard to know whether Baz Luhrmann's third feature is a rollercoaster ride of complete awfulness or a work of true brilliance. Recalling the frenetic, vulgar style of Ken Russell's films of the 1970s, Luhrmann's reinvention of Victorian music hall pastiche is at first bewildering and then completely seductive. Supercharged by Nicole Kidman's breathlessly sexy performance as Satine, Ewan McGregor's genuine sincerity as the love-struck writer and Jim Broadbent's unfettered bombast as the Moulin's manager, this is one thespian showpiece. Scripted by Luhrmann in collaboration with regular cohort Craig Pearce, the film also takes delight in plucking clichés from the future, whether they be lines of dialogue (Christian: 'Love is like oxygen, love is a many splendored thing!') or snatches of popular songs from the likes of Elton John, The Beatles and Sting. Above all, though, it's a visual revelation, with digital technology and model work bringing turn-of-the-century Montmartre vibrantly to life.

• *Satine* Nicole Kidman, *Christian* Ewan McGregor, *Toulouse Lautrec* John Leguizamo, *Harold Zidler* Jim Broadbent, *Duke of Worcester* Richard Roxburgh, *the unconscious Argentinean* Jacek Koman, *Satie* Matthew

Above: 'All you need is love': Nicole Kidman and Ewan McGregor trip the light fantastic in Baz Luhrmann's courageous, ground-breaking and triumphant *Moulin Rouge!* (from Fox)

Whittet, *Marie* Kerry Walker, *Audrey* David Wenham, *China Doll* Natalie Mendoza, *green fairy* Kylie Minogue, *Le Petomane* Keith Robinson, Garry McDonald, Caroline O'Connor, Christine Anu, Lara Mulcahy, Deobia Oparei, Linal Haft, Peter Whitford, Norman Kaye, Arthur Dignam, Carole Skinner, Jonathan Hardy.
• *Dir* Baz Luhrmann, *Pro* Luhrmann, Martin Brown and Fred Baron, *Co-Pro* Catherine Knapman, *Assoc Pro* and *Pro Des* Catherine Martin, *Screenplay* Luhrmann and Craig Pearce, *Ph* Donald McAlpine, *Ed* Jill Bilcock, *M* Craig Asrmstrong; songs performed by John Leguizamo, Jim Broadbent, Marilyn Manson and Danny Saber, Christina Aguilera, Lil' Kim, Mya and Pink, Rufus Wainwright, Marius DeVries, Ewan McGregor, Jacek Koman, Garry McDonald, Kylie Minogue, Ozzy Osbourne and Matthew Whittet, Nicole Kidman, Natalie Mendoza, Lara Mulcahy and Caroline O'Connor, Valeria, Placido Domingo and Alessandro Safina, Richard Roxburgh, Bono, Gavin Friday and Maurice Seezer, Anthony Weigh, José Feliciano, Alka Yagnik, David Bowie and Massive Attack, *Costumes* Catherine Martin and Angus Strathie, *Choreography* John O'Connell.

Fox/Bazmark-Fox.
128 mins. USA/Australia. 2001. Rel: 7 September 2001. Cert 12.

Muhammad Ali – The Greatest
★★★★

Like Michael Mann's *Ali*, this feature-length documentary looks at the career of the celebrated boxer between 1964 and 1974. The film's last quarter – set in Zaire and dealing with the fight with Foreman: the 'Rumble in the Jungle' – is good enough although hardly exceptional, but the earlier part of the film, shot in black and white, is truly special. The filmmaker, William Klein, first found fame as a photographer who exhibited in galleries and his pictures prove that black and white images, richly atmospheric and cinematically treated here, were his natural medium. He may have limited footage of the actual matches, but the way his camera captures the ambience of Ali's world at that time is art of the highest order.
[*Mansel Stimpson*]

• *With* Muhammad Ali, John Lennon, Paul McCartney, Ringo Starr, Sonny Liston, James X, Malcolm X, Floyd Patterson, Norman Mailer, Sam X, George Foreman, Don King, Mobutu Sese Seko, Joe Frazier, etc.
• *Dir* William Klein, *Ed* Francine Grubert, Eva Zora, Isabelle Rathéry and Emmanuelle Le Ray, *M* Mickey Baker, Umban and Le Wac.

Delphine Advico Films-Optimum Releasing.
111 mins. France. 1975. Rel: 8 February 2002. Cert 15.

Left: Dreams are made of this: Laura Elena Harring and Justin Theroux in David Lynch's sumptuously surreal *Mulholland Dr.* (from Pathé)

Mulholland Dr. ★★★

A limousine draws to a halt on Mulholland Drive, Los Angeles, and a man pulls a gun on his passenger, a beautiful, elegantly attired brunette. Seconds later, another car ploughs into the limo, killing everybody but the woman. Not remembering anything (or who she is), the brunette hides out in a nearby apartment and is befriended by its tenant, a wide-eyed Canadian actress who has just arrived in LA to become 'a movie star'... *Mulholland Dr.* is a model of magnificent direction, outstanding acting, consummate production design and unrepentant weirdness. Originally conceived as a TV pilot in the tradition of *Twin Peaks*, the film was developed into a feature when the ABC network pulled the plug on it for being too slow and too strange. Writer-director David Lynch then added another 45 minutes and has released it as an incomprehensible movie validated under the seal of being, well, positively Lynchian. A stylish accumulation of intriguing details, the film teasingly draws the viewer into its labyrinthine world and then absconds with the plot. Still, even an unfulfilled Lynch movie has its many rewards (Naomi Watts is sensational), but it would be nice if the director would eventually provide us with a conclusive ending.

• *Adam Kesher* Justin Theroux, *Betty Elms/Diane Selwyn* Naomi Watts, *Rita/Camilla Rhodes* Laura Elena Harring, *Coco Lenoix* Ann Miller, *Det Harry McKnight* Robert Forster, *Vincenzo Castigliane* Dan Hedaya, *Joe* Mark Pellegrino, *Det Domgaard* Brent Briscoe, *Cynthia* Katharine Towne, *Louise Bonner* Lee Grant, *Gene* Billy Ray Cyrus, *Jimmy Katz* Chad Everett, *Lorraine* Lori Heuring, *Billy* Michael Des Barres, *Wilkins* Scott Coffey, *Cowboy* Lafayette Montgomery, Rita Taggart, James Karen, Scott Wulff, Angelo Badalementi, Jeanne Bates, Marcus Gragam, Melissa Crider, Kate Forster, Rebekah Del Rio.
• *Dir* and *Screenplay* David Lynch, *Pro* Mary Sweeney, Alain Sarde, Neal Edelstein, Michael Polaire and Tony Krantz, *Ex Pro* Pierre Edelman, *Ph* Peter Deming, *Pro Des* Jack Fisk, *Ed* Mary Sweeney, *M* Angelo Badalementi; songs performed by Connie Stevens, Rebekah Del Rio, Linda Scott, David Lynch and John Neff, Sunny Boy Williams, and Milt Buckner, *Costumes* Amy Stofsky.

Les Films Alain Sarde/Canal Plus/Picture Factory/ Asymmetrical-Pathé.
146 mins. USA/France. 2001. Rel: 4 January 2002. Cert 15.

Murder by Numbers ★★★

Raised by materially comfortable, self-seeking parents, the bright but irresponsible Richard Haywood and Justin Pendleton strike up a singular relationship. Way ahead of their league at school, they decide to act out the perfect crime, just because they can. With scrupulous planning, they carry out an infallible murder, an act of abomination designed to fool the police. However, homicide investigator Cassie Mayweather relies more on instinct than on the sophisticated tools of her trade. And she smells a rat… The notorious Leopold and Loeb murder case has served such movies as Hitchcock's *Rope* (1948), *Compulsion* (1959) and *Swoon* (1992). *Murder by Numbers* is the first, however, to transpose the events to a contemporary setting. So, while the psychologi-

Right: Histoire Extraordinaire: Daniel Mesguich and Catherine Deneuve suffer an Eastern makeover in Peter Hyams' staggeringly mundane *The Musketeer* (from Buena Vista)

cal motivation of the Nietzschean 'superman' is no longer new, the modern forensic techniques to undermine it are. That is not to say that the interaction between the intellectually precocious Haywood and Pendleton is not engrossing (particularly as played by Gosling and Pitt), but that the minutiae of the scientific investigation is more so. It is unfortunate, then, that the parallel plot featuring the wise-cracking Mayweather is so trite.

• *Cassie Mayweather* Sandra Bullock, *Richard Haywood* Ryan Gosling, *Justin Pendleton* Michael Pitt, *Ray* Chris Penn, *Sam Kennedy* Ben Chaplin, *Lisa Mills* Agnes Bruckner, *Captain Rod Cody* R D Call, *Al Swanson* Tom Verica, *Olivia Lake* Krista Carpenter, *with* Janni Brenn, John Vickery, Michael Canavan.
• *Dir* Barbet Schroeder, *Pro* Schroeder, Richard Crystal and Susan Hoffman, *Ex Pro* Sandra Bullock and Jeffrey Stott, *Co-Pro* Frank Capra III, *Screenplay* Tony Gayton, *Ph* Luciano Tovoli, *Pro Des* Stuart Wurtzel, *Ed* Lee Percy, *M* Clint Mansell, *Costumes* Carol Oditz.

Warner/Castle Rock-Warner.
120 mins. USA. 2001. Rel: 28 June 2002. Cert 15.

The Musketeer ★★

While Febre, the treacherous right-hand man of Cardinal Richelieu, threatens to plunge France into war with Spain and England, aspiring Musketeer D'Artagnan tries to enlist the co-operation of the king's jaded guardsmen… The apparent excuse for

filming *The Three Musketeers* yet again was to introduce an Eastern element into the fight sequences (à la *Brotherhood of the Wolf*, also set in period France). Indeed, these scenes are something else, particularly the finale in which D'Artagnan battles the evil Febre across a network of tall ladders. It's a shame, though, that more attention wasn't paid to the script, a limp, pedestrian adaptation of Alexandre Dumas' literate, stirring romp. Besides the weak dialogue, the film is madly miscast, badly dubbed (listen to the creek of Tim Roth's leather jacket!) and muddily photographed. Only Roth's delicious villain and the beautiful location work prevent this from being total pap.

• *Queen of France* Catherine Deneuve, *Francesca* Mena Suvari, *Cardinal Richelieu* Stephen Rea, *Febre* Tim Roth, *D'Artagnan* Justin Chambers, *Aramis* Nick Moran, *Bonacieux* Bill Treacher, *Louis XIII* Daniel Mesguich, *Porthos* Steven Speirs, *Athos* Jan Gregor Kremp, *Rochefort* David Schofield, *Madame Lacross* Isilla Chelton, *young D'Artagnan* Maximilian Dolbey, *Dumas* Bertrand Witt, *with* Jean-Pierre Castaldi, Luc Gentile, Jeremy Clyde.
• *Dir* and *Ph* Peter Hyams, *Pro* Moshe Diamant, *Ex Pro* Rudy Cohen, Mark Damon, Steve Paul, Frank Hübner and Romain Schroeder, *Co-Pro* Jan Fantl, *Screenplay* Gene Quintano and Fabrice Ziolkowski, *Pro Des* Philip Harrison, *Ed* Terry Rawlings, *M* David Arnold, *Costumes* Raymond Hughes and Cynthia Dumont, *Choreographer* Xiong Xin Xin.

Miramax/Universal/MDP Worldwide/Crystal Sky/ApolloMedia/Q and Q Media/Carousel Picture Co/Film Fund Luxembourg-Buena Vista.

104 mins. UK/Germany/USA/Luxembourg. 2001.
Rel: 21 June 2002. Cert PG.

My Brother Tom ★★★

Jessica and Tom collide in suburban Hertfordshire and embark on a wild teenage infatuation fuelled by hormones, anger and a desperate denial of sexual abuse. Framed by leafy woods and secret ponds, they give each other pet names, swim naked and eat roots in a desperately skewed reaction to their 'real' lives. But it is only a matter of time before society invades their made-up Eden with the moral codes they were trying to escape… A contemporary coming of age movie darkly laced with raw tragedy, the film extracts some electric performances from its young stars (Ben Whishaw won a BIFA for Most Promising Newcomer and Jenna Harrison was picked for the role from an A-Level Drama workshop) but suffers from a self-conscious 'rawness-as-bad-video' approach and a narrative paced past the point of boredom. On top of that, the emotionally pornographic atmosphere it exudes threatens to leave the audience feeling like voyeuristic pervs.
[*Adam Keen*]

• *Jessica* Jenna Harrison, *Tom* Ben Whishaw, *Sarah* Honeysuckle Weeks, *Ian* Michael Erskine, *Jack* Adrian Rawlins, *Jessica's mum* Judith Scott, *gang leader* Michael Tucek, Jonathan Hackett, Richard Hope, Patrick Godfrey.
• *Dir* Dom Rotheroe, *Pro* Carl Schonfeld, *Ex Pro* Robin Gutch, Roger Shannon, Paul Trijbits and Paul Webster, *Screenplay* Alison Beeton-Hilder and Dom Rotheroe, *Ph* Robby Muller, *Pro Des* Isolde Sommerfeldt, *Ed* David Charap, *M* Annabelle Pangborn, *Costumes* Sarah Bleninsop and Lee Croucher.

British Screen/Channel 4 Films/Film Council/Trijbits Productions/WOW Productions.
110 mins. UK/Germany. 2001. Rel: 16 November 2001. Cert 18.

The Mystic Masseur ★¹⁄₂

Trinidad; 1943/Oxford, 1954. The son of a revered masseur, schoolteacher Ganesh Ramsumair returns to his country village to attend his father's funeral. There, he is coaxed into a marriage with the beautiful daughter of an admiring neighbour and decides to capitalise on his education by writing a book. Meanwhile, to pay the bills, he sets up as a masseur in his own right… It is unfortunate that the first movie adaptation of a work by the Nobel Prize-winning novelist V S Naipaul should be so unremittingly dull. The material itself is enormously interesting, though: the Indian community in the West Indies, the power of mystical massage, the tug-of-war between romantic commitment and creative expression, and so on. However, leading actor Aasif Mandvi conveys none of the charisma of Ganesh, the plotting is terminally ponderous and the delineation of character both condescending and one-dimensional.

• *Ramlogan* Om Puri, *Mr Stewart* James Fox, *Ganesh Ramsumair* Aasif Mandvi, *Beharry* Sanjeev Bhaskar, *Leela* Ayesha Dharker, *Partap* Jimi Mistry, *Auntie* Zohra Segal, *Suruj* Sakina Jaffrey, *Mrs Cooper* Grace Maharaj, *young Partrap* Danesh Khan, *Narayan* Keith Hazare Imambaksh, *Governor* Pip Torrens.
• *Dir* Ismail Merchant, *Pro* Nayeem Hafizka and Richard Hawley, *Ex Pro* Paul Bradley and Lawrence Duprey, *Screenplay* Caryl Phillips, *Ph* Ernie Vincze, *Pro Des* Lucy Richardson, *Ed* Roberto Silvi, *M* Richard Robbins and Zakir Hussain, *Costumes* Michael O'Connor.

Merchant Ivory Prods/Pritish Nandy Comm/Video Associates-Miracle Communications.
118 mins. UK/India. 2001. Rel: 29 March 2002. Cert PG.

Above: Mystical masala: Aasif Mandvi ponders his lines in Ismail Merchant's thin and ponderous *The Mystic Masseur* (from Miracle Communications)

New Year's Day ★'/₂

On New Year's Day, Jake and Steven decide to kill themselves. The only survivors of a school skiing trip, they decide that they have nothing left to live for. But first, Steven reasons, they must achieve a number of objectives: to sample a full range of illegal drugs, punch a policeman, crash a car, kill a large animal and so on... When building a film around a roster of proposed goals it is advisable to make the tone and protagonists as true-to-life as possible. Unfortunately, *New Year's Day* opens with a hopelessly phoney, meretricious prologue from which it never recovers. Furthermore, the material craves for a touch of surreal style, which it is sorely denied (Lindsay Anderson would have had a field day with this stuff), while the film is neither dark enough nor suitably credible to work on its own terms. If either of the leading characters had been invested with an iota of charm or sympathy, then this uneven, unpleasant and unbelievable mess might have had something to work with. And what on earth is Jacqueline Bisset doing appearing in a bit part?

• *Veronica* Marianne Jean-Baptiste, *Shelley* Anastasia Hille, *Jake* Andrew Lee Potts, *Steven* Bobby Barry, *Robin* Michael Kitchen, *Mrs Fisher* Sue Johnston, *Mr Diamond* Ralph Brown, *Geraldine* Jacqueline Bisset, *Ben* Gregg Prentice, *Trout* Zoe Thorne, *Vicky* Hannah Faulkner, *Heather* Emilie Francois, *with* Liam Barr, Ryan Davenport, Nicole Charles, Cecilia Noble, Burt Caesar, Graham Bill, Michael Attwell, Hayley Nott.
• *Dir* Suri Krishnamma, *Pro* Stephen Cleary and Simon Channing-Williams, *Ex Pro* David Forrest and Beau Rogers, *Co-Pro* Charles Steel, Marianne Slot and Vibeke Windelov, *Co-Ex Pro* Cameron McCracken and Pippa Cross, *Screenplay* Ralph Brown, *Ph* John de Borman, *Pro Des* Eve Stewart, *Ed* Adam Ross, *M* Julian Nott; Schubert; songs performed by Technique, Sparks, Ice 9 and Andrew Lee Potts, Bobby Barry, The Flaming Lips, The Fun Lovin' Criminals, Herp Albert, Leonard Cohen, A.B. Didgeridoo Oblivion, Paul Weller, and Nina Simone, *Costumes* Frances Tempest, *Sound* Kevin Brazier and Stephen Griffiths, *Airbag man* Garrick Woodruff.

Flashpoint/Liberator Prods/British Screen/BskyB/Canal Plus/Alchymie/Granada Film-Optimum Releasing. 101 mins. UK/France. 1999. Rel: 2 November 2001. Cert 18.

Nightshift ★★'/₂

Philippe Le Guay's first feature starts well, showing his total command of the director's craft and presenting an intriguing and relatively unfamiliar theme: the power exercised by a bully in the workplace who tries to humiliate a new employee. Marc Barbé and Gérald Laroche as aggressor and married victim play well, but, frustratingly, the film loses its way. This is partly due to improbabilities in the plot development and the behaviour of the characters. Yet even more disconcerting is the way that the film handles its sudden shift into quite different territory when it suggests underlying homosexual feelings. In this day and age it should be possible to portray candidly and with insight a gay sado-masochistic bond between the two men. But *Nightshift* leaves this as a subtext and bafflingly refuses to face up to the true nature of its story.
Original title: *Trois Huit*.
[*Mansel Stimpson*]

• *Pierre* Gérald Laroche, *Fred* Marc Barbé, *Carole* Luce Mouchel, *Victor* Bastien Le Roy, *Franck* Bernard Ballet, *Danny* Alexandre Carrière, *Alain* Michel Cassagne.
• *Dir* Philippe Le Guay, *Pro* Bertrand Faivre and Adeline Lecallier, *Screenplay* Olivier Dazat, Regis Franc and Philippe Le Guay, *Ph* Jean-Marc Fabre, *Pro Des* Jimmy Vansteenkiste, *Ed* Emmanuelle Castro, *M* Yann Tiersen, *Costumes* Anne Schotte.

France 3 Cinema/Canal Plus/Les Productions Lazennec/ Studio Images 7-Metro Tartan. 97 mins. France. 2000. Rel: 1 February 2002. Cert 15.

No Man's Land ★★★★

Bosnia; June 1993. After a night of jokes and irreverent banter, a group of Bosnian soldiers awake to find themselves in the firing line on the Serbian border. Within minutes they are all dead, save for Tchiki. Shot through the shoulder, Tchiki scrambles into a trench and waits for the cover of night. However, he is disturbed by two Serbian scouts, one of whom places the body of his friend Tsera onto an activated mine, thus turning the Bosnian into a human booby trap. Tchiki kills the first Serb but is unable to finish the other one off. Thus trapped in no man's land, the Serb and Bosnian trade insults as their respective sides, the UN peacekeeping forces and the media decide what to do next... An articulate satire on the absurdity of war, *No Man's Land* manages to sustain a constant frisson of suspense while injecting healthy doses of humour. Aided by crisp photography and superlative performances, it provides the intimacy of a good play (in the manner of Brecht and Beckett), while maintaining the immediacy and scope of a film. And even as events spiral into ever-increasing realms of farce, former documentary filmmaker Dabis Tanović keeps it all absolutely real, complete with a bitter aftertaste of stinging irony. Winner of the Oscar for Best Foreign-Language Film.

• *Tchiki* Branko Djuric, *Nino* Rene Bitorajac, *Cera* Filip Sovagović, *Sergeant Marchand* Georges Siatidis, *Colonel Soft* Simon Callow, *Jane Livingstone* Katrin

Cartlidge, *Captain Dubois* Serge-Henri Valcke, *Michel* Sacha Kremer.

• *Dir, Screenplay* and *M* Danis Tanović, *Pro* Frédérique Dumas-Zajdela, Marc Baschet and Cedomir Kolar, *Ph* Walther Vanden Ende, *Pro Des* Dusko Milkavec, *Ed* Francesca Calvelli, *Costumes* Zvonka Makuc, *Sound* Michael Billingsley.

Noé Prods/Fabrica Cinema/Man's Films/Casablanca/ British Screen/Canal Plus, etc-Momentum Pictures. 97 mins. France/Italy/Belgium/UK/Slovenia/Switzerland. 2001. Rel: 17 May 2002. Cert 15.

Nobody Someday ★★★★

It's hardly an easy task for a documentary to be more interesting than its subject and Robbie Williams, as a subject, hardly elicits excitement. The cocky poster boy of British pop who has made arrogance his trademark, Robbie has already been the topic of two documentaries, *Some Mothers Do 'Ave 'Em* (1998) and *It Ain't Half Hot Mum* (1999). Here, writer-director Brian Hill follows him on his five-week, 15-city tour of Europe, just as he has given up drugs and alcohol; he insists on camera that he is a boring pop star and that most of his songs are 'crap'. This hardly bodes well for a riveting insight into the demons of rock- 'n'roll. But then Robbie, who was determined that this portrait be an honest one, is no cutting edge icon- oclast, conceding that, 'I don't mind being called "uncool" – I was in Take That.' What *Nobody Someday* is, then, is a compelling, funny and tragic portrait of an icon who has come to terms with his own short- comings ('the only opinion I have about anything is me'), of the extraordinary demands on his small army of security guards and of the terrible cost of celebrity. And the music isn't half bad, either.

• With Robbie Williams, *musical director* Guy Chambers, *guitar* Gary Nuttall, *guitar* Fil Eisler, *bass guitar* Yolanda Charles, *drums* Chris Sharrock, *key- boards/guitar* Claire Worall, *personal manager* Josie Cliff, *tour manager* Andy Franks, *accountant* Tom Golseth, etc.
• *Dir* and *Screenplay* Brian Hill, *Pro* Caroline Levy, *Ex Pro* Tim Clark, David Enthoven and Gabby Chelmicka, *Ph* Simon Niblett and Michael Timney, *Ed* Stuart Briggs, *M* Guy Chambers; Carl Orff; songs performed by Robbie Williams, *Sound* Andrew Boag, Ian MacLagan and George Foulgham.

Century Films/IE Music-UIP. 90 mins. UK. 2001. Rel: 4 January 2002. Cert 15.

Not Another Teen Movie ★★¹⁄₂

Joel Gallen makes his big screen debut with this paro- dy of the most memorable 'teen' movies of the 80s and 90s, while lifting the entire plot from *She's All That.*

Jake Wyler, head hunk of John Hughes High, bets he can turn plain Jane Briggs into the prom queen. True to form, all it takes to turn Janey from pooch to princess is a new hairdo and the removal of her glass- es. *Not Another Teen Movie* takes a stab at just about every entry in the teen genre but falls short of similar genre-spoofing parodies like *Airplane!* and *Scary Movie*. It's all too clear that Gallen and his writers are aficionados of teen films: John Hughes' repertoire in particular. Instead of the scathing humour needed to pull off the joke, Gallen opts for a more loving homage that, ironically, turns this into just another teen movie. [*Scot Woodward Myers*]

• *Janey Briggs* Chyler Leigh, *Jake Wyler* Chris Evans, *Priscilla* Jaime Presley, *Austin* Eric Christian Olsen, with Mia Kirshner, Deon Richmond, Eric Jungmann, Ron Lester, Lacey Chabert, Ed Lauter, Paul Gleason, Mr T, Randy Quaid, Molly Ringwald.
• *Dir* Joel Gallen, *Pro* Neal H Mortitz, *Ex Pro* Brad Luff and Michael Rachmil, *Screenplay* Michael G Bender, Adam Jay Epstein, Andrew Jacobson, Phil Beauman and Buddy Johnson, *Ph* Reynaldo Villalobos, *Pro Des* Joseph T Garrity, *Ed* Stephen Welch, *M* Theodore Shapiro, *Costumes* Florence- Isabelle Megginson.

Columbia Pictures/Original Film-Columbia TriStar. 89 mins. USA. 2001. Rel: 24 May 2002. Cert 15.

Above: Welcome to Bosnia: the late Katrin Cartlidge plays hard-boiled war correspondent Jane Livingstone in Danis Tanoviæ's compelling and ironic *No Man's Land* (Momentum Pictures), which won the Oscar for Best Foreign Language Film

Ocean's Eleven ★★★★¹/₂

Danny Ocean has spent four years behind bars and, in the interim, has lost his wife to a multi-billionaire casino owner. Now he's out and wants to make up for lost time. Immediately violating his parole, Danny flits all over the country to enlist the singular talents of ten world-class thieves. His goal: to lift $150 million from the vaults of three Vegas casinos and to win back the heart of his ex... As a heist movie, *Ocean's Eleven* is a 24-carat gem. Tooled to precision, it is a cut above such specimens as *Snatch*, *Heist* and *The Score* and has a stellar lustre second to none. It is also a substantial improvement on the 1960 original, which brought together the celebrity muscle of Frank Sinatra, Dean Martin, Sammy Davis Jr, Peter Lawford and Joey Bishop. Downgrading their salaries by half, Clooney and his accomplices deliver priceless deadpan performances, with only Don Cheadle's cockney explosives expert proving to be a major misfire (for some reason, Cheadle refused a credit, as he did for *Rush Hour 2*). Expertly crafted (like the heist itself), meticulously detailed (ditto) and effortlessly witty, *Ocean's Eleven* is not only a superlative caper but a classic love story, every bit as intelligent and understated as *Casablanca*.

• *Danny Ocean* George Clooney, *Linus* Matt Damon, *Terry Benedict* Andy Garcia, *Rusty Ryan* Brad Pitt, *Tess Ocean* Julia Roberts, *Virgil Malloy* Casey Affleck, *Turk Malloy* Scott Caan, *Reuben Tishkoff* Elliott Gould, *Frank Catton* Bernie Mac, *Saul Bloom* Carl Reiner, *Livingston Dell* Eddie Jemison, *Yen* Shaobo Qin, Cecelia Birt, Lennox Lewis, Wladimir Klitschko, Joe Ladue, Michael Delano, Robin Sachs, Jerry Weintraub, Henry Silva, Eydie Gormé, Angie Dickinson, Steve Lawrence, Wayne Newton, Richard Reed, and (uncredited) *Basher Tarr* Don Cheadle, *with* Hollie Marie Combs, Topher Grace, Joshua Jackson, Barry Watson, Shane West.
• *Dir* Steven Soderbergh, *Pro* Jerry Weintraub, *Ex Pro* John Hardy, Susan Ekins and Bruce Berman, *Co-Pro* R J Louis, *Screenplay* Ted Griffin, *Ph* Peter Andrews (aka Steven Soderbergh), *Pro Des* Philip Messina, *Ed* Stephen Mirrione, *M* David Holmes; songs performed by David Holmes, Handsome Boy Modeling School, Perry Como, Norman Greenbaum, Berlin, Quincy Jones, Elvis Presley, Liberace, Percy Faith and His Orchestra, etc, *Costumes* Jeffrey Kurland.

Warner/Village Roadshow Pictures/NPV Entertainment/Section Eight-Warner.
116 mins. USA/Australia. 2001. Rel: 15 February 2002. Cert 12.

Offending Angels ★★¹/₂

Sam and Baggy share a comfortable terraced house in London but cannot seem to commit to anything resembling a future. Squandering their time on childish antics, they seem trapped in a no man's land of porn, pizza and trips to the pub. Then their guardian angels turn up to lend a helping hand, but they aren't exactly equipped to cope with the human side of their assignment... A British variation on *City of Angels* (itself a remake of Herzog's *Wings of Desire*), this first-time effort from producer-director-writer-star Andrew Rajan is full of good things. The shorthand that Rajan establishes between his two main protagonists is deftly done and there is an offbeat sweetness that is quite affecting for a story about a couple of good-for-nothing layabouts. However, the story is not strong enough to support such niceties and the occasional shift in tone seriously undermines any emotional value.

• *Paris* Susannah Harker, *Sam* Andrew Lincoln, *Zeke* Shaun Parkes, *Baggy* Andrew Rajan, *Alison* Paula O'Grady, *with* Marion Bailey, Michael Cochrane, Sophie Dix, Sean Gallagher, Louise Delamere, Jack Davenport, Steve Mangan.
• *Dir* and *Pro* Andrew Rajan, *Ex Pro* Jeremy Hewitt, Mike Lozowski, Victoria Owen and Rupert Rossander, *Screenplay* Rajan and Tim Moyler, *Ph* Alvin Leong, *Pro Des* Annie Gosney, *Ed* Roger Burgess and Catherine Fletcher, *M* Martin Ward, *Costumes* Michelle Jones.

Pants Prods-Guerilla Films.
93 mins. UK. 2000. Rel: 19 April 2002. Cert 15.

The Officers' Ward ★★★★★

France; 1914-18. Without realising that the war has begun, Lieutenant Adrien Fournier is hit by enemy fire and loses half his face. Soaked in the blood of other soldiers and unable to speak, he arrives at the officers' ward in an army hospital far from the front line. There, he slowly confronts the reality that he will never be the same again... In an age that promotes cosmetic perfection from every angle, it is sobering to sit through a 132-minute film about disfigurement. Indeed, the intensity is such that, at times, one wants to put it down like a difficult book, and return to it when one is feeling stronger. Yet the drama's cumulative effect is spiritually liberating. François Dupeyron may not be the finest director working in France (his *A Strange Place to Meet* was both plodding and irritating), but here he has done his subject proud. Few war films can boast as many powerful, moving and devastating sequences without showing a single scene of combat. And few have managed to convey the cruelty and compassion of the human condition with such poetic, unsentimental clarity.
Original title: *La Chambre des officiers*.

• *Adrien Fournier* Éric Caravaca, *Henri* Denis Podalydès, *Pierre* Grégori Derangere, *Anaïs* Sabine

Azema, *the surgeon* André Dussollier, *Marguerite* Isabelle Renauld, *Alain* Jean-Michel Portal, *Clémence* Geraldine Pailhas, *Adrien's sister* Circé Lethem, *with* Guy Tréjan, Xavier de Guillebon, Catherine Arditi, Paul Le Person.
• *Dir* and *Screenplay* François Dupeyron, from the novel by Marc Dugain, *Pro* Michèle and Laurent Petin, *Ph* Tetsuo Nagata, *Pro Des* Patrick Durand, *Ed* Dominique Faysee, *M* Arvo Pärt, *Costumes* Catherine Bouchard.

ARP/France 2 Cinema/Canal Plus-Optimum Releasing. 132 mins. France. 2001. Rel: 22 March 2002. Cert 15.

The One ★★¹/₂

A former agent for the Multiverse Bureau of Investigation, Gabriel Yulaw has routinely violated his sacrosanct knowledge of wormhole transportation. Systematically popping into parallel universes, Yulaw has eliminated 122 of his alternate life-forces in order to harness the strength and powers of his doppel-gängers. Now he has just one more alter ego to kill before upsetting the balance of the cosmos to become the Only One, a deity of unimaginable power… While adopting an audacious premise and borrowing liberally from other movies (*Double Impact*, *Twin Dragons*, *Maximum Risk*, *The Matrix*), *The One* at least has the courage of its convictions. From the aggressive exposition and gravity-defying stunts to the heavy rock score and spectacular closing shot, the film certainly delivers, or at least tries to. And, for all its derivative swipes, it does introduce some novel extremes of its own, not least when Jet Li uses a pair of motorbikes for hand-to-hand combat. It's complete rubbish, of course, but it moves at a rate of knots and boasts some flashy production values.

• *Gabe/Yulaw/Lawless* Jet Li, *Roedecker* Delroy Lindo, *TK/Massie Walsh* Carla Gugino, *Funsch* Jason Statham, *Aldrich* James Morrison, *Yates* Dylan Bruno, *D'Antoni* Richard Steinmetz, *Sgt. Siegel* Dean Norris.
• *Dir* James Wong, *Pro* Glen Morgan and Steven Chasman, *Ex Pro* Lata Ryan, Charles Newirth, Todd Garner and Greg Silverman, *Screenplay* Wong and Morgan, *Ph* Robert McLachlan, *Pro Des* David L Snyder, *Ed* James Coblentz, *M* Trevor Rabin, *Costumes* Chrisi Karvonides-Dushenko, *Sound* Geoffrey G Rubay, Ann Scibelli and Harry Cohen, *Visual effects* Eric Durst.

Columbia Pictures/Revolution Studios/Hard Eight Pictures-Columbia TriStar. 87 mins. USA. 2001. Rel: 12 April 2002. Cert 15.

Original Sin ★★¹/₂

Successful Cuban entrepreneur Luis Vargas sends off for his American mail order bride in this late 19th century period piece. When the beautiful and enig-matic Julia Russell turns up, the chemistry is unden-iable and the two are wed. But it isn't long before Julia reveals herself to be professional con woman Bonny Castle, taking Vargas for everything he's got… and then disappears. Obsessed with his own need for vengeance, Vargas tracks Bonny down, finding her partner, several plots for murder and the lengths to which he'll go for love. Two of Hollywood's sexiest actors and the sultry Cuban setting do little to inject the necessary steam into this limp adaptation of Cornell Woolrich's novel.
[*Scot Woodward Myers*]

• *Luis Antonio Vargas* Antonio Banderas, *Julia Russell/Bonny Castle* Angelina Jolie, *Billy/Walter Downs/Mephisto* Thomas Jane, *Alan Jordan* Jack Thompson, *Colonel Worth* Gregory Itzin, *Augusta Jordan* Allison Mackie, *Sara* Joan Pringle, *Emily Russell* Cordelia Richards.
• *Dir* Michael Cristofer, *Pro* Denise Di Novi, Kate Guinzburg and Carol Lees, *Ex Pro* Sheldon Abend, Ashok Amritraj and David Hoberman, *Screenplay* Michael Cristofer, based on the Cornell Woolrich novel *Waltz into Darkness*, *Ph* Rodrigo Prieto, *Pro Des* David J Bomba, *Ed* Eric A Sears, *M* Terence Blanchard, *Costumes* Donna Zakowska.

DiNovi Pictures/Epsilon Motion Pictures/Hyde Park Entertainment/Intermedia Films/ MGM/UGC International/Via Rosa Productions-Fox. 116 mins. France/USA. 2000. Rel: 5 October 2001. Cert 18.

Osmosis Jones ★★★

Little does he know it, but Frank is far more than just a loser dad with disgusting personal habits. His body comprises the City of Frank and is populated (and protected) by a host of animated cells. When the lethal Thrax invades the City, it's up to rebellious white blood cell Osmosis Jones and his cold tablet partner Drix to save the City – along with Frank's life… Cutting between the real, live-action world of Bill Murray's disgusting Frank and the animated splendour of the City, *Osmosis Jones* is really a lot of fun. Of course, the animated portions steal the show with especially brilliant voice casting. It's only the pop soundtrack, with its incessant and distracting back-beat, that detracts from this enjoyable romp.
[*Scot Woodward Myers*]

• *Frank* Bill Murray, *Osmosis Jones* Chris Rock, *Thrax* Laurence Fishburne, *Drix* David Hyde Pierce, *Leah* Brandy Norwood, *the mayor* William Shatner, *Tom Colonic* Ron Howard, *Kidney Rock* Kid Rock, *Mrs Boyd* Molly Shannon, *Bob* Chris Elliott, *Shane* Elena Franklin.

Above: Ghost of a chance: James Bentley and Alakina Mann are haunted by spectral intruders in Alejandro Amenábar's *The Others* (from Buena Vista), a masterpiece of stylish suspense

• *Dirs* Bobby Farrelly and Peter Farrelly, *Animation Dirs* Piet Kroon and Tom Sito, *Pro* Dennis Edwards, Bobby Farrelly, Peter Farrelly, Zak Penn and Bradley Thomas, *Screenplay* Marc Hyman, *Ph* Mark Irwin, *Pro Des* Steve Pilcher (animation) and Sydney J Bartholomew Jr (live action), *Ed* Lois Freeman-Fox, Stephen Schaffer and Sam Seig, *M* Randy Edelman; songs performed by De La Soul and Elizabeth 'Yummie' Bingham, Foreigner, Nappy Roots, Craig David, Brandy, Trick Daddy, KC and the Sunshine Band, Gilbert O'Sullivan, Moby, Kid Rock, Sophie Ellis Bextor, Uncle Kracker, Solange, R Kelly, St Lunatics, Sunshine Anderson, Debelah Morgan, etc, *Costumes* Pamela

Withers, *Sound* Randy Thom.

Conundrum Entertainment-Warner.
95 mins. USA. 2001. Rel: 2 November 2001. Cert PG.

The Others ★★★★

It is 1945 in Jersey, the war is recently over and the magisterial, very English Grace (another great accent from Nicole Kidman) is left on her own with her two photosensitive children in a vast empty house (boasting 50 rooms, no less). With her husband still away at the front and the servants having taken flight the previous week, Grace is relieved to see the friendly face of Mrs Mills, who turns up in answer to her ad for a new housekeeper. However, Grace never posted the advertisement and is not sure how Mrs Mills might cope with her errant daughter, a compulsive liar who claims that she sees 'others' in the house, intruders who slip through the locked doors with apparent ease... The haunted house thriller has never been an easy oeuvre to pull off, as exemplified by such recent, middling attempts as *The Haunting, House on Haunted Hill* and *What Lies Beneath*. However, by going back to the basics of a good story and artful construction – and by drawing on the power of the audience's imagination – the 29-year-old Chilean director Alejandro Amenábar has created a chilling, thrilling ghost story second to none. By setting the film in the past (and on an island few people know well), Amenábar immediately creates a setting where anything can happen within its own logic. Immaculately crafted, superbly played and refreshingly free of digital effects and superfluous music, *The Others* takes its time and cranks up the suspense with a masterful grip.
FYI: Amenábar's last film, the Spanish *Open Your Eyes*, was remade as *Vanilla Sky* – starring Nicole Kidman's then-husband Tom Cruise.

• *Grace* Nicole Kidman, *Bertha Mills* Fionnula Flanagan, *Charles* Christopher Eccleston, *Lydia* Elaine Cassidy, *Mr Tuttle* Eric Sykes, *Anne* Alakina Mann, *Nicholas* James Bentley, Renée Asherson, Gordon Reid, Keith Allen.
• *Dir, Screenplay* and *M* Alejandro Amenábar, *Pro* Fernando Bovaira, José Luis Cuerda and Sunmin Park, *Ex Pro* Tom Cruise, Paula Wagner, Bob Weinstein, Harvey Weinstein and Rick Schwartz, *Ph* Javier Aguirresarobe, *Pro Des* Benjamin Fernández, *Ed* Nacho Ruiz Capillas, *Costumes* Sonia Grande, *Sound* Isabel Diaz Cassou, *Dialogue coach* Sandra Frieze.

Miramax Internatonal/Dimension Films/Cruise-Wagner Prods/Sogecine/Las Producciones Del Escorpión-Buena Vista.
104 mins. USA/Spain. 2001. Rel: 2 November 2001. Cert 12.

Left: Cop's a robber: Steve Coogan samples the big screen to varying results, in John Duigan's sporadically amusing *The Parole Officer* (from UIP)

Pandaemonium ★★★

England; 1795-1816. As the likes of Wordsworth, Lord Byron and Robert Southey await the announcement of the new Poet Laureate, Samuel Taylor Coleridge makes an unexpected appearance, the worse for opium. Casting his mind back to his first meeting with Wordsworth, Coleridge recalls his early days as a poet, husband, father and champion of a literary break from the artificiality of neo-classical verse... An attempt to contemporise the lives of Wordsworth and Coleridge, the ill-named *Pandaemonium* does more for their verse than their characters. Visually luminous and lushly scored, the film seldom ascends above the lustre of soap opera, but captures the verbal alchemy of Coleridge's words with a passionate immediacy. It also has some fun at the expense of Wordsworth (improbably played by John Hannah), who, strolling through the heather, mutters 'I wandered lonely as a cow.' 'Perhaps 'cloud' would be better, William,' chips in his sister, Dorothy. There are plenty of good ideas at work here – as well as some revelations – but the protagonists fail to inhabit their own lives.

• *William Wordsworth* John Hannah, *Samuel Taylor Coleridge* Linus Roache, *Sara Coleridge* Samantha Morton, *Dorothy Wordsworth* Emily Woof, *Mary Wordsworth* Emma Fielding, *John Thelwall* Andy Serkis, *Robert Southey* Samuel West, *Walsh* Michael N Harbour, *Tom Poole* William Scott-Masson, *Dr Gillman* Clive Merrison, *Humphry Davy* Dexter Fletcher, *Lord Byron* Guy Lankester, *Reverend Holland* John Standing, *Andrew Crosse* Andy De La Tour, Andrea Lowe, Jacqueline Defferary, John Kane, Glyn Owen, Peter Harkness, Juno Temple, Leo Temple.
• *Dir* Julien Temple, *Pro* Nick O'Hagen, *Ex Pro* Mike Phillips, Tracey Scoffield and David M. Thompson, *Line Pro* Jane Robertson, *Screenplay* Frank Cottrell Boyce, *Ph* John Lynch, *Pro Des* Laurence Dorman, *Ed* Niven Howie, *M* Dario

Marianelli, *Costumes* Annie Symons, *Handwriting doubles* Neil Bromley and Patricia Lovett.

Optimum Releasing/BBC Films/Mariner Films/Arts Council of England/Moonstone Entertainment-Optimum Releasing. 124 mins. UK/USA. 2000. Rel: 14 September 2001. Cert 12.

Panic Room ★★★¹/₂

It is a dark and stormy night and Meg Altman and her young daughter, Sarah, are spending their first evening in their new home, a large, empty house on New York's Upper West Side. For the three intruders who break in that night, Meg and Sarah are not meant to be there. Escaping into the security of an electronically controlled chamber – the panic room – mother and daughter wait for the trespassers to leave. But what the intruders have come for – a bounty worth millions – happens to be hidden inside the secret chamber… As with most efficient thrillers, the premise behind *Panic Room* is deliciously simple. Atmospherically controlled and elegantly shot, the film reveals the masterful stamp of director Fincher (*Se7en*, *The Game*, *Fight Club*) from the outset, complete with his trademark tracking shots through minuscule spaces. Although the villains prove to be stereotypically one-dimensional, Forest Whitaker's gentle giant is permitted a degree of humanity, while the vacillating mother-daughter relationship is deftly judged by Jodie Foster and newcomer Kristen Stewart (the latter revealing the tomboyish qualities of Jodie at the same age). And in spite of the obvious contrivance of the plot, the suspense is effectively maintained.

• *Meg Altman* Jodie Foster, *Burnham* Forest Whitaker, *Raoul* Dwight Yoakam, *Junior* Jared Leto, *Sarah Altman* Kristen Stewart, *Stephen Altman* Patrick Bauchau, *Lydia Lynch* Ann Magnuson, *Evan Kurlander* Ian Buchanan, *sleepy neighbour* Andrew

Kevin Walker, *cops* Paul Schulze, Mel Rodriguez.
• *Dir* David Fincher, *Pro* Gavin Polone, Judy Hofflund, David Koepp and Ceán Chaffin, *Screenplay* Koepp, *Ph* Conrad W Hall and Darius Khondji, *Pro Des* Arthur Max, *Ed* James Haygood and Angus Wall, *M* Howard Shore, *Costumes* Michael Kaplan.

Indelible Pictures/Columbia-Columbia TriStar.
111 mins. USA. 2002. Rel: 3 May 2002. Cert 15.

The Parole Officer ★★¹/₂

Manchester; the present. Following his enormous success on television in his comic incarnations of Alan Partridge and Paul Calf, Steve Coogan takes on his first feature in a starring role. And here's the problem: while never less than watchable on the big screen, Coogan is neither that plausible as a human being nor is he that funny. Falling off a chair for the film's opening gag is not a promising start. But *The Parole Officer* does pick up steam, boasts first-rate production values and includes a perky debut from the 17-year-old Emma Williams (who could be England's answer to Kirsten Dunst). Above all, the idea of a parole officer being inept at everything but crime is a good one, but it's largely squandered in a film with far too much dead air. Nevertheless, there are some comic highlights, not least Emma Williams' attempt to dispose of a human head and a fertility statue's erection that takes on a life of its own.

• *Simon Garden* Steve Coogan, *Emma* Lena Headey, *George* Om Puri, *Jeff* Steven Waddington, *Colin* Ben Miller, *Victor's wife* Jenny Agutter, *Kirsty* Emma Williams, *Inspector Burton* Stephen Dillane, *Victor* Omar Sharif, Emma Gilmour, Justin Burrows, Kate Deakin, Hazel Douglas.
• *Dir* John Duigan, *Pro* Duncan Kenworthy, Andrew Macdonald and Callum McDougall, *Screenplay* Steve Coogan and Henry Normal, *Ph* John Daly, *Pro Des* Tom Brown, *Ed* David Freeman, *M* Alex Heffes; songs performed by Supertramp, Nina Simone, S Club 7, Marvin Gaye, David Bowie, Atomic Kitten, etc, *Costumes* Alex Caulfield.

DNA Films/Universal Pictures/Film Council/Figment Films/Toledo Pictures-UIP.
94 mins. UK. 2001. Rel: 10 August 2001. Cert 12.

Pasty Faces ★

Glasgow/Los Angeles/Las Vegas; today. Dejected by their failure to make an impression in Scottish showbusiness, out-of-work actors Mickey and Joe decide to join their friend Stevie in Hollywood. However, Stevie, who lives in a bus, turns out to be no more successful than his kinsmen. So the lads decide to head to Vegas to make their fortune… The prospect of a low-budget comedy about Glaswegian losers attempting to make it in America is not an appetising one, and this drably photographed

effort does it no favours. Bereft of wit, invention and comic timing, this is the sort of comedy in which, when somebody says 'Bobby's no pervert', we cut to a shot of Bobby humping a blow-up doll. And the scene in which a fifth-rate producer pitches an idea for *Braveheart 2* has to be a low point in the cinema of the Third Millennium.

• *Mickey* David Paul Baker, *Joe MacDonald* Alan McCafferty, *Steve* Gary Cross, *Lena* Chloe Annett, *Jackie* Cora Bissett, *Bobby* Martin McGreechin.
• *Dir* and *Screenplay* David Paul Baker, *Pro* Christopher Figg and Alasdair Waddell, *Ex Pro* Angad Paul, Rupert Preston and Alan Martin, *Co-Pro* Caroline Waldron, *Ph* Martin Parry, *Pro Des* Alan Payne, *Ed* Fiona MacDonald.

Noel Gay Motion Pictures/Lonewolf Prods-Metrodome.
89 mins. UK. 2000. Rel: 13 July 2001 (Scotland only). Cert 15.

Pauline & Paulette ★★¹/₂

Lochristi, Belgium; the present. Pauline is not the brightest bloom in the garden but she's happy with her life of watering the flowerbeds, running errands for her sister Martha and pasting pictures of flowers into her scrap book. Then Martha dies and Pauline has to be looked after by one of her other two sisters: Paulette, who runs a fabric shop in the local town, and Cecile, who lives with her boyfriend in Brussels… What might have been quite disarming as a one-hour TV play is somewhat lost on the cinema screen. Nevertheless, there is a tenderness and gentle humour here that is quite beguiling. First-time director Lieven Debrauwer, who drew on his childhood memories for his material, never pushes the comedy too far and has elicited peerless performances from his two celebrated leads. Still, a real story would have been nice.

• *Pauline Declercq* Dora Van Der Groen, *Paulette* Ann Petersen, *Cécile* Rosemarie Berghmans, *Albert* Idwig Stéphane, *Martha* Julienne De Bruyn, *butcher's wife* Camilia Blereau, *Marie-José* Magda Cnudde.
• *Dir* Lieven Debrauwer, *Pro* Dominique Janne, *Co-Pro* Arlette Zylberberg, *Screenplay* Debrauwer and Jacques Boon, *Ph* Michel van Laer, *Pro Des* Hilde Duyck, *Ed* Philippe Ravoet, *M* Frederic Devreese; Tchaikovsky, Johann Strauss Jr, *Costumes* Erna Siebens.

Dominique Janne/Fonds Film in Vlaanderen/Canal Plus-Columbia TriStar.
78 mins. Belgium/Netherlands/France. 2001. Rel: 12 April 2002. Cert PG.

Peaches ★

This is an uninspired retread of the old story in which a bunch of lads aim for one last grasp at a summer of love before getting real jobs and developing an emotion or

two. Matthew Rhys stars as Frank, who has dropped out of college with no ambition beyond sampling as many 'peaches' as he can in the fleshly orchard of London. His equally laddish mates, none of whom is remotely interesting (no matter how many silly poses they strike), join him… Adapted by Nick Grosso from his stage play, itself notable only for giving Ben Chaplin a break, *Peaches* is a lumpy bowl of waxed fruit, colourful on the outside yet patently fake and utterly unappetising.
FYI: Though set in Camden, the film was shot mostly in Dublin.
[*Adam Keen*]

• *Frank* Matthew Rhys, *Cherry* Kelly Reilly, *Johnny* Justin Salinger, *Pete* Matthew Dunster, *Pippa* Sophie Okonedo, *Niki* Emily Hillier, *Linda* Stephanie Bagshaw.
• *Dir* Nick Grosso, *Pro* Ronan Glennane, *Ex Pro* Paul Ward, Nicholas O'Neill and Rod Stoneman, *Screenplay* Nick Grosso, *Ph* Brendan Galvin, *Pro Des* Jessica Coyle, *Ed* Niamh Fagan, *Costumes* Barbara Heffernan.

Stone Ridge Entertainment/Irish Film Board-Optimum Releasing.
85 mins. Ireland. 2000. Rel: 12 October 2001. Cert 15.

The Piano Teacher ★★★¹/₂

Vienna, Austria; the present. Michael Haneke has always been a provocative director, not for what he displays on screen but for what he conceals. Isabelle Huppert's Erika Kohut is a woman who conceals much. On the outside an emotionally aloof, artistically disciplined and spartanly attired piano teacher, on the inside she is a woman of wild and degrading sexual appetites. An ice queen to her students, Erika speaks forcefully about the emotional voice of her idols Schubert and Schumann, while in her private moments she mutilates her genitals with a razor blade. Hers is a fascinating character and Haneke guides her emotional transition with a sure hand. The film is a masterful character study, a cold, cruel and compelling exploration of the undercurrent of human depravity. Mlle Huppert is simply outstanding, deservedly winning the best actress prize at the 2001 Cannes festival.
Original title: *Die Klavierspielerin*.

• *Erika Kohut* Isabelle Huppert, *Walter Klemmer* Benoît Magimel, *Erika's mother* Annie Girardot, *Anna Schrober* Anna Sigalevitch, *Mrs Schrober* Susanne Lothar, *Dr Blonskij* Udo Samel, *Mrs Blonskij* Cornelia Köngden, *baritone* Thomas Weinhappel, *violinist* Luz Leskowitz.
• *Dir and Screenplay* Michael Haneke, from the novel by Elfriede Jelinek, *Pro* Veit Heiduschka, Marin Karmitz and Alain Sarde, *Ex Pro* Michael Katz and Yvon Crenn, *Ph* Christian Berger, *Pro Des* Christoph Kanter, *Ed* Monika Willi and Nadine Muse, *M* Chopin, Haydn, Schubert, Beethoven, J S Bach, Schönberg, Rachmaninoff, Brahms, etc, *Costumes* Annette Beaufaÿ.

Wega Film/MK2 SA/Les Films Alain Sarde/ARTE France

Cinéma-Artificial Eye.
130 mins. Austria/France/Germany. 2001. Rel: 9 November 2001. Cert 18.

Planet of the Apes ★★¹/₂

When his chimpanzee vanishes during a routine research flight, astronaut Leo Davidson breaks protocol and goes looking for him. Davidson is then sucked into a time warp and ends up crash-landing on a planet that is dominated by apes. In a perverse reversal of his own world, Davidson finds that here humans are used as slave labour and treated like animals… As a director of such wry vision, Tim Burton seemed the ideal man to revisit the Darwinian man-vs-ape scenario originally envisioned in Pierre Boulle's 1959 novel. In the wake of five films and two TV series, Burton has mounted a colossal, sometimes quite exciting behemoth of missed opportunities. Not only does Mark Wahlberg deliver a sensationally dull reading of the misplaced astronaut (a lug who seems to take the evolutionary conundrum in his stride), but the fact that he, the reigning apes and the primitive humans all use the same vocabulary is a joke (the potential for linguistic aerobics is cruelly squandered). Which leaves only Tim Roth (turning in a remarkable performance of noble, bestial savagery as General Thade) and the impressive production values, showcasing a budget well north of $100 million.

• *Captain Leo Davidson* Mark Wahlberg, *General Thade* Tim Roth, *Ari* Helena Bonham Carter, *Atar* Michael Clarke Duncan, *Karubi* Kris Kristofferson, *Daena* Estella Warren, *Limbo* Paul Giamatti, *Krull* Cary-Hiroyuki Tagawa, *Sandar* David Warner, *Tival* Erick Avari, *Nova* Lisa Marie, *with* Luke Eberl, Glenn Shadix, Chris Ellis, Anne Ramsay, Andrea Grano, Michael Jace, Deep Roy, Philip Tan, Rick Baker, *woman in cart* Linda Harrison, and (uncredited) *Thade's father* Charlton Heston.
• *Dir* Tim Burton, *Pro* Richard D Zanuck, *Ex Pro* Ralph Winter, *Screenplay* William Broyles Jr, Lawrence Konner and Mark Rosenthal, *Ph* Philippe Rousselot, *Pro Des* Rick Lebenzon, *Ed* Chris Lebenzon, *M* Danny Elfman, *Costumes* Colleen Atwood, *Make-up design* Rick Baker.

Fox/Zanuck Co-Fox.
120 mins. 2001. USA. Rel: 17 August 2001. Cert 12.

The Pledge ★★★

Just six hours before his retirement, veteran homicide detective Jerry Black finds himself at the scene of the horrific murder of an eight-year-old girl. Forced to break the news to the child's parents, Jerry swears to the mother – on his 'soul's salvation' – that he will find the killer. Months later, as he attempts to adjust to a life of leisurely reflection, Jerry finds himself becoming obsessed by the details of the murder. Following the confession of a simple-minded suspect, the case has been closed, but Jerry has a hunch that the man – who has since committed suicide – was innocent... A character study of uncommon texture, *The Pledge* affords Jack Nicholson yet another opportunity to provide a magnificent, intuitive performance. Furthermore, with his eye for visual detail and nose for atmosphere, director Sean Penn has fashioned a psychological thriller that refuses to play by the rules. And that is both its strength and, perhaps, its undoing. Such downbeat irony may work wonders on the printed page, but bounced off a series of accomplished star cameos, it fails to find an authentic voice. This film should shatter the sensibilities of the viewer. At its best, it merely perturbs and intrigues.

• *Jerry Black* Jack Nicholson, *Toby Jay Wadenah* Benicio Del Toro, *Stan Krolak* Aaron Eckhart, *doctor* Helen Mirren, *Gary Jackson* Tom Noonan, *Lori* Robin Wright Penn, *Annalise Hansen* Vanessa Redgrave, *Jim Olstad* Mickey Rourke, *Eric Pollack* Sam Shepard, *Helen Jackson* Lois Smith, *Floyd Cage* Harry Sean Stanton, *Margaret Larsen* Patricia Clarkson, *Rudy* Beau Daniels, *Strom* Dale Dickey, *Monash Deputy* Costas Mandylor, *Duane Larsen* Michael O'Keefe, *Chrissy* Pauline Roberts, *Jean* Eileen Ryan, Wendy Morrow Donaldson, P Adrien Dorval, Kathy Jensen, Lucy Schmidt, Brittany Tiplady.
• *Dir* Sean Penn, *Pro* Penn, Michael Fitzgerald and Elie Samaha, *Ex Pro* Andrew Stevens, *Screenplay* Jerzy Kromolowski and Mary Olson-Kromolowski, from the book by Friedrich Dürrenmatt, *Ph* Chris Menges, *Pro Des* Bill Groom, *Ed* Jay Cassidy, *M* Hans Zimmer and Klaus Badelt; songs performed by Jerry Hannan, Flywheel, Steve Earle, Metallica, Kenny Rogers, and David Baerwald, *Costumes* Jill Ohanneson.

Morgan Creek/Franchise Pictures/Clyde is Hungry Films-Warner.
123 mins. USA. 2000. Rel: 12 October 2001. Cert 15.

Pokémon 3 Spell of the Unknown ★★

Misty is a lonely little girl who misses her father. When the enigmatic Pokémon Entei appears to her, it uses her despair to create a crystal tower where both she, and later, Mrs Delia Ketchum are imprisoned. It's up to perennial Pokémon hero Ash Ketchum to rescue Misty and his mother! ... *Pokémon 3* is more than the episodic amalgams of its predecessors and actually approaches something akin to an animated feature. While simplistic in its approach, there is some appeal to the creative visual designs. Furthermore, the story about how isolated children feel is quite touching. [*Scot Woodward Myers*]

• Voices: *Ash Ketchum/Mrs Delia Ketchum* Veronica Taylor, *Misty/Jessie* Rachael Lillis, *Brock/James* Eric Stuart, *Meowth* Maddie Blaustein, *Pikachu* Ikue Ootani, *Professor Oak* Stan Hart, *with* Ken Gates, Amy Birnbaum, Dan Green.

• *Dir* Kunihiko Yuyama and Michael Haigney, *Pro* Norman J Grossfeld, Yukako Matsusako, Takemoto Mori and Choji Yoshikawa, *Ex Pro* Alfred Kahn, Takashi Kawaguchi and Masakazu Kubo, *Screenplay* Norman J Grossfeld and Michael Haigney, *Ph* Hisao Shirai, *Art Dir* Katsuyoshi Kanemura, *Ed* Toshio Henmi and Yutaka Ita, *M* Ralph Schuckett.

4 Kids Entertainment/Kids WB/Nintendo Company Ltd./ Pikachu Project 2000/ Shoakuken/TV Tokyo-Warner. 73 mins. Japan/USA. 2001. Rel: 13 July 2001. Cert U.

Pollock ★★★

Reclusive and socially insecure, Jackson Pollock only seems to come alive in the presence of paint or alcohol. Then, a fellow abstract painter, Lee Krasner, sees an urgent, inspiring originality in the artist's work and discerns a kindred spirit in the man behind the diffident, retiring mask. It is the beginning of a remarkable partnership and the unleashing of a singular talent... As any screen biography will tell you, to be a genius you need to be an abusive alcoholic and a severely unhinged human being. *Pollock* meets these requirements with gusto, with director Ed Harris, 50, playing the beast in various shades of black during the last 15 years of the artist's life before his tragic death at age 44. What this biopic does do well is shed some light on the creative process of the so-called 'Jack the Dripper', an artist who found 'pure form' in the apparently random whirlpools of his paint. Marcia Gay Harden won an Oscar for her performance as Pollock's wife, Lee Krasner (whose own career flourished after his death), but Amy Madigan (Mrs Ed Harris) is every bit as impressive as a formidable Peggy Guggenheim.

• *Jackson Pollock* Ed Harris, *Lee Krasner* Marcia Gay Harden, *Dan Miller* Tom Bower, *Ruth Kligman* Jennifer Connelly, *Howard Putzel* Bud Cort, *Tony Smith* John Heard, *Willem DeKooning* Val Kilmer, *Sande Pollock* Robert Knott, *Charles Pollock* David Leary, *Peggy Guggenheim* Amy Madigan, *Edith Metzger* Sally Murphy, *Clement Greenberg* Jeffrey Tambor, *Stella Pollock* Sada Thompson, *with* Molly Regan, Stephanie Seymour, Matthew Sussman, Norbert Weisser, Eulal Grace Harden, Tom McGuinness, Katherine Wallach, Barbara Garrick, and John Madigan (voice only).
• *Dir* Ed Harris, *Pro* Harris, Fred Berner, James Francis Trezza and Jon Kilik, *Ex Pro* Peter M Brant and Joseph Allen, *Co-Pro* Cecilia Kate Roque, *Assoc Pro* Candy Trabucco, *Screenplay* Barbara Turner and Susan J Emshwiller, based on the book *Jackson Pollock: An American Saga* by Steven Naifeh and Gregory White Smith, *Ph* Lisa Rinzler, *Pro Des* Mark Friedberg, *Ed* Kathryn Himoff, *M* Jeff Beal; songs performed by The Port of Harlem Jazzmen, Benny Goodman, Burl Ives, Buddy Tate, Nappy Brown, Duke Ellington, Billie Holiday, Louis Armstrong, Herbie Duncan, Tom Waits, etc, *Costumes* David C Robinson.

Brant-Allen Films-Columbia TriStar.
123 mins. USA. 2000. Rel: 24 May 2002. Cert 18.

The Pornographer ★'/2

Paris; today. A filmed called *The Pornographer* inevitably sets up certain expectations. Yet after an early sequence of penetrative sex, the film sinks into a morose, seemingly aimless contemplation of a man – a porno director – trying to come to terms with the emptiness of his life. At its most profound, it does give pornography an artistic frisson (as in the description of a blowjob by the film's protagonist), but it is the banality of the medium that director Bonello would seem to be celebrating. Apparently inspired by an exhibition of abstract paintings by Mark Rothko, the film is every bit as abstruse as it sounds.

• *Jacques Laurent* Jean-Pierre Léaud, *Joseph* Jérémie Renier, *Jeanne* Dominique Blanc, *Richard* Thibault de Montalembert, *Louis* André Marcon, *Monika* Alice Houri, *Jenny* Ovidie, *Olivia Rochet* Catherine Mouchet, *Carles* Laurent Lucas.
• *Dir* and *Screenplay* Bertrand Bonello, *Pro* Carole Scotta, *Ex Pro* Barbara Letellier and Stéphane Choquette, *Ph* Josée Deshaies, *Art Dir* Romain Denis, *Ed* Fabrice Rouaud, *M* Laurie Markovitch, *Costumes* Romane Bohringer.

Haut et Court & In Extremis Images/Téléfilm Canada-Metro Tartan.
108 mins. France/Canada. 2001. Rel: 19 April 2002. Cert 18.

Presque Rien ★★★'/2

While spending the summer at the family beach house, 18-year-old Mathieu meets local boy Cédric and the two become lovers… Less a 'gay romance' than a raw look at first loves and how alternately exhilarating yet debilitating they can be. Lead actor Jérémie Elkaïm lends such a tangible pain to his portrayal of Mathieu that you can't help but want to reach out and protect him. Younger sister Annick is perfectly embodied by Marie Matheron in all her teen snide-ness. The film isn't exactly linear and segments hint at a broader tragedy and an attempted suicide that is never quite revealed. As if, despite what we are privy to on screen, there's a deeper secret pain not meant to be shared. Cursed with the ugliest promotional poster imaginable, this is an honest, tender little film that deserves a wider audience.
English title: *Come Undone.*
[*Scot Woodward Myers*]

• *Mathieu* Jérémie Elkaïm, *Cédric* Stéphane Rideau, *Mother* Dominique Reymond, *Annick* Marie Matheron, *Sarah* Laetitia Legrix, *Pierre* Nils Öhlund, *psychiatrist* Réjane Kerdaffrec.
• *Dir* Sebastien Lifshitz, *Pro* Cecile Amillat and Jean-Christophe Colson, *Screenplay* Stephane Bouquet and Sebastien Lifshitz, *Ph* Pascal Poucet, *Pro Des*

Roseanna Sacco, *Ed* Yann Dedet, *M* Perry Blake, *Costumes* Elisabeth Mehu.

Lancelot Films/Maris Films/RTBF/Arte France Cinéma/Canal Plus-Peccadillo Pictures.
100 mins. France/Belgium. 2000. Rel: 26 October 2001. Cert 18.

The Princess Diaries ★★★'/2

San Francisco; today. *Pygmalion* is one of those scenarios that can go on being re-invented until the cows come home. Here, we have a gawky, nerdy schoolgirl whose sole ambition in life is to be invisible, an objective that seems halfway fulfilled when, at the beginning of the film, a callous lad sits on her, apologising, 'Oh, I didn't see you.' Mia Thermopolis' worst fear is public speaking (an exercise that makes her sick – literally), so when she discovers that she is the heir apparent to the (fictitious) European principality of Genovia, her natural response is to run away. Luckily, though, the reigning queen is Julie Andrews, who made her name playing Eliza Doolittle in *My Fair Lady* on Broadway. Unlike last year's *Pygmalion* clone *Miss Congeniality*, *The Princess Diaries* is a funny and touching morality tale, distinguished by some class acts from Ms Andrews (naturally), Garry Marshall regular Hector Elizondo (as a sly chauffeur-cum-babysitter) and Heather Matarazzo as Mia's geeky best friend. As Mia herself, Anne Hathaway injects some generous brio, while the film's little pleasures accumulate to create an extremely satisfactory whole that should delight family audiences tired of flatulence jokes.
FYI: The film was shot on the same soundstage used for *Mary Poppins*, while Marshall now owns the house Julie Andrews lived in at the time.

• *Mia Thermopolis* Anne Hathaway, *Joseph* Hector Elizondo, *Lilly Moscovitz* Heather Matarazzo, *Lana Thomas* Mandy Moore, *Helen Thermopolis* Caroline Goodall, *Michael Moscovitz* Robert Schwartzman, *Queen Clarisse Renaldi* Julie Andrews, *Mr O'Connell* Sean O'Bryan, *Josh Bryant* Erik von Detten, *Jeremiah Hart* Patrick Flueger, *vice principal Gupta* Sandra Oh, Kathleen Marshall, Joel McCrary, Juliet Elizondo, Bob Glaudini, Barbara Marshall, Tracy Reiner, Patrick Richwood, John McGivern, Nicholle Tom, *himself* William Brown Jr, mayor of San Francisco, and (uncredited) Larry Miller.
• *Dir* Garry Marshall, *Pro* Whitney Houston, Debra Martin Chase and Mario Iscovich, *Co-Pro* Ellen H Schwartz, *Screenplay* Gina Wendkos, *Ph* Karl Walter Lindenlaub, *Pro Des* Mayne Berke, *Ed* Bruce Green, *M* John Debney; songs performed by Krystal Harris, Steps, Nelly Furtado, Hanson, Aaron Carter, Pink, Mandy Moore, Youngstown, Myra, Backstreet Boys, B*witched, etc, *Costumes* Gary Jones.

Walt Disney Pictures/Brownhouse-Buena Vista.
115 mins. USA. 2001. Rel: 21 December 2001. Cert U.

Right: All fangs bright and beautiful: Stuart Townsend and the late Aaliyah in Michael Rymer's entertaining *Queen of the Damned* (from Warner)

Queen of the Damned ★★★

This further instalment of Anne Rice's *The Vampire Chronicles* is a minor effort compared to *Interview with the Vampire*, but it has been under-rated for all that. Director Michael Rymer keeps it moving throughout its 101 minutes, supplying a fair mix of humour, tension and special effects. The appealing Stuart Townsend takes on the lead role of the vampire Lestat and Marguerite Moreau is a pleasing heroine, so it was probably a mistake to sell it on the name of the late Aaliyah, whose title role is not that large. It may be unsophisticated tosh, but it can still provide a fun night out for the right audience. Judge it by the complaint of one vampire to another whose reappearance is delayed: '200 years and not a word from you.'
[*Mansel Stimpson*]

• *Lestat* Stuart Townsend, *Akasha* Aaliyah, *Jesse Reeves*

Marguerite Moreau, *Marius* Vincent Perez, *David Talbot* Paul McGann, *Maharet* Lena Olin, *with* Christian Manon, Claudia Black, Bruce Spence, Matthew Newton, Jonathan Davis.
• *Dir* Michael Rymer, *Pro* Jorge Saralegui, *Ex Pro* Su Armstrong, Andrew Mason, Bill Gerber and Bruce Berman, *Screenplay* Scott Abbott and Michael Petroni, *Ph* Ian Baker, *Pro Des* Graham 'Grace' Walker, *Ed* Dany Cooper, *M* Richard Gibbs and Jonathan Davis; songs performed by Jonathan Davis and Shankar, Dry Cell, Static X, Papa Roach, Candyhateful, Tricky, Earshot, Godhead, Disturbed, Deftones, kidneythieves, Wayne Static, etc, *Costumes* Angus Strathie, *Sound* Tim Walston, *Visual effects* Gregory L McMurry.

Warner/Village Roadshow/NPV Entertainment/Material-Warner.
101 mins. USA. 2002. Rel: 12 April 2002. Cert 15.

Left: Cuba Gooding Jr (right) and Lucille Ball lookalike reveal a talent for understated comedy in Jerry Zucker's uninspired *Rat Race* (from Pathé)

Rape Me

See *Baise-Moi*

Rat Race ★★

Director Jerry Zucker may be famed for such comedies as *Airplane!* but this comedy of greed, a modern variant on *It's a Mad Mad Mad Mad World* (1963), confirms once again that films sink or swim with their script. Scenarist Andy Breckman starts with a promising idea, with six individuals gambling in Las Vegas being invited to compete in a cross-country race to New Mexico. On a 'first come first served' basis, two million dollars await whoever arrives quickest, while the organiser (John Cleese) has his own hidden agenda. But the script's lack of imaginative invention continually renders this much less diverting than you would expect. Fans of *Bean* may be disconcerted to find Rowan Atkinson merely one of the ensemble, but he's the one who fares best.
[*Mansel Stimpson*]

• *Enrico Pollini* Rowan Atkinson, *Donald P Sinclair* John Cleese, *Owen Templeton* Cuba Gooding Jr, *Randall Pear* Jon Lovitz, *Nick Schaffer* Breckin Meyer, *Vera Baker* Whoopi Goldberg, *Duane Cody* Seth Green, Kathy Najimy, Amy Smart, Dave Thomas, Paul Rodriguez, Dean Cain, Charlotte Zucker, Kate Zucker, Bob Zucker, Wayne Knight, Kathleen Marshall, Colleen Camp, Rance Howard.
• *Dir* Jerry Zucker, *Pro* Sean Daniel, Janet Zucker and Jerry Zucker, *Ex Pro* James Jacks and Richard Vane, *Sc* Andy Breckman, *Ph* Thomas E Ackerman, *Prod Des* Gary Frutkoff, *Ed* Tom Lewis, *M* John Powell and James McKee Smith, *Costumes* Ellen Mirojnick.

Alphaville Films/Fireworks Entertainment/Paramount-Pathé.
112 mins. Canada/USA. 2001. Rel: 11 January 2002. Cert 12.

Read My Lips ★★★

Carla Bhem is a hearing-impaired secretary employed by a property development company in Paris. Falling behind with her work, she hires an assistant, the handsome, gauche Paul Angeli, who turns out to be on parole from prison… Jacques Audiard is good at textures and selective close-ups and has prised a mesmerising performance from his leading lady, Emmanuelle Devos. In fact, the director exerts a remarkable control over his imagery, subtly fraying the viewer's nerves through what is and isn't seen. The film is at its most successful in its first third, as it peels away our preconceptions of its heroine as victim or femme fatale. Carla is certainly a victim of the male-dominated workplace, but she has turned her disability to her advantage: with the assistance of a neatly concealed hearing aid she can hear well enough but can also lip-read. This latter gift proves to be a godsend for Paul, who uses her to

Right: Jacques
Audiard directs a
scene from *Read
My Lips* (Pathé), his
highly textured but
ultimately implausi-
ble thriller

spy on his boss from the roof of the club where he
works which (conveniently) overlooks his employer's apartment. Unfortunately, the energy level
drops in the middle section and is over-compensat-
ed for in the last third by a ludicrous finale that just
doesn't make sense.
Original title: *Sur mes lèvres.*

• *Paul Angeli* Vincent Cassel, *Carla Bhem*
Emmanuelle Devos, *Marchand* Olivier Gourmet,
Masson Olivier Perrier, *Annie* Olivia Bonamy, *Morel*
Bernard Alane, *Josie Marchand* Cecile Samie, *Keller*
Pierre Diot, *with* David Saracino, Christophe
Vandevelde, Serge Boutleroff.
•*Dir* Jacques Audiard, *Pro* Jean-Louis Livi and
Philippe Carcassonne, *Ex Pro* Bernard Marescot,
Screenplay Audiard and Tonino Benacquista, *Ph*
Matthieu Vadepied, *Pro Des* Michel Barthélémy, *Ed*
Juliette Welfling, *M* Alexandre Desplat, *Costumes*
Virginie Montel.

Sédif/Ciné B/Pathé Image/France 2 Cinéma/Canal Plus-
Pathé.
119 mins. France. 2001. Rel: 24 May 2002. Cert 15.

Recess: School's Out ★★

As his friends set off for their various summer camp
vacations, T J Detweiler is left to play on his own. He
then notices a sinister green light emanating from the
windows of his school and sets out to investigate.

However, his parents and the police dismiss his alarm
as the product of an over-active imagination. Good
news, then, for the dastardly Benedict (voiced by
James Woods), who is using the school as a base for
his operation to take over the world's weather system... As the possibilities of animated cinema are
expanded with films like *Toy Story, Chicken Run* and
Shrek, it's hard to embrace something as mundane as
this big-screen version of the popular TV show. While
Recess is not really a bad film per se, its anodyne qualities barely commend it. Furthermore, the prospect of
kids struggling to save the future of the world is so
old-hat that the stench of mothballs stings one's finer
sensibilities. Sadly, young fans of the original will no
doubt have nothing to complain of.

• **Voices:** *Vince* Rickey D'Shon Collins, *Mikey* Jason
Davis, *Gretchen* Ashley Johnson, *T J Detweiler* Andy
Lawrence, *Gus* Courtland Mead, *Spinelli* Pam Segall,
Principal Prickly Dabney Coleman, *Mikey's singing
voice* Robert Goulet, *Becky* Melissa Joan Hart,
Fenwick Peter MacNicol, *Ms Finster/Mrs Detweiler*
April Winchell, *Benedict* James Woods, *Miss Grotke*
Allyce Beasley, Clancy Brown, E G Daily, R Lee
Ermey, Clyde Kusatsu, Charles Kimbrough, Andrea
Martin, Phil Proctor, Jack Riley, Kath Soucie, Robert
Stack, Ken Swofford, Nick Turturro.
• *Dir* Chuck Sheetz, *Pro* Paul Germain, Joe
Ansolabehere and Stephen Swofford, *Screenplay*
Jonathan Greenberg, *Art Dir* Eric Keyes, *Ed* Nancy
Frazen, *M* Denis M. Hannigan, *Sound* Ronald Eng.

Walt Disney Pictures/Walt Disney Television Animation-Buena Vista.
83 mins. USA. 2000. Rel: 13 July 2001 (Scotland). Cert U.

Return to Never Land ★★★

The first of a slew of projected animated sequels (including *Cinderella II*, *Dumbo II* and *The Jungle Book II*), *Return to Never Land* was made by Disney's TV arm but released in cinemas to capitalise on the Presidents Day holiday weekend in the US. While it would be easy to dismiss the project as an opportunistic ploy to exploit the cherished memory of J M Barrie's immortal creation, Barrie himself might well have approved. He himself expanded on his original play a number of times (with a book, silent screenplay and self-financed public statue), while the theme of keeping the magic of childhood imagination alive is advocated by the sequel's story. Jane, the 12-year-old daughter of Wendy Darling, takes on the mantle of contemporary cynicism by rejecting Peter Pan as 'a lot of foolish nonsense'. Such scepticism is put to the test, however, when Jane is spirited away from war-torn London to Never Never Land, all part of a plot by Captain Hook. Sticking slavishly to the sentiments and pictorial style of the original 1953 film, the sequel is enchanting and accomplished if not exactly brimming with visual inspiration.

• **Voices:** *Jane/young Wendy* Harriet Owen, *Peter Pan* Blayne Weaver, *Captain Hook* Corey Burton, *Smee* Jeff Bennett, *Wendy* Kath Soucie, *Danny* Andrew McDonough, *Edward* Roger Rees, *with* Spencer Breslin, Jim Cummings, Frank Welker.

• *Dir* Robin Budd and Donovan Cook, *Pro* Christopher Chase, Michelle Robinson and Dan Rounds, *Screenplay* Temple Mathews and Carter Crocker, *Art Dir* Wendell Luebbe, *Ed* Anthony F Rocco and Daniel Lee, *M* Joel McNeely.

Walt Disney Pictures/Walt Disney Television Animation-Buena Vista.
72 mins. USA. 2002. Rel: 22 March 2002. Cert U.

Revelation ★★

As the planets line up for a rare conjunction, reclusive billionaire Magnus Martel worries about the state of the world. For centuries, a sacred box called the Loculus has been guarded by the Knights Templar but is now secreted off the Mediterranean. Somebody called the Grand Master wants it for some untold evil, so Magnus enlists his estranged son, Jake, to retrieve it before all Hell breaks loose… Writer-director Stuart Urban previously brought us the painful *Preaching to the Perverted*, and while his visual eye has improved in the intervening four years, his direction of actors hasn't. Terence Stamp and Udo Kier send the whole thing up,

James D'Arcy and Natasha Wightman offer little charisma and Ron Moody seems a perverse choice to play Isaac Newton. Nevertheless, the film has its atmospheric moments, although it's dreadfully over-written. [*Charles Bacon*]

• *Lord Magnus Martel* Terence Stamp, *Jake Martel* James D'Arcy, *Mira* Natasha Wightman, *Father Ray Connolly* Liam Cunningham, *librarian* Derek Jacobi, *New Age man* Heathcote Williams, *Sir Isaac Newton* Ron Moody, *Grand Master* Udo Kier, *Harriet Martel* Celia Imrie, *with* Pip Torrens, Oliver Ford Davies, Charlotte Weston, Vernon Dobtcheff, Earl Cameron.
• *Dir* and *Screenplay* Stuart Urban, from an original idea by Frank Falco, *Pro* Urban and Jonathan Woolf, *Co-Pro* Pat Harding, *Ph* Sam McCurdy, *Pro Des* James Merifield, *Ed* Julian Rodd, *M* Edmund Butt, *Costumes* John Krausa, *Visual effects* Paul Franklin.

Romulus Films/Cyclops Vision-Miracle Communications.
111 mins. UK. 2001. Rel: 12 April 2002. Cert 15.

Riding in Cars with Boys ★★

Wallingford, Connecticut; 1961-86. On the way to meet up with her ex-husband, aspiring writer Beverly Donofrio reflects on the life that has constantly scuppered her creative goals. With her is Jason, her 20-year-old son, for whom she has put her career on hold. However, Jason has come to a point in his maturation when he is no longer prepared to take on the guilt for his mother's disappointments… Regardless of how true to the real facts Morgan Upton Ward's long-winded adaptation may be, the result reeks of phoniness. A trawl through the lower depths of white trash Americana, the film plies us with tales of unwanted pregnancy (not one but two), unemployment, alcoholism, imprisonment and heroin dependency. Furthermore, far too much is demanded of Drew Barrymore, who has to (unconvincingly) age from 15 to 36 and spends far too much time crying (an activity that is plainly not her creative forte). Much better is Brittany Murphy as Beverly's best friend, who bears an uncanny resemblance to Lorraine Bracco, who plays Barrymore's mother. So, shoot the casting director and buy the book.

• *Beverly Donofrio* Drew Barrymore, *Ray Hasek* Steve Zahn, *Fay Forrester* Brittany Murphy, *Jason aged 20* Adam Garcia, *Mrs Donofrio* Lorraine Bracco, *Mr Donofrio* James Woods, *Tina* Sara Gilbert, *Bobby* Desmond Harrington, *Lizard* David Moscow, *Amelia aged 20* Maggie Gyllenhall, *Tommy Butcher* Peter Facinelli, *Janet Donofrio aged 19* Marisa Ryan, *Beverly aged 11* Mika Boorem, *Amelia aged eight* Skye McCole Bartusiak, *Jason Donofrio aged eight* Logan Lerman, *Jason aged six* Cody Arens, *Uncle Lou* Vincent Pastore, *Aunt Ann* Maryann Urbano, John Bedford Lloyd, Robert Greenhut, Tracy Reiner,

Right: Interstate of Siege: A scene from John Dahl's pulse-accelerating *Roadkill* (from Fox)

Shirley Rosie Perez.
• *Dir* Penny Marshall, *Pro* James L Brooks, Lawrence Mark, Sara Colleton, Richard Sakai and Julie Ansell, *Ex Pro* Morgan Upton Ward and Bridget Johnson, *Screenplay* Morgan Upton Ward, based on the book by Beverly Donofrio, *Ph* Miroslav Ondrícek, *Pro Des* Bill Groom, *Ed* Richard Marks and Lawrence Jordan, *M* Hans Zimmer and Heitor Pereira; songs performed by Lou Monte, The Everly Brothers, Billy Idol, Cyndi Lauper, Eurythmics, Sonny & Cher, The Jelly Beans, Billy Joe Royal, Neil Sedaka, Gerry & The Pacemakers, Freddie and The Dreamers, The Supremes, James Brown, Sir Douglas Quintet, Wilson Pickett, Skeeter Davis, The Chiffons, Big Brother and the Holding Company, The Doobie Brothers, Three Dog Night, Harry Nilsson, Vic Damone, etc, *Costumes* Cynthia Flynt.

Columbia Pictures/Gracie Films-Columbia TriStar. 131 mins. USA. 2001. Rel: 7 December 2001. Cert 12.

Roadkill ★★★★

Formulaic thrillers are seldom this good. Giving Steven Spielberg's classic *Duel* (1971) a teenage overhaul, scripters Clay Tarver and J J Abrams have cooked up an ingenious story hatched from a very simple idea. A pair of brothers on the lonely road from Salt Lake City to Boulder, Nevada, play a practical joke on a trucker over their CB radio. Disguising his voice as a woman's, Lewis Thomas arranges to meet the stranger at a motel room that he happens to know is occupied by a short-tempered businessman. Taking the room next door, the siblings eavesdrop on the encounter, which backfires horrendously when the businessman

has his lower jaw ripped off his face. Now the trucker – going under the CB handle of 'Rusty Nail' – wants to play his own practical joke on the boys… Filming on the most desolate freeways of the US (on the Interstate 80 in Nevada), director John Dahl has recreated the Wild West on asphalt, where the comforting rules of homogenised America don't apply. And like the driver of the monster truck in *Duel*, Rusty Nail is never really seen, being a disembodied voice with a seemingly ubiquitous presence. Thus, the suspense is ratcheted up considerably while, as the trucker's prey, Steve Zahn and Paul Walker bring considerable empathy and plausibility to their roles.
US title: *Joy Ride*; formerly known as *Squelch*.

•*Fuller Thomas* Steve Zahn, *Lewis Thomas* Paul Walker, *Venna* Leelee Sobieski, *Charlotte* Jessica Bowman, *with* Stuart Stone, Basil Wallace, Brian Leckner, Kenneth White, Michael McCleery, Satch Huizenga, and (uncredited) Ted Levine as the voice of Rusty Nail.
• *Dir* John Dahl, *Pro* J J Abrams and Chris Moore, *Ex Pro* Arnon Milchan, Patrick Markey and Bridget Johnson, *Screenplay* Abrams and Clay Tarver, *Ph* Jeffrey Jur, *Pro Des* Rob Pearson, *Ed* Eric L Beason, Scott Chestnut, Todd E Miller and Glen Scantlebury, *M* Marco Beltrami; songs performed by Sinomatic, Paco, Alien Crime Syndicate, Sarah Slean, Old 97's, Ultra V, Embrace, Deep Audio, Brenda Lee, Caroline Lavelle, etc, *Costumes* Terry Dresbach.

Regency Enterprises/Bad Robot/Liveplanet/Epsilon Motion Pictures-Fox.
97 mins. USA. 2001. Rel: 26 April 2002. Cert 15.

Left: The killer inside me: Newcomer Stefano Cassetti in the title role of Cédric Kahn's fascinating *Roberto Succo* (from Artificial Eye)

Roberto Succo ★★★¹/₂

Meeting in a bar in Toulon, southern France, Léa and Kurt immediately form an attachment, in spite of an age difference of ten years. She is a 16-year-old virgin, he a compulsive liar who tells her, almost instantly, that he loves her. He also drives her around in a variety of different cars and constantly switches his version of events, explaining that he is Dutch, English, maybe even Italian. Meanwhile, a dedicated detective is investigating a series of apparently random and unconnected car thefts, muggings, rapes and murders... Meticulously reconstructed from witness statements and police reports, *Roberto Succo* is a credible and presumably accurate chronicle of the crime spree of the eponymous serial killer from Mestre, Italy. With two of the most graphic scenes cut from the completed film and Succo's more gruesome acts confined to police photos, the film is an objective portrait (marvellously played by the non-professional Stefano Cassetti) untainted by moral judgment. Writer-director Cédric Kahn (*L'Ennui*) leaves no doubt in our minds that Succo was an unscrupulous monster, but he refuses to demonise him, resulting in a fascinating if ultimately emotionally detached film.

• *Kurt/Roberto Succo* Stefano Cassetti, *Léa* Isild Le Besco, *Major Thomas* Patrick Dell'isola, *Denis* Vincent Deneriaz, *Delaunay, Thomas' assistant* Aymeric Chauffert, *Swiss schoolteacher* Viviana Aliberti, *Céline Simon* Estelle Perron, *Cathy* Leyla Sassi.
• *Dir* and *Screenplay* Cédric Kahn, *Pro* Gilles Sandoz and Patrick Sobelman, *Ph* Pascal Marti, *Pro Des* François Abelanet, *Ed* Yann Dedet, *M* Julien Civange; songs performed by Culture Club, Marianne Faithfull, George McRae, and Jesse Green,

Costumes Nathalie Raoul.

Agat Films & Cie/Diaphana Films/France 3 Cinéma/ Canal Plus-Artificial Eye.
125 mins. France/Switzerland. 2001. Rel: 7 June 2002. Cert 15.

Rock Star ★★★

Chris Cole is lead singer of Blood Pollution, a tribute band to heavy rockers Steel Dragon. However, Chris' obsession for reproducing the exact sound of his idols is beginning to get up the collective nose of his fellow band members. Just then, Chris gets a call from the head honcho of Steel Dragon itself... An engrossing if superficial look at the 1980s hard rock scene, Stephen Herek's film is accomplished without being stylish, while John Stockwell's script is intriguing if not exactly revelatory. Mark Wahlberg, a former rock star himself (as Marky Mark), is actually perfect for the role of the initially devotional and committed wannabe and later as the strutting and sometimes confused moth trapped in the glare of his own celebrity. More problematic is Jennifer Aniston who, as an icon herself, never successfully disappears inside her character, the actress' familiar smile and facial tics overshadowing the anonymity of Chris' grounded girlfriend. Yet in spite of the film's conventional narrative arc (rags to riches, drugs, sex and more rock'n'roll), *Rock Star* has a number of nice touches: Wahlberg practising his English accent in the mirror ('I loke pussy'), the hedonistic post-first night party and the presence of Rachel Hunter – Mrs Rod Stewart – as one of the neglected celebrity wives. Previously known as *Metal God* (a much better title).

• *Chris Cole* Mark Wahlberg, *Emily Poule* Jennifer Aniston, *Bobby Beers* Jason Flemyng, *Rob Malcolm* Timothy Olyphant, *Mats* Timothy Spall, *Kirk Cuddy* Dominic West, *Tania Asher* Dagmara Dominczyk, *AC* Jason Bonham, *Joe Jr* Matthew Glave, *Mrs Cole* Beth Grant, *Mr Cole* Michael Shamus Wiles, *AC's wife* Rachel Hunter, Jeff Pilson, Zakk Wylde, Blas Elias, Brian Vander Ark.
• *Dir* Stephen Herek, *Pro* Robert Lawrence and Toby Jaffe, *Ex Pro* Steven Reuther, George Clooney and Mike Ockrent, *Screenplay* John Stockwell, *Ph* Ueli Steiger, *Pro Des* Mayne Berke, *Ed* Trudy Ship, *M* Trevor Rabin; songs performed by Steel Dragon, Blood Pollution, Culture Club, AC/DC, Jennifer Aniston, Bon Jovi, Kiss, Def Leppard, Frankie Goes To Hollywood, Ted Nugent, Foghat, Talking Heads, Mötley Crüe, Zakk Wylde, Everclear, Marky Mark & The Funky Bunch, etc, *Costumes* Aggie Guerard Rodgers.

Warner/Bel-Air Entertainment/Maysville Pictures-Warner. 105 mins. USA. 2001. Rel: 11 January 2002. Cert 15.

Rollerball ★★

San Francisco/Kazakhstan/Mongolia; 2005. The original *Rollerball*, released in 1975 and starring James Caan, was set in 2018 in a world where poverty no longer existed and where Bach, Tchaikovsky and Shostakovich was the music of choice. This was a classy and contemplative, if somewhat ponderous, film. The remake introduces a totally new story and replaces the original timbre with a pumped-up, chaotically edited, trashy style, complete with daft script and heavy metal music. Only the hero's name, Jonathon, remains the same. As for the bloodsport itself, a confusing cross between roller derby, basketball, hockey and motorcycling, this is reduced to a free-for-all, WWF/Gladiator style knockabout on a figure-eight course. Unfortunately, the message of ratings meaning more than human life is over-worked to death, while Chris Klein proves to be a decidedly weak leading man (some edge, intelligence and ambiguity would've been nice).
FYI: This is the second Norman Jewison movie that director John McTiernan has remade, following his far more accomplished encore of *The Thomas Crown Affair*.

• *Jonathon Cross* Chris Klein, *Petrovich* Jean Reno, *Marcus Ridley* LL Cool J, *Aurora* Rebecca Romijn-Stamos, *Sanjay* Naveen Andrews, *Denekin* Oleg Taktarov, *Serokin* David Hemblen, *herself* Pink, *with* Paul Heyman, Janet Wright, Andrew Bryniarski, Kata Dobo, Eugene Lipinski, Jean Brassard, Peter Blake.
• *Dir* John McTiernan, *Pro* McTiernan, Charles Roven and Beau St Clair, *Ex Pro* Michael Tadross, *Screenplay* Larry Ferguson and John Pogue, based on the short story and screenplay by William Harrison, *Ph* Steve Mason, *Pro Des* Norman Garwood and Dennis Bradford, *Ed* John Wright, *M* Eric Serra, *Costumes* Kate Harrington, *Visual effects* John Sullivan.

MGM/Mosaic Media-Columbia TriStar. 98 mins. USA. 2002. Rel: 28 June 2002. Cert 15.

The Royal Tenenbaums ★★★★¹/₂

New York City; the present. The Tenenbaums are an exceptional family. At least, they were. Royal Tenenbaum, a prominent litigator, and his wife, Etheline, an eminent archaeologist, had three children, all geniuses in their own way. While still at high school, Chas Tenenbaum was a gifted international trader and invented a species of Dalmatian mice; Margot, adopted, had her first play performed on the night of her 11th birthday; and Richie, the youngest, picked up a tennis racket and won the US Nationals three years in a row. Then, when Royal left home, the Tenenbaums' brilliance was erased by 'two decades of betrayal, failure and disaster'… It's not often that a filmmaker with an independent sensibility can marshal such a stellar cast and pull off his unique vision with such masterful aplomb. Partly inspired by the profiles of unconventional personalities featured in the pages of *New Yorker* magazine, Wes Anderson and Owen Wilson's rich, literate screenplay started with its bizarre dramatis personae and evolved from there. That this remarkable cast embodies these individuals so precisely is a joy to behold, while the visual detail – the ubiquitous presence of Third World cabs, the meticulous manifestation of the characters' traits – is constantly rewarding. Indeed, *The Royal Tenenbaums* is more than just a film, it is a symbiosis of talent and original ideas that demands to be seen over and over again and then bottled as inspiration for future filmmakers.

• *Royal Tenenbaum* Gene Hackman, *Etheline Tenenbaum* Anjelica Huston, *Chas Tenenbaum* Ben Stiller, *Margot Tenenbaum* Gwyneth Paltrow, *Richie Tenenbaum* Luke Wilson, *Eli Cash* Owen Wilson, *Henry Sherman* Danny Glover, *Raleigh St Clair* Bill Murray, *Dusty* Seymour Cassel, *Pagoda* Kumar Pallana, *narrator* Alec Baldwin, *young Chas Tenenbaum* Aram Aslanian-Persico, *young Margot Tenenbaum* Irene Gorovaia, *young Richie Tenenbaum* Amedeo Turturro, *Dudley Heinsbergen* Stephen Lea Sheppard, *Peter Bradley* Larry Pine, *with* Don McKinnon, Andrew Wilson, Rex Robbins, *paramedic* Brian Tenenbaum.
• *Dir* Wes Anderson, *Pro* Anderson, Barry Mendel and Scott Rudin, *Ex Pro* Rudd Simmons and Owen Wilson, *Screenplay* Anderson and Wilson, *Ph* Robert Yeoman, *Pro Des* David Wasco, *Ed* Dylan Tichenor, *M* Mark Mothersbaugh; Ravel; songs performed by

Elliot Smith, The Clash, Bob Dylan, Nico, Paul Simon, The Ramones, Nick Drake, The Velvet Underground, John Lennon, The Rolling Stones, The Beach Boys, Emitt Rhodes, etc, *Costumes* Karen Patch, *Dialect coach* Judy Dickerson.

Touchstone Pictures/American Empirical-Buena Vista. 110 mins. USA. 2001. Rel: 15 March 2002. Cert 15.

Rush Hour 2 ★★★

Hong Kong/Los Angeles/Las Vegas; the present. While showing his American colleague the sights of his native city, Hong Kong's Chief Inspector Lee is drawn into a case involving the murder of two US customs officials. So, while James Carter attempts to enjoy himself, Lee battles with the Triads, an old enemy of his father's and a mysterious, very beautiful kung fu virtuoso... Building on the winning chemistry between Jackie Chan's resourceful, moral cop and Chris Tucker's loud-mouthed walking disaster zone, this costly follow-up to the surprise hit of 1998 gives its stars some suitably impressive set-pieces. It's all good fun (if a little obvious), while it's refreshing to have a non-English baddie this time round (Zhang Ziyi reprising her turn from *Crouching Tiger, Hidden Dragon*). Still, with a budget of $90 million (compared to the original's $30m), one might have expected a more exciting – and original – plot. And, in spite

of the occasional nasty device (a mini-grenade cellotaped inside Chan's mouth), there's no sense of any real danger. But then this is a summer movie packaged entirely around the personalities of its stars.

• *James Carter* Chris Tucker, *Inspector Lee* Jackie Chan, *Ricky Tan* John Lone, *Hu Li* Zhang Ziyi, *Isabella Molina* Roselyn Sanchez, *Steven Reign* Alan King, *Agent Sterling* Harris Yulin, *Captain Chin* Kenneth Tsang, *with* Lucy Lin, Mei Ling Wong, William Tuen, Ernie Reyes Jr, Jeremy Piven, Joel McKinnon Miller, Saul Rubinek, Gianni Russo, and (uncredited) *Kenny* Don Cheadle.
• *Dir* Brett Ratner, *Pro* Arthur Sarkissian, Roger Birnbaum, Jonathan Glickman and Jay Stern, *Ex Pro* Andrew Z Davis, Michael De Luca and Toby Emmerich, *Screenplay* Jeff Nathanson, *Ph* Matthew F Leonetti, *Pro Des* Terence Marsh, *Ed* Mark Helfrich, *M* Lalo Schifrin; songs performed by Michael Jackson, Chris Tucker, The Beach Boys, Hikaru Utada and Foxy Brown, Puff Daddy and Faith Evans, The Police, Ludacris and Nate Dogg, Curtis Mayfield, King Curtis, The JB's, Billy Preston, The Commodores, Chic, Coco Lee, etc, *Costumes* Rita Ryack, *Special effects* Mike Meinardus, *Stunts* Conrad E Palmisano.

New Line Cinema-Entertainment.
90 mins. USA. 2001. Rel: 3 August 2001. Cert 12.

Above: Family values: Luke Wilson, Gwyneth Paltrow, Gene Hackman, Ben Stiller, Anjelica Huston, Danny Glover and Kumar Pallana in Wes Anderson's idiosyncratic, profound and extremely funny *The Royal Tenenbaums* (from Buena Vista)

Saving Silverman
See *Evil Woman*

Scary Movie 2 ★½
Everything that made *Scary Movie* so enjoyable is sadly missing in this horrific sequel. While the first film tackled a wide range of source material with gusto and creativity, its limp follow-up covers no new ground and generates almost no humour. Director Keenen Ivory Wayans, who usually has a fantastic eye for comedy, can't breathe life into this hurried script from brothers Shawn and Marlon Wayans. If you can make it past the tedious opening spoof on *The Exorcist*, you might get a random chuckle from a few gags, the best being when the Wayans poke fun at themselves and their own careers. Sadly, in their hurry to capitalise on the success of the hysterical *Scary Movie*, all they have managed to do is scupper this potentially lucrative franchise.
[*Scot Woodward Myers*]

• *Ray Wilkins* Shawn Wayans, *Shorty Meeks* Marlon Wayans, *Cindy Campbell* Anna Faris, *Brenda Meeks* Regina Hall, *Buddy* Chris Masterson, *Father McFeely* James Woods, *Professor Oldman* Tim Curry, Kathleen Robertson, Tori Spelling, Chris Elliott, Veronica Cartwright, Andy Richter, Natasha Lyonne, David Cross, Vitamin C, Richard Moll.
* *Dir* Keenen Ivory Wayans, *Pro* Eric L Gold, *Ex Pro* Peter Schwerin, Bob Weinstein, Harvey Weinstein and Brad Weston, *Screenplay* Shawn Wayans, Marlon Wayans, Alyson Fouse, Greg Grabianski, Dave Polsky, Michael Anthony Snowden and Craig Wayans, *Ph* Steven Bernstein, *Pro Des* Cynthia Kay Charette, *Ed* Thomas J Nordberg, Richard Pearson and Peter Teschner, *M* Randy Spendlove, *Costumes* Valari Adams and Mary Jane Fort.

Dimension Films/Brillstein-Grey Entertainment/
Gold-Muller Productions/Wayans Bros Entertainment-
Buena Vista.
82 mins. USA. 2001. Rel: 7 September 2001. Cert 18.

The Score ★★★★
Montreal; Québec; today. No sooner has Nick Wells decided to pack in his life of crime than he is made an offer he can't refuse: $4 million for stealing a sceptre from the basement of Montreal's Customs House. However, he is having to make a couple of compromises: working in his own city and teaming up with a young thief he doesn't even know... As heist films get increasingly complicated, it's nice to come across one that is as concerned with the characters as the plotting. Of course, it's in the nature of the genre that 'the plot thickens', but the twists in this refreshingly straightforward yarn never let you see them coming. Consequently, the suspense is that much greater,

while the opportunity to watch Brando, De Niro and Norton bat off each other is one of the thespian treats of the year. Riveting stuff.

• *Nick Wells* Robert De Niro, *Jackie Teller/Brian* Edward Norton, *Diane* Angela Bassett, *Max Baron* Marlon Brando, *Burt* Gary Farmer, *Steven* Jamie Harrold, *Danny* Paul Soles, Martin Drainville, Serge Houde, Jean René Ouellet, Richard Waugh, Mark Camacho, Bobby Brown, Christian Jacques, Henry Farmer, Cassandra Wilson, Mose Allison.
• *Dir* Frank Oz, *Pro* Gary Foster and Lee Rich, *Ex Pro* Adam Platnick and Bernie Williams, *Screenplay* Kario Salem, Lem Dobbs and Scott Marshall Smith, from a story by Salem and Daniel E Taylor, *Ph* Rob Hahn, *Pro Des* Jackson De Govia, *Ed* Richard Pearson, *M* Howard Shore; songs performed by G Club, Cannonball Adderly with Miles Davis, Cassandra Wilson, Thelonious Monk, Clifford Brown, Mose Allison, Dee Cernile, and Diana Krall, *Costumes* Aude Bronson-Howard.

Mandalay Pictures/CP Medien/MP
Management/Horseshoe Bay/Lee Rich-Pathé.
124 mins. USA/Germany. 2001. Rel: 28 September 2001.
Cert 15.

The Scorpion King ★★★
Mathayus is the last in a line of heroic assassins known as Akkadians, warriors who substitute the thespian salutation 'break a leg' with 'die well'. When the tyrannical warlord Memnon has all but subjugated or slain the nations of the desert, Mathayus is the last hope the people have. But Memnon has a deadly advantage over his rivals: he has in his command a seer who can foretell the future... With its tongue wedged squarely in its lantern jaw, *The Scorpion King* is a pumped-up, high-octane rollercoaster ride of spectacular fights and derring-do set in a time before the first pharaohs. Unremittingly brutal, but sparing us the gore of the Ridley Scott school of violence (sickening sound effects aside), this off-shoot of *The Mummy Returns* is a lively, dynamic entertainment for teenage boys of all ages. Its trump card, though, is the presence of WWF phenomenon The Rock (aka Dwayne Douglas Johnson), an able replacement for Arnold Schwarzenegger in his earlier incarnation as Conan the Barbarian. With his monumental physique, sly sense of humour and beguiling innocence, The Rock is destined to be a familiar sight on marquees for years to come. Filmed entirely in California.

• *Mathayus* The Rock, *Memnon* Steven Brand, *The Sorceress* Kelly Hu, *Philos* Bernard Hill, *Arpid* Grant Heslov, *Takmet* Peter Facinelli, *Thorak* Ralf Moeller,

Left: He Will Rock You II: Kelly Hu waits for The Rock to drive his point home in Chuck Russell's pumped-up spectacle, *The Scorpion King* (from UIP)

Balthazar Michael Clarke Duncan, *King Pheron* Roger Rees, *Queen Isis* Sherri Howard, *with* Branscombe Richmond, Conrad Roberts, Joseph Ruskin, Al Leong.
• *Dir* Chuck Russell, *Pro* Stephen Sommers, Sean Daniel, James Jacks and Kevin Misher, *Ex Pro* Vince McMahon, *Screenplay* Sommers, William Osborne and David Hayter, from a story by Sommers and Jonathan Hales, *Ph* John R Leonetti, *Pro Des* Ed Verreaux, *Ed* Michael Tronick and Greg Parsons, *M* John Debney; 'I Stand Alone' performed by Godsmack, *Costumes* John Bloomfield.

Universal/WWF Entertainment/Alphaville/Misher Prods-UIP.
91 mins. USA. 2001. Rel: 19 April 2002. Cert 12.

Le Secret ★★★★¹/₂

Marie and François Colvant are the perfect couple. After 12 years of marriage and the birth of their son, Paul, they are as affectionate and happy together as ever. And while Marie is off selling encyclopaedias door-to-door, François stays at home to tend their son. Then, for no apparent reason, Marie offers herself to an enigmatic black American... The last thing the cinema needs is another film about an adulterous wife, but few models have felt as authentic as this disturbing drama. From the early scenes of domestic harmony to the later emotional fallout, Virginie Wagon's examination of an inexplicable breakdown in marital trust leaps off the screen. Even Marie and François' two-year-old boy seems as unquestionably a piece of the picture as any child featured in a movie. But the trump card of *Le Secret* is the ubiquitous presence of the little-known French actress Anne Coesens (a coquettish yet steely cross between Rachel Griffiths and Saffron Burrows), who gives a performance of breath-catching depth, spontaneity and truth. All things being equal, she should be a major star in a very short time.

• *Marie Colvant* Anne Coesens, *François Colvant* Michel Bompoil, *Bill West* Tony Todd, *Paul* Quentin Rossi, *Marie's mother* Jacqueline Jehanneuf, *Rémy* Aladin Reibel, *Séverine* Valérie Vogt, *Luc* Frédéric Sauzay, *Ana* Natalya Ermilova, *Mélanie* Charlotte Pradon.
• *Dir* Virginie Wagon, *Pro* François Marquis, *Screenplay* Wagon and Erick Zonca, *Ph* Jean-Marcc Fabre, *Pro Des* Brigitte Brassart, *Ed* Yannick Kergoat, *M* various; songs performed by Mercury Rev, Dick Dale & His Del-Tones, Chuck Berry, and The Centurions, *Costumes* Brigitte Slama.

Les Productions Bagheera/France 3 Cinéma/Diaphane Films/Canal Plus/Sofica S, etc-Optimum Releasing. 109 mins. France. 2000. Rel: August 2001. Cert 18.

Serendipity ★★★★¹/₂

New York City; the present. 'Serendipity', according to Webster's, means 'an aptitude for making fortunate discoveries accidentally'. It is a favourite word of Sara, who likes to think of life as part of a grander scheme. So when she meets Jonathan while Christmas shopping for her boyfriend, she leaves the future of any possible liaison in the hands of fate. She writes her name and number inside a copy of Gabriel Garcia Marquez' *Love in the Time of Cholera*, while he scribbles his details on the back of a five-dollar bill. Sara then cashes in the fiver and sells the Marquez to a second-hand bookshop. Should either of them reclaim the other's name and number, then they are most certainly destined to be together... Gliding into the enchanted footsteps of *Sleepless in Seattle*, *Serendipity* is a heady cocktail for die-hard romantics. Both Cusack and Beckinsale prove to be most engaging leads, while Jeremy Piven (Cusack's best friend in real life) is exceptionally good as Cusack's confidante and right-hand man. The film's twists and turns are skilfully navigated by Marc Klein's ingenious script, while director Peter Chelsom (*Hear My Song*, *The Mighty*) brews up a perfect blend of romantic fantasy and lightweight comic likeability. Thus, judged by the parameters of its genre, *Serendipity* is at the very top its class. Utterly charming.

• *Jonathan Trager* John Cusack, *Sara Thomas* Kate Beckinsale, *Eve* Molly Shannon, *Dean Kansky* Jeremy Piven, *Lars Hammond* John Corbett, *Halley Buchanan* Bridget Moynahan, *Bloomingdale salesman* Eugene Levy, *Caroline Mitchell* Lucy Gordon, Mike

Benitez, Pamela Redfern, Evan Neuman, Kevin Rice, Leo Fitzpatrick, Victor Young, Eve Crawford, Marcia Bennett, Jamie Goodwin, David Sparrow, and (uncredited) Buck Henry.
• *Dir* Peter Chelsom, *Pro* Simon Fields, Peter Abrams and Robert L Levy, *Ex Pro* Bob Osher, Julie Goldstein and Amy Slotnick, *Co-Pro* Amy Kaufman and Andrew Panay, *Co-Ex Pro* Robbie Brenner, *Screenplay* Marc Klein, *Ph* John De Borman, *Pro Des* Caroline Hanania, *Ed* Christopher Greenbury, *M* Alan Silvestri; songs performed by Chantal Kreviazuk, Louis Armstrong, David Gray, Annie Lennox, Wood, Daryl Hall and John Oates, Mint Royale, Sourcerer, Don Byron, Shawn Colvin, Nick Drake, Ronan Keating, Evan and Jaron, etc, *Costumes* Marie-Sylvie Deveau and Mary Claire Hannon.

Miramax/Tapestry Films/Simon Fields Prods-Buena Vista. 90 mins. USA. 2001. Rel: 26 December 2001. Cert PG.

Sex & Lucía ★★★

On his birthday, in the Mediterranean, Lorenzo has a night of passion that he will never forget. Years later, in Madrid, he is struggling with his second novel and is propositioned by a statuesque beauty in a bar. She confesses to having read his first novel over and over again and has been stalking him. Unable to resist her infatuation, and beauty, Lorenzo embarks on a relationship that has far-reaching consequences on both his fiction and his past... Julio Medem has always been a consummate storyteller, spinning out his plots in elliptical strands of fate tinged with irony. Here, he guides six characters together in an increasingly claustrophobic tale of passion, lost love and the storytelling process itself. Unlike Claude Lelouch, who's also rather fond of epic, predestined romances, Medem distances himself from any undue surges of romanticism, preferring to play out his melodrama in hushed tones and muted colours. With his eye for the designer-friendly image and his use of billboard-ready stars, Medem presents an alluring package (there's plenty of sex, by the way), but it's a more sensual than emotionally gripping experience.

• *Lucía* Paz Vega, *Lorenzo* Tristán Ulloa, *Elena* Najwa Nimri, *Carlos/Antonio* Daniel Freyre, *Belén* Elena Anaya, *Luna* Silvia Llanos, *Pepe* Javier Cámara, *Manuela, Belén's mother* Diana Suárez.
• *Dir* and *Screenplay* Julio Medem, *Pro* Fernando Bovaira and Enrique López Lavigne, *Ex Pro* Anna Cassina, *Line Pro* Teresa Cepeda, *Ph* Kiko de la Rica, *Art Dir* Montse Sanz, *Ed* Iván Aledo, *M* Alberto Iglesias, *Costumes* Estíbaliz Markiegui.

Alicia Produce/Sogecine/Canal Plus-Metro Tartan. 128 mins. Spain/France. 2001. Rel: 10 May 2002. Cert 18.

Left: Gwyneth Paltrow throws her weight around as Jack Black looks on in the Farrelly brothers' thought-provoking farce, *Shallow Hal* (from Fox)

Shallow Hal ★★★¹/₂

Hal Larsen is the living embodiment of the average male – ie, he is hypnotised by the marketing of cosmetic perfection as the ideal of beauty. However, after getting stuck in a lift with a self-help guru, he is released from this 'hypnotism' and from then on sees the inner beauty of those around him made flesh. He then meets the shy, lonely, 308-pound Rosemary Shanahan and cannot believe his good fortune… In an extraordinary about-turn, Peter and Bobby Farrelly – the brothers who made fun of diarrhoea, flatulence, physical deformity, bestiality, bad hair, masturbation, dwarfs and albinos in their previous five movies – here pay homage to the disadvantaged in a sweet and romantic fable. A sort of *What Women Want* welded on to *The Truth About Cats and Dogs*, *Shallow Hal* is an original film with a neat gimmick empowered by another marvellous turn from Gwyneth Paltrow. While looking absolutely gorgeous, the actress manages to convey her awkward mental bulk while progressively drawing us into the inner beauty of the 'marginalised' character she is playing. Credit this as a thought-provoking comedy with not so much a dark edge as a mottled centre.

• *Rosemary Shanahan* Gwyneth Paltrow, *Hal Larsen* Jack Black, *Mauricio* Jason Alexander, *Steve Shanahan* Joe Viterelli, *Jill* Susan Ward, *Walt* Rene Kirby, *himself* Tony Robbins, *Lindy* Manon Von Gerkan, Bruce McGill, Zen Gesner, Brooke Burns, Joshua 'Li'l Boy' Shintani, Laura Kightlinger, Jill Christine Fitzgerald, and (uncredited) *Mrs Larsen* Nora Dunn.
• *Dir* Peter and Bobby Farrelly, *Pro* Peter and Bobby Farrelly, Bradley Thomas and Charles R Wessler, *Screenplay* Peter and Bobby Farrelly and Sean Moynihan, *Ph* Russell Carpenter, *Pro Des* Sydney J Bartholomew Jr, *Ed* Christopher Greenbury, *M* Ivy; songs performed by Sheryl Crow, P J Harvey,

Coldplay, Joel Evans, Ivy, Jeff Beck, Phoenix, Kings of Convenience, Rosey, Madredeus, Lucinda Williams, The Foundations, Elvis Sinatra, Darius Rucker, John Frusicante, Ellis Paul, Randy Weeks, Shelby Lynne, Neil Young, Cake, Edison Lighthouse, etc, *Costumes* Pamela Withers.

Twentieth Century Fox/Conundrum Entertainment-Fox. 113 mins. USA. 2001. Rel: 1 February 2002. Cert 12.

Shiner ★★★★

East London; today. Billy 'Shiner' Simpson has spent 30 years working up to this moment. Having just moved into a luxurious new house, he has invested his remaining, hard-earned dosh on a lavish, legitimate boxing pageant, complete with fireworks, showgirls and Sky Sports coverage. After a lifetime of working on the fringes of the boxing world, Shiner is about to become a rich man off the blood and sweat of his very own son – Eddie 'Golden Boy' Simpson. However, the support act is not up to much, the American promoter is appalled by the tattiness of the venue and the police turn up to lock Shiner away... Welcome back Michael Caine, we have missed you. Not since *Get Carter* 30 years ago has Caine seemed so at home as a foul-mouthed, East End hard man, oozing charisma and sardonic humour in between bursts of snarling savagery. When he derides a boxing contender with the riposte, 'When did he last work out? He looks like Hattie fucking Jacques!', we know we can just sit back and enjoy the ride. There's also sterling work from the supporting cast – in particular Frank Harper, Claire Rushbrook and Nicola Walker – and a strong story charged with equal parts black humour and stomach-knotting tension.

• *Billy 'Shiner' Simpson* Michael Caine, *Frank Spedding* Martin Landau, *Georgie* Frances Barber, *Stoney* Frank Harper, *Mel* Andy Serkis, *Eddie 'Golden Boy' Simpson*

Right: Coastal order: Judi Dench attempts to set Kevin Spacey right in Lasse Hallström's moving and picturesque *The Shipping News* (from Buena Vista)

Matthew Marsden, *Ruth* Claire Rushbrook, *Karl* Danny Webb, *Gibson* Kenneth Cranham, *Chris* David Kennedy, *DI Grant* Peter Wight, *DS Garland* Nicola Walker, *Vic* Gary Lewis, *Mikey Peck* Derrick Harmon, *Mel's girlfriend* Siobhan Fogarty, Josephine Butler, Malcolm Tierney, Helen Grace, Anna Mountford, Robin Kermode, George Innes.
• *Dir* John Irvin, *Pro* Geoffrey Reeve and Jim Reeve, *Ex Pro* Laura Townsley and Barry Townsley, *Co-Ex Pro* Guy Collins and Neil Bowman, *Line Pro* Al Burgess, *Screenplay* Scott Cherry, *Ph* Mike Molloy, *Pro Des* Austen Spriggs, *Ed* Ian Crafford, *M* Paul Grabowsky; songs performed by AC/DC, Gay Dad, and Andy Williams, *Costumes* Stephanie Collie.

IAC Films/Wisecroft/Visionview-Momentum Pictures. 99 mins. UK. 2000. Rel: 14 September 2001. Cert 18.

The Shipping News ★★★¹/₂

Since Quoyle was almost drowned by his father when he was a boy, he has never been able to take control of his life. Now a lowly ink-setter in upstate New York, he is seduced by an intemperate man-eater and, as her husband, ends up paying her bills and bringing up her daughter. Then, following her death, he is enticed to build a new life on the desolate coast of Newfoundland… A melancholy, wistful tale of bruised, fragile people set in the bleak landscape of Newfoundland, *The Shipping News* inhabits its own unique universe with some distinction. While the cosmopolitan all-star cast initially distracts from the film's reality, the actors' commitment to their roles quickly and deftly establishes the singular colour of the dramatis personae. Indeed, this is an actors' paradise, although the evocative photography and timeless landscape is just as much a character in the film. As with most literary adaptations, there is a surfeit of incident, although the textual power of Annie Proulx'

writing certainly shines through, fortifying a most unusual and affecting film.

• *Quoyle* Kevin Spacey, *Wavey Prowse* Julianne Moore, *Agnis Hamm* Judi Dench, *Jack Buggit* Scott Glenn, *Beaufield Nutbeem* Rhys Ifans, *Tert Card* Pete Postlethwaite, *Petal* Cate Blanchett, *Billy Pretty* Gordon Pinsent, *Dennis Buggit* Jason Behr, *Cousin Nolan* Marc Lawrence, Larry Pine, Jeanetta Arnette, Robert Joy, Ken James, Katherine Moenning, Nancy Beatty, Deborah Grover.
• *Dir* Lasse Hallström, *Pro* Irwin Winkler, Linda Goldstein Knowlton and Leslie Holleran, *Ex Pro* Bon Weinstein, Harvey Weinstein and Meryl Poster, *Co-Pro* Diana Pokorny, *Screenplay* Robert Nelson Jacobs, *Ph* Oliver Stapleton, *Pro Des* David Gropman, *Ed* Andrew Mondshein, *M* Christopher Young, *Costumes* Renée Ehrlich Kalfus, *Sound* Michael Kirchberger, *Dialect coach* Nadia Venesse.

Miraxmax-Buena Vista. 117 mins. USA. 2001. Rel: 1 March 2002. Cert 15.

Shooters ★★

In the graffiti-scarred streets of contemporary London, kids are constantly on the look out for 'something to shoot and something to shoot up with'. It is into this new world of guns and drugs that Gilly emerges, having served six years for the murder of a woman killed by his best friend Justin. Justin is still the only person that Gilly can turn to, but in the interim he has invested Gilly's ill-gotten gains into a drugs-for-guns enterprise. Justin has just one week to recoup Gilly's money, but it's a week that might never end… Since the actor-writers Andrew Howard and Louis Dempsey settled on the idea for a British gangster movie, its release eight years later seems redundant to say the least. Shot on a shoestring and thoroughly unpleasant, *Shooters* offers nothing new to an exhausted genre. However, after a slow start, the film does gain some dramatic momentum, but it's still little more than a showcase for the intense screen presence of its star, Andrew Howard.

• *Max Bell* Adrian Dunbar, *'J' aka Justin* Andrew Howard, *Gilly* Louis Dempsey, *Marie* Melanie Lynskey, *Det Inspector Sarah Pryce* Emma Fielding, *Eddie* Matthew Rhys, *Jackie Jr* Gerard Butler, *Charlie Franklin* Jason Hughes, *Freddy Guns* Ioan Gruffud, *Skip* Jamie Sweeney, *Sgt. Webb* David Kennedy, *Pac* Ranjit Krishnamma, *Glenn* Glenn Durfort, Walter Roberts, Treva Etienne, Raquel Cassidy, Joanne Young, Neil Howard.
• *Dir* Colin Teague and Glenn Durfort, *Pro* Margery Bone, *Ex Pro* George Skene, *Co-Ex Pro* Jan Bruinstroop, *Screenplay* Gary Young, Andrew Howard and Louis Dempsey, *Ph* Tom Erisman, *Pro Des* Robin Tarsnane, *Ed* Kevin Whelan, *M* Kemal Ultanur; songs performed by Lo-Fidelity All-Stars, The Seventh Messiah, and Leftfield, *Costumes* Vivienne Low, *Sound* Future Post.

PFG Entertainment/Coolbeans Films/Catapult Prods-Universal Pictures International.
95 mins. UK/Netherlands/USA. 2000. Rel: 18 January 2002. Cert 18.

Showtime ★

Los Angeles; the present. When no-nonsense veteran cop Mitch Preston fires his gun at a TV news cameraman, his precinct is hit with a $10 million lawsuit. As a compromise, the network suggests that Preston star in a new reality TV cop show, *Showtime*, partnered with the camera-friendly patrol officer Trey Sellars. With no option but to toe the line, Preston teaches Trey a few things about real law-enforcement, while Trey gets Preston to see that there's more to life than crime-busting… Had Robert De Niro's hardened cop been remotely credible or Eddie Murphy's character witty, then this mechanical mishmash of *48 HRS*, *The Hard Way* and *15 Minutes* may have had something to work with. As it is, *Showtime* is exactly the sort of generic pap that De Niro's Mitch Preston derides, making this derivative star vehicle all the more embarrassing. Frankly, De Niro and Murphy ought to be ashamed of themselves for being associated with such drivel.

• *Trey Sellars* Eddie Murphy, *Mitch Preston* Robert De Niro, *Chase Renzi* Rene Russo, *Captain Winship* Frankie R Faison, *himself* William Shatner, *Caesar Vargas* Pedro Damian, *ReRun* T J Cross, *Lazy Boy* Mos Def, *Brad Slocum* Peter Jacobson, *Annie* Drena De Niro, *himself* Johnnie L Cochran Jr, Zaid Farid, Nestor Serrano, Ken Campbell, Linda Hart, Kadeem Hardison, Joy Bryant, Judah Friedlander, Angela Rosa Alvarado.

• *Dir* Tom Dey, *Pro* Jorge Saralegui and Jane Rosenthal, *Ex Pro* Will Smith, James Lassiter, Eric McLeod and Bruce Berman, *Screenplay* Keith Sharoin, Alfred Gough and Miles Millar, from a story by Saralegui, *Ph* Thomas Kloss, *Pro Des* Jeff Mann, *Ed* Billy Weber, *M* Alan Silvestri; songs performed by Shaggy and Babyface, Junior Wells, James Brown, Ray Charles, Sergent Garcia, Latrelle, etc.

Warner/Village Roadshow/NPV Entertainment/Material/Tribeca-Warner.
95 mins. USA. 2002. Rel: 3 May 2002. Cert 12.

Sidewalks of New York ★★★

Unlike Woody Allen's contemplations of love and sex in Manhattan, *Sidewalks of New York* embraces more than just the cultural elite. Here, the writer-director-producer-actor Edward Burns taps into several social strata as he explores the irrational permutations of the mating game. Framing his romantic mosaic with vox pox interviews with his characters, Burns threads together the lives of a dentist carrying out an adulterous affair, a doorman obsessed by his ex-wife, a TV producer thrown out on his ear by his girlfriend, a schoolteacher coming to terms with solitude, a real estate agent who suspects her husband of having an affair and a waitress locked into a dead-end relationship with the aforementioned dentist. Gradually, the paths of these transitional romantics intertwine, leading to a satisfactory if bittersweet finish. Adopting a light, spontaneous tone, Burns sheds precious new light on the war of the sexes, but he has rustled up an engaging cross-section of characters, beautifully played by an illustrious cast. Once again, Brittany Murphy proves that she is a star on the rise, while Stanley Tucci (appropriating a Woody Allen whine) is hilarious as a man who cannot see beyond his penis.

• *Tommy* Edward Burns, *Maria* Rosario Dawson, *Carpo* Dennis Farina, *Annie* Heather Graham, *Ben* David Krumholtz, *Ashley* Brittany Murphy, *Griffin* Stanley Tucci, *Gio/Harry* Michael Leydon Campbell, *Hilary* Nadia Dajani, *Shari* Aida Turturro, *with* Penny Balfour, Kathleen Doyle, Tim Jerome, Libby Langdon, Callie Thorne.
• *Dir* and *Screenplay* Edward Burns, *Pro* Burns, Margot Bridger, Cathy Schulman and Rick Yorn, *Ph* Frank Prinzi, *Ed* David Greenwald, *M* Vivaldi, *Music consultant* Laura Ziffren; songs performed by Cake, American Paint, World Party, Chet Baker, Peter Yorn, Ben Folds Five, Django Reinhardt, Departure Lounge, Gift Horse, Chris Tart, Stan Getz, etc, *Costumes* Catherine Thomas.

Marlboro Road Gang/Artists Production Group-Helkon SK.
108 mins. USA. 2000. Rel: 5 April 2002. Cert 15.

Right: Jason Schwartzman and James King try the latest in millinery fashion in Dewey Nicks' wacky and distasteful *Slackers* (from Momentum Pictures)

Slackers ★★★

On the verge of scamming their way through their final exams, con artists Dave, Jeff and Sam are found out by the college weirdo 'Cool Ethan'. In return for the latter's silence, the trio agree to trick Ethan's dream babe into falling in love with him… Aspiring to the heights of *There's Something About Mary*, *Slackers* neither produces the belly laughs nor sufficient human empathy to join such vaunted company, but it certainly has its moments. While the film begins fairly conventionally, its subversive vein starts throbbing 20 minutes in. It's a good ploy, as what follows gets increasingly weird, funny and surprising. Jason Schwartzman, so good in *Rushmore*, repeats his schtick as the school oddball with a vengeance and, among other things, gets to suck the elevated left nipple of hospital patient Mamie Van Doren (prompting a nurse to bellow: 'Put the sponge down and get away from the bed', as if coaxing a criminal away from a crime scene). There are also surprise cameos from Cameron Diaz, Gina Gershon and Leigh Taylor Young (the last named a star of the 1970s and ex-wife of Ryan O'Neal, who gets to proclaim 'I love to suck cock'). But *Slackers* is more about great moments than sustained comedy, although debuting director Dewey Nicks is obviously a talent to watch.

• *Dave* Devon Sawa, *Cool Ethan* Jason Schwartzman, *Angela* James King, *Jeff* Michael Maronna, *Sam* Jason Segel, *Reanna* Laura Prepon, *Mrs Van Graaf* Mamie Van Doren, *Mr Leonard* Joe Flaherty, *Valerie Patten* Leigh Taylor Young, *Charles Patton* Sam Anderson, *with* Gedde Watanabe, Michael McDonald, Jonathan Kasdan, Cameron Diaz, and (uncredited) Gina Gershon.

• *Dir* Dewey Nicks, *Pro* Neal Moritz and Erik Feig, *Ex Pro* Patrice Theroux, *Co-Pro* Louis G Friedman, *Screenplay* David H Steinberg, *Ph* James Bagdonas, *Pro Des* Bill Arnold, *Ed* Larry Block, *M* Joey Altruda, Venus Brown, Printz Board and Justin Stanley; Richard Wagner, Elgar, *Costumes* Jennifer Levy.

Alliance Atlantis-Momentum Pictures.
86 mins. USA. 2001. Rel: 10 May 2002. Cert 15.

Snow Dogs ★½

A famous dentist (only in America), who apparently hates teeth, finds out on the death of his biological mother that he was adopted. And so he heads out to Alaska to hear his real mother's will and discovers that he has inherited a pack of aggressive Siberian huskies… The ultimate lowbrow McEntertainment from Disney, *Snow Dogs* was conceived by a team of five writers and is a corporate mess. From the clichéd, meddlesome score to the phenomenal miscasting (forget logic and genetics), this really is an embarrassment for all concerned. Only the pack of animatronically enhanced huskies saves the film from being a total dog.

• *Ted Brooks* Cuba Gooding Jr, *Thunder Jack* James Coburn, *Dr Rupert Brooks* Sisqo, *Amelia Brooks* Nichelle Nichols, *George* M Emmet Walsh, *Peter Yellowbear* Graham Greene, *Ernie* Brian Doyle-Murray, *Barb* Joanna Bacalso, *with* Jean-Michel Pare, Michael Bolton, Frank C Turner.
• *Dir* Brian Levant, *Pro* Jordan Kerner, *Ex Pro* Christine Whitaker and Casey Grant, *Screenplay* Jim Kouf, Tommy Swerdlow, Michael Goldberg, Mark Gibson and Philip Halprin, 'suggested' by the book

Left: Frost in Alaska: Joanna Bacalso and Cuba Gooding Jr in Brian Levant's overstated, illogical and generally embarrassing *Snow Dogs* (from Buena Vista)

Winterdance by Gary Paulesen, *Ph* Thomas Ackerman, *Pro Des* Stephen Lineweaver, *Ed* Roger Bondelli, *M* John Debney, *Costumes* Monique Prudhomme.

Walt Disney Pictures/Galapagos Prods-Buena Vista. 99 mins. USA. 2001. Rel: 31 May 2002. Cert PG.

Solas ★★★¹/₂

Seville; today. Visiting the city where her belligerent husband is in hospital, an elderly woman stays with her daughter, María. The latter has problems of her own, being an alcoholic and also having to decide whether to have an abortion as her truck-driver lover suggests… This well-intentioned first feature from Spanish writer/director Benito Zambrano suffers from two serious defects. Structurally it lacks a centre, divisively paying equal attention to María and to her mother's encounter with a solitary old man who is clearly more sympathetic than her husband. As for the film's close, it betrays the honesty of what has preceded it by becoming romanticised and sentimental. But the acting is excellent, and the film's welcome humanity echoes the classic films of Vittorio De Sica.
English title: *Alone.*
[*Mansel Stimpson*]

• *Rosa Jiménez Peña, Maria's mother* María Galiana, *María* Ana Fernández, *Vecino* Carlos Álvarez-Novoa, *doctor* Antonio Perez Dechent, *María's father* Paco de Osca, *Juan* Juan Fernández, *El Gordo* Miguel Alcibar. • *Dir* and *Screenplay* Benito Zambrano, *Pro* Antonio P Pérez, *Ph* Tote Trenas, *Pro Des* Lalo Obrero, *Ed* Fernando Pardo, *M* Antonio Meliveo; 'Woman' sung by Neneh Cherry.

Canal Sur Television S.A./Canwest Entertainment/Fireworks Pictures/Maestranza Films S.L./Via Digital-Artificial Eye. 101 mins. Spain. 1999. Rel: 20 July 2001. Cert 15.

Someone Like You

See *Animal Attraction*

The Son of Two Mothers

See *Comédie de l'innocence*

The Son's Room ★★★★¹/₂

How do you continue the function of daily life when inwardly you have been arrested? This beautifully crafted film probes deep into the core of the human psyche – uncovering our preoccupation with death and the sense of loss it can leave behind. As if dedicated to all those who have lost a person in tragic circumstances, Nanni Moretti's film articulates the emotional repercussions of a family torn apart by grief. The mother's insurmountable pain; the father's guilt that plays and replays itself; and the sister's anger – each despair reflecting the other and threatening to separate the family forever. Like the father's occupation (a psychiatrist), this film collates the fantastical and the real to formulate a sympathetic human study of pain in a world without spiritual faith.
Original title: *La stanza del figlio.*
[*Eva Marie Bryer*]

• *Giovanni* Nanni Moretti, *Paola* Laura Morante, *Irene* Jasmine Trinca, *Andrea* Giuseppe Sanfelice,

Arianna Sofia Vigliar, *headmaster* Renato Scarpa, *priest* Roberto Nobile.
• *Dir* Nanni Moretti, *Pro* Angelo Barbagallo and Nanni Moretti, *Screenplay* Nanni Moretti, Linda Ferri and Heidrun Schleef, *Ph* Giuseppe Lanci, *Pro Des* Giancarlo Basili, *Ed* Esmeralda Calabria, *M* Nicola Piovani, *Costumes* Maria Rita Barbera.

Bac Films/Canal Plus/Rai Cinemafiction/Sacher Film/Telepiu-Momentum Pictures.
99 mins. Italy/France. 2001. Rel: 15 February 2002. Cert 15.

Soul Survivors ★★

Cassie the college co-ed gets a little wild at a party and snogs her ex-boyfriend Matt, sending her current squeeze Sean into a rage. Then she and Sean get into a car accident but she's the only one who walks away alive. Suddenly, her social life is infested by strange men in masks and spooky people who can only speak portentously. And, over there in the shadows, doesn't that stalker look astonishingly like Sean? … Writer-director Stephen Carpenter was groomed on low-budget horror, and is here given a break with a serviceable idea and Artisan Entertainment's studio money. Unfortunately for him and a few of the more talented co-stars, the film, for all its flashy moves, is contrived, derivative and dull, comparing poorly to recent highs in the psycho-horror-thriller-with-a-twist genre (like *The Others*). [*Adam Keen*]

• *Sean* Casey Affleck, *Matt* Wes Bentley, *Cassie* Melissa Sagemiller, *Annabel* Eliza Dushku, *Raven* Angela Featherstone, *Jude* Luke Wilson, *Dr Haverston* Allen Hamilton.
• *Dir* Stephen Carpenter, *Pro* Stokely Chaffin and Neal H Moritz, *Ex Pro* Jonathan Shestack and Michele Weisler, *Screenplay* Stephen Carpenter, *Ph* Fred Murphy, *Pro Des* Larry Fulton, *Ed* Janice Hampton and Todd C Ramsay, *M* Daniel Licht, *Costumes* Denise Wingate.

Lost Soul Productions/Neal H. Moritz Productions/Artisan Entertainment-Momentum.
85 mins. USA. 2001. Rel: 11 January 2002. Cert 12.

South West Nine ★★★

Richard Parry's deeply committed feature debut surveys life in Brixton today with social awareness and a welcome cinematic flair. The energy generated recalls *Human Traffic*, which came from the same producer. But Parry is also the writer and in that role he proves less adept. He sets up an opening scene which seems to indicate that one of the five leading characters will be shot, and then goes back in time to thread together various storylines touching on such matters as drug-taking, gentrification and Brixton's ethnic mix. Fine in

theory, the writing becomes contrived, heavy-handed and manipulative, as well as introducing late on at least one character who is wholly unpersuasive. Ultimately a misfire, it's nevertheless promising and worth a look. [*Mansel Stimpson*]

• *Freddy* Wil Johnson, *Jake* Stuart Laing, *Mitch* Mark Letheren, *Kat* Amelia Curtis, *Helen* Orlessa Edwards, *Sal* Nicola Stapleton, *Rafaela* Zebida Gardener-Sharper.
• *Dir* Richard Parry, *Pro* Allan Niblo, *Ex Pro* Marie Louise Queally and Renata S Aly, *Co-Pro* Nigel Warren-Green, *Screenplay* Steve North and Richard Parry, *Ph* Graham Fowler, *Pro Des* Rob Lunn, *Ed* Christine Pancott, *M* David Bradnum, *Costumes* John Krausa.

Fruit Salad/Irish Screen/Allan Niblo-Fruit Salad Dist.
98 mins. UK/Ireland. 2001. Rel: 12 October 2001. Cert 18.

Spider-Man ★★★½

On a field trip to the science lab at Columbia University, school outsider Peter Parker is bitten by a genetically modified super-spider. The next day, he realises that he no longer needs his spectacles, that he is endowed with an almost extrasensory perception and can scale walls. Transformed from campus dweeb to superhero, Parker decides to set a few wrongs right… The great strength of Spider-Man is his vulnerability. Unlike his square-jawed predecessors, Spider-Man is in essence just a lovestruck schoolboy bestowed with supernatural powers. Consequently, we can both identify with him and thrill at his newfound strength and aerial agility. It was genius, then, to cast Tobey Maguire – the thinking teenager's Everyboy – as the hero, a young actor who embodies everything that is normal, credible and virtuous in today's adolescent world. For Maguire is a *reactive* performer, a star who can speak volumes with his eyes and resist the onslaught of the special effects department. As the (Mary) Jane to his Tarzan, Kirsten Dunst is less successful, failing to represent the comic-book tone of the movie (Scarlett Johansson would have been superb), although Willem Dafoe is appropriately unnerving and repellent as the villain. The film itself lacks the distinctive originality of, say, *X-Men*, but its engaging hero and human centre ensure the dawn of a profitable franchise.

• *Peter Parker/Spider-Man* Tobey Maguire, *Norman Osborn/Green Goblin* Willem Dafoe, *Mary Jane Watson* Kirsten Dunst, *Harry Osborn* James Franco, *Ben Parker* Cliff Robertson, *May Parker* Rosemary Harris, *J Jonah Jameson* J K Simmons, *Maximilian Fargas* Gerry Becker, *Joseph 'Robbie' Robertson* Bill Nunn, *Henry Balkan* Jack Betts, *General Slocum* Stanley Anderson, *Flash Thompson* Joe Manganiello, *with* Ron Perkins, K K Dodds, Ted Raimi, Bruce Campbell, Larry Joshua, Macy Gray, Lucy Lawless, Stan Lee.
• *Dir* Sam Raimi, *Pro* Laura Ziskin and Ian Bryce,

Ex Pro Avi Arad and Stan Lee, *Co-Pro* Grant Curtis, *Screenplay* David Koepp, baded on the Marvel comicbook by Stan Lee and Steve Ditko, *Ph* Don Burgess, *Pro Des* Neil Spisak, *Ed* Bob Murawski and Arthur Coburn, *M* Danny Elfman, *Costumes* James Acheson, *Sound* Stephen Hunter Flick and Susan Dudeck, *Visual effects* John Dykstra.

Columbia Pictures/Marvel Entertainment-Columbia TriStar. 121 mins. USA. 2002. Rel: 14 June 2002. Cert 12.

Spy Game ★★★

Washington DC; April 1991. As veteran CIA operative Nathan Muir works out his last day before retirement, he is called in to brief his superiors on his protégé, Tom Bishop, who has been arrested in China on charges of espionage. Realising that Bishop is about to be sacrificed on the grounds of political expediency, Muir plots to have him rescued behind the CIA's back... Tony Scott is one of the most competent action directors working in Hollywood, so it's a shame that he's taken on such a cumbersomely structured, largely sedentary endeavour. The potentially most exciting sequences – set in Vietnam, West Berlin and Beirut – are all revealed in flashback, thus depriving the viewer of any sense of being in the moment. The other problem is that the two central protagonists never share a scene in the film's present tense, leaving the real chemistry to evolve between Redford and his resourceful secretary, played to perfection by Marianne Jean-Baptiste. Nevertheless, the minutiae of the 'spying game' are beautifully observed, as is Muir's smug one-upmanship on his CIA superiors.

• *Nathan Muir* Robert Redford, *Tom 'Boy Scout' Bishop* Brad Pitt, *Elizabeth Hadley* Catherine McCormack, *Charles Harker* Stephen Dillane, *Troy Folger* Larry Bryggman, *Gladys Jennip* Marianne Jean-Baptiste, *Li* Ken Leung, *Harry Duncan* David Hemmings, *Dr Byars* Matthew Marsh, *Robert Aiken* Todd Boyce, *Vincent Vy Ngo* Michael Paul Chan, *Fred Kappler* Bill Buell, *Schmidt* Joerg Stadler, *Ambassador Cathcart* Iain Smith, *Sheik Salameh* Nabil Massad, *Anne Cathcart* Charlotte Rampling, Garrick Hagon, Andrew Grainger, Shane Rimmer, James Aubrey, Benedict Wong, Stuart Milligan, Omid Djalili, Amidou, Mohamed Picasso, Dale Dye.
• *Dir* Tony Scott, *Pro* Douglas Wick and Marc Abraham, *Ex Pro* Armyan Bernstein, Iain Smith, Thomas A Bliss and James W Skotchdopole, *Screenplay* Michael Frost Beckner and David Arata, *Ph* Dan Mindel, *Pro Des* Norris Spencer and Chris Seagers, *Ed* Christian Wagner, *M* Harry Gregson-Williams; Vivaldi; songs performed by The Rolling Stones, Dire Straits, Dean Martin, Cory Cullinan, Nigel Kennedy, Jimi Hendrix, etc, *Costumes* Louise Frogley, *Military consultant* Freddie Joe Farnsworth.

Beacon Pictures/Toho-Towa Co., etc-Entertainment. 126 mins. USA/Japan. 2001. Rel: 23 November 2001. Cert 15.

Star Wars: Episode II – Attack of the Clones ★★

The galaxy is in trouble. Thousands of solar systems are threatening to withdraw from the Galactic Republic and so senator Padmé Amidala, former

queen of Naboo, turns up to lend her support. However, on her arrival at Coruscant, an attempt is made on her life. And so Jedi knight Obi-Wan Kenobi and his apprentice Anakin Skywalker are assigned to guard her. Then, following a further assassination attempt, Obi hotfoots it to the waterlogged planet of Kamino to hunt down Padmé's assailant… Seldom has the summer season been served by such an interminable, plodding and *boring* blockbuster. From the uninspired casting of Christopher Lee as the villain to the sappy Ken and Barbie romance, *Attack of the Clones* stinks to high Heaven. Visually, yes, the film is stunning, but how many Yes album covers can you drool over for two hours-plus? This prequel sequel is nailed to the service of plot and exposition over content, with all the best bits consigned to the background. The dialogue and acting is also exceptionally bad, while John Williams' incessant score blankets the whole film in a hermetically sealed universe of its own making. In short, this must be the most expensive power-nap ever committed to celluloid.

• *Obi-Wan Kenobi* Ewan McGregor, *Padmé Amidala* Natalie Portman, *Anakin Skywalke*r Hayden Christensen, *Supreme Chancellor Palpatine* Ian McDiarmid, *Mace Windu* Samuel L Jackson, *Count Dooku* Christopher Lee, *C-3PO* Anthony Daniels, *R2-D2* Kenny Baker, *Yoda* Frank Oz, *Shmi Skywalker* Pernilla August, *Jango Fett* Temuera Morrison, *Senator Bail Organa* Jimmy Smits, *Cliegg Lars* Jack Thompson, *Zam Wesell* Leeanna Walsman, *Jar Jar Binks* Ahmed Best, *Dormé* Rose Byrne, *Sio Bibble* Oliver Ford Davies, *Dexter Jettser* Ronald Falk, *Captain Typho* Jay Laga'aia, *Watto* Andrew Secombe, *Queen Jamillia* Ayesha Dharker, *Boba Fett* Daniel Logan, *Owen Lars* Joel Edgerton, *voice of Taun We* Rena Owen, *Hermione Bagwa* Susie Porter.
• *Dir* and *Ex Pro* George Lucas, *Pro* Rick McCallum, *Screenplay* Lucas and Jonathan Hales, from a story by Lucas, *Ph* David Tattersall, *Pro Des* Gavin Bocquet, *Ed* and *Sound* Ben Burtt, *M* John Williams, *Costumes* Trisha Biggar, *Visual effects* John Knoll, Pablo Helman, Ben Snow and Dennis Muren.

Lucasfilm/Fox-Fox.
143 mins. USA. 2001. Rel: 16 May 2002. Cert U.

startup.com ★★★★

startup.com is a documentary that follows the creation and subsequent demise of one of the many failed dot-com businesses that have crippled the American economy. We follow old high school buddies Kaleil Isaza Tuzman and Tom Herman as they orchestrate the rise of govWorks.com, a website that will allow people to interact and do online business with local government. Between May 1999 and December 2000, they manage to raise over $64 million from appallingly naïve capital investment firms without ever producing a product. Shortly after they actually do manage to launch govWorks, their site is 'hacked' and the company ruined. Scattered throughout, we meet various family members, watch girlfriends come and go, and see exactly what dollar values some friendships actually have. Apparently squandering other people's money is hard on personal relationships. *startup.com* is a damning and unflinching look at everything wrong with the

American ideal of getting something for nothing and the price we all pay for indulging it.
[*Scot Woodward Myers*]

• With Kaleil Isaza Tuzman, Tom Herman, Kenneth Austin, Tricia Burke, Roy Burston, David Camp, Jose Feliciano.
• *Dir* Chris Hegedus and Jehane Noujaim, *Pro* D A Pennebaker, *Ex Pro* Hegedus, Noujaim and Frazer Pennebaker, *Ph* Noujaim, *Ed* Hegedus, Noujaim and Erez Laufer.

Noujaim Films/Pennebaker Hegedus Films-Artificial Eye. 107 mins. USA. 2001. Rel: 7 September 2001. Cert 15.

Storytelling ★★★¹/₂

A creative writing student at a second-rate college, Vi is desperate to impress her Pulitzer Prize-winning professor. After dismissing her disabled boyfriend's heartfelt essay as 'shit', the Professor gives Vi something very real to write about. Later, a failed actor and lawyer attempts to make a documentary about contemporary teenage life in suburbia, focusing on an apathetic senior high school student from an 'everyday' family in New Jersey... Todd Solondz' stark, bitter humour is an acquired taste and this, his third film, is a surprising follow-up to his epic ensemble masterpiece *Happiness* (1998). Running at a terse 86 minutes, *Storytelling* is thin and often ponderous but is still so original, unpredictable and articulate that, in the stale smog of contemporary urban cinema, it is a breath of fresh air. A confrontational, sparse treatise on narrative and reality, the film dissects the nature of fiction and documentary. Its first segment, subtitled *Fiction*, is actually a shocking examination of the predicament of putting reality into words, while the second, *Nonfiction*, illustrates how video documentation can distort, inadvertently turning tragedy into black farce. Of course, this will not be to everybody's fancy, but *Storytelling* has a sting that is indelible.

• *Fiction*: *Vi* Selma Blair, *Gary Scott* Robert Wisdom, *Marcus* Leo Fitzpatrick, *Catherine* Aleksa Palladino, *Amy* Maria Thayer, *Elli* Angela Goethals.
• *Nonfiction:* *Toby Oxman* Paul Giamatti, *Marty Livingston* John Goodman, *Consuelo* Lupe Ontiveros, *Mikey Livingston* Jonathan Osser, *Scooby Livingston* Mark Webber, *Brady Livingston* Noah Fleiss, *Fern Livingston* Julie Hagerty, *Mike* Mike Schank, *Mr DeMarco* Xander Berkeley, *Mr Kirk* Steve Railsback, *Toby's editor* Franka Potente, *himself* Conan O'Brien.
• *Dir* and *Screenplay* Todd Solondz, *Pro* Ted Hope and Christine Vachon, *Ex Pro* David Linde, Amy Henkels and Mike De Luca, *Ph* Frederick Elmes, *Pro Des* James Chinlund, *Ed* Alan Oxman, *M* Belle & Sebastian and Nathan Larson, *Costumes* John Dunn, *Cerebral palsy consultant* Robert Kahoud.

New Line Cinema/Good Machine International/Killer Films -Entertainment.
86 mins. USA. 2001. Rel: 30 November 2001. Cert 18.

Strictly Sinatra ★★★¹/₂

Glasgow; the present. Toni Cocozza is a second-rate Scottish-Italian crooner whose repertoire is strictly Sinatra. Then, one night, a local gangster 'requests' that Toni sing Elvis Presley's 'In the Ghetto', a performance that wins the singer new fans. Although warned by his pianist to avoid such dubious company, Toni is inexorably sucked into the criminal underworld, a situation that has both its advantages and drawbacks... A little short on the laughs that buoyed Bill Forsyth's Scottish gangster venture *Comfort and Joy* (1984), *Strictly Sinatra* does have its charms, supplied mostly by its cast. Again, Ian Hart reveals more layers to his seemingly endless talent, while Kelly Macdonald is luminous as Toni's maybe girlfriend, with Brian Cox and Alun Armstrong lending sterling support. The film's downside is its overly familiar milieu (do we *really* need another British gangster film?), although this is offset by a wonderful soundtrack.
FYI: Ian Hart sings all his own songs – in the manner of Sinatra, at that – although he has never sung on film before.

• *Toni Cocozza* Ian Hart, *Irene* Kelly Macdonald, *Chisholm* Brian Cox, *Bill Collins* Alun Armstrong, *Michelangelo* Tommy Flanagan, *Connolly* Iain Cutherbertson, *Dainty* Una McLean, *Aldo* Alex McAvoy, *Rod Edmunds* Jimmy Yuill, Richard E Grant, Jimmy Tarbuck, Paul Dennan, Alex Howden, Jamie Murphy, Jimmy Chisholm, Iain Fraser.
• *Dir* and *Screenplay* Peter Capaldi, *Pro* Ruth Kenley-Letts, *Assoc Pro* Elaine Collins, *Ph* Stephen Blackman, *Pro Des* Martyn John, *Ed* Martin Walsh, *M* Stanislas Syrewicz; songs performed by Ian Hart, Bobby Goldsboro, The Flamingos, Tony Christie, Lewis Taylor, Pilot, Al Martino, and The Bluetones, *Costumes* Kate Carin.

DNA Films/Universal Pictures International/Arts Council of England/Saracen Street Prods/National Lottery-UIP. 97 mins. UK. 2000. Rel: 9 November 2001. Cert 15.

Suspicious River ★★

As perverse, pretentious and beautifully shot as most Canadian films that make it to Britain, this is a double tale of infidelity from Lynne Stopkewich, whose first feature, *Kissed*, was an arthouse hit about necrophilia. Here, the main story focuses on Leila Murray, a young housewife who works as receptionist at a motel on the river of the title. There, for the price of a room, Leila treats male guests to a blowjob, but then falls in with an abusive man who wants more for his money. The subplot, which mirrors Leila's own childhood, features a young girl whose mother is having an affair. Potentially, this is interesting material, but Stopkewich pitches her scenes at such a flat tempo that any dramatic traction is undermined. Then, as Leila's trance switches into nightmare mode, the stories get totally muddled, resulting in confusion and alienation. A serious attempt to explore the ramifications of sexual abuse, *Suspicious River* fails either to convince or to shock. All rather depressing.

• *Leila Murray* Molly Parker, *Gary Jensen* Callum Keith Rennie, *young girl* Mary Kate Welsh, *Rick Schmidt* Joel Bissonnette, *Millie* Deanna Milligan, *mother* Sarah Jane Redmond, *father* Norman Armour, *uncle* Byron Lucas, *ball cap man* Michael Shanks, Paul Jarrett, Don S Davis, Jay Brazeau, Ingrid Tesch.
• *Dir* and *Screenplay* Lynne Stopkewich, from the book by Laura Kasischke, *Pro* Michael Okulitch and Raymond Massey, *Ex Pro* Hamish McAlpine and Werik Stensrud, *Ph* Gregory Middleton, *Pro Des* Don MacAulay, *Ed* Allan Lee, *M* Don MacDonald; songs performed by Wild Strawberries, Jack Harlan, The Be Good Tanyas, Tom Wilson, The Devlins, Veal, The Michael Chase Band, Sean McDonald, Cowboy Junkies, etc, *Costumes* Sheila White, *Sound* James Genn.

TVA International, etc-Metro Tartan.
93 mins. Canada. 2000. Rel: 31 August 2001. Cert 18.

Sweet November ★'/₂

San Francisco; the present. Nelson Moss, a high-flying advertising executive, lives off adrenaline and has no time for relaxation, reflection or redemption. However, when he's forced to take a written driving test, he encounters Sara Deever, who would seem to have all the time in the world. Yet, for all her lazy afternoons frolicking with dogs and children, Sara's days are numbered... Sometimes films can be like buses, and after the tragic and visually sumptuous *Autumn in New York*, this looks like the back of one. With a robotic performance from Keanu Reeves, a grating one from Charlize Theron and a San Francisco filmed through orange gauze, *Sweet November* is not so much sweet as glutinous. An archly manipulative remake of the 1968 weepy which starred Sandy Dennis and Anthony Newley, it is about as credible and moving as a Hallmark greetings card.

• *Nelson Moss* Keanu Reeves, *Sara Deever* Charlize Theron, *Chaz* Jason Isaacs, *Vince* Greg Germann, *Abner* Liam Aiken, *Raeford Dunne* Robert Joy, *Angelica* Lauren Graham, *Brandon* Michael Rosenbaum, *Edgar Price* Frank Langella, *Manny* Jason Kravits, Ray Baker, Tom Bullock, Adele Proom, Elizabeth Weber, Susan Zelinsky.
• *Dir* Pat O'Connor, *Pro* Erwin Stoff & Deborah

Aal, Steven Reuther and Elliot Kastner, *Ex Pro* Wendy Wanderman, *Co-Pro* Marty Ewing, *Assoc Pro* Jodi Ehrlich, *Screenplay* Kurt Voelker, from a story by Voelker and Paul Yurick, *Ph* Edward Lachman, *Pro Des* Naomi Shohan, *Ed* Anne V Coates, *M* Christopher Young; songs performed by Bt, Robbie Williams, Paula Cole and Dolly Parton, Jump With Joey, Barenaked Ladies, k.d. lang, Bobby Darin, Jackie Wilson, Enya, Tracy Dawn, Stevie Nicks, Keanu Reeves, Amanda Ghost, etc, *Costumes* Shay Cunliffe, *Sound* Tim Walston.

Warner/Bel-Air Entertainment/3 Arts Entertainment-Warner.
120 mins. USA. 2001. Rel: 13 July 2001. Cert 12.

Swordfish ★★★'/₂

Gabriel Shear is a driven, unflinching and calculating machine, a criminal who moves in a world far beyond the resources of the law. Resolved to fight global terrorism with terrorism, he recruits the world's number one hacker, Stanley Jobson, offering him a reunion with his daughter and $10 million in return for his services. Shear then takes 22 hostages in a spectacular heist aimed at relieving the government of nine billion dollars in laundered drug money... As a slab of turbo-charged escapism for the boys, *Swordfish* delivers in wheelbarrows. There are guns, girls, computers and, at a cost of $500,000 (in addition to her normal salary), a shot of Halle Berry's sensational breasts. Add a terrific return to form for John Travolta (as a villain of epic amorality), a creditable leading man in Hugh Jackman and a handful of eye-popping set-pieces (Jackman hacking into a top-secret file with a gun at his head and a girl at his fly, an explosion filmed in slow motion in a 360 degree pan, a bus lifted off the freeway by helicopter) and you have a near-perfect popcorn movie for the summer. Of course, it's still a popcorn movie and never once attempts to sound a note of credibility. But that's Joel Silver for you.

• *Gabriel Shear* John Travolta, *Stanley Jobson* Hugh Jackman, *Ginger* Halle Berry, *Agent Roberts* Don Cheadle, *Marco* Vinnie Jones, *Senator Reisman* Sam Shepard, *Melissa* Drea De Matteo, *Holly* Camryn Grimes, *AD Joy* Zach Grenier, *Axl Torvalds* Rudolf Martin, Angelo Pagán, Chic Daniel, Laura Lane, William Mapother, and (uncredited) Tate Donovan
• *Dir* Dominic Sena, *Pro* Joel Silver and Jonathan D Krane, *Ex Pro* Jim Van Wyck and Bruce Berman, *Co-Pro* Dan Cracchiolo and Skip Woods, *Screenplay* Woods, *Ph* Paul Cameron, *Pro Des* Jeff Mann, *Ed* Stephen Rivkin, *M* Christopher Young and Paul Oakenfold, *Costumes* Ha Nguyen, *Sound* Dane A. Davis, *Voice coach* Jess Platt.

Warner/Village Roadshow/NPV Entertainment-Warner.
99 mins. USA/Australia. 2001. Rel: 27 July 2001. Cert 15.

Tears of the Black Tiger ★★★★

This pastiche from Thailand blends action and an ill-fated romance as the bandit known as the Black Tiger seeks to develop the childhood bond between himself and the girl whose father is now governor of the province and opposed to their union. Apparently drawing on past styles in Thai cinema, it's also accessible to Western audiences because its references range from silent cinema to Leone, Peckinpah and Sirk while also prompting thoughts of *Gone With the Wind* and *Johnny Guitar*. As for the music track, it incorporates songs and a theme from Dvorak's New World Symphony, thus adding, if possible, to the camp mode. Well sustained and not without a touch of genuine emotion, this extraordinary film also boasts colour tones halfway between *The Umbrellas of Cherbourg* and the lost glories of Trucolor!
Original title: *Fa Talai Jone.*
[*Mansel Stimpson*]

• *Seua Dum, Black Tiger* Chartchai Ngamsan, *Rumpoey* Stella Malucchi, *Mahesuan* Supakorn Kitsuwon, *Police Captain Kumjorn* Arawat Ruangvuth, *Fai* Sombat Metanee, *Phya Prasit* Pairoj Jaisingha, *Rumpoey's maid* Naiyana Sheewanun.
• *Dir* Wisit Sartsanatieng, *Pro* Nonzee Nimibutr, *Ex Pro* Pracha Maleenont, Brian L Marcar, Adirek Wattaleela, *Screenplay* Wisit Sartsanatieng, *Ph* Nattawut Kittikhun, *Pro Des* Ake Eiamchurn, *Ed* Dusanee Puinongpho, *M* Amornpong Methakunawat, *Costumes* Chaiwichit Somoboon.

Aichi Arts Center/Film Bangkok/Five Star Productions Inc. 110 mins. Thailand. 2001. Rel: 24 August 2001. Cert 18.

The Texas Chainsaw Massacre 2 ★

Local radio DJ Vantia 'Stretch' Block listens on the phone while two hellions drive through Texas. After they play a game of 'chicken' with a blue pickup truck, they have an unfortunate encounter with its chainsaw-wielding passenger. Seems the Sawyer boys are at it again while their dad is in town winning the local chilli cook-off with his 'secret ingredient' of human flesh. Enter Dennis Hopper as the misunderstood lawman bent on vengeance. He too prefers to use a chainsaw to mete out justice. All the while, Leatherface tries to 'court' Stretch. That is, until he's gutted… Director Tobe Hooper can't decide whether his film (hitting UK screens after 15 years' resistance from the BBFC) is a slasher flick, a black comedy, or therapy for a demented childhood. Inane plotting, coupled with tedious music, terrible acting, and even worse dialogue make this one of the most lamentable movies ever made. It's amazing that Hooper squandered his *Poltergeist* pay cheque to make it.
[*Scot Woodward Myers*]

• *Lieutenant 'Lefty' Enright* Dennis Hopper, *Vantia 'Stretch' Block* Caroline Williams, *Cook* Jim Siedow, *Chop Top* Bill Moseley, *Leatherface* Bill Johnson, *Grandpa* Ken Evert, *L G McPeters* Lou Perry, *with* Harlan Jordan, Kirk Sisco, Joe Bob Briggs.
• *Dir* Tobe Hooper, *Pro* Yoram Globus and Menahem Golan, *Screenplay* L M Kit Carson, *Ph* Richard Kooris, *Pro Des* Cary White, *Ed* Alain Jakubowicz, *M* Tobe Hooper and Jerry Lambert, *Costumes* Carin Hooper, *Special make-up effects* Tom Savini.

Cannon Films-Blue Dolphin. 100 mins. USA. 1986. Rel: 5 October 2001. Cert 18.

Thir13en Ghosts ★★

Having fallen on hard times, a humble maths teacher and widowed father of two cannot believe his luck when he is left a house in his uncle's will. But this is no ordinary house, being the life's work of a brilliant but demented supernaturalist… Like an antique Rubik's cube on acid, the house of glass designed by the mad

Above: Art of glass: Tony Shalhoub looks on as Matthew Lillard comes a cropper in Steve Beck's demented *Thir13en Ghosts* (from Columbia TriStar)

professor is a wonder to behold. With its mobile, see-through panels, perpetual reinvention and astronomical instruments, the structure is a filmmaker's dream – and a gift to a production designer. Sean Hargreaves has risen to the challenge with aplomb but is let down shamefully by his director, who has reduced a wonderful idea (purloined from the 1960 film of the same name) to a demented mess in which self-parody degenerates into amateurish farce. There are a couple of nice death scenes (J R Bourne is sliced neatly in two by a sheet of glass), but the rest is garbage.

• *Arthur Kriticos* Tony Shalhoub, *Kalina Seyler* Embeth Davidtz, *Dennis Rafkin* Matthew Lillard, *Kathy Kriticos* Shannon Elizabeth, *Maggie Jones* Rah Digga, *Uncle Cyrus Kriticos* F Murray Abraham, *Bobby Kriticos* Alec Roberts, *Ben Moss* J R Bourne, *Damon* Matthew Harrison.
• *Dir* Steve Beck, *Pro* Gilbert Adler, Joel Silver and Robert Zemeckis, *Ex Pro* Dan Cracchiolo and Steve Richards, *Co-Pro* Terry Castle, *Screenplay* Neal Marshall Stevens and Richard D'Ovidio, from a story by Robb White, *Ph* Gale Tattersall, *Pro Des* Sean Hargreaves, *Ed* Derek G Brechin and Edward A Warschilka, *M* John Frizzell; songs performed by Rah Digga, and Tricky, *Costumes* Jenni Gullett, *Visual effects* Dan Glass (!), *Sound* Dane A Davis.

Columbia/Warner/Dark Castle Entertainment-Columbia TriStar.
91 mins. USA. 2001. Rel: 8 March 2002. Cert 15.

This Filthy Earth ★★★

Eking out a living on their late father's land, Kath and Francine have found contentment in their own company and that of Kath's illegitimate three-year-old daughter, Etta. But when Kath turns 21, Etta's father, Buto, proposes marriage so that he can take over the management of the sisters' farm for himself... A loose adaptation of Emile Zola's *Earth* (*La Terre*, 1887), Andrew Kötting's second theatrical feature (following *Gallivant*) certainly lives up to its name. From the opening shot of mud and manure to the ensuing doses of sperm, urine, puss and blood, *This Filthy Earth* is not so much a movie as a primal, visceral experience. Recalling the spirit of Rabelais, Hieronymous Bosch, Thomas Hardy and Francis Bacon, Kötting's unique vision cannot be judged by other films, but by the accumulated potency of its own imagery. Like a home movie that has encountered a literary melodrama, it attains a timeless power that is all the more remarkable for coming out of contemporary England (filmed in Wensleydale, of all places). Of course, most people will hate it and you'll want to sterilise your hands afterwards.

• *Buto Lowam* Shane Attwool, *Francine* Rebecca Palmer, *Kath* Demelza Randall, *Lek* Xavier Tchili,

Joey Ryan Kelly, *Megan* Eve Steele, *Armandine Lowam* Ina Clough, *Papa Lowam* Dudley Sutton, *Jesus Christ aka Terence Lowam* Peter-Hugo Daly, *Etta* Etta Kötting, Benji Ming, Bill Rodgers, George Neville, Rachel Kirk, Robert Hickson.
• *Dir* Andrew Kötting, *Pro* Ben Woolford, *Ex Pro* Robin Gutch, *Assoc Pro* Christopher Collins, *Screenplay* Kötting and Sean Lock, *Ph* N G Smith and Gary Parker, *Pro Des* Judith Stanley-Smith, *Ed* Cliff West, *M* and *Sound* David Burnand, *Costumes* Jane Heather.

FilmFour/The Film Council/East London Film Fund/Yorkshire Media Production Agency/British Screen/BskyB/Tall Stories-FilmFour.
111 mins. UK. 2001. Rel: 2 November 2001. Cert 15.

Thunderpants ★½

Born with two stomachs and an uncontrollable sphincter, Patrick Smash has grown up an isolated, smelly child. Then, at the age of ten, he is befriended by the school's brainy nerd, Alan A Allen, who invents an ingenious contraption that can contain Patrick's inadvertent emissions. He calls it his 'Thunderpants'... Adopting the same non-specific time-frame he used for his version of *The Borrowers* (1997), director Pete Hewitt has produced a fanciful farce that appeals to the lowest common denominator... of seven-year-olds. While a comedy devoted to the perils of farting could prove liberating to children and grownups, the one-joke premise quickly loses gas. It is unfortunate, too, that Hewitt is guilty of encouraging his cast to overact to embarrassing extremes (Simon Callow is unforgivable), while he fails to give his inexperienced lead actor Bruce Cook any direction at all. So, another soul-destroying low point for the British film industry, only marginally redeemed at the 11th hour by quite funny turns from Paul Giamatti and Ned Beatty as American space personnel.

• *Patrick Smash* Bruce Cook, *Alan A Allen* Rupert Grint, *Sir John Osgood* Simon Callow, *Sir Anthony Silk QC* Stephen Fry, *Miss Rapier* Celia Imrie, *Johnson J Johnson* Paul Giamatti, *Ed Sheppard* Ned Beatty, *Mrs Smash* Bronagh Gallagher, *Mr Smash* Victor McGuire, *Placido P Placeedo* Adam Godley, *with* Leslie Phillips, Robert Hardy, Joshua Herdman, Anna Popplewell, Colin Stinton.
• *Dir* Pete Hewitt, *Pro* Hewitt, Graham Broadbent and Damian Jones, *Ex Pro* François Ivernel and Cameron McCracken, *Co-Pro* Sally French, *Screenplay* Phil Hughes, from an original story by Hewitt, *Ph* Andy Collins, *Pro Des* Chris Roope, *Ed* Michael Parker, *M* Rupert Gregson-Williams, *Costumes* Ann Maskrey.

Pathé Pictures/Sky/Film Council/Mission Pictures/CP Medien/Working Title-Pathé.
87 mins. UK/Germany. 2002. Rel: 24 May 2002. Cert PG.

A Time for Drunken Horses ★★★★

In the mountainous region that separates Iran from Iraq, Kurdish smugglers pour alcohol into their horses' water so that the animals can better withstand the cold. It is in this world that young Ayoub, a Kurdish orphan, is forced to work in order to support himself and his five siblings. In particular need of help is Ayoub's badly handicapped brother, Madi, who is given only four weeks to live if he doesn't receive surgery. So Ayoub joins the smugglers, carrying enormous loads on his back and risking life and limb from the cold, the treacherous terrain and marauding snipers... Applying a painterly eye to his first-hand knowledge of this true story, writer-director Bahman Ghobadi has created a poignant and credible document of a people little known beyond their own borders. Using non-professionals from the village where he himself grew up, Ghobadi elicits an almost documentary-like realism, while the simple, plaintive voice-over chills the marrow. Starkly picturesque and virtually devoid of music, this is one film that, without the slick devices of mainstream cinema, goes straight for the heart.

FYI: Bahman Ghobadi played the role of Reeboir in the award-winning Kurdish drama *Blackboards* (2000).
Original title: *Zamani Baraye Masti Asbha*.

• *Ayoub* Ayoub Ahmadi, *Roujin* Roujin Younesi, *Ameneh* Ameneh Ekhtiar-Dini, *Madi* Madi Ekhtiar-Dini, Nezhad Ekhtiar-Dini.
• *Dir, Screenplay* and *Pro Des* Bahman Ghobadi, *Pro* Bahman, *Ph* Saed Nikzat, *Ed* Samad Tavazoi, *M* Hossein Alizadeh.

Bahman Ghobadi Films/Farabi Cinema Foundation/BBC-Millenium Film.
80 mins. Iran. 2000. Rel: 17 August 2001. Cert PG.

The Time Machine ★★★★

New York; 1899/2030/2037/802,701 AD. On the surface, H G Wells' early novels were jolly entertaining romps, yet underneath they contained much serious thought and some profound contemplations on the future of mankind. Here, the accent is on adventure and romance, and a thoroughly visual experience it is, containing one of the most awe-inspiring sequences in contemporary cinema. Realising that he cannot alter the predestined path of fate, pioneering scientist Alex Hartdegen pushes back the dimensions of recognised physics to embrace the future. And so, enshrined in the glistening craft of the title, our hero is transported through the changing seasons of his New York apartment, with plants growing and receding at rapidly increasing rates as the camera pulls back to reveal a world transforming before our very eyes. Wisely, the film does not take itself too seriously and

Above: Flatulence rules: Bruce Cook is fitted with the latest in wind instruments in Pete Hewitt's witless, truly awful *Thunderpants* (from Pathé)

Above: Future
tense: Guy Pearce
tinkers with a
quantum leap in
The Time Machine
(Warner), directed
by H G Wells'
great-grandson,
Simon

there are some wonderful gags (including an excerpt
from Andrew Lloyd Webber's future musical of the
eponymous novel) and some deftly drawn characters.
Even the Central Park mugger (at the film's beginning) is memorable. True, the film loses some of its
emotional ballast in its second half, but it remains an
eye-popping, mind-frying experience throughout.
FYI: The director, who previously brought us *The Prince
of Egypt*, is the real-life great-grandson of H G Wells.

• *Prof Alexander Hartdegen* Guy Pearce, *Mara*
Samantha Mumba, *Uber-Morlock* Jeremy Irons, *Vox*
Orlando Jones, *Dr David Philby* Mark Addy, *Emma*
Sienna Guillory, *Mrs Watchit* Phyllida Law, *Kalen*
Omero Mumba, *Toren* Yancey Arias, *flower shop
worker* Alan Young.
• *Dir* Simon Wells, *additional direction* Gore
Verbinski, *Pro* Walter F Parkes and David Valdes, *Ex
Pro* Laurie MacDonald, Arnold Leibovit and Jorge
Saralegui, *Co-Pro* and *Screenplay* John Logan, *Ph*
Donald M McAlpine, *Pro Des* Oliver Scholl, *Ed*
Wayne Wahrman, *M* Klaus Badelt, *Costumes* Deena
Appel and Bob Ringwood, *Visual effects* James E
Price, *Special effects* Matt Sweeney, *Morlock makeup
effects* Stan Winston Studio.

Warner/DreamWorks/Parkes/MacDonald-Warner.
95 mins. USA. 2002. Rel: 31 May 2002. Cert PG.

Together ★★★¹/₂

Stockholm; 1975. Anna has separated from her husband Lasse, moved next door and come out. Göran's
sister Elisabeth has left her husband and, with her
two children in tow, has moved in with Göran and
Anna. Meanwhile, Göran's promiscuous girlfriend
Lena has reached her first orgasm in Lasse's bed. Yes,
it's another typical day in the lives of a group of veg-
etarian misfits who find that living together isn't all
it's cracked up to be... Having shown a deft touch for
humanist comedy with his *Show Me Love* (aka
Fucking Åmål), writer-director Lukas Moodysson
turns his attention to the hippie culture of the 1970s
with equally pleasing results. As the sound of Abba's
'SOS' sets the satirical tone from the outset, the film
ambles into the lives of these off-centre people with
an affection and gentle mockery that is irresistible.
There are no belly laughs or bracing revelations, just
a warm glow born of the recognition of the absurdity of the human race.
Original title: *Tillsammans.*

• *Elisabeth* Lisa Lindgren, *Rolf* Michael Nyqvist,
Göran Gustaf Hammarsten, *Lena* Anja Lundqvist,
Anna Jessica Liedberg, *Lasse* Ola Norell, *Klas* Shanti
Roney, *Stefan* Sam Kessel, *Eva* Emma Samuelsson,
Fredrik Henrik Lundström, *Margit* Therese
Brunnander, *Ragnar* Claes Hartelius, *Tet* Axel Zuber,

Birger Sten Ljunggren, Lars Frode, Cecilia Frode, Olle Sarri, Emil Moodysson.
• *Dir* and *Screenplay* Lukas Moodysson, *Pro* Lars Jönsson, *Co-Pro* Peter Aalbaek Jensen, *Assoc Pro* Anna Anthony and Kermit Smith, *Ph* Ulf Brantås, *Pro Des* Carl Johan De Geer, *Ed* Michal Leszczylowski and Fredrik Abrahamsen, *Costumes* Mette Möller.

Memfis Film/Zentropa Entertainment/Keyfilms Roma/ Nordisk Film, etc-Metrodome.
106 mins. Sweden/Denmark/Italy. 2000. Rel: 13 July 2001. Cert 15.

Tosca ★★

Puccini's popular dramatic opera set in Rome in 1800 here receives a strong performance with the celebrated husband and wife team of Angela Gheorghiu and Roberto Alagna as the ill-fated lovers and Ruggero Raimondi as the villainous Scarpia. The Covent Garden Orchestra under Antonio Pappano backs them up splendidly, but the same cannot be said of filmmaker Benoît Jacquot, who bulldozes through the suspension of disbelief required by opera. Frequent returns to the recording studio seen in black and white, the distracting use of digital video for location shots and other filmic trickery render the film a major disappointment. But luckily you can hear without seeing, since the soundtrack is available on CD. [*Mansel Stimpson*]

• *Floria Tosca* Angela Gheorghiu, *Mario Cavaradossi* Roberto Alagna, *Baron Scarpia* Ruggero Raimondi, *Spoletta* David Cangelosi, *Sciarrone* Sorin Coliban, *Sacristan* Enrico Fissore, *Angelotti* Maurizio Muraro.
• *Dir* and *Screenplay* Benoît Jacquot, *Pro* Daniel Toscan du Plantier and Frederic Sichler, *Ph* Romain Winding, *Pro Des* Sylvain Chauvelot, *Ed* Luc Barnier, *M* Giacomo Puccini; *libretto* Luigi Illica and Giuseppe Giacosa, *Costumes* Christian Gasc.

Euripide Prods/Axiom Films/Veradia Film/France 3 Cinéma/Integral Films/Canal Plus, etc-Axiom Films.
120 mins. France/UK/Germany/Italy. 2001. Rel: 10 May 2002. Cert PG.

The Town is Quiet

See *La Ville est tranquille*

Training Day ★★★★

Rookie cop Jake Hoyt is assigned one day in the trenches of Los Angeles' more volatile areas in order to qualify for his position as undercover narcotics detective. However, all his months of training go for nought as his instructor, Alonzo Harris, bucks the principles of the constabulary rulebook, forcing Hoyt to re-evaluate the

very notion of law and order. Alonzo argues that in order to hunt the wolf you need to become a wolf, but at what cost to your soul? … As an exposé of the thin moral ground that separates the law enforcers from the lawbreakers in LA's urban war zone, *Training Day* is a glitzy, pumped-up action thriller. Stylishly photographed and endowed with colourful street dialogue by scenarist David Ayer (who spent his teens living in the tough neighbourhood of South Central LA), the film combines gloss and grit in a heady cocktail that elevates it above the norm of formulaic cop movies. However, it is the steel-plated, explosive performance from Denzel Washington that makes this something special, being a forceful study of warped heroism and one of the most compelling character studies of the new millennium.

• *Det Sgt Alonzo Harris* Denzel Washington, *Jake Hoyt* Ethan Hawke, *Roger* Scott Glenn, *Paul* Dr Dre, *Sandman's wife* Macy Gray, *Sammy* Snoop Dogg, *Stan Gursky* Tom Berenger, *Smiley* Cliff Curtis, *Doug Rosselli* Harris Yulin, *Lou Jacobs* Raymond J Barry, *Lisa* Charlotte Ayanna, *Sara* Eva Mendez, *Tim* Nick Chinlund, Jaime P Gomez, Raymond Cruz, Noel Guglielmi, Samantha Becker, Denzel Whitaker.
• *Dir* Antoine Fuqua, *Pro* Jeffrey Silver and Bobby Newmyer, *Ex Pro* Davis Guggenheim and Bruce Berman, *Co-Pro* David Wisnievitz, Scott Strauss and David Ayer, *Assoc Pro* Susan E Novick, *Screenplay* Ayer, *Ph* Mauro Fiore, *Pro Des* Naomi Shohan, *Ed*

Above: Real-life wife and husband Angela Gheorghiu and Roberto Alagna test out Angela's new six-pack in Benoît Jacquot's disappointing treatment of Puccini's *Tosca* (from Axiom Films)

Right: Factory fodder: Steve Coogan (centre) having a high time in Michael Winterbottom's creditable and often hilarious *24 Hour Party People* (from Pathé)

Conrad Buff, *M* Mark Mancina; songs performed by Franky Perez, Dr Dre, Buena Vista Social Club, Elvis Crespo, Papa Roach, 2Pac Shakur and the Outlawz, Cypress Hill, P Diddy and David Bowie, Nelly, etc, *Costumes* Michele Michel.

Warner/Village Roadshow/NPV Entertainment/ Outlaw-Warner.
122 mins. USA. 2001. Rel: 1 February 2002. Cert 18.

24 Hour Party People ★★★★

The story of Manchester's legendary Factory Records, based on co-founder Tony Wilson's eponymous book. Wilson turns everyone else's idea of total incompetence into art, leaving audiences still choosing between exceptional genius or complete prat. Make your own mind up about someone who compares Happy Mondays' Shaun Ryder with Keats. Steve Coogan introduces more than a touch of Alan Partridge in his uncannily accurate portrayal of Wilson in Michael Winterbottom's hilarious tale of rock and roll anarchy. But there's a background intensity – the death of Joy Division's Ian Curtis and the reality of drug abuse and violence undermining Wilson's hippy Hacienda club – and the frothy TV newsman Wilson screaming in frustration, 'I'm a serious journalist. I was at Cambridge.' The same Wilson, blissfully high, closes with a surreal vision of himself as God. There's a message here about the alienation of genius

confronting reality – nicely done.
[*Graham Clayton*]

• *Tony Wilson* Steve Coogan, *Alan Erasmus* Lennie James, *Lindsay Wilson* Shirley Henderson, *Rob Gretton* Paddy Considine, *Martin Hannett* Andy Serkis, *Ian Curtis* Sean Harris, *Bernard Sumner* John Simm, *Roger Ames* Keith Allen, *with* Ralf Little, Danny Cunningham, Chris Coghill, Paul Popplewell, Ron Cook, Dave Gorman, Peter Kay, Paul Ryder, Tim Horrocks, Peter Gunn, Margi Clarke, Martin Coogan, Helen Schlesinger, Mark E Smith and (uncredited) Shaun Ryder, Christopher Eccleston, Kenny Baker, Mark Tildesley, etc.
• *Dir* and *Ed* Michael Winterbottom, *Pro* Andrew Eaton, *Ex Pro* Henry Normal, *Co-Pro* Gina Carter, *Screenplay* Frank Cottrell Boyce, *Ph* Robby Muller, *Pro Des* Mark Tildesley, *M* Liz Gallacher; songs performed by Happy Mondays, The Buzzcocks, John Martyn, Siouxsie and The Banshees, The Jam, Prince Far 1 and The Arabs, Joy Division, Margi Clarke, A Guy Called Gerald, Moby, Orbital, The Sex Pistols, New Order, Iggy Pop, The Stranglers, The Clash, Blackfoot Sue, John Simm, DSK, etc, *Costumes* Natalie Ward and Stephen Noble, *Special consultant* Tony Wilson.

Film Consortium/United Arists/Film Council/FilmFour/ Wave Pictures/Revolution Films/Baby Cow-Pathé.
113 mins. UK. 2002. Rel: 5 April 2002. Cert 18.

U

Wilson Dominic Chianese, *Gloria* Myra Lucretia Taylor, *Detective Dean* Zeljko Ivanek, *Detective Mirojnick* Gary Basaraba, *with* Michelle Monaghan, Larry Gleason, Anne Pitoniak.
• *Dir* Adrian Lyne, *Pro* Lyne and G Mac Brown, *Ex Pro* Pierre-Richard Muller and Lawrence Steven Meyers, *Screenplay* Alvin Sargent and William Broyles Jr, *Ph* Peter Biziou, *Pro Des* Brian Morris, *Ed* Anne V Coates, *M* Jan A P Kaczmarek, *Costumes* Ellen Mirojnick.

Fox/Monarchy Enterprises/Epsilon Motion Pictures-Fox. 123 mins. USA. 2002. Rel: 7 June 2002. Cert 15.

Urban Ghost Story ★★★★

Glasgow, Scotland; today. 12-year-old Lizzie Fisher has recently survived a traumatic car accident in which her friend, Kevin, was killed. In fact, for just three minutes, Lizzie was clinically dead herself. Now she's back, living with her single mum and little stepbrother in a squalid high-rise daubed by graffiti and populated by junkies. If life couldn't get much worse, an unseen entity starts moving the furniture around and making a hell of a racket... As much a damning social comment on contemporary Britain as a chilling ghost story, this directorial debut from Britain's youngest producer (who, at 20, entered *The Guinness Book of Records*) is one of the most realistic portrayals of spectral intrusion ever committed to celluloid. Utilising a grimy visual palette and some unsettling sound effects, *Urban Ghost Story* succeeds in chilling the marrow by a number of means. Newcomer Heather Ann Foster is totally credible as the alienated Lizzie, while the actual poltergeist activity is never laboured, allowing the imagination to take over. If Ken Loach, not Tobe Hooper, had made *Poltergeist*, this is how it might have turned out.

• *John Fox* Jason Connery, *Kate Fisher* Stephanie Buttle, *minister* James Cosmo, *Mrs Ash* Elizabeth Berrington, *Kerrie* Nicola Stapleton, *Lizzie Fisher* Heather Ann Foster, *Quinn* Andreas Wisniewski, *loan shark* Billy Boyd, *social worker* Siri O'Neal, *Mr Ash* Kenneth Bryans, *Mrs Miller* Carolyn Bonnyman, *Alex Fisher* Alan Owen, *with* Stephen MacDonald, Julie Austin, Nicola Greene, Nicolas Von Schlippe, David Haddow, Aaron White.
• *Dir* Genevieve Jolliffe, *Pro* Chris Jones, *Ex Pro* David Hardwick, *Assoc Pro* Ian Hierons, *Screenplay* Jones and Jolliffe, *Ph* Jon Walker, *Pro Des* Simon Pickup, *Ed* Eddie Hamilton, *M* Rupert Gregson Williams, *Costumes* Linda Haysman.

Living Spirit/Jones/Jolliffe Prods-Ratpack Films/Visual Entertainment. 90 mins. UK. 1998. Rel: 13 July 2001. Cert 15.

Left: Brought to book: Diane Lane is drawn to a man and his hardbacks in Adrian Lyne's powerful, exquisitely nuanced *Unfaithful* (from Fox)

Unfaithful ★★★★

While the surfaces of Adrian Lyne's latest sexual thriller glimmer with their usual lustre, they do not detract from the human undertow at the heart of the matter. The matter is with Connie Sumner, a mother and housewife in her late thirties who finds something missing in what was perhaps a perfect life. Maybe she didn't even know it was missing until she, literally, bumps into an impossibly attractive French bookseller in his late twenties. One thing leads to another, but in a cyclical fashion, seducing both Constance and the viewer into the world of this charismatic Lothario. Alvin Sargent and William Broyle's script is deeply layered, with air bubbles of humour occasionally escaping to the surface from a deep well of emotion, much of it unspoken. Grounding the film's reality in his focus on everyday activities and objects, Lyne subtly ruffles the domestic balance as he draws the viewer into his inexorable drama.
FYI: This is the fourth Americanisation of a French original Richard Gere has starred in, following *Breathless*, *Sommersby* and *Intersection*.

• *Edward Sumner* Richard Gere, *Connie Sumner* Diane Lane, *Paul Martel* Olivier Martinez, *Bill Stone* Chad Lowe, *Tracy* Kate Burton, *Sally* Margaret Colin, *Charlie Sumner* Erik Per Sullivan, *Frank*

Right: Face to face: Tom Cruise and Cameron Diaz are beautiful for a moment in Cameron Crowe's *Vanilla Sky* (from UIP), a self-assured contemplation of disfigurement and vanity

Va savoir ★★★¹/₂

Long (which is no surprise) but light in tone (which is), Jacques Rivette's latest film has a theatre background and echoes Iris Murdoch in offering a complex tale of changing relationships among a wide group of characters. Set mainly in Paris, it also carries echoes of Pirandello's *As You Desire Me*, which is being staged, and adds a quest for a missing manuscript of a Goldoni play. Initially, Jeanne Balibar's actress seems insufficiently engaging to be a central figure but this feeling passes, and *Va savoir* settles into a witty and appealingly literate divertissement. In a good cast, Hélène de Fougerolles is particularly attractive and the film's take on French life and culture is sometimes reminiscent of the later work of Claude Sautet – but he probably wouldn't have ended the film with a song by Peggy Lee! [*Mansel Stimpson*]

• *Cammille B* Jeanne Balibar, *Sonia* Marianne Basler, *Dominique 'Do'* Hélène de Fougerolles, *Madame Desprez* Catherine Rouvel, *Ugo* Sergio Castellitto, *Pierre* Jacques Bonnaffe, *Arthur* Bruno Todeschini.
• *Dir* Jacques Rivette, *Ex Pro* Martine Marignac, Maurice Tinchant, *Screenplay* Pascal Bonitzer, Christine Laurent, Jacques Rivette, *Ph* William Lubtchansky, *Pro Des* Emmanuel de Chauvigny, *Ed* Nicole Lubtchansky, *Costumes* Laurence Struz Christine Laurent.

Centre National de la Cinematographie/Cofimage 12/ Eurimages/France 2 Cinema/ Gimages 4/Kinowelt Filmproduktion/Canal Plus/Mikado Films/Pierre Grise Productions/Procirep/VM Productions-Artificial Eye. 154 mins. France/Italy

Vanilla Sky ★★★★

Manhattan, New York; some time whenever. In spite of his father's aversion to the homogenisation of America, David Aames has embraced it wholeheartedly. Rich, successful and handsome, David is living the American dream. But then, on the toss of a coin, everything can change. David's 'fuck buddy' Julie Gianni starts to stalk him and then he falls in love with his best friend's girlfriend. But should that drive a man to murder? ... A 1997 Spanish film of extraordinary invention and chutzpah, *Abre los ojos* (*Open Your Eyes*) introduced Tom Cruise to its director Alejandro Amenábar as well as to its star Penélope Cruz. Duly gobsmacked by the experience, Cruise signed Amenábar to direct *The Others* (as a vehicle for his then-wife Nicole Kidman) and optioned the remake rights for *Open Your Eyes*. Cameron Crowe, who directed Cruise to an Oscar nomination as *Jerry Maguire*, had also seen *Open Your Eyes* and was eager to re-interpret it for an American audience. And so what was originally a dark and edgy psychological thriller has been opened out into the most expensive mind-fuck ever committed to film, garnished with Crowe's characteristically terrific dialogue. Crowe has also grown considerably as a filmmaker, bringing a style and drama to Amenábar's original vision that takes the breath away. Addressing such primal issues as identity, reality, death, vanity and the after-life, *Vanilla Sky* will provide cerebral nutrition for many and substantial irritation for the less self-indulgent.

• *David Aames* Tom Cruise, *Sofia Serrano* Penélope Cruz, *Curtis McCabe* Kurt Russell, *Brian Shelby* Jason Lee, *Edmund Ventura* Noah Taylor, *Julie Gianni* Cameron Diaz, *Thomas Tipp* Timothy Spall,

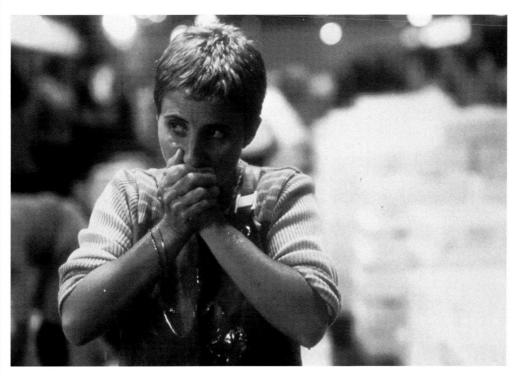

Rebecca Dearborn Tilda Swinton, *Aaron* Michael Shannon, *Colleen* Shalom Harlow, *Peter Brown* Johnny Galecki, *Libby* Alicia Witt, Delaina Mitchell, Oona Hart, Ivana Milicevic, Cameron Watson, W Earl Brown, Ken Leung, Conan O'Brien, Stacey Sher, Alice Crowe, Jonathan Sanger, Tommy Lee, Cindy Crowe, Laura Fraser, and (uncredited) *Steven Spielberg lookalike* Steven Spielberg.

• *Dir* and *Screenplay* Cameron Crowe, *Pro* Crowe, Tom Cruise and Paula Wagner, *Ex Pro* Jonathan Sanger and Danny Bramson, *Ph* John Toll, *Pro Des* Catherine Hardwicke, *Ed* Joe Hutshing, *M* Nancy Wilson; songs performed by Paul McCartney, Radiohead, Red House Painters, REM, Looper, John Coltrane, The Impressions, Creeper Lagoon, Peter Gabriel, Jeff Buckley, Cameron Diaz, Sigur Rós, Josh Rouse, The Chemical Brothers and Beth Orton, Leftfield and Afrika Bambaata, Underworld, Joan Osborne, Bob Dylan, U2, The Monkees, Todd Rundgren, The Rolling Stones, Sinéad O'Connor, The Beach Boys, etc, *Costumes* Betsy Heimann.

Paramount/Cruise/Wagner/Vinyl Films-UIP. 136 mins. USA. 2001. Rel: 25 January 2002. Cert 15.

La Ville est tranquille ★★★★

In brutal contrast to Robert Guédiguian's last feature, the warm and whimsical *A l'Attaque!* (qv), this is a bleak and damning indictment of contemporary Western society. Setting the film in his home town of Marseille (as per usual), Guédiguian has rounded up his familiar repertoire of actors and scrubbed the charm off their complexions. Explaining that as he now feels things 'are a bit better' with the world, Guédiguian has taken the liberty of a darker approach to the 'quiet town' he knows so intimately, tackling such issues as racism, prostitution, heroin addiction, divorce, unemployment, debt, adultery, deceit, self-delusion, drug dealing and even assassination. Developing a number of story strands and cutting back and forth between them, he peers into the blackest recesses of a multi-layered society and gives them a chilling, credible resonance. This is a moving, disturbing experience distinguished by another outstanding performance from Ariane Ascaride (as a grandmother who prostitutes herself to pay for her daughter's heroin habit), but one not without humour or even hope. At times the film does seem to stand still, but such narrative stasis merely adds to the potency of an emotionally wrenching finale.

English title: *The Town is Quiet.*

• *Michèle* Ariane Ascaride, *Paul* Jean-Pierre Darroussin, *Gérard* Gérard Meylan, *Claude* Pierre Banderet, *Abderramane* Alexandre Ogue, *Jean, Paul's father* Jacques Boudet, *Paul's mother* Pascale Roberts, *Fiona, Michèle's daughter* Julie-Marie Parmentier, *Yves Froment* Jacques Pieiller, *Viviane Froment* Christine Brücher, *René* Philippe Leroy-Beaulieu, *pianist* Julien Sevan Papazian.

• *Dir* Robert Guédiguian, *Pro* Guédiguian, Gilles Sandoz and Michel Saint-Jean, *Screenplay* Guédiguian and Jean-Louis Milesi, *Ph* Bernard Cavalie, *Pro Des* Michel Vandestien, *Ed* Bernard Sasia, *M* Jacques Menichetti, *Costumes* Catherine Keller.

Agat Films et Cie/Diaphana Dist./Canal Plus-Artificial Eye. 133 mins. France. 2000. Rel: 19 October 2001. Cert 18.

Right: The Life Boat: a scene from Richard Linklater's metaphysical and audacious *Waking Life* (from Fox)

Waking Life ★★

One day a young man 'wakes up' to find himself privy to a series of profound contemplations on what it means to be alive, human and so on. But is it all a dream anyway? This would make a great radio play, albeit a rather short one. As it is, Richard Linklater, director of *Slacker*, *Dazed and Confused* and *Before Sunrise*, has fashioned an animated philosophical treatise, the first cartoon to be shot with a hand-held camera. What he's done is to film over 60 characters waxing metaphysical and then got 31 artists to paint over the frames, thus creating a head trip that might've been cool in the 1960s (depending on what type of mushrooms you were ingesting). At 99 minutes, this more than outstays its welcome, while the constantly floating images induce seasickness. Still, if one is prepared to stick with it, there are a few priceless observations ('We're really asleep in life's waiting room'). For the record, the singular animation technique is called 'interpolated rotoscoping', previously used for Ralph Bakshi's *The Lord of the Rings* (1978).

• *Voices*: Wiley Wiggins, Julie Delpy, Adam Goldberg, Ethan Hawke, Lara Hicks, Nicky Katt, Lorelei Linklater, Richard Linklater, Steven Soderbergh, etc.
• *Dir* and *Screenplay* Richard Linklater, *Pro* Anne Walker-McBay, Tommy Pallotta, Palmer West and Jonah Smith, *Ex Pro* Jonathan Sehring, Caroline Kaplan and John Sloss, *Ph* Richard Linklater and Tommy Pallotta, *Art Dir* Bob Sabiston, *Ed* Sandra Adair, *M* Glover Gill; Chopin; songs performed by TOSCA, *Sound* Tom Hammond.

Independent Film Channel Productions/Thousand Words/Line Research/Detour-Fox.
100 mins. USA. 2001. Rel: 19 April 2002. Cert 15.

Warm Water Under a Red Bridge ★★

Having lost his job, Yosuke is almost apologetic when he asks for his redundancy cheque. Mild-mannered to say the least, Yosuke is having a hard time from his wife, has sold his house for half its market value and cannot seem to get another job. Then, prompted by a homeless philosopher, he decides to seek out a golden statue hidden in a distant house beside a red bridge. There, he meets Saeko, a pretty young confectioner who mounts him five minutes after he has introduced himself. And, during their impromptu coitus, she drenches him in a spectacular torrent of water that issues from her loins... A shaggy dog story with a surreal edge, *Warm Water* superimposes the mystical heritage of Japan onto the country's current social malaise. The result is anything but successful, being an aimless fable that seems to have no idea where it's going. Visually unprepossessing and over-long, the film strives for a poetic humour and erotic frisson but comes off as merely self-indulgent.

• *Yosuke Sasano* Koji Yakusho, *Saeko Aizawa* Misa Shimizu, *Mitsu Aizawa* Mitsuko Baisho, *Gen* Mansaku Fuwa, *Taro* Kazuo Kitramura, *Masayuki Uomi* Isao Natsuyagi.
• *Dir* Shohei Imamura, *Pro* Hisa Ino, *Ex Pro* Masaya Nakamura, *Screenplay* Imamura, Motofumi Tomikawa, Daisuke Tengan and Henmi Yo, *Ph* Shigeru Komatsubara, *Pro Des* Hisao Inagaki, *Ed* Hajime Okayasu, *M* Shinichiro Ikebe.

Nikkatsu Corp/BBC Four-Metro Tartan.
119 mins. Japan. 2001. Rel: 15 March 2002. Cert 15.

The Warrior ★★¹/₂

An assassin in the employ of a tyrannical warlord has a change of heart when he is ordered to raze a peasant village to the ground. Cutting his hair and abandoning his sword, he sets off with his son for the mountains. However, the warrior's former colleagues are ordered to track him down and bring back his head... Asserting his stamp as a master of the *National Geographic* photo-op, first-time feature director Asif Kapadia is nothing if not ambitious. Employing 600 extras and stretching his tale from the sand dunes of Rajasthan to the snow-carpeted Himalayas, the Hackney-born commercials director has done his forebears' country proud. Opting for a simple narrative and minimal dialogue, Kapadia has produced a fable that strives for poetic resonance at the expense of credibility. Part of the problem is that much of the film feels posed, while Kapadia too often ignores the everyday detail that might have brought his story to life. Adapted from a Japanese folk tale.

• *Lafcadia, the Warrior* Irfan Khan, *Katiba, the warrior's son* Puru Chhibber, *lord* Anupam Shyam, *blind woman* Damayanti Marfatia, *restaurant girl* Karuna Sarah Davis, *with* Sheikh Annuddin, Manoj Mishra, Sunita Sharma, Prabhuram, Pushpa Negi.
• *Dir* Asif Kapadia, *Pro* Bertrand Faivre, *Ex Pro* Paul Webster and Hanno Huth, *Co-Pro* Elinor Day, *Screenplay* Kapadia and Tim Miller, *Ph* Roman Osin, *Pro Des* Adrian Smith, *Ed* Ewa J Lind, *M* Dario Marianelli, *Costumes* Louise Stjernsward, *Sound* Andy Shelley.

FilmFour/The Bureau/Senator Films/British Screen/Equinoxe-Film Four.
86 mins. UK/France/Germany/India. 2001.
Rel: 3 May 2002. Cert 12.

We Were Soldiers ★★★★

Ia Drang Valley, the Central Highlands of South Vietnam; November 1965. 450 men of the 1st Battalion of the 7th Cavalry of the US army land in the so-called 'Valley of Death' and find themselves surrounded by more than 2000 soldiers of the People's Army of Vietnam… Since 1998 all war films have been measured by the standards set by *Saving Private Ryan* and this is no *Private Ryan*. Adapted from the autobiographical account *We Were Soldiers Once… And Young* by Lieutenant General Harold G Moore (played here by Mel Gibson) and the war correspondent Joseph L Galloway (Barry Pepper), the film is well made, expertly scored and allows the viewer a rare glimpse into the enemy camp (Moore calls his book a 'tribute' to 'the hundreds of young men … who died by our hand in that place'). The war scenes, too, are brutal and exhausting – and intensely gory – but the presence of Gibson hints at Hollywood packaging and takes away from the sheer immediacy, chaos and credibility of the conflict. Had Moore been portrayed as a more fallible, human solider – rather than the heroic, charming, humorous and indestructible officer we see on screen – then our sympathies may have been more effectively engaged. By any criteria, *We Were Soldiers* is a fine war film – but it's not the great one that it could have been.

• *Hal Moore* Mel Gibson, *Julie Moore* Madeleine Stowe, *Maj Bruce 'Snakeshit' Crandall* Greg Kinnear, *Sgt-Maj Basil Plumley* Sam Elliott, *Lt Jack Geoghegan* Chris Klein, *Barbara Geoghegan* Keri Russell, *Joe Galloway* Barry Pepper, *Lt Col Nguyen Huu An* Don Duong, *with* Ryan Hurst, Robert Bagnell, Marc Blucas, Desmond Harrington, Dylan Walsh, Adrian Grenier, Edwin Morrow, Mike White, Mark McCracken, Jsu Garcia, Andrew Wallace.
• *Dir* and *Screenplay* Randall Wallace, *Pro* Wallace, Bruce Davey and Stephen McEveety, *Ex Pro* Jim Lemley and Arne L Schmidt, *Co-Pro* Danielle Lemmon and Stephen Zapotoczny, *Ph* Dean Semler, *Pro Des* Tom Sanders, *Ed* William Hoy, *M* Nick Glennie-Smith, *Costumes* Michael T Boyd, *Sound* Geoffrey G Rubay, *Military technical adviser* Jason Powell.

Paramount/Icon/Wheelhouse-Icon.
138 mins. USA. 2002. Rel: 8 March 2002. Cert 15.

What's Cooking? ★★★★

Take one meddlesome African-American mother-in-law, a Jewish lesbian (and her girlfriend), a Mexican matriarch (and her new boyfriend) and a Vietnamese student (and his gun). Add a number of disparate friends, in-laws and relations, and leave them all to stew over Thanksgiving weekend… As a Kenyan-born Englishwoman of Indian descent, writer-director Gurinder Chadha (*Bhaji on the Beach*) was bound to have a fresh perspective on life in Los Angeles. That she has chosen the traditional weekend of Thanksgiving as her time-frame and a cast of Jewish-American, African-American, Mexican and Vietnamese characters, makes her banquet of embarrassment and discord all the more appetising. With its energetic soundtrack and vivid dramatis personae, *What's Cooking?* juggles a variety of comic styles with a warmth and perception that's slow to build but is finally both engaging and revelatory. Indeed, this is a rich feast for both the heart and mind.

• *Trin Nguyen* Joan Chen, *Carla* Julianna Margulies, *Elizabeth Avila* Mercedes Ruehl, *Rachel Seelig* Kyra Sedgwick, *Audrey Williams* Alfre Woodard, *Javier Avila* Victor Rivers, *Anthony Avila* Douglas Spain, *Sofia Avila* Maria Carmen, *Gina Avila* Isidra Vega, *Daniel* A Martinez, *Duc Nguyen* Francois Chau, *Jimmy Nguyen* Will Yun Lee, *Jenny Nguyen* Kristy Wu, *Joey Nguyen* Brennan Louie, *Gary Nguyen* Jimmy Pham, *Grandma Nguyen* Kieu Chinh, *Ruth Seelig* Lainie Kazan, *Herb Seelig* Maury Chaykin, *Aunt Bea* Estelle Harris, *Jerry* Andrew Heckler, *Ronald Williams* Dennis Haysbert, *Michael Williams* Eric K George, *Grace Williams* Ann Weldon, *Paula Moore* Sharren Mitchell, *James Moore* Gregory Itzin, *Monica Moore* Marian Parris, Elena Lopez, Richard Yniguez, Eva Rodriguez, Chao-Li Chi, Chad Todhunter, Scotty Nguyen, Albie Selznick, Suzanne Carney, Ralph Manza, Brittany Jean Henry, Frank Novak.
• *Dir* Gurinder Chadha, *Pro* Jeffrey Taylor, *Ex Pro* Abe Glazer, *Co-Ex Pro* David Forrest and Beau Rogers, *Screenplay* and *Assoc Pro* Chadha and Paul Mayeda

Right: Vile bodies: Nora Dunn and Danny DeVito in Sam Weisman's patronising, homophobic, offensive and generally execrable *What's the Worst That Could Happen?* (from Fox)

Berges, *Ph* Jong Lin, *Pro Des* Stuart Blatt, *Ed* Janice Hampton, *M* Craig Pruess, *Costumes* Eduardo Castro.

Flashpoint/Stagescreen Prods/Sundance Institute-Redbus. 109 mins. USA/UK. 2000. Rel: 31 August 2001. Cert 12.

What's the Worst That Could Happen? ★

When crack burglar Kevin Caffrey breaks into the magnificent pile of Boston tycoon Max Fairbanks, he is caught red-handed. Worse, Fairbanks tells the police that the ring on Caffrey's finger is stolen and so gets to keep it as a memento (how satisfying to steal from a thief!). As it happens, the ring is a love token from Caffrey's new girlfriend and so the burglar embarks on an elaborate crusade to retrieve it... The worst that could happen is that a perfectly reasonable novel by Donald E Westlake could be translated into such mush. Part of the problem is that we are expected to believe that Danny DeVito is a smart, cultured and physically irresistible guy who has a wife and two mistresses and is even fancied by his butch head of security. The other problem is that the film is patronising, homophobic and offensive, while the only two good jokes are milked into curd.

• *Kevin Caffrey* Martin Lawrence, *Max Fairbanks* Danny DeVito, *Berger* John Leguizamo, *Gloria* Glenne Headly, *Det Alex Tardio* William Fichtner, *Amber Belhaven* Carmen Ejogo, *Jack Caffrey* Bernie Mac, *Earl Radburn* Larry Miller, *Lutetia Fairbanks* Nora Dunn, *Walter Greenbaum* Richard Schiff, *Ann Marie* Ana Gasteyer, *with* Siobhan Fallon, Lenny Clarke.
• *Dir* Sam Weisman, *Pro* Lawrence Turman, David

Hoberman, Ashok Amritraj and Wendy Dytman, *Ex Pro* John Morrissey, Martin Lawrence and David Nicksay, *Co-Pro* Peaches Davis, *Screenplay* Matthew Chapman, *Ph* Anastos Michos, *Pro Des* Howard Cummings, *Ed* Garth Craven and Nick Moore, *M* Tyler Bates, *Costumes* Jeffrey Kurland.

Turman-Morrissey Co/Hyde Park Entertainment/MGM-Optimum Releasing.
98 mins. USA. 2001. Rel: 28 June 2002. Cert 15.

When Love Comes ★★¹/₂

This contemporary piece by New Zealander Garth Maxwell portrays the world of pop music, but far less endearingly than Allison Anders did in *Grace of My Heart*.

Central here are the splendid Rena Owen of *Once Were Warriors*, who deserves a better role than that of a former star still hoping for a comeback, and a younger lesbian couple (Brunning and Hawthorne) looking for the break which will make their name as a musical double-act. Linking the characters are Owen's supportive gay friend (Prast) and his drug-taking lover (O'Gorman), who writes lyrics for the girls. This is by no means the worst film of the year, but passing echoes of *A Star is Born* only confirm how totally forgettable this is in comparison.
[*Mansel Stimpson*]

• *Katie Keen* Rena Owen, *Mark* Dean O'Gorman, *Stephen* Simon Prast, *Fig* Nancy Brunning, *Sally* Sophia Hawthorne, *Eddie* Simon Westaway, *Magazine reporter* Judith Gibson.
• *Dir* Garth Maxwell, *Pro* Jonathan Dowling and Michele Fantl, *Screenplay* Maxwell, Rex Pilgrim and Peter Wells, *Ph* Darryl Ward, *Pro Des* Grace Mok, *Ed* Cushla Dillon, *M* various, *Costumes* Kirsty Cameron.

New Zealand Film Commission/MF Films-Millivres Multimedia.
93 mins. New Zealand. 1998. Rel: 6 July 2001. Cert 18.

Whipped ★★

Zeke, Eric and Brad, three 30-something skirt-chasers, have been friends since college. Each Sunday they meet at their local diner to share bawdy talk of the women they've seduced the night before. It's a tradition that's threatened when they learn that they've each fallen for the same girl. Mia sees different qualities in each man and seems to be each one's ideal woman. The pursuit of their dream girl strains their long-time friendship but also reveals the true character of each man... Written, directed and produced by Peter M Cohen, *Whipped* is an enjoyable enough comedy if you relish seeing men emasculated and believe that lesbians have only one goal in life: to destroy heterosexual men.
[*Scot Woodward Myers*]

• *Mia* Amanda Peet, *Brad* Brian Van Holt, *Eric* Judah Domke, *Zeke* Zorie Barber, *Jonathan* Jonathan Abrahams, *Liz* Callie Thorne, *with* Bridget Moynahan, Aviva Gale, Taryn Reif, David J Cohen, Leslie Cohen, Peter M Cohen.
• *Dir, Pro* and *Screenplay* Peter M Cohen, *Ex Pro* Anthony Armetta and Taylor MacCrae, *Co-Pro* Zorie Barber and Andrew R Shakman, *Assoc Pro* Bo Bazylevsky, *Line Pro* Jill Rubin, *Ph* Peter B Kowalski, *Pro Des* Katherine M Szilagyi, *Ed* Tom McArdle, *M* Michael Montes, *Costumes* Karen Kozlowski.

Intermedia Films/Hi-Rez Films-Pathé.
82 mins. USA. 2000. Rel: 13 July 2001. Cert 18.

Wild About Harry ★★★¹/₂

Belfast, Northern Ireland; the present. Naff TV host Harry McKee may have a devoted following of blue-rinsed old dears, but he's not a nice bloke. An over-weight womaniser and heavy drinker, he's in the throes of an acrimonious divorce when an unforeseen act of violence stops the process in its tracks. Beaten up by thugs, Harry enters a coma and emerges six days later unable to remember anything beyond the age of 18. Starting from scratch is a painful process: Harry is appalled to learn that he is a complete bastard, his mother is dead and that Elton John is gay... There is very little new about *Wild About Harry* (think *Big* meets *Regarding Henry*), but by taking two threadbare premises and weaving them together, first-time scripter Colin Bateman has fashioned a fresh and colourful new quilt. Brendan Gleeson makes an engaging 18-year-old, just as he is convincing as a charismatic and obnoxious cad, while there are splendid turns from Tara Lynn O'Neil and Henry Deazley as his non-plussed kids. The film also manages to be sweet and touching without ever becoming maudlin, while it never labours a scene (witness the sequence in which father and son open their hearts to each other). Only a subplot involving James Nesbitt as a disgraced homo-sexual doesn't quite work, but even this has its pay-off.

• *Harry McKee* Brendan Gleeson, *Ruth McKee* Amanda Donohoe, *Walter Adair* James Nesbitt, *J J McMahon* Adrian Dunbar, *Miss Boyle* Bronagh Gallagher, *Lily* Ruth McCabe, *Tara Adair* Doon MacKichan, *Professor Simmington* Paul Barber, *Frankie* George Wendt, *Billy McKee* Henry Deazley, *Claire McKee* Tara Lynn O'Neil, Billy Donnelly, Terence Corrigan, Pat Shortt, Kathy Kiera Clarke, Eileen Pollock, Frank Carson, Claire Cogan, Julian Simmons, *radio commentator* John Peel.
• *Dir* Declan Lowney, *Pro* Robert Cooper and Laurie Borg, *Ex Pro* Nik Powell, Rainer Mockert and David M. Thompson, *Co-Pro* Torsten Lesculy, *Co-Ex Pro* Kevin Jackson, Gary Smith and Chris Craib, *Line Pro* Jennifer McAufield, *Screenplay* Colin Bateman, *Ph* Ron Fortunato, *Pro Des* Claire Kenny, *Ed* Tim

Waddell, *M* Murray Gold; songs performed by Brendan Gleeson, The Rubettes, Elton John, Bob Marley and The Wailers, Mungo Jerry, James Nesbitt, Basement Jaxx, Deep Purple, Al Green, Charlotte, Groove Armada, Average White Band, etc, *Costumes* Diana Moseley.

BBC Films/Scala/MBP/Wave Pictures/Winchester Films/ National Lottery/Arts Council of Northern Ireland/ Northern Ireland Film Commission-Winchester Film Dist.
91 mins. UK/Germany/Ireland. 2000. Rel: 26 October 2001. Cert 15.

Women Talking Dirty ★★

When Cora and Ellen independently seek the refuge of their local Edinburgh pub, they discover a mutual disappointment in their men. Cora, heavily pregnant, has been smacked about by her French boyfriend, while Ellen, craving children, has been belittled by her errant husband. It's the beginning of a beautiful rela-tionship – until Cora's libido gets the better of her... Continuing the recent trend of female buddy movies (*Beautiful Creatures*, *High Heels and Low Lifes*, *Me Without You*), this mis-titled venture is most notable for being the first production from Elton John and David Furnish's Rocket Pictures. Unfortunately, as comediennes go, Helena Bonham Carter is no Minnie Driver and most of the humour in this amorphous comedy falls flat. Failing to create credible characters or any sense of drama, director Coky Giedroyc (*Stella Does Tricks*) keeps the action moving at a brisk pace but it just doesn't go anywhere. If only these women *did* talk dirty, then we might have had something to write home about.

• *Cora O'Brien* Helena Bonham Carter, *Ellen Quinn* Gina McKee, *Emily Boyle* Eileen Atkins, *George* Kenneth Cranham, *Stanley* James Nesbitt, *Daniel* James Purefoy, *Bill O'Brien* Ken Drury, *Claude* Julien Lambroschini, *Janine* Barbara Rafferty, *Irene O'Brien* Elaine C Smith, *Ronald* Richard Wilson, Carter Ferguson, Karen Kyle, Nicole Marie Hood, Julie Austin.
• *Dir* Coky Giedroyc, *Pro* David Furnish and Polly Steele, *Ex Pro* J E Beaucaire, Jean Doumanian and Elton John, *Co-Ex Pro* Letty Aronson and John Logigan, *Screenplay* Isla Dewar, *Ph* Brian Tufano, *Pro Des* Lynne Whiteread, *Ed* Patrick Moore and Budge Tremlett, *M* Simon Boswell; Rachmaninoff; songs performed by Imogen Heap, Dolly Parton, Bananarama, Dinah Washington, Sheryl Crow, Naked Funk, Diana Krall, Marianne Faithful, The Honeyz, Trisha Yearwood, Lulu, Kate Bush, The Village People, etc, *Costumes* Michele Clapton, *Ellen's cartoons* Bob Dewar, *Dialect coach* Julia Wilson Dickson.

Magnolia Prods/Sweetland Films/Rocket Pictures-UIP.
97 mins. UK/USA. 1999. Rel: 7 December 2001. Cert 15.

Y

Right: Mexican stand-off: Gaël García Bernal and Diego Luna in Alfonso Cuarón's international hit, *Y Tu Mamá Tambien* (from Icon)

Y Tu Mamá Tambien ★★★¹/₂

When their girlfriends leave for Europe on vacation, best friends Julio and Tenoch, both 17, find boredom settling in quickly. Then, to their surprise, their offer of a trip to the beach is taken up by Luisa Cortés, a beautiful 28-year-old Spanish woman, the wife of Tenoch's cousin... *Y Tu Mamá Tambien* is ostensibly about two friends on the brink of manhood who discover that there's more to life than sex, drugs and alcohol. And yet the film, for all its liberating sexual talk (and frequent nudity), works best as a colourful, panoramic view of contemporary Mexico. As the lecherous trio looks in vain for the illusory beach dubbed 'Heaven's Mouth', our protagonists' physical journey proves far more interesting than their emotional one. Indeed, the boys first meet their sexual catalyst, Luisa, in the very presence of the President and then, as they search for their sexual Eden, numerous layers of Mexico are peeled away until, on a secluded, idyllic beach, their personal nirvana is achieved – far from the limousines and flag-waving pomp that informs the life of Tenoch's father. It is a moment of fleeting happiness, driven home when the narrator informs us that the native fisherman befriended by the trio ends up working as a janitor for a luxurious, beach-front hotel. Indeed, the film works best as an allegory, supplanting the loss of innocence experienced by the boys for that of Mexico itself. **English title:** *And Your Mother Too.*

• *Luisa Cortés* Maribel Verdú, *Julio Zapata* Gaël García Bernal, *Tenoch Iturbide* Diego Luna, *Ana Morelos* Ana López Mercado, *Cecilia Huerta* María Aura, *Diego 'Saba' Madero* Andrés Almeida, *Montes de Oca* Juan Carlos Remolina, *Jesús 'Chuy' Carranza* Silverio Palacios, *narrator* Daniel Giménez Cacho.
• *Dir* Alfonso Cuarón, *Pro* Alfonso Cuarón and Jorge Vergara, *Ex Pro* Sergio Agüero, David Linde and Amy Kaufman, *Co-Pro* Sandra Solares, *Screenplay* Alfonso Cuarón and Carlos Cuarón, *Pro Des* Miguel Angel Álvarez, *Ed* Alfonso Cuarón and Alex Rodríguez, *M* various; songs performed by Bran Van 3000, Eek-a-Mouse, Molotov y Dub Pistols, Supernova, Eagle Eye Cherry, Natalie Imbruglia, Brian Eno, Frank Zappa, etc, *Costumes* Gabriela Diaque.

Jorge Vergara/Producciones Anhelo-Icon.
106 mins. Mexico. 2001. Rel: 12 April 2002. Cert 18.

Zoolander ★★¹/₂

Derek Zoolander is the world's most famous male supermodel. But when he loses the Male Model of the Year title (which he has held for three consecutive terms), he wonders if there's more to life than being really, really, really good-looking...
The reason that Ben Stiller was so funny in *There's Something About Mary* and *Meet the Parents* is that he remained essentially straight in the face of escalating silliness. Here, he uses all his resources (and friends and family) to try and prove that he can be funny himself. Affecting an odd accent and a bizarre stare, he creates something that might have been amusing at the tail end of a dinner party but which can hardly sustain an entire movie. For all its occasional belly laughs, *Zoolander* is little more than a rehash of the *Dumb and Dumber* formula, relocated to the world of male fashion modelling. Of course, this narcissistic arena is ripe for Stiller's lampooning, but he seems unable to let a joke be. When Zoolander misspells 'day', it would have been funnier if he'd just let it go at D-A-Y-E. But, no, Stiller has him spell it D-A-I-Y-E, stooping to the intellectual level of his own protagonist. Incidentally, with the writer-producer-director-star cast as the world's most beautiful man, this prompts uncomfortable comparisons with Barbra Streisand's vanity project, *The Mirror Has Two Faces*.

• *Derek Zoolander* Ben Stiller, *Hansel* Owen Wilson, *Jacobim Mugatu* Will Ferrell, *Matilda Jeffries* Christine Taylor, *Katinka* Milla Jovovich, *Maury Ballstein* Jerry Stiller, *Larry Zoolander* Jon Voight, *J P Prewitt* David Duchovny, *Scrappy Zoolander* Judah Friedlander, *Todd* Nathan Lee Graham, Christian Slater, Cuba Gooding Jr, Steve Kmetko, Tommy Hilfiger, Donald Trump, Victoria Beckham, Natalie Portman, Fabio, Lennie Kravitz, Gwen Stefani, Heidi Klum, Paris Hilton, David Bowie, L'il Kim, Stephen Dorff, Garry Shandling, Claudia Schiffer, Sandra Bernhard, Lukas Haas, Veronica Webb, *evil DJ* Justin Theroux, Andy Dick, Jennifer Coolidge, Nora Dunn, Jerry Stahl, Richard Stanley, Svetlana, *John Wilkes Booth* James Marsden, Richie Rich, and (uncredited) Anne Meara, Winona Ryder, *Luke Zoolander* Vince Vaughn, Emma Bunton, Billy Zane.
• *Dir* Ben Stiller, *Pro* Stiller, Scott Rudin and Stuart Cornfeld, *Ex Pro* Joel Gallen, Adam Schroeder and Lauren Zalaznick, *Co-Pro* Celia Costas, *Assoc Pro* Monica Levinson, *Screenplay* Stiller, Drake Sather and John Hamburg, *Ph* Barry Peterson, *Pro Des* Robin Standefer, *Ed* Greg Hayden, *M* David Arnold; John Barry, Richard Strauss; songs performed by Frankie Goes To Hollywood, Orgy, Mike Simpson, The Wallflowers, Wham!, The Hollies, Rufus Wainwright, Loverboy, David Holmes, BT, David Bowie, Michael Jackson, No Doubt, Mystikal, The Crystal Method, Herbie Hancock, Walter Murphy, etc, *Costumes* David C Robinson

Paramount/Village RoadshowVH1/NPV Entertainment/ Red Hour Prods-UIP.
89 mins. USA. 2001. Rel: 30 November 2001. Cert 12.

Video Releases
from July 2001 through to June 2002

by Daniel O'Brien

After the Storm

Based on a story by Ernest Hemingway, this passable melodrama involves a luxury yacht, a violent storm and two sets of salvage hunters. Dwelling on the theme of romantic betrayal, director Guy Ferland gets things off to a slow start, building up the tension and dramatic force in the last half hour. There's a case for arguing that Hemingway's work doesn't really lend itself to cinematic treatment. For all its merits, *After the Storm* won't silence the doubters. Leading man Benjamin Bratt, best known as Julia Roberts' ex-boyfriend, is a solid actor but lacks star power. The Belize locations are easy on the eye, though.
• Also starring Armand Assante, Stephen Lang, Jennifer Beals, Mili Avital.
High Fliers. November 2001. Cert 15.

American Psycho 2

Whatever its faults, Mary Harron's *American Psycho* (2000) at least captured the darkly satirical edge of Brett Easton Ellis' novel, aided by Christian Bale's deadpan performance as the narcissistic yuppie nutter Patrick Bateman. In *American Psycho 2*, Mila Kunis stars as Rachel Newman, Bateman's only surviving victim. Having given her would-be killer a taste of his own lethal medicine, Rachel enrols in college. Unfortunately, she's developed a liking for serial murder herself and starts bumping off fellow students who get in her way. William Shatner co-stars as Dr Daniels, an FBI profiler turned college professor. Will he figure out what the hell is going on? With a script this poor, it really doesn't matter. Wide of girth and unlikely of hair, Shatner hams it up with his usual self-mocking panache. It's acting, Jim, but not as we know it.
• *Dir* Morgan J Freeman.
Entertainment in Video. April 2002. Cert 18.

Arachnid

Many full moons ago, Jack Sholder directed the enjoyable s-f horror film *The Hidden* (1987), starring the then-fashionable Kyle

MacLachlan as an undercover alien avenger. Fifteen years later, Sholder is still turning out monster movies, of which *Arachnid* is a fair example. Investigating a series of mysterious deaths on a remote island, a team of government scientists discovers a new species of spider. Are these aggressive, virus-carrying creepy-crawlies

Above: The disappointing sequel to *American Psycho* had Bateman's only surviving victim (Mila Kunis) taking up some serial-killing of her own. *American Psycho 2* (from Entertainment)

connected with the crashed UFO found nearby? Could be. Pitched somewhere between *Arachnophobia* (1990) and *Kingdom of the Spiders* (1977), Sholder's film offers good special effects, reasonable scares and more laughs than the makers intended. Co-star Jeffrey Combs, veteran of such horror flicks as *Re-Animator* (1985), *From Beyond* (1986) and *The Frighteners* (1996), adds a touch of spooky class. While *Arachnid* is unlikely to achieve the cult status of *Tarantula* (1955), it's a lot better than *The Giant Spider Invasion* (1975).
• Also starring Andrew Divoff, Mark Frost, Isabel Brook.
Mosaic. February 2002. Cert 15.

Attraction

A radio talk show counsellor becomes obsessed with his ex-lover, then decides to pursue her best friend, an actress. Initially playing the two women against each other, he soon becomes uncertain as to what – or who – he wants. Writer-director Russell De Grazier explores the darker side of human relationships, touching on jealousy and stalking, without producing a perceptive or memorable film. The plot becomes twist-heavy, leading to an abrupt, unsatisfying conclusion.
• Starring Matthew Settle, Tom Everett Scott, Gretchen Mol, Samantha Mathis.
High Fliers. September 2001. Cert 15.

Backflash

Robert Patrick's recent exposure in *The X-Files* has brought some of his lesser efforts out of the woodwork. In this dull thriller, Patrick plays Ray, a discontented video store manager. Hitting the road, he picks up a sultry hitchhiker, Harley (Jennifer Esposito), only to wish he'd let her walk. Tempted by easy money and the prospect of some excitement, Ray agrees to impersonate Harley's husband as part of an elaborate fraud scheme. What could possibly go wrong? Perfectly cast as the liquid metal cyborg assassin in *Terminator 2: Judgement Day*

(1991), Patrick is still looking for his ideal flesh-and-blood role. Patrick fans claim that *Backflash* improves with a second viewing.
• *Director* Phillip Jones.
Third Millennium. January 2002. Cert 15.

Beethoven's 4th

Ten years ago the first *Beethoven* (1992) was a big hit, with audiences unable to resist the cute St Bernard dog and his lovable antics. Three sequels on, the formula is looking extremely tired. Judge Reinhold, who took over from original star Charles Grodin for *Beethoven's 3rd*, returns as the bemused family patriarch. The glory days of *Gremlins* (1984) and *Beverly Hills Cop* (1984) must seem very far away.
• *Director* David Mickey Evans
Universal Pictures. June 2002. Cert U.

The Book That Wrote Itself

This poorly produced, intermittently funny Irish comedy is virtually a one-man show. Writer-director Liam O Mochain stars as an aspiring novelist whose literary 'masterpiece' is rejected by every publisher on the grounds that the story is ridiculous. Determined to prove them wrong, he attempts to live out his book's plot, recording his experiences with a video camera. No great shakes as a filmmaker, O Mochain shows some comic imagination, though the material is stretched very thin to achieve feature length. One of the best sequences takes place at the Venice Film Festival, with O Mochain's character interacting with real-life celebrities George Clooney, Kenneth Branagh, Chazz Palminteri and Melanie Griffith.
• Also starring Antoinette Guiney, Orlaith Rafter, Paul Mahon, Philip Owen.
West We Will Go. June 2002. Cert 15.

Boycott

On 1 December 1955, Alabama resident Rosa Parks, a middle-aged black woman, refused to give up her seat in the whites-only section of a crowded bus. Arrested for this breach of segregation law, Parks quickly

became a cause celebre, prompting a massive black boycott of public transport. A true-life story well worth telling, *Boycott* avoids the TV-movie-of-the-week approach, delivering a powerful and moving drama. Iris Little-Thomas gives a fine performance as Parks, who wouldn't surrender her dignity to an oppressive, racist society.
• Also starring Jeffrey Wright, Terrence Dashon Howard, Carmen Ejogo, C C H Pounder.
Dir Clark Johnson.
High Fliers. October 2001. Cert 15.

Call Me Claus

It sounds awful: Santa Claus, played by the late great Nigel Hawthorne, persuades Whoopi Goldberg to take his place. In fact, this feelgood Yuletide fantasy is surprisingly entertaining, despite obvious debts to *A Christmas Carol* and *Miracle on 34th Street*. Goldberg plays Lucy Cullins, a jaded television producer for a home-shopping channel. In need of an inexpensive actor to play Father Christmas, she hires Chris (Hawthorne), who turns out to be the real thing. After 200 years on the job, Chris faces mandatory retirement and has to find a replacement by Christmas Eve. After a slow start, *Call Me Claus* is solid, predictable entertainment, which keeps the sentiment to a minimum. Hawthorne and Goldberg make for an effective, if unlikely comedy team. Probably not the movie swansong Hawthorne would have liked, however.
• *Dir* Peter Werner.
Columbia TriStar. December 2001. Cert PG.

Cheap Killers

Producer-writer Wong Jing and director Clarence Fok scored a major cult hit with *Naked Killer* (1992), a chic, utterly absurd tale of rival hit-women. This 1998 saga of the Hong Kong underworld attempts the same pseudo-noir approach, lending its violent set pieces a pop-video ambience. Wong has been turning out high-energy, low-style exploitation for over 20 years. Fok is more

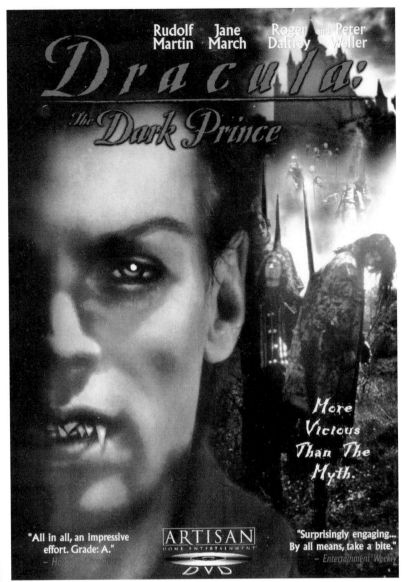

RUDOLF
MARTIN

JANE
MARCH

Roger and Peter
Daltrey Weller

Dracula:
The Dark Prince

More
Vicious
Than The
Myth.

"All in all, an impressive
effort. Grade: A."
– Ho...

ARTISAN
HOME ENTERTAINMENT
DVD

"Surprisingly engaging...
By all means, take a bite."
– Entertainment Weekly

ambitious, directing the enjoyable time-travel fantasy *The Iceman Cometh* (1989), starring Yuen Biao and Maggie Cheung. Boasting character names such as Sam Cool and Discipline King, *Cheap Killers* will probably please *Naked Killer*'s fans, despite the lack of lesbian assassins. Viewers who regarded the earlier movie as a camp load of old nonsense are unlikely to be converted.
• Starring Sunny Chan, Kathy Chow, Alex Fong, Stephen Fung.
Hong Kong Classics. February 2002. Cert 18.

Children of the Corn – Revelation

Even die-hard *Corn* fans – if they exist – will be disappointed with this weak seventh instalment. Bored with their smalltown existence in the Bible Belt, the demonic kids now hang around a derelict apartment block in Omaha, Nebraska. Meanwhile, a young woman searching for her grandmother runs into all kinds of trouble. The only name actor in the cast is Michael Ironside, a quality bad guy in films such as *Scanners* (1980) and *Total Recall* (1990). Cast as an unlikely priest, Ironside drifts in and out of the narrative to no great purpose. Faced with an admittedly uphill task, director Guy Magar and scriptwriter S J Smith simply give up. As the '15' certificate suggests, the gore factor has been toned down from the previous films, leaving horror fans little reason to watch. The only revelation here is that this dead-end franchise can still turn a profit.
• Also starring Claudette Mink, Kyle Cassie, Troy Yorke.
Buena Vista. February 2002. Cert 15.

Common Ground

A moving look at intolerance towards homosexuality, *Common Ground* combines three stories linked by a Vietnam war veteran, running the gamut from a Wren dishonourably discharged from the Navy in 1954 to the contemporary marriage of two gay men.
• Starring Edward Asner, Beau Bridges, Margot Kidder, Eric Stoltz.
Dir Donna Deitch.
Paramount. May 2002. Cert 15.

Contagion

Since hanging up his *Robocop* body armour, Peter Weller has enjoyed a low-key film career, with the notable exception of *Naked Lunch* (1991). This low-grade science fiction thriller isn't going to change anything. Co-star William Hurt won an Academy Award for his performance in *Kiss of the Spider Woman* (1985), which now seems ancient history. Infected by one of those nasty man-made viruses, Weller is pursued across the USA by Hurt's government investigator. Throwing in shady cover-ups and personal betrayal, the script is a hopeless case from the start.
• Also starring Natascha McElhone.
High Fliers. October 2001. Cert 15.

Dark Prince – The Legend of Dracula

Crassly marketed as '*Braveheart* meets *Interview with the Vampire*,' this American TV movie tells the gory true-life story of Vlad the Impaler, the no-nonsense 15th century tyrant often cited (unconvincingly) as Bram Stoker's inspiration for Count Dracula. More of a gory swashbuckler than a horror film, *Dark Prince* stars intense German actor Rudolf Martin, who played Dracula in an episode of *Buffy the Vampire Slayer*. The script, by Thomas Baum, doesn't flinch from depicting some of Vlad's notorious real-life atrocities, but is less successful in attempting to give him a quasi-supernatural dimension. Director Joe Chappelle,

who cut his scary teeth on the mediocre *Halloween: The Curse of Michael Myers* (1995), does much better here. While the TV budget precludes large-scale battle scenes, Chappelle does make good use of the authentic Romanian locations and supporting cast, which includes Jane March, Peter Weller (who'd make a good vampire himself) and Who frontman Roger Daltrey.
• Original title: *Dark Prince – The True Story of Dracula* (which it patently isn't).
High Fliers. August 2001. Cert 18.

Dead or Alive

This is an extraordinary 1999 Japanese thriller, pitting local gangsters against Chinese interlopers, with a world-weary cop caught in between. Directed by Takashi Miike, who made the unsettling *Audition*, this violent, often surreal yakuza drama takes the genre to strange new places. Featuring a gay man murdered mid-sodomy, huge quantities of cocaine and a dazzling restaurant shootout, *Dead or Alive* is a striking, if perverse, achievement.
• Starring Riki Takeuchi, Sho Aikawa, Renji Ishibashi, Hitoshi Ozawa, Susumu Terajima, Ren Osugi.
Tartan Asia Extreme. June 2002. Cert 18.

Double Take

Yet another reworking of Mark Twain's *The Prince and the Pauper*. A business executive and a streetwise hustler exchange identities after a passport switch. Designed as an action comedy showcase for Orlando Jones and Eddie Griffin, this convoluted farce never catches fire. Loosely based on the British film *Across the Bridge* (1957), starring the late Rod Steiger, the script throws in the CIA, political strife in Mexico and assassination. *Trading Places* (1983) did it a lot better.
• Dir George Gallo.
Buena Vista. December 2001. Cert 12.

Get Well Soon

Vincent Gallo and Courtney Cox star in this reasonable romantic comedy. Ambitious high school student Kevin (Gallo) dumps long-term girlfriend Lily (Cox) and heads for Los Angeles in search of media stardom. Changing his name to Bobby Bishop, he sells out and finds fame, fortune and ego massage as a late-night chat show host. Soon disenchanted with 'Bobby', Kevin wants to win back Lily, his first love, even if it means abandoning the Hollywood high life. Despite a few nods to the much darker *Network* (1976), writer-director Justin McCarthy keeps things upbeat. While the moody, introspective Gallo and the chirpy Cox are an unlikely screen couple, the combination works well.
• Also starring Jeffrey Tambor, Tate Donovan.
High Fliers. May 2002. Cert 15.

Gonin

One of the most exciting, innovative thrillers in years, this 1995 Japanese production leaves most Hollywood examples of the genre standing. Five losers team up to rob a 'respectable' yakuza clan of 100 million yen. A one-eyed gay hitman ('Beat' Takeshi Kitano) is dispatched to settle the score. Writer-director Takashi Ishii, who began his career in comic books, delivers a visually audacious, extremely well-acted drama. Flash frames, slow motion, jump cuts and discoloration are expertly employed to produce a dreamlike disorientation, while ingenious sound design, noir-style lighting and bold colour schemes evoke a hellish, unfeeling world where brutal violence erupts out of nowhere. The gang members, who include a busted cop, failed businessman, lovelorn pimp and male prostitute, represent the dark underbelly of Japan's apparently well-ordered society. The film also touches on the country's 'burst bubble' economy, the stigma of unemployment and trial by media. Alongside the social comment, *Gonin* offers an unusually frank depiction of homosexuality, both tender and sado-masochistic. This is one film that really does require two viewings for a full appreciation. And Goro Tasukawa's outstanding score deserves a CD release.
• Also starring Koichi Sato, Masahiro Motoki, Jinpachi Nezu, Naoto Takenaka, Toshiyuki Nagashima.
MIA/Tokyo Bullet. December 2001. Cert 18.

Good Advice

Successful Wall Street broker Ryan Turner (Charlie Sheen) seems to have it all: a great job, a beautiful girlfriend named Cindy, and a whole lot of casual screwing on the side. However, Turner is fired and dumped in rapid succession, while Cindy disappears on a long holiday. Serves him right. As it happens, Cindy writes an agony column, 'Ask Cindy', for the local paper, offering 'advice for the lovelorn'. In need of money, Turner takes over the column while Cindy is away, turning 'Ask Cindy' into a huge success. Unwilling to blow his cover, Turner pretends that he is Cindy, working from home to avoid detection. All kinds of complications ensue, Turner falling for the paper's editor without being able to reveal his 'true' identity. Though hardly a classic of the romantic comedy genre, *Good Advice* is enjoyable viewing, with director Steve Rash moving the predictable plot along at a brisk pace. Sheen and co-star Denise Richards are now a real-life couple; they got married in June 2002.
• Also starring Angie Harmon.
Mosaic. May 2002. Cert 15.

Highway

This is a road movie that begins in Las Vegas and ends in Seattle, stirring up a lot of dust but little else. Pool boy Jack (Jared Leto) and lifeguard Pilot (Jake Gyllenhaal) are bored with their loser lifestyles. While Pilot has been dealing drugs on the side, it's Jack who ends up in big trouble, caught with a mobster's wife. Getting the hell out of Vegas, the boys hit the highway, picking up hitchhiker Cassie (Selma Blair) en route. Needless to say, their past sins soon catch up with them. While leading man

Jared Leto showed promise in *Fight Club* and *Requiem for a Dream*, he needs to find a better starring vehicle than this lame action comedy. Fans of deceased Seattle grunge rocker Kurt Cobain may be intrigued by one of the subplots.

Entertainment in Video. Cert 18. June 2002.

The Huntress – Her Name is Cat

This 1998 Hong Kong babes'n'bullets fest stars Almen Wong as Cat, a *Nikita/Black Cat/Naked Killer*-style hit lady. Short on plot, character and logic, the film unwinds as a series of high-chic action set pieces. Raised in poverty, Cat is big on feral aggression, underlined by amplified panther snarls as she goes into action (the film's Cantonese title translates as 'Panther Girl'). The supporting characters include Cat's lesbian boss, Sister Shin; a single parent cop (Michael Wong); a rival killer (Noelle Tzik), and a whole lot of Triad bad guys. The film's biggest asset is a publicity still of former model Wong in an electric blue plastic bikini, with matching thigh-length boots and sidearm. This image has inspired an American action figure and, one suspects, a fair amount of teenage self-abuse. Apparently, the outfit was neither comfortable nor hard-wearing.

Hong Kong Classics. June 2002. Cert 18.

I Can't Sleep

See *Sleepless*

Iron-Fisted Monk

Hong Kong superstar Sammo Hung made his 1977 directing debut with this Ching Dynasty tale of righteous vengeance. Hung plays Husker, a miller who turns fighting Shaolin monk after the death of his master. When the local Manchu ruler embarks on a campaign of rape and murder, Husker and his Buddhist *sifu* (teacher) decide to take a stand. While Sammo Hung is one of Hong Kong's best filmmakers, *Iron-Fisted Monk* is very much an apprentice work. Working

from a thin script, Hung throws in split-screens, vertical wipes and freeze-frames to no great purpose. The female characters are stereotyped as either victims or shrews, existing only to be brutalised by the monstrous chief villain. Hung stages an unpleasant, uncomfortably prolonged rape scene, cut by over a minute for this belated UK premiere. Given the film's grim tone, the broad comedy interludes seem incongruous by Western standards. The final battle is well handled, though one of the Manchu bad guys seems to have no idea why he's fighting to the death.

Hong Kong Legends/Medusa. October 2001. Cert 18.

The Irrefutable Truth About Demons

See *The Truth About Demons*

Jane Doe

This hard-edged independent movie stars Calista Flockhart as a pathetic, destitute drug addict. Several billion lightyears removed from *Ally McBeal*, *Jane Doe* offers an unflinching, sexually frank portrayal of street life, balancing its downbeat quality with a sense of tenderness and some unexpected story turns. Noted for her emaciated figure, Flockhart is physically ideal for the title character. Winner of the Best Feature Award at the New York International Film Festival.

• *Dir* Paul Peditto.

MIA. April 2002. Cert 15.

Joe Dirt

From the people who brought you *Deuce Bigalow: Male Gigolo* (1999)… David Spade stars as natural born loser Joe Dirt, poor-but-honest white trash, in this dismal comedy. Searching for his long-lost family, Joe encounters various weird and wacky characters, ending up in Los Angeles (where else?). Christopher Walken contributes one of his trademark bonkers cameos, which is the only reason to sit through this trash. To

quote one of Spinal Tap's reviews, executive producer Adam Sandler is 'treading water in a sea of retarded sexuality.' Not so much *Joe Dirt* as *Jack Sh*t*.

• Also starring Brittany Daniel, Dennis Miller.

Columbia TriStar. November 2001. Cert 12.

Last Cry

See *Sexual Predator*

Liberty Stands Still

Hailed as the straight-to-video event of the year, this high-concept hostage thriller boasts a solid star line-up. Linda Fiorentino plays arms dealer Liberty, who finds herself at the wrong end of Wesley Snipes' high-powered rifle. She's also handcuffed to a hot dog stand fitted with high explosives. It seems that Fiorentino and husband Oliver Platt are indirectly responsible for the death of Snipes' wife, and he's going to make them pay. While the premise is reasonable, *Liberty Stands Still* says little about the ethics of the arms trade, political corruption and individual responsibility. Nor does it really work as a thriller, dissipating the 'real-time' tension with monotonous rapid-fire editing. Snipes' grieving avenger, an ex-CIA man, becomes wearying, leaving the viewer more interested in Fiorentino and Platt.

• Also with Martin Cummings, Jonathan Scarfe, Hart Bochner.

Dir Kari Skogland.

High Fliers. June 2002. Cert 15.

A Map of the World

Sigourney Weaver and Julianne Moore star in this thoughtful, if harrowing, tale of child abuse and infant death, set in the Midwest of the United States. Weaver plays an outspoken school nurse, accused of an appalling crime, already condemned by smalltown prejudice. Director Scott Elliott, making his feature debut, avoids easy sentiment and ready answers. A mother herself, Weaver's character remains an enigma, the film shying away from a safe happy ending. Weaver

regards the film as one of her best: 'American audiences … are conditioned to seeing predictable emotionalism in films and *A Map of the World* didn't do that.'
• Also starring David Strathairn, Chloë Sevigny.
High Fliers. March 2002. Cert 15.

Once in the Life

Laurence Fishburne wrote, produced, directed and starred in this film version of his own play. A downbeat New York tale of junkies and dealers, *Once in the Life* is an impressive if uneven piece of work, blending violence, humour, rhyming narrative and sentiment. British actor Eamonn Walker gives a commanding performance as an ex-con, now married and supposedly straightened out, who tangles with a Chinese Triad. As one character puts it: 'Once in the life, always in the life.' Jazz musician Branford Marsalis contributes a fine score.
• Also starring Titus Welliver, Annabella Sciorra.
High Fliers. January 2002. Cert 18.

On the Edge

Engrossing look at a 19-year-old lad who is committed to a psychiatric hospital after driving a stolen car over a cliff. With sympathetic characters and an honest portrayal of mental instability, this Irish drama addresses serious issues with some skill.
• Starring Cillian Murphy, Stephen Rea, Tricia Vessey.
Dir John Carney.
Universal. May 2002. Cert 15.

Possessed

Supposedly based on the 'true' story that inspired William Peter Blatty's novel *The Exorcist*, this feeble supernatural melodrama makes the Devil look extremely dull. Produced for cable television, *Possessed* is closer in quality to *Hudson Hawk* (1991). Director Steven E De Souza – who made his name scripting the action blockbuster *Die Hard* (1988) – displays the same lack of visual flair that characterised *Street Fighter* (1994), his directing debut. Even allowing for its small screen origins, *Possessed* is flat, indifferently staged and unscary. Leading man Timothy Dalton is not a convincing screen priest. Co-star Christopher Plummer, who battled the undead in *Vampires in Venice* (1988), goes through the motions with little enthusiasm. For all its crass pretensions, William Friedkin's 1973 film of the Blatty novel at least delivered a few visceral shocks.
• Also starring Henry Czerny.
Mosaic. July 2001. Cert 15.

Red Wolf

A 1995 Hong Kong take on Steven Seagal's *Under Siege* (1992), directed by Yuen Woo Ping. Kenny Ho stars as Alan, an unhappy security guard working on an ocean liner. Villains Ngai Sing and Elaine Lui plot to steal the ship's cargo, high-quality uranium, and only one man can stop them. Unfortunately, it's not Jackie Chan, Jet Li, Chow Yun-Fat, Sammo Hung, Donnie Yen, Yuen Biao or even Jimmy Wang Yu; it's unconvincing action man Ho. Yuen Woo Ping is one of the world's greatest action choreographers, having worked on *Once Upon a Time in China* (1991), *Fist of Legend* (1994), *The Matrix* (1999) and *Crouching Tiger, Hidden Dragon* (2000). And his films as a director include the outstanding *Magnificent Butcher* (1979), *Dreadnought* (1981), *Iron Monkey* (1993) and *Tai Chi Master* (1993, aka *Twin Dragons*). But *Red Wolf* is a major disappointment, poorly scripted and indifferently staged. Exactly why Hong Kong Legends selected this film for a special 'Platinum Edition' will remain one of life's small mysteries.
• Also starring Christy Chung.
Hong Kong Legends/Medusa. February 2002. Cert 18.

Replicant

Having demonstrated his versatility playing identical twins in *Double Impact* (1991), Jean-Claude Van Damme treats the world to another dual role. *Replicant* casts Van Damme as both a serial killer and the non-homicidal clone created to bring him in. Or take him out. Back in straight-to-video land, where he surely belongs, Van Damme goes through the motions, soft-spoken and moody between the punch-ups. Co-star Michael Rooker, best known for his chilling performance in *Henry: Portrait of a Serial Killer* (1990), acts Jean-Claude off the screen. Compared to Hong Kong stars such as Jackie Chan and Jet Li, Van Damme's martial arts moves look decidedly lacklustre. That said, *Replicant* is no better or worse than the bulk of the Van Damme filmography.
• *Dir* Ringo Lam.
Also with Catherine Dent, Ian Robison.
Columbia TriStar. January 2002. Cert 18.

Route 666

Clever title, no? FBI agents Lou Diamond Phillips and Lori Petty are escorting a fugitive mob witness through the Arizona desert when they stumble across a little-known highway. Nicknamed Route 666, this particular back road is haunted by zombies, victims of a nasty chaingang murder many years before. Still aggrieved after all this time, the vengeful undead rise from the blacktop, attacking unwary travellers with hammer drills and steamrollers. Meanwhile, a team of enthusiastic, if incompetent, Mafia hitmen continue their dogged pursuit of our heroes. Director William Wesley does fairly well with a hackneyed script that blends the usual zombie clichés with a touch of post-*Scream* self-parody. While the shock moments don't always work, despite some effective zombie make-up, the eerie desert setting adds a genuine frisson. If former *Young Gun* Phillips and failed *Tank Girl* Petty are not the most scintillating leads, they at least know how to shoot and run. The film has been compared by some to the work of Quentin Tarantino, which isn't such a big compliment these days. Just remem-

ber: 'Once on the road to Hell, there's no turning back'.
• Also starring Steven Williams.
High Fliers. February 2002. Cert 18.

Sexual Predator

This is one of those tedious 'erotic thrillers' which offers precious little of either commodity. A parole officer (Angie Everhart) becomes involved with a dubious 'fashion' photographer (Richard Grieco), stripping off at the drop of a lens cap. Columbia TriStar must have better soft-porn titles lurking in their back catalogue. The BBFC have cut this release by 52 seconds, removing footage of 'potentially harmful sexual activity'. How about potentially brain-numbing straight-to-video drivel?

• Also known as *Last Cry*.
Dir Robert Angelo and Rob Spera.
Columbia TriStar. December 2001. Cert 18.

Sleepless

Dario Argento's gruesome thriller has been hailed as a return to form for the giallo master after years of tiresome self-plagiarism. Released in Italy as *Nonhosonno/I Can't Sleep*, the film reunites Argento with Goblin, the musicians responsible for the classic *Suspiria* (1976) score. Max Von Sydow stars as a retired policeman who goes back into action when a supposedly closed case bursts wide open in a flood of gore. Unfortunately, *Sleepless* doesn't live up to the advance hype, exhibiting Argento's weaknesses far more than his

strengths. The script is thin, boasting just a handful of good ideas, and the dubbed supporting cast barely register. The killer's anonymous female victims are uniformly unsympathetic, doing little to alter Argento's image as a rampant misogynist. The film does include the novelty of murder by cor anglais, however.
• MIA. January 2002. Cert 18.

Slow Burn

See *Wilder*

Stormriders

Andrew Lau Wei Keung's 1998 swordplay epic was a smash hit in its native Hong Kong, out-grossing *Crouching Tiger, Hidden Dragon* by nearly 3-1. Based on a popular comic book, *Stormriders* tells the story of Wind (Ekin Cheng) and Cloud (Aaron Kwok), two martial arts masters employed by Lord Conquer. After ten years of loyal service, the duo discovers that Conquer murdered their fathers and so vow a bloody revenge. Filled to bursting with zero-gravity fight scenes, *Stormriders* delivers the action goods. What it lacks is the mythic quality of earlier Hong Kong films such as Tsui Hark's *Zu: Warriors from the Magic Mountain* (1983). The uneven CGI effects are a mixed blessing. Co-star Aaron Kwok is also a hugely successful pop star.
• Also starring Shinichi 'Sonny' Chiba, Kirsty Yeung, Shu Qi, Michael Tse, Lai Yiu Cheung.
MIA. October 2001. Cert 12.

Stranger Inside

Made for American cable television, this is a grim-as-hell prison drama about a mother and daughter reunited behind bars. Director Cheryl Dunye, who also co-wrote the script, manages to generate viewer involvement despite unsympathetic characters. Give or take a few lapses into WIP (Women in Prison) cliché, *Stranger Inside* carries an unexpected emotional charge.
• Starring Yolonda Ross, Davenia McFadden, Rain Phoenix.
High Fliers. December 2001. Cert 18.

Styx

This is a formula heist movie starring Peter Weller, Angus McFadyen and straight-to-video favourite Bryan Brown. Featuring the usual plot twists and double-crosses, *Styx* falls several million miles short of *Reservoir Dogs* and *The Usual Suspects*. Director Alex Wright handles the action with little flair. Good title, though.
• High Fliers. January 2002. Cert 18.

Sugar and Spice

When a football cheerleader becomes pregnant by her star quarterback boyfriend, the happy couple are disowned by their families and face a bleak future. Luckily, the teenage mother's fellow dancers decide to support her, even if it means turning to crime. After the embarrassment of *Live Virgin* (US: *American Virgin*), star Mena Suvari seemed headed for a rapid career-fade. Despite the lame premise, *Sugar and Spice* is a watchable teen comedy, performed with some verve. It's certainly better than *The Musketeer*.
• Also starring Marla Sokoloff,
Marley Shelton.
Dir Francine McDougall.
Entertainment in Video. September 2001.
Cert 15.

Sunset Strip

Covering the lives of a group of wannabes over a 24-hour period on Hollywood's Sunset Strip in 1974, this is an agreeable ensemble comedy that covers familiar territory with some nuance. Great soundtrack, too.
• Starring Anna Friel, Rory Cochrane,
Simon Baker, Nick Stahl, Adam Goldberg,
Tommy Flanagan, John Randolph, Jared
Leto.
Dir Adam Collis.
Twentieth Century Fox. December 2001.
Cert 15.

Tesis

Alejandro Amenábar's success with *The Others* has prompted interest in the writer-director's earlier work, made in his native Spain. *Tesis* is his 1995 debut feature, a provocative thriller about voyeurism and obsession. Student Angela (Ana Torrent) is researching a thesis on the ever-contentious theme of screen violence. Searching through a gore-freak's video collection, she unearths a tape which appears to be a genuine 'snuff' movie. Angela shares this sinister discovery with fellow student Chema (Rafael Martinez) and the intrepid pair attempt to track down the people responsible. The most likely suspect is Bosco (Eduardo Noriega), a charismatic yet callous student who both attracts and repels Angela. Determined to solve the mystery, Angela places herself in extreme danger and looks likely to become the next snuff 'star'. While the plot has major holes – such as Angela's refusal to simply call the police – Amenábar keeps the tension level high. While *Tesis* may not bear close scrutiny, exploiting the appetite for violence it claims to condemn, the film delivers the scary goods with a vengeance.
• Tartan Video. December 2001. Cert 18.

The Third Miracle

In this effective thriller, Ed Harris plays a priest who investigates supposed miracles for the Catholic Church. On the verge of losing his faith, he encounters a woman (Anne Heche) apparently blessed with healing powers. Boasting a better than average script, the film conjures a strong supernatural atmosphere. Bing Crosby aside, few actors make for believable screen priests. Looking dogged in his dog collar, Father Ed at least comes across as a dedicated professional. Meanwhile, Heche's elfin, ethereal features are ideally suited for her otherworldly character.
• Buena Vista. October 2001. Cert 15.

Thug Life

It's business as usual down the LA 'hood, where rivals gangs vie for money, power and women. Popular (?) rappers Willie D, Lady of the Rage and Napoleon lead the cast of this formula melodrama, which has nothing new to say about Black America's urban strife.
• *Dir* Greg Carter.
MIA. June 2002. Cert 18.

Ticker

Some people predicted great things for actor Tom Sizemore after *Saving Private Ryan*. This mediocre thriller is probably not what they had in mind. Sizemore plays another cop-on-the-edge, who teams up with bomb squad veteran Steven Seagal to take out terrorist Dennis Hopper. While the combination of Seagal and Hopper sounds like a dream team for fans of high-camp, heavy-duty action nonsense, neither actor looks very enthusiastic. Director Albert Pyun previously gave the world *The Sword and the Sorcerer* (1982) and *Adrenalin – Fear the Rush* (1995), and supposedly learned his filmmaking craft from master director Akira Kurosawa. He must have skipped a lot of classes.
• Also starring Rozonda 'Chilli' Thomas,
Peter Greene.
Universal Pictures. June 2002. Cert 15.

Time Lapse

Ever wonder what Roy Scheider has been up to since *Jaws*? This lame thriller won't encourage further research. Government agent Clayton Pierce (William McNamara) is on undercover assignment to nail drug-dealing terrorists. Except they're actually trading in nuclear weapons. Upset at this development, Pierce guns down a lot of bad guys but finds his troubles are only beginning. Director David Worth has his work cut out, contending with a confused, feebly plotted script involving double crosses, chess games, an 'oblivion' serum and dead people who may still be alive. Even old pro Scheider just goes through the motions.
• Also starring Dina Meyer, Henry Rollins.
Metrodome. January 2002. Cert 15.

The Truth About Demons

Originally released as *The Irrefutable Truth About Demons*, this low-budget New Zealand horror movie, heavily influenced by Jacques Tourneur's *Night of the Demon*, deserves marks for effort. An anthropologist tangles with a satanic cult and finds his life in extreme danger. Writer-director Glenn Standring delivers several scares and a fair shock ending. Despite its shaky production values and story clichés, *The Truth About Demons* has a disturbing atmosphere as the hero's sense of reality is gradually eroded.

• Starring Karl Urban, Katie Wolfe, Sally Stockwell, Jonathon Hendry.

High Fliers. September 2001. Cert 18.

Tuesdays with Morrie

Sold as 'Jack Lemmon's last and most moving film', this is a shamelessly manipulative tale redeemed by a genuinely touching star performance. Lemmon plays Morrie, a retired lecturer who learns he is terminally ill. Encountering a former pupil, Mitch (Hank Azaria), now a discontented sports journalist, Morrie teaches him how to appreciate the important things in life. Director Mick Jackson piles on the sentiment and only an actor of Lemmon's calibre can overcome the script's trite homilies. *Simpsons* regular Azaria does what he can with an unconvincing character. Supposedly based on a true story.

• **Odyssey. January 2002. Cert PG.**

2000 AD

Hong Kong heartthrob Aaron Kwok stars as a video game genius who uncovers a conspiracy to unleash a millennium bug that will wreck South East Asia's economy. Director Gordon Chan, who made the excellent *Fist of Legend* (1994), delivers a hi-tech s-f fantasy with a breakneck pace. Enhanced by skilful editing and impressive visual effects, *2000 AD* also boasts Yuen Tak's outstanding action choreography. The confused script, heavily rewritten during production, is another matter.

• **Hong Kong Legends/Medusa. September 2001. Cert 18.**

Vacas

In *Vacas/Cows*, Spanish writer-director Julio Medem chronicles the lives and times of two Basque families over several generations. Beginning in 1895 with a blackly comic meditation on the indignities of survival, this fast-paced saga takes in clan feuds, forbidden love, the American Dream and the Spanish Civil War. Life is hard, unpredictable and often short. Only the ever-watchful cows seem to have things in perspective. Made back in 1992, Medem's audacious debut feature packs a whole novel's worth of incident into a brisk 96 minutes.

• Starring Emma Suarez, Carmelo Gomez, Ana Torrent, Karra Elejalde.

Tartan. June 2002. Cert 15.

Wilder

Not a biopic of the late great Billy Wilder, but another maverick cop thriller. This OK effort stars Pam Grier as Della Wilder, a veteran law enforcement officer and single mother. Having played a straitlaced police sidekick in Steven Seagal's *Above the Law/Nico* (1988), Grier clearly relishes the chance to cut loose as a dedicated cop who knows the streets and won't take any jive. Dutch actor Rutger Hauer, the patron saint of straight-to-video action movies, lends solid back-up.

• *Dir* Rodney Gibbons.

High Fliers. December 2001. Cert 18.

Wishmaster 3 – Devil Stone

Blonde yet troubled student Diana (A J Cook) solves a mysterious ancient puzzle, which proves a bad move. Before anyone can yell *Hellraiser*, a demon is unleashed, which murders Diana's Limey professor (Jason Connery) and possesses his corpse. Looking to unlock the gates of Hell, the demon marks time by slicing up Diana's college buddies. The original *Wishmaster* (1997), executive-produced by Wes Craven, at least featured *Candyman* star Tony Todd and Robert Englund, the one and only Freddie Krueger. Two sequels on and the producers can only afford ex-pat Brit actor Connery. Clearly patterned on the hit *Buffy the Vampire Slayer* TV series, *Wishmaster 3* is rapidly sunk by awful spe-

cial effects, non-characters, clunky dialogue and a general lack of talent. Directed by Chris Angel, which sounds like someone's idea of a joke. 'Stunningly poor' said the *Southern Daily Echo*.

• Also starring John Novak, Daniella Evangelista.

Mosaic. December 2001. Cert 18.

Wishmaster 4 – The Prophecy Fulfilled

Wishmaster 3 director Chris Angel returns for this fourth instalment, which manages to be even worse. As before, an evil djinn dupes unwary victims into making three wishes, prompting the inevitable bloody carnage. This time out, the bad genie possesses an attorney (subtext?), commits a few murders and falls in love. The gory killings are nasty rather than horrific, while the cut-price special effects verge on the amateurish.

• Starring Michael Trucco, Tara Spencer Nairn.

Mosaic. June 2002. Cert 18.

Zombie Flesh Eaters 2

Originally released as *Zombie 3* (1988), this spaghetti shocker was intended as Lucio Fulci's sequel to his hit *Zombie 2* (1979), aka *Zombie Flesh Eaters*, itself an unofficial prequel to George Romero's superior *Dawn of the Dead* (1978), aka *Zombies*. Unfortunately, Fulci fell ill during production and Bruno Mattei, a hack of no discernible talent, directed most of the film. The negligible plot centres on the 'Death-1 Compound virus', which turns ordinary human beings into flesh-munching zombies. As government scientists try to find a cure, a small group of humans fight for survival. While by no means a great movie, *Zombie Flesh Eaters* had a certain schlock conviction. Aside from some decent gore effects, *Zombie Flesh Eaters 2* is truly terrible, with an absurd script, bad dubbing and braindead characters. The unusually talkative zombies are less than terrifying, though one severed head proves very lively. Uncut, if anyone cares.

• Vipco. Cert 18. March 2002.

Faces of the Year

ERIC BANA

Born: 9 August 1968 in Melbourne, Australia
Previous occupation: stand-up comic
The films: *The Castle, Chopper, Black Hawk Down, The Nugget*
Next up: The title role in *The Hulk*, directed by Ang Lee. So Bana's future is assured, then
TV: *Full Frontal* (1993), *Eric, The Eric Bana Show, Something in the Air*
In a nutshell: One of the more unlikely actors to break into movies of late, Bana made his name as a stand-up comic in his native Australia. He was then selected by the real-life killer Mark 'Chopper' Read to play him in his screen biography. Bana won the Australian Oscar for his performance and next played a US marine in the box-office smash *Black Hawk Down*. Paul Hogan was never this versatile
Furthermore: Bana originally turned down his agent's request to audition for the title role in *Chopper*. He intended to finish his honeymoon first
He said it: 'The benefit of being in my position is that you get a lot more scripts to read – but then you have less time to read them'

PAUL BETTANY

Born: 27 May 1971 in London, England, raised in Willesden and Harlesden
Previous occupation: busker ('I love playing guitar, but I play like a cobbler')
The films: *Bent* (1997), *The Land Girls, Coming Home* (TVM), *After the Rain, Gangster No. 1, The Suicide Club, Kiss Kiss Bang Bang, Dead Babies* (aka *Mood Swingers*), *A Knight's Tale, A Beautiful Mind* (with Russell Crowe), *The Reckoning* (aka *Morality Play*), *Heart of Me,* Lars von Trier's *Dogville* with Nicole Kidman
Next up: He will star opposite Russell Crowe (again) in the 19th century naval drama *The Far Side of the World* for Peter Weir. He's also lined up to play The Rolling Stones' deceased guitarist Brian Jones in Paul McGuigan's biopic and may star in Mike Figgis' *By Grand Central Station I Sat Down and Wept*, from the novel by Elizabeth Smart. There's also talk of the tennis-themed *Wimbledon* in which he would star opposite Kirsten Dunst for director Richard Loncraine.
TV: *Sharpe's Waterloo* (1997), *Killer Net, Every Woman Knows a Secret, David Copperfield* (as James Steerforth)
In a nutshell: Tall (6'3") English actor with a passing resemblance to the younger Michael Caine. Exhibited a chilling presence in *Gangster No. 1*, then revealed a talent for comedy when he played (a naked) Geoffrey Chaucer in *A Knight's Tale*, for which he was voted Best Supporting British Actor by the London Film Critics' Circle. He was also quite prominent in a film called *A Beautiful Mind*.
Furthermore: When executive producer Stephen Evans offered Bettany a 'pay or play' deal to star in *The Reckoning*, he defended his decision by saying: 'I thought, "We've got to hang on to this guy." It is difficult to finds true movie stars. They don't grow on trees'
He said it: 'It's really difficult to talk about acting because you either sound like a cunt or… I hear a lot of actors say, "Oh, acting is better than working." If it genuinely doesn't cost them anything, then they are better than me'

JOSH HARTNETT

Born: 21 July 1978 in San Francisco, California
Full name: Joshua Daniel Hartnett
The films: *Halloween H20: 20 Years Later* (1998), *Debutante* (aka *Modern*

Girl), *The Faculty*, *The Virgin Suicides*, *Here On Earth*, *Blow Dry*, *Town & Country*, *O*, *Pearl Harbor*, *40 Days and 40 Nights*, *Black Hawk Down*

Next up: Hartnett's next film will most likely be *Wicker Park*, the American remake of the 1996 French thriller, *L'Appartement*. Hartnett will have the lead, as a New York man who fixates on a woman he believes is his long-lost love. Paul McGuigan (*Gangster No. 1*, *The Reckoning*) is pencilled in to direct. Hartnett is also lined up to star in an untitled police drama to be directed by Ron Shelton, with Harrison Ford

TV: *Cracker* (1997)

In a nutshell: Lanky, 6'3" method actor who captured the hearts of teenage girls with his performance as the vulnerable Danny Walker in *Pearl Harbor*. Cemented his stardom with solo billing above the title in *Black Hawk Down*, this time a commercial *and* critical hit. With his looks, physique and dedication, Hartnett could find a permanent niche in the Hollywood landscape

He said it: 'As far as jobs go, I'm doing all right', although 'One day I would love to be a painter'

SCARLETT JOHANSSON

Born: 22 November 1984 in New York, New York

The films: *North* (1994), *Just Cause*, *If Lucy Fell*, *Manny & Lo*, *Fall*, *Home Alone 3*, *The Horse Whisperer*, *My Brother the Pig*, *The Man Who Wasn't There*, *Ghost World*, *An American Rhapsody*, *Eight Legged Freaks*

Next up: *Thumbsucker*, a drama directed and written by Mike Mills and starring Elijah Wood, her *North* co-star

In a nutshell: Intelligent, precocious actress who emerged from 'wise child' roles to play sardonic and/or precocious teenagers. Quite what she was doing in *Eight Legged Freaks*, then, is a mystery (although she did play a sardonic/preco-

cious teenager)

Furthermore: Scarlett was just eight years old when she made her professional debut in *Sophistry*, a play off-Broadway. Her co-star was Ethan Hawke

They said it: 'She's a terrific actress: funny, bright and wise beyond her years' – Terry Zwigoff, director of *Ghost World*

KEIRA KNIGHTLEY

Born: 22 March 1985 in London

The films: *Innocent Lies* (aka *Halcyon Days*) (1995), *Star Wars: Episode One – The Phantom Menace*, *The Hole*, *Bend It Like Beckham*

Next up: The French film *Monsieur N.*, directed by Antoine de Caunes and co-starring Elsa Zylberstein and Stephen Fry

TV: *Coming Home* (1998), *Oliver Twist* (as Rose Fleming), *Princess of Thieves*, *Doctor Zhivago* (as Lara)

In a nutshell: Willowy, stunningly attractive English actress described as the next Julie Christie. Having had a bigger part in *Star Wars: Episode One – The Phantom Menace* than most people realised (she doubled for Natalie Portman, with whom she shares a con-siderable likeness), she landed the second

female lead in *The Hole* and the surprise hit *Bend it Like Beckham*.

Furthermore: Her mother is the dramatist and novelist Sharman Macdonald, who penned the award-winning play *When I Was a Girl I Used to Scream and Shout*

HEATH LEDGER

Born: 4 April 1979 in Perth, Australia

Full name: Heath Andrew Ledger

The films: *Blackrock*, *Paws*, *10 Things I Hate About You*, Gregor Jordan's *Two Hands*, *The Patriot*, *A Knight's Tale*, *Four Feathers*, *Monster's Ball*, *The Sin Eater*

Next up: The title role in *Ned Kelly*, Gregor Jordan's big-screen adaptation of the Booker Prize-winning novel by Peter Carey, co-starring Geoffrey Rush and Rachel Griffiths

TV: *Home and Away* (1988), *Ship to Shore*, *Sweat*, *Roar*, *Bush Patrol*

In a nutshell: The latest in a line of Strine stars to sweep Hollywood off its feet, Heath scored in *10 Things I Hate About You*, played Mel Gibson's heroic son in *The Patriot* and then rocked the medieval world in *A Knight's Tale*. His string of celebrity girlfriends (Jordana

Brewster, Heather Graham, Tara Reid) hasn't exactly harmed his emerging profile, either. Oh, and he was dubbed 'the new Matt Damon' by a fan in *Josie and the Pussycats* (starring Tara Reid)

Furthermore: He turned down the title role in *Spider-Man*

They said it: 'He's got it pretty well wired for his age' – Mel Gibson

BRITTANY MURPHY

Born: 10 November 1977 in Atlanta, Georgia

Real name: Sharon Murphy

The films: *Family Prayers* (1993), *Clueless*, *Freeway*, *Drive*, *Double Jeopardy* (TVM), *The Prophecy II* (aka *God's Army II*), *Bongwater*, *Phoenix*, *Zack and Riba*, *David and Lisa* (TVM), *Falling Sky*, *The Devil's Arithmetic*, *Drop Dead Gorgeous*, *Girl Interrupted*, *Common Ground* (TVM), *Trixie*, *Angels!*, *Cherry Falls*, *Sidewalks of New York*, *Summer Catch*, *Don't Say a Word*, *Riding in Cars With Boys*, *8 Mile*, *Spun*, *Molly Gunn* (title role)

Next up: Shawn Levy's *Just Married*, in which she and Ashton Kutcher play newlyweds whose honeymoon in Venice turns into a nightmare

TV: *Drexell's Class* (1991), *Almost Home*, *Sister Sister*, *King of the Hill* (voice only)

In a nutshell: Since her breakthrough performance in *Clueless* (1995) as the fashion victim Tai Fraiser, Brittany kept a pretty low profile in a slew of either modest parts or modest projects. Then she attracted the attention of critics again in the tragic role of the suicidal Daisy in *Girl, Interrupted* (1999). In the meantime she had honed her craft as a consummate character actress, equally adept at all-out drama or comedy. More recently, she's been taking showier roles in higher-profile pictures (*Don't Say a Word*, *Riding in Cars with Boys*) and is now poised to become a major, major star. And she's still only 24

She said it: 'This [acting] isn't my life. I'm working on working to live, as opposed to living to work'

THE ROCK

Born: 2 May 1972 in Hayward, California

Real name: Dwayne Douglas Johnson

The films: *The Mummy Returns*, *The Scorpion King*

Next up: A film based on the life of the Hawaiian King Kamehameha, whom The Rock will play (was Kamehameha *really* that muscly?)

In a nutshell: The Rock, all 6'5" and 250-plus-pounds of him, is the son of the wrestler Rocky Johnson and grandson of the World Wrestling Federation champ Peter Maivia. After becoming a six-time WWF champ himself – and a sporting phenomenon – he flexed his way into the cinema as the mythical Egyptian warrior the Scorpion King in *The Mummy Returns*. He repeated the role in *The Scorpion King*, which grossed over $157 million worldwide.

Furthermore: He earned a degree in criminology at the University of Miami and penned the No 1 bestseller *The Rock Says…*

He said it: 'My goal in the World Wrestling Federation and that whole sports entertainment industry was to be the absolute best, hands down. I'm not saying, "Dustin Hoffman look out, 'cause The Rock is coming to Hollywood!" But in my genre, whatever that may be, I'll work as hard as I can to be the best.' And: 'Having done my first film – boy, *this* is what I want to do'

They said it: 'This guy has the whole

package – Dwayne's really smart, he's got a lot of charm and a great sense of humour, he's good-looking, and he has a big fan base. And he can kick the shit out of people' – Stephen Sommers, director of *The Mummy Returns*

NAOMI WATTS

Born: 28 September 1968 in Shoreham, England
Previous occupation: model
The films: *For Love Alone* (1986), *Flirting* (with Nicole Kidman), *Matinee*, *Wide Sargasso Sea*, *Gross Misconduct*, *The Custodian*, *Tank Girl*, *Persons Unknown*, *Children of the Corn IV: The Gathering*, *Under the Lighthouse Dancing*, *Dangerous Beauty* (aka *A Destiny of Her Own*), *Babe: Pig in the City* (voice only), *Strange Planet*, *Ellie Parker* (title role), *Down*, *Mulholland Dr.*, *Plots with a View*, *The Ring*, *Le Divorce*
Next up: *Ned Kelly*, with Heath Ledger (qv) and Geoffrey Rush, and probably the romance *21 Grams*, in which she will star opposite Benicio Del Toro and Sean Penn for director Alejandro Gonzalez Inarritu
TV: *Home and Away* (as Julie Gibson), *Brides of Christ*, *Sleepwalkers*
In a nutshell: Beautiful, talented, vulnerable and daring performer who put in her time before deservedly winning ecstatic reviews for David Lynch's *Mulholland Dr.* Also attracted some attention when she accompanied her good friend Nicole Kidman to the premiere of *The Others*. Intriguingly, Naomi and Nicole do share a lot of physical characteristics.
Furthermore: Her father was the sound engineer for Pink Floyd. Oh, and Naomi spelled backwards reads 'I moan'
She said it: 'I want to be brave. I want to explore a side of myself that is blocked or afraid or ashamed and see what that conjures up in me'
They said it: 'I consider her a sister. So now, seeing her gain the success, it's like seeing my sister get all that she wants' –

Nicole Kidman, who befriended Naomi, aged 15, at a casting call for a swimsuit gig

ZHANG ZIYI

Born: 9 February 1980 in Beijing
The films: *The Road Home* (1999), *Crouching Tiger, Hidden Dragon*, *Rush Hour 2*, *The Legend of Zu* (aka *Zu Warriors*), *Warrior* (aka *Musa*), *Hero*
Next up: *2046*, in which she plays a working woman in a futuristic Hong Kong
In a nutshell: Described by *Rush Hour 2* director Brett Ratner as 'the Audrey Hepburn of Asia', Ziyi went from sharing a room with five other people to starring in Zhang Yimou's award-winning *The Road Home*. However, it was her performance as a martial arts vixen in *Crouching Tiger, Hidden Dragon* (the highest-grossing foreign-language film of all time) and the role of the villainous Hu Li in *Rush Hour 2* that cemented her stardom
Furthermore: *People* magazine included her in its '50 Most Beautiful People in the World' feature in 2001
She said it: 'In an ideal world, I'd love to be cast with Al Pacino. I realise there's a huge age gap, but that doesn't seem to matter'

TEN YEARS AGO

Faces of the Year: Halle Berry, Caroline Goodall, Woody Harrelson, Samuel L Jackson, Anthony LaPaglia, Juliette Lewis, Luke Perry, Brad Pitt, Marisa Tomei, Polly Walker

Film World Diary
July 2001 – June 2002

JULY 2001

The strike to be staged by the Screen Actors' Guild, threatened six months ago, has been amicably resolved • Following her break-up with **Benjamin Bratt**, her main squeeze for four years, **Julia Roberts** seeks the solace of her ex-husband, **Lyle Lovett** • *The Fast and the Furious* grosses $100 million in the US • **Harrison Ford** helps rescue **Cody Clawson**, a 13-year-old boy stranded south of Yellowstone National Park in Wyoming. Appearing in his Bell 206 Jet Ranger helicopter, Ford gives the boy a hug and a handshake which, Cody tells his mother, was better than an autograph • A cat fight breaks out on the set of *Wise Girls* after **Mira Sorvino** reprimands her co-star **Mariah Carey** for turning up three hours late for work. Mariah responds by hurling a salt shaker at Sorvino and, according to an onlooker, 'the next thing you know the girls were rolling around on the floor, punching, scratching, pulling hair' • A spokesman for **Tom Cruise** confirms that the actor has been 'dating' **Penélope Cruz**, his co-star in *Vanilla Sky* • *Jurassic Park III* grosses $100m in the US • A criminal complaint is lodged by Animal Amnesty against **Pedro Almodóvar** for the alleged killing of four bulls during the shooting of his latest movie. The film, *Talk to Her*, is the story of a female bullfighter • **Colin Farrell** marries actress **Amelia Warner** (*Quills*) on a beach in Tahiti. No friends or family members are present • *Dr. Dolittle 2* grosses $100m in the US • *The Mummy Returns* grosses $200m in the US – and over $400m worldwide.

AUGUST 2001

Pierce Brosnan ties the knot with TV broadcaster **Keely Shaye-Smith** at the 800-year-old Ballintubber Abbey, in County Mayo, Ireland • It's official: **Penélope Cruz** moves into the Los Angeles home of **Tom Cruise** • **Catherine Deneuve**, 57, is chosen as the new face of L'Oréal and is to launch a hair-care product for mature women • **Jean-Paul Belmondo** suffers a stroke in Corsica and is rushed to a Paris hospital. His condition is said to be serious • *Planet of the Apes* grosses $100m in the US • The *National Enquirer* reveals that **Elizabeth Taylor**, 69, has found a new boyfriend: **Jeff Goldblum**, 48 • In the US, *Rush Hour 2* grosses $100m in its first week, a record for a comedy • **Peter Bart**, editor of *Variety*, is suspended on charges of racism and ordered to attend a 'diversity course' • *American Pie 2* grosses $100m in the US • **Aaliyah** is killed when her private plane crashes on take-off in the Bahamas • **Natasha Lyonne** is charged with driving under the influence after wrapping her Dodge Dollar Rent-a-Car around a road sign in Miami Beach • The *Daily Express* reveals that **Julia Roberts** has run off with a married man, the cameraman **Danny Moder**, whom she met on the set of *The Mexican* • Production on **Darren Aronofsky**'s sci-fi epic *The Last Man* is put back to 2002, when co-star **Cate Blanchett** will have had her baby (which is due in December).

SEPTEMBER 2001

Geena Davis marries neurosurgeon **Dr Reza Jarrahy** in the small town of Wainscott on Long Island, New York • **Anne Heche**, 32, marries the cameraman **Coleman Laffoon**, 27, whom she met while he was making a documentary about her former lover, **Ellen DeGeneres** • *Rush Hour 2* grosses $200m in the US • **Rosanna Arquette** reveals that she is engaged to the 'entertainment executive' **David Codikow**. The couple plan to marry some time next year • **Kate Winslet** separates from her husband, the assistant director **Jim Threapleton**. The couple were married in November 1998 and have one daughter, Mia • In the wake of the terrorist attacks on the World Trade Center and the Pentagon, Hollywood studios cancel the release of the **Anthony Hopkins-Chris Rock** comedy *Bad Company* (about a CIA agent fighting terrorists in New York), the **Tim Allen** farce *Big Trouble* (about a bomb that ends up on a plane) and the **Arnold Schwarzenegger** action-thriller *Collateral Damage* (about a fire-fighter who hunts down terrorists who have killed his wife and son). In addition, Sony delays production on the **Jennifer Lopez** vehicle *Tick-Tock*, the story of an FBI agent on the trail of a terror-ist planting bombs in Los Angeles shopping malls, while Twentieth Century Fox suspend their fire-fighting drama *Truck 44* • Equity, the British actors' union, announces that strike action will

resume from December should a settlement fail to be reached with the Producers Alliance for Cinema and Television. Actors are asking for a greater share of DVD sales and various other residual payments • *The Princess Diaries* grosses $100m in the US • **Jodie Foster** gives birth to a baby boy, Kit, her second child • At the instigation of **Kathy Bates**, the American Academy of Motion Picture Arts and Sciences donates $1 million to the families of the victims of the World Trade Centre disaster • **Stephen Daldry**, director of *Billy Elliot* and *The Hours*, marries his long-standing American girlfriend, Lucy, in secret • In spite of their attempts to keep it secret, the growing friendship between **George Clooney** and **Renée Zellweger** is leaked by a friend of the latter who reveals that 'they're acting like a married couple' •

Left: By August, Tim Burton's 're-imagining' of *Planet of the Apes* had grossed $100 million in the United States

Sharon Stone is rushed to hospi-tal with a subarachnoid brain haemorrhage • **Jennifer Lopez**, wearing a classical gown of Chantilly lace and silk made for her by Valentino, marries dancer **Cris Judd** in a glitzy ceremony in Los Angeles.

OCTOBER 2001

Minnie Driver calls off her engagement to **Josh Brolin**, thus depriving herself of the chance to become the daughter-in-law of **Barbra Streisand**. Streisand had even written a song espe-cially for the wedding • **Sylvester Stallone** and his wife **Jennifer Flavin** are expecting their third child. The bundle should arrive next May • Following the bar-room brawl in April which landed him in prison, **Vince Vaughn** gets into another scrape at the 22nd birthday party of **Rachael Leigh Cook**. After a tussle with an unnamed male guest, the actor is hurled out of the Los Angeles

Goodbar venue by two security guards • In the US, DVD sales of *Snow White and the Seven*

Dwarfs reach a record one mil-lion units within the space of 24 hours on release.

Left: By November, the worldwide gross of *Bridget Jones's Diary* (starring Renée Zellweger) had hit $250 million

NOVEMBER 2001

Bridget Jones's Diary grosses $250m worldwide • **Elizabeth Hurley** announces that she is three months' pregnant. She says

the father-to-be is the American millionaire and film producer **Steve Bing** • **Ben Stiller** and his actress wife **Christine Taylor** are

expecting their first child – next spring • *Monsters, Inc.* grosses over $100m at the US box-office in under ten days • **Tom Cruise** and

Nicole Kidman settle the details of their divorce out of court: Nicole gets the apartment in Sydney and the $10m mansion in Los Angeles, Tom gets the 130-acre ranch in the ski resort of Telluride, the apartment in Manhattan and the house in London • Two months after her separation from Jim Threapleton, Kate Winslet is said to be in love with Sam Mendes, the British Oscar-winning director of *American Beauty* and *Road to Perdition* • Word has it that Kim Basinger, 48 next month, is romantically involved with the rap star Eminem, 29. The actress is playing Eminem's mother in his first film, *8 Mile* • The singer-songwriter Anno Birkin, the 20-year-old son of the director and screenwriter Andrew Birkin (*The Cement Garden, Salt On Our Skin*), is killed in a car crash in Italy. Anno's aunt is the actress Jane Birkin • On its opening weekend, *Harry Potter and the Philosopher's Stone* smashes box-office records on both sides of the Atlantic • Julia Roberts' ex, Benjamin Bratt, and former Bond girl Talisa Soto go on a date and become an item • *Billy Elliot* director Stephen Daldry marries his long-term girlfriend Lucy in New York • Ewan McGregor and his wife celebrate the birth of their second daughter • Andie MacDowell, 43, marries Rhett DeCamp Hartzog, 43, a travelling jewellery salesman, in a private ceremony in Asheville, North Carolina. The couple met in high school Bible Club in South Carolina but only fell in love a year ago • Carol Burnett marries the musician Brian Miller at a quiet ceremony in Los Angeles. Miller, 45, is 23 years Ms Burnett's junior • Actor Tom Sizemore (*Saving Private Ryan*) pops the question to his girl-friend, former Hollywood Madam Heidi Fleiss. The wedding is set for 2002 • Liza Minnelli announces her engagement to the music producer David Gest, whom she is to marry in March at St Patrick's Cathedral in New York. Michael Jackson will give her away and Elizabeth Taylor will be her maid of honour.

DECEMBER 2001

Above: Nicole Kidman arrives at the premiere of *The Others* at the end of October

Another star breaks another record. It is announced that Arnold Schwarzenegger will receive $30 million for reprising his title role in *Terminator 3: Rise of the Machines* • Robert Zemeckis marries for the second time (his first wife was the actress Mary Ellen Trainor), tying the knot with the actress Leslie Harter in Venice, Italy • Cate Blanchett is the proud mother of a baby boy, Dashiell John, who is born in London • Arnold Schwarzenegger suffers several fractured ribs after falling off his motorcycle in California • It's official: Kate Winslet is divorced from her husband of three years, assistant director James Threapleton • Charles Bronson's battle with Alzheimer's is made public, in spite of efforts by his family to keep the news secret • Ashley Judd marries the Edinburgh-born racing driver Dario Franchitti at Skibo Castle, Scotland, the very same pile where Guy and Madge Ritchie exchanged their vows. Edward Norton and Salma Hayek are there to cheer the couple on • Nicole Kidman is reportedly dating the Italian filmmaker Fabrizio Mosca • Winona Ryder is arrested for shoplifting, charged with felony grand theft by the Beverly Hills police department. The actress is caught on video removing security sensors from clothes, hair accessories and jewellery worth in the region of $4700, bagging them and then leaving the store, Saks Fifth Avenue • Joan Collins announces her engagement to the Peruvian-born Percy Gibson, who, at 36, is 32 years her junior • Apparently, Keanu Reeves turns his romantic gaze from occasional girlfriend Amanda de Cadenet to the unknown **Rachael Jones**, a 26-year-old newsreader from Hull whom he has met in Sydney • The Oscar-winning cinematographer **Janusz Kaminski** (*Schindler's List, Saving Private Ryan*) files for divorce from his wife of six years, **Holly Hunter**. Kaminski cites the old 'irreconcilable differences' • The actress **Frances Fisher** (*Titanic, True Crime*) is hospitalised with second-degree burns to her hands following a fire at her home in British Columbia • *The Lord of the Rings: The Fellowship of the Ring* grosses $100m in the US • *Ocean's 11* grosses $100m in the US.

JANUARY 2002

Ben Kingsley is made a knight in the New Year's Honours • *The Lord of the Rings: The Fellowship of the Ring* grosses $200m at the US box-office • **Drew Barrymore** moves out of the home she has shared with her husband **Tom Green** for almost six months • Film producer **Steve Bing** reveals to friends that he thinks the father of **Elizabeth Hurley**'s unborn child is actually **Matthew Perry** • *Harry Potter and the Philosopher's Stone* grosses $300m in the US, making it the top money-making film of 2001 • **Minnie Driver** is hauled over the coals in the UK media for calling **Judi Dench** 'a small, round, middle-aged, mothering type' who, in Hollywood, 'would melt into the crowd in a second.' In Britain, you do not mess with Dame Judi • Outside a Seattle cinema **John Guth**, 32, and **Jeff Tweiten**, 24, start queuing to see *Star Wars Episode II: Attack of the Clones*, which opens in May • *Amélie* grosses over $100m worldwide, becoming the first French film to do so • **Kim Delaney** (*That Was Then…This is Now, Mission to Mars*, TV's *NYPD Blue*) is arrested on charges of drunken driving, but refuses to take a blood-alcohol test. After pleading no contest to reckless driving, the actress is sentenced to two years' summary probation, fined $300 and ordered to complete a safe-driving class • *Monsters, Inc.* grosses $250m in the US and $300m worldwide, almost simultaneously.

FEBRUARY 2002

A Beautiful Mind grosses $100 million in the US • **Nicolas Cage** and **Lisa Maria Presley** break off their engagement but insist that they are still good friends • *Black Hawk Down* grosses $100m in the US • **Uma Thurman** and her husband, Oscar nominee **Ethan Hawke** (*Training Day*), are the proud parents of baby Roan, a boy • After 'dumping' **Minnie Driver**, **Harrison Ford** appears to be very much in tandem with **Calista Flockhart**, according to the tabloids. But spare no tears for Minnie, who is now reported to be in the arms of **David Schwimmer**.

MARCH 2002

Charlie Sheen is so smitten with his new girlfriend, **Denise Richards**, that he has obeyed her command to get rid of his prized collection of porn videos. Indeed, he has handed them all out to the crew members of his current movie • Apparently, **Kate Hudson** is joining the ranks of **Tom Cruise, Michelle Pfeiffer** and **Calista Flockhart** to become the latest celebrity looking for a child to adopt. However, Kate and her rocking husband **Chris Robinson** are opting for a four-to-five-year-old! • According to *National Enquirer*, **Hugh Grant** and **Sandra Bullock** are Hollywood's 'hot new item' • A public showing of the surveillance tape that convicted **Winona Ryder** of shoplifting reveals that the actress did not cut tags off the items she 'stole'. According to her lawyer, the tape, 'contrary to public perception… exonerates her. I'd say this is a case of prosecution interrupted' • **Michelle Rodriguez** (*Girlfight, Resident Evil*) is arrested for attacking her 'roommate' • **Roseanne**'s third husband, her former bodyguard **Ben Thomas**, serves her with divorce papers. They share one child, six-year-old Buck • **Liza Minnelli** marries the Broadway producer **David Gest**, making him her fourth husband • On her honeymoon in London, Liza is mugged by a gang of youths as her Mercedes idles at traffic lights. The star mistook the thieves for autograph hunters and rolled down the car window to greet them. However, when they tried to snatch a crucifix from around her neck, Ms Minnelli's chauffeur speeded off. The actress-singer said later, 'I feel fine. They were just a couple of kids fooling around. I am a New

Right: An historic Academy Award ceremony: Halle Berry won an Oscar for her performance in *Monster's Ball.*

history to win the Oscar for Best Actress, for her role in *Monster's Ball.* Reduced to sobbing convulsions, the star declared that 'This moment is so much bigger than me. This moment is for Dorothy Dandridge, Lena Horne, Diahann Carroll. It's for the women that stand beside me, Jada Pinkett, Angela Bassett, Vivica Fox, and it's for every nameless, faceless woman of colour that has a chance because tonight the door has been opened…' Previous Best Actress African-American nominees **Diana Ross**, **Cicely Tyson**, **Diahann Carroll**, **Whoopi Goldberg** and **Angela Bassett** all went home empty-handed • **Bo Derek**, 45, shows off her new boyfriend, TV star **John Corbett** (*Northern Exposure*, *Sex and the City*) • *Ice Age* becomes the first 2002 release to gross over $100 million in the US • **Billy Bob Thornton** and **Angelina Jolie** adopt a nine-month-old Cambodian orphan, Maddox • **James Gandolfini** files for divorce from his wife **Marcy Wudarski**, much to her surprise, apparently • Following her break-up with **Val Kilmer**, **Daryl Hannah** appears to be in romantic cahoots with **Mickey Rourke** • And **Jon Voight**, 63, father-in-law of **Billy Bob Thornton**, 46, is now dating **Nastassja Kinski**, 42.

Yorker, after all. I am used to it' • **Naomi Campbell** wins a High Court ruling against her former assistant **Vanessa Frisbee**, who revealed intimate details about Naomi's unholy bedlock with **Joseph Fiennes**. For spilling the beans, Frisbee was reportedly paid £25,000 by the *News of the World*

• At the Los Angeles nightspot AD, **Drew Barrymore** surprises onlookers by openly dancing with two women who kiss her naked breasts. Only when a fellow dancer began taking photographs did Drew and her chums beat a hasty retreat • **Halle Berry** becomes the first black woman in

APRIL 2002

According to *National Enquirer* (them again), **Pamela Anderson** is diagnosed with hepatitis C, a potentially fatal disease • **Tawny Kitain**, Tom Hanks' romantic co-star in *Bachelor Party* (1984), is arrested for assaulting her husband **Chuck Finley**, the 6'6", 240-pound pitcher for the Cleveland Indians baseball team. The former actress is jailed for two days and issued with a restraining order. According to police, Tawny, now known as Julie, repeatedly kicked her hus-

band and twisted his ear • **George Clooney** is reportedly now dating the softcore porn actress **Krista Allen** • *The Lord of the Rings: The Fellowship of the Ring* grosses $300m at the US box-office • Lovebirds **Leonardo DiCaprio** and Brazilian supermodel **Gisele Bündchen** go their separate ways • As do **Gwyneth Paltrow** and **Luke Wilson**… • Word has it that **Harrison Ford** and **Calista Flockhart** are already considering marriage • *Vanilla*

Sky grosses $100 million in the US • **Geena Davis**, 45, and her husband Reza are the proud parents of a baby girl • On the same day, **Julianne Moore**, 41, gives birth to another girl, Liv Helen • On the same day, **Ben Stiller** and his actress wife **Christine Taylor** celebrate the birth of *their* baby girl • **Pamela Anderson** and the musician **Kid Rock** get engaged • The actor and former child star **Robert Blake** is officially charged with the murder of his wife, **Bonny**

Lee Bakley, who was shot dead in his car last May • **Jennifer Lopez** celebrates the opening of her Cuban restaurant, Madre's, in Pasadena, California. First-night guests include **Ben Affleck, Brooke Shields** and **Nicole Kidman**, while Lopez' first husband, **Ojani Noa**, will run the joint • **Elizabeth Hurley** gives birth to a baby boy, Damian Charles. The child's father, cited by Ms Hurley to be the producer **Steve Bing**, has requested that DNA tests be carried out to determine whether or not the baby is really his • *Monsters, Inc.* pulls in $500 million worldwide, becoming the highest-grossing computer-animated film in history • Less than a year after his well-publicised split from **Julia Roberts**, **Benjamin Bratt** escorts actress **Talisa Soto** down the aisle in an intimate family ceremony in his native San Francisco.

MAY 2002

Spider-Man sets new box-office records in the US as it grosses $114.8 million in its first weekend, becoming the first film to top $100m in its initial three days. It then breaks the four-day record by pulling in $125.8m • **Sharon Stone** is rushed to a San Francisco hospital with a migraine. Following a nearly fatal aneurysm last year, the star feared a repeat of the condition • *Spider-Man* grosses $200m in under ten days • **Leonardo DiCaprio** honours his bet to **Tobey Maguire** that *Spider-Man* could not break the opening-day records set by *Titanic*. He hands over $5000 to his good friend • *A Beautiful Mind* grosses $300 million worldwide • **Julia Roberts** appears before Congress to lobby for $15 million for research on the rare neurological disorder Rett Syndrome, which attacks girls in early childhood. In a voice charged with emotion, Roberts tells a House of Representatives sub-committee, 'This disease strikes girls too young to comprehend what is happening' • *Star Wars: Episode II – Attack of the Clones* grosses $100 million in under four days at the US box-office, but fails to dent the record set by *Spider-Man*. Meanwhile, *Spider-Man* continues to break box-office records, becoming the first film to gross as much as $46m in its third weekend on release • **Claudia Schiffer** ties the knot with film producer **Matthew Vaughn** at their baronial home, Coldham Hall in Stanningfield, near Bury St Edmunds in Suffolk. Guests at the event include **Boris Becker, Vinnie Jones** and **Guy Ritchie** • *Spider-Man* grosses $300m in the US • *Star Wars Episode II: Attack of the Clones* grosses $200m in the US • According to *National Enquirer*, **Julia Roberts** pays her boyfriend's wife a six-figure sum in order to secure his divorce.

JUNE 2002

Two rural councils in Norfolk overturn the censor's 12 certificate of *Spider-Man*. Following protests from parents and children disappointed at the strict rating bestowed by the BBFC, cinemas in Cromer, Dereham and Fakenham will show the film with a PG certificate accompanied by a warning that some scenes may be unsuitable for children under eight. A spokesman for the censor notes that, 'we classify films on behalf of local authorities and so the district councils are quite entitled to change the classification. However, we considered *Spider-Man* to be verging on a 15 certificate because of the levels of violence in the film' • DNA tests reveal that the multi-millionaire producer Steve Bing – heir to a £275 million fortune - is the father of **Elizabeth Hurley**'s son, Damian Charles. Under Californian law, this would entitle Ms Hurley to millions of dollars in child support, at least until the boy is 18. This must come as something of a shock to Bing as an alleged ex-lover, Brenda Swanson, is suing him for $15 million for calling her 'a liar' after she revealed that they were having an affair while he was dating Hurley Charlie Sheen and Denise Richards tie the knot in an intimate Catholic ceremony • *Spider-Man* grosses $500 million worldwide • **Michael Jagger**, producer of *Enigma*, is made a knight in the Queen's Birthday honours • **Daryl Hannah**, 41, takes up with publicity-seeking magician-cum-stuntman **David Blaine**, 29 • *Scooby-Doo* grosses $100 million – in just ten days on release in the US • *The Sum of All Fears* grosses $100 million in the US • Rumour has it that the two-year-old marriage of **Billy Bob Thornton** and **Angelina Jolie** is on the rocks • *Lilo & Stitch* grosses $100 million in the US • *Spider-Man* grosses $400 million in the US • **Julia Roberts** appears to be on the verge of formalising her love for her cameraman boyfriend Daniel Moder. Could there be wedding bells in July? • *Spider-Man* grosses $700 million worldwide.

Movie Quotations of the Year

Self-satisfied bachelor Will Freeman: 'I am an island. I am bloody Ibiza!' Hugh Grant in *About a Boy*

Belinda, the second wife of Muhammad Ali, putting down a certain boxing promoter: 'Don King talks black, lives white, thinks green.' Nona Gaye in *Ali*

'What may be drinkable for a Slav may not be drinkable for a human being.' A wisecracking SS officer discussing water purification, in Costa-Gavras' *Amen*

Glamorous movie star Gwen Harrison, to her assistant: 'Nobody knows what it is like being me. Did we brush my teeth?' Catherine Zeta-Jones in *America's Sweethearts*

Nigel Powers, Austin's insensitive father: 'There are two things I despise: people who are completely intolerant of other cultures, and the Dutch.' Michael Caine in *Austin Powers in Goldmember*

Terry Collins, proffering his opinion of his companion-in-crime, Kate Wheeler: 'Kate is an iceberg waiting for the Titanic.' Billy Bob Thornton in *Bandits*

Schizophrenic John Forbes Nash Jr to his new colleagues at Princeton: 'I'm actually quite well balanced. I have a chip on both shoulders.' Russell Crowe in *A Beautiful Mind*

Frank to his suspicious wife, Teresa: 'I'm not having an affair. I don't have the energy for it.' Tom Wilkinson in *Before You Go*

Tony, revealing his true colours to David Beckham fan Jess Bhamra. 'No, Jess, I really like Beckham.' Ameet Chana in *Bend It Like Beckham*

Arthur Herk, to his maid: 'It's my house, you work here and I want to suck your toes.' Stanley Tucci in *Big Trouble*

Amnesiac Jason Bourne to Marie Kreutz, having been asked to forget her: 'How could I forget you? You're the only person I know.' Matt Damon to Franka Potente in *The Bourne Identity*

Julie Styron, trying to look on the bright side of her redundancy: 'Maybe it's a blessing in disguise. [beat] A brilliant disguise.' Stockard Channing in *The Business of Strangers*

'In war anything can be true. Even a lie.' Cate Blanchett as *Charlotte Gray*

The prison warden Dorleac, musing on the prospect of divine intervention: 'God isn't in France at this time of year.' Michael Wincott in *The Count of Monte Cristo*

Jed, on the first three couplings of a couple: 'Once is an accident. Twice is a coincidence. Three is a 'thing'.' Kenny Doughty in *Crush*

Lap dancer Jo to client: 'Excuse the smell of my breasts. They're lactating.' Jennifer Tilly in *Dancing at the Blue Iguana*

Loser Conor O'Neil to threatening gang (prior to shoving his head through a bar window): 'No one can kick my ass better than me.' Keanu Reeves in *Hardball*

Pinky Pincus: 'My motherfucker's so cool, when he goes to sleep, the sheep count him.' Ricky Jay in *Heist*

Diego, a sabre-toothed tiger from about 20,000 years ago, glancing at Stonehenge: 'Modern architecture! It'll never last.' From *Ice Age*

Optimistic film director: 'This movie is going to make *House Party* look like *House Party 2!*' Chris Rock in *Jay and Silent Bob Strike Back*

Lt Melanie Ballard, proving that she's just a pretty face: 'What would happen if we blew up the nuclear power station? There'd be a huge explosion, right?' Natasha Henstridge in *John Carpenter's Ghosts of Mars*

19th century aristocrat Leopold, the third Duke of Albany, after being transported to 21st century New York: 'What has happened to the world? You have every convenience, every comfort, yet no time for integrity.' Hugh Jackman to Meg Ryan in *Kate & Leopold*

'Normally, I'm quite a self-defecating guy.' Dinner date of the obsessively linguistic Jessica Stein – in *Kissing Jessica Stein*

Mike Bassett: 'Why do I do this job? It's a good question and absolutely impossible to answer with a quick two-word response, so there's no point in me even trying. The glory.' Ricky Tomlinson in *Mike Bassett: England Manager*

Prophetic Pre-Cog Agatha: 'I'm tired of the future.' Samantha Morton in *Minority Report*

Nurse, to Hank Grotowski (Billy Bob Thornton), after he has brought his father into the nursing home: 'You must love him very much.' Hank: 'No. I don't. But he's my father.' From *Monster's Ball*

'We scare because we care.' Corporate slogan of *Monsters, Inc.*

Aspiring dramatist Christian: 'Above all things I believe in love! Love is like oxygen. Love is a many-splendored thing, love lifts us up where we belong, all you need is love!' Ewan McGregor in *Moulin Rouge!*

Danny Ocean, questioning his ex-wife, Tess, about her new boyfriend, rich casino owner Terry Benedict: 'Does he make you laugh?' Pause. Tess: 'He doesn't make me cry.' George Clooney and Julia Roberts in *Ocean's Eleven*

Danny Walker as the Japanese bomb Hawaii: 'I think World War II just started.' Josh Hartnett in *Pearl Harbor*

Reporter, interviewing Jackson Pollock (Ed Harris) about his abstract art: 'How do you know when you've finished a painting?' Pollock: 'How do you know when you've finished making love?' From *Pollock*

'That which doesn't kill you... makes you want to die.' Adam Garcia in *Riding in Cars with Boys*

A distracted Chris Cole, surprised to see his girlfriend Emily at an after-gig party: 'I thought you were in Seattle!' Emily, confused: 'We are in Seattle.' Mark Wahlberg and Jennifer Aniston in *Rock Star*

Etheline Tenenbaum, on discovering that her daughter smokes: 'How long have you been a smoker?' Margot Tenenbaum: '22 years.' Etheline: 'I think you should quit.' Anjelica Huston and Gwyneth Paltrow in *The Royal Tenenbaums*

Fred, the narcissist, to his friend Velma: 'Dorky chicks like you turn me on too.' Freddie Prinze Jr in *Scooby-Doo*

Billy, summing up his enigmatic philosophy of the world: 'All I know is that women are shaped like leaves and men fall.' Gordon Pinsent in *The Shipping News*

'If we can get a picture of Julia Roberts in a thong we can get a picture of this weirdo.' J Jonah Jameson (J K Simmons), editor of *The Daily Bugle*, determined to print photographic evidence of *Spider-Man*

Intergalactic bounty hunter Jango Fett: 'I'm just a simple man trying to make his way in the universe.' Temuera Morrison in *Star Wars: Episode II – Attack of the Clones*

Russian President Nemerov preparing for war after a nuclear bomb has wiped out Baltimore: 'These days it is better to appear guilty than impotent.' Ciarán Hinds in *The Sum of All Fears*

Billy, to his glamorous best friend, David Aames: 'You're rich and you're handsome and I'm drunk and from Ohio.' David: 'You're not from Ohio.' Billy: 'I know.' Jason Lee and Tom Cruise in *Vanilla Sky*

Sergeant Major Basil Plumley, reacting to his commanding officer's comparison of their fate to the massacre at Little Bighorn: 'Sir, Custer was a pussy.' Sam Elliott in *We Were Soldiers*

QUOTES, OFF-SCREEN
(that is, notable lines not scripted)

'For some reason, I'm more appreciated in France than I am at home. The subtitles must be incredibly good.' Woody Allen

'I'm a wimp. Just say it. I'm always a wimp at these things.' Halle Berry, on her tearful acceptance speech at the Oscars

'I was afraid that Gwyneth would want to date me after our film, like she did with Brad Pitt.' Jack Black, on his *Shallow Hal* co-star

'I just said I had a girlfriend and this girl jumped under the subway, and another girl in front of my office drank poison. It made me very, very nervous and sad.' Jackie Chan, on the burden of being a sex symbol

'Unless you are born Daniel Day-Lewis you are never going to be like Daniel Day-Lewis.' Cameron Diaz, Daniel Day-Lewis' co-star in *Gangs of New York*

'Filmmakers should think about the kind of proposals they're offering; they're

not presenting solutions, but they should help get things moving in the right direction.' Robert Guédiguian, director of *À l'Attaque!* and *La Ville est tranquille*

'He is married to a beautiful woman, and I'd sooner sleep with her than have an affair with him.' Angelina Jolie setting the record straight on Antonio Banderas, her co-star in *Original Sin*

'Stand next to Will Smith and do exactly what Barry tells you to do.' Tommy Lee Jones, star of Barry Sonnenfeld's *Men in Black* and *Men in Black II*, on the secret of comedy

'At least I can wear high heels again.' Nicole Kidman, looking on the bright side of her divorce from Tom Cruise

'When walking around London I always have a quick look in the skips. One man's rubbish is another man's treasure, and I am that 'another man'.' Leslie Phillips

'I just don't think I can do this kind of movie anymore... They should stop me. I'm like a compulsive romantic-comedy actor.' Meg Ryan, promoting her latest role as a ditzy romantic in *Kate & Leopold*

'Trends are so fleeting that new clothes are a bad investment.' Winona Ryder

'I run into people all the time who are paralysed by the fact that they might fail. To me, there's no failure. This is all an exploration.' John Sayles on the politics of making film

'There's a wonderful delusional quality I possess that allows me to attempt things that are really bad ideas.' Will Smith

'Dating in college and dating in Hollywood are actually really similar in that the relationships don't last long.' Julia Stiles

'It's not that actors are stupid, it's just that a lot of them don't over-complicate their thought processes.' Rachel Weisz

'Billy Bob and I have a kind of a male love for each other... You know, in a prison way.' Bruce Willis, on Billy Bob Thornton, his *Armageddon* and *Bandits* co-star

Soundtracks

So, on a purely aural level, how will you remember 2002? It's unlikely that any strains from the year's most popular movies – *Harry Potter and the Philosopher's Stone*, *The Lord of the Rings* or *Spider-Man* – will have squirreled their way into your memory. Or, for that matter, anything from the five scores nominated for an Oscar. Soundtracks laden with songs continue to dominate the marketplace, while the really good instrumental music seems to arrive from overseas. By far the richest scores of the year accompanied *Amélie*, *Dark Blue World*, *Invincible*, *Lantana* and *Monsoon Wedding*, all non-UK and non-US releases.

True, there was the brilliant *Black Hawk Down*, but that was composed by the Frankfurt-born **Hans Zimmer**. And there are two other exceptions: *Mulholland Dr.* and *Unfaithful*, the former scored by **Angelo Badalamenti**, the latter by Poland's **Jan A P Kaczmarek**. One would be forgiven for thinking that Badalamenti, too, is a foreigner, although the composer was actually born Andy Badale in Brooklyn, New York. Nonetheless,

his haunting waves of synthesiser and electric guitar could not be further removed from the standard orchestral wallpaper of most Hollywood fare. Badalamenti's music inhabits the fabric of the film to such an extent that, without it, a major character would be missing.

On the other hand, composers like **John Williams** drown their movies in symphonic overkill. No sooner has *Harry Potter* started than Williams' familiar music wells up to suffocate any charm or individuality the film may have had. Likewise, every visual gag in *Spy Kids 2* is emasculated by the orchestra underlining the joke. If a gag is funny, it's funny; it doesn't need a trombone to dig you in the ribs.

Music certainly has its place but more and more it's being used just because it's regarded as an essential ingredient of the filmmaking process. Alfred Hitchcock's *The Birds* had nary a note on its soundtrack – ditto Michael Haneke's highly unsettling *Funny Games* – and both films were the more powerful for it.

About a Boy
Engagingly agreeable, uplifting collection of snappy ballads and themes from pop auteur **Badly Drawn Boy** (aka **Damon Gough**). Dig a little deeper, though, and you'll find an album that resonates with more than its subject.

Ali
A magical catalogue of class acts (Aretha, Al Green, R Kelly, Alicia Keys, David Elliott as Sam Cooke) brings the enchantment and power of a singular period hauntingly to life. Few compilations waft off the hi-fi with such a redolent stamp of a movie.

Amélie
Like the film it accompanies, this is an uplifting, soul-enhancing smorgasbord of quintessentially French and eternally romantic sounds. Drawn from four of his previous albums and incorporating new compositions, this should cement the reputation of **Yann Tiersen** for good. Exhilarating, reflective, mischievous and totally wonderful.

Atlantis:
The Lost Empire
Unlike live-action movies which are often drowned by orchestral wallpaper, cartoons more often than not *require* a musical counterpoint. After all, both the animated image and the incidental score are synthetic artistic conceits. **James Newton Howard**, who previously scored *Space Jam* and *Dinosaur*, has at his command a wide range of emotional buttons, exemplified by this picturesque work. By turns bombastic, comic and soaringly romantic, it is a composition of considerable breadth and technical confidence.

Bandits
Satisfyingly cool, groovy and rousing assortment of tracks from Dylan, Aretha, Tanita Tikaram, Mark Knopfler, Pete Yorn, Jimmy Page and Robert Plant, Grover Washington Jr and Bill Withers and, of course, Bonnie Tyler, the wild-haired chanteuse who ties together the destiny of Bruce Willis and Cate Blanchett. Rock on.

Bend It Like Beckham
As much a pleasure as it is a revelation, this not only highlights such Western acts as Basement Jaxx, Texas and Blondie but supplies a whole range of Anglo-Asian music. From the frenzied reggae-ska of Backyard Dog to the seductive Eastern promise of Delhi-born Gunjan, this album is a joyous, infectious education.

Black Hawk Down
An explosive profusion of Middle Eastern percussion and wind instruments, traditional orchestra, really weird stuff and haunting vocals, this is **Hans Zimmer**'s most awesome soundtrack since, well, *Gladiator*. Five-star material. Only sadness: Omar Sharif's 'Dhibic Roob' from the film didn't make it onto the CD.

Charlotte Gray
Yet another sterling work from **Stephen Warbeck**, Britain's most consistently satisfying composer of late. Here, Warbeck whips up a lush, soaring work of orchestral

melody with distinctive cameos from the flute, guitar and piano. Definitely a score to wallow in.

Dark Blue World

Another evocative, stirring work from the Czech composer **Ondrej Soukup**, who previously scored Jan Sverak's *Kolya*. Whether summoning up bucolic rhythms, soaring excitement, the shadow of doomed love or military bluster, Soukup delivers the goods. There's also a sprinkling of wartime ballads (in Czech) that seals this soundtrack's uniqueness.

Divine Secrets of the Ya-Ya Sisterhood

Eccentric, eclectic, exotic and above all brimming with heart and soul, this is a divine collection indeed. From the urban folk-blues of Taj Mahal via old standards reinterpreted by Macy Gray, Tony Bennett and Alison Krauss, to the traditional Cajun songs of Ann Savoy (sung in French), this is another gem from producer T Bone Burnett (he who produced the Grammy-winning CD *O Brother, Where Art Thou?*).

Dog Soldiers

Majestic, overblown and totally inappropriate for the film it serves, this is a highly accomplished calling card for its composer, **Mark Thomas**. The filmmakers got a good deal for their money; it's just a shame they blew it on the wrong movie.

Enigma

Nobody can accuse **John Barry** of being experimental, yet his char-

acteristic wash of piano and strings seems to suit just about anything, be it an old-fashioned love story, futuristic thriller or exotic melodrama. Here, he conjures up a lush, densely emotional work that serves both the film's dramatic and romantic moods and provides the perfect sonic accompaniment to this quintessentially Barryesque film.

Ghost World

Steve Buscemi would approve. Here's a weird collection of antediluvian blues that the film's director, Terry Zwigoff, has pieced together from his musical ramblings. The names won't mean anything to most filmgoers, but there's a raw, bittersweet quality to the numbers that is quite disarming.

Gosford Park

Boasting as varied a collection of moods as the film's disparate dramatis personae would warrant, this is a stately, refined and melodic work from the periodically exemplary **Patrick Doyle**. There are also five delicious songs by Ivor Novello, delivered with crisp bonhomie by Jeremy Northam, plus a couple of poignant numbers sung by the composer's daughter, Abigail (with lyrics by Robert Altman, no less).

I Am Sam (instrumental)

In spite of the occasional lapse into bathos, this is one of the year's most distinctive scores. A bright showcase for the virtuosity

of guitarists George Doering and Heitor Pereira, **John Powell**'s sparky composition extends the instrument's range with some amazing arrangements while introducing a spectrum of other sounds (ukulele, percussion, violins, digital blips, clapping) into the bargain.

I Am Sam (vocal)

Both a showcase for some of the music industry's most credible acts and a valentine to the songwriting skills of Lennon & McCartney, this is an unalloyed pleasure. Revisiting the sounds of 'Two of Us' (courtesy of Aimee Mann and Michael Penn), 'You've Got to Hide Your Love Away' (Eddie Vedder), 'Strawberry Fields Forever' (Ben Harper), 'Julia' (Chocolate Genius) and 'Let It Be' (Nick Cave), the CD presents a gilt-edged trip down memory lane.

In the Bedroom

Sparse, plaintive and sometimes almost subliminal work from **Thomas Newman**, enhanced by the haunting sound of the Newark Balkan Chorus. Not to everyone's taste, but a mature, telling companion piece to Todd Field's heartrending film

Invincible

This is a hypnotic, ethereal, reassuringly magical and even profound work from **Hans Zimmer** and **Klaus Badelt**, augmented by snippets of Beethoven and Handel, plus two nostalgic numbers from Max Raabe.

Above left to right: Crouching Tiger, Hidden Dragon, O Brother, Where Art Thou?, Pearl Harbor *and* Requiem For a Dream

Kissing Jessica Stein

An upbeat collection of femme-oriented ballads set to one of the year's funniest and freshest films, this attractive package includes gems from Sarah Vaughan, Ella Fitzgerald, Dinah Washington, Diana Krall and Billie Holiday.

Lantana

One of the year's most distinctive soundtracks, a smoky, resonant, jazzy, almost mesmerising score that leisurely builds up an emotional head of steam. **Paul Kelly**, described as Australia's answer to Bob Dylan (which is stretching it a bit), started from a single riff on an electric guitar, improvised for a couple of hours and then drew what he needed from the session. There are also five excellent Latin-American tracks, including the heartbreakingly elegiac 'Te Busco' from Celia Cruz.

The Lord of the Rings: The Fellowship of the Ring

A solid, rousing soundtrack from the Canadian master of the moody motif, this won **Howard Shore** the Oscar for Best Score. A dark, grandiose work with tinges of Celtic lyricism, this is to be commended for its significant power and scope, as well as for its refreshingly varied passages, by turns epic, romantic and magical. Enya supplies the two songs.

Monsoon Wedding

Addictively joyous, ethnically rich celebration of everything from traditional Punjabi ballads to bhangra rock, threaded through an evocative score from **Mychael Danna**, this really is an exotic, mysterious and life-enhancing album.

Monsters, Inc.

Uproariously buoyant, giddy, jazzy and even, at times, balletic instrumental score from **Randy Newman**. Without doubt one of the year's more joyous treats, kicking off with the Oscar-winning track 'If I Didn't Have You', sung by John Goodman and Billy Crystal.

Mulholland Dr.

About as perfect an aural accompaniment as one could ask to David Lynch's haunting, irritating and superbly crafted film. Once again, **Angelo Badalamenti** summons up a powerful beauty, albeit mottled with the ebb and flow of apocalyptic synth, weird piano chords and the odd incongruous vocal number. And you couldn't get much odder than Joe Melson's indelible, heart-stopping *Llorando* sung by Rebekah Del Rio. Musically, this is where dreams and nightmares come to play.

Riding in Cars with Boys

Call them naff, simplistic and downright sentimental, but the songs of the early 1960s had a timeless resonance and innocence that nobody today would even *dare* emulate. Here, there are some true gems: Sonny & Cher's 'I Got You Babe', Billy Joe Royal's 'Down in the Boondocks', Skeeter Davis' 'End of the World'... A fine collection, capped off with **Hans Zimmer** and **Heitor Pereira**'s medley of incidental themes entitled, endearingly, 'Our Little Bit of Score'.

The Royal Tenenbaums

A suitably idiosyncratic soundtrack to one of the year's most original and stylish films. **Mark Mothersbaugh** (formerly of the rock band Devo) supplies the incidental music, a combination of rowdy percussion and classical harp and strings, interlaced with lyrical numbers from Emitt Rhodes, Elliot Smith and Nick Drake, plus more eccentric offerings by Nico and Bob Dylan.

The Scorpion King (instrumental)

After the mandatory hard-rock intro, **John Debney**'s score settles down to its robust, epic and sweeping agenda. Utilising the full brawn of the Hollywood Studio Symphony, Debney's riffs prove to be a dynamic counterpoint to the star's musculature, melding echoes of the mysterious East with a traditional orchestral

gust. For devotees of Godsmack and Rob Zombie there is also a full shrapnel version.

Shallow Hal

An exceptionally strong selection of tracks, this reflects the Farrellys' switch to the mainstream, but in a good way. Here are ace turns from Sheryl Crow, Ellis Paul, Rosey, Darius Rucker (of Hootie and the Blowfish), P J Harvey and Shelby Lynne. Sterling stuff.

Spirit: Stallion of the Cimarron

Richly emotive and satisfyingly melodic companion to the old-fashioned cartoon, with eight new power ballads from Bryan Adams and a superlative score from **Hans Zimmer**.

Unfaithful

Subtle, atmospheric yet emotionally overwhelming score from the consummate Polish composer **Jan A P Kaczmarek**, whose lush musical palette ideally matches Adrian Lyne's luxuriant imagery. Some may find it repetitive, but it works.

Vanilla Sky

Probably the year's most thrilling collection of tracks and Cameron Crowe's best soundtrack to date (and that's saying something). Besides Paul McCartney's naff title song (which was inexplicably nominated for an Oscar), there's great stuff from REM (the previously unrecorded 'All the Right Friends'), Radiohead, Bob Dylan, Jeff Buckley, Red House Painters, Sigur Ros, Beth Orton and The Chemical Brothers and even Cameron Diaz.

We Were Soldiers

Although an 'inspired by' CD, this happens to be one of the strongest compilations of the year, with especially powerful tracks from Johnny Cash (with Dave Matthews faintly accompanying him), Train, Montgomery Gentry, Joseph Klina MacKenzie and, get this, the United States Military Academy Cadet Glee Club and Metro Voices. All rather moving.

Internet

by Daniel O'Brien

A selection of notable websites relating to the year's most popular stars and most successful films.

JACKIE CHAN

The Official Jackie Chan Web Page (www.jackie-chan.com) is comprehensive and well laid out. The numerous sections include My Legend, My Photos, My Movies, My Travelog and My Schedule. There's also a plug for the upcoming *Shanghai Knights*. Chan doesn't shy away from discussing his early career problems, when he was labelled box office poison. Hardly earth-shattering but a good starting point.

GEORGE CLOONEY

The Complete George Clooney Site (http://members.lycos.nl/Reinfilmindex_2/georgeclooney.html) offers a fair selection of colour pictures, film and television credits, awards and trivia. Fans may want to check out www.clooneyfiles.com first. Formerly known as Julie's George Clooney Page, this site is comprehensive and easy to use, if not visually exciting. There's even information on Clooney's stunt doubles.

SACHA BARON COHEN

The official Ali G website (www.alig.com) is written in Ali G-speak, directing visitors to Da Facts, Da Gospel and so on. Hardcore fans will probably love it. There are plugs for the movie *Ali G Indahouse* and a fictional (?) book, *Da Joy of Bonin*. Click for a larger picture at your own risk. Needless to say, there's no mention of Sacha Baron Cohen himself.

RUSSELL CROWE

Maximum Russell Crowe (www.geocities.com/Hollywood/Cinema/1501/maximum_us.html) is a frighteningly comprehensive fansite. While the dark green backdrops and pink-on-black text are a little hard on the eye, fans will have no complaints. The exhaustive photo gallery includes pictures of Crowe in *Neighbours* and a production of *The Rocky Horror Show*. This award-winning site is endorsed by the star himself: 'The favourite fan site. The best fan site, the one you should be using.'

TOM CRUISE

At present, the Cruiser doesn't seem well served by fansites. The Complete Tom Cruise site (http://members.lycos.nl/Reinfilmindex_2/tomcruise.html) was still under construction in mid-September 2002. Tom Cruise's Corner (www.geocities.com/amie_07/tom.html) uses hard-to-read yellow-on-black text. On the plus side, there are over 700 pictures.

CAMERON DIAZ

The Secret Files of Cameron Diaz (http://georgeastridge.freeyellow.com/Diaz.html) contains no secrets whatsoever. The introduction also concedes that Diaz 'may not be the best actress ever, or even a particularly good one…' What it does offer is a picture gallery, quotes, a filmography and links. The images are of variable quality and searches are regularly interrupted by adverts for a dating service (not with Cameron Diaz). The Best of Cameron Diaz (www.cameron-diaz.com) includes a detailed biography and good picture resolution. While this site features stills from just six of Diaz's films, there are loads of them.

HUGH GRANT

Hugh Grant fans in search of hard facts should check out Poppy's Hugh Grant Page (www.geocities.com/Hollywood/Land/4637/hughbk1). This reasonable site features the usual biography, photo gallery, reader reviews, feedback and links. Unfortunately, Poppy hasn't updated her Page recently, ending with news on the 'forthcoming' *Bridget Jones's Diary*. Myhrmaid's Kiss Hugh Grant Page (www.geocities.com/themyhrmaids/kisshugh) enables fans to 'plant a lipsticked kiss on Hugh's face'. And that's all. Students of Grant's early, pre-Hollywood work will be pleased to learn that *The Lair of the White Worm* (1988) has its own fansite (www.geocities.com/lairof). This contains *everything* you could want to know about Ken Russell's camp classic.

ANGELINA JOLIE

Ultimate Angelina Jolie (www.celebrity-fansites.com/stars/angelina_jolie) is a fair bare-bones fansite, offering 280 images of the *Tomb Raider* star. Wuthering Jolie (www.wutheringjolie.com/angelina.html) is more ambitious, featuring a cool ice-blue dragon logo. The various sections are basic, yet well designed. Curious fans can check out a gallery of the star's various tattoos, and information on her broth-

er. There's also a major plug for a replica Lara Croft back pack, accompanied by a big photograph. The site refers to financial problems, which may account for the eye-straining yellow-on-black biography page.

NICOLE KIDMAN
Look no further than www.teamnicole.com, which greets visitors with a large colour photo of Nicole Kidman holding a red rose. Devoid of gossip on Kidman's private life, teamnicole.com claims to be 'The only site dedicated to the professional career of Nicole Kidman.' Featuring over 3,500 pictures, it's certainly well-designed and easy to use.

CHRISTOPHER LEE
The Official Christopher Lee Web (http://christopherleeweb.com/) contains everything a fan could want to know about the *Lord of the Rings* and *Star Wars* bad guy. This detailed, well-designed site has small but clearly laid out sections. Visitors can indulge in Fun and Games, read detailed fan reviews, purchase a Saruman bust at the store, watch Lee on television and vote for their favourite Lee DVD commentary. The Scrapbook section includes Lee's school certificate, school awards, exam results and enlistment papers. A high point is the vast picture gallery, featuring hundreds of rare photographs from Lee's personal collection. The more unusual stills include Lee made up as Prince Philip for the tv movie *Charles and Diana* (1982). The last picture taken of Lee with the late Peter Cushing, a close friend and regular co-star, is extremely poignant.

EWAN MCGREGOR
Ewan McGegor's official resume can be found on his agents' website (www.pfd.co.uk). Those in search of a less formal site can check out The Best of Ewan McGregor (www.bestofewan.com), which offers pictures, wallpapers, links and a printable calendar. McGregor voyeurs will be disappointed to learn that there are no nude photos on offer – this is one site that respects Ewan McGregor as an artist. The Best of Ewan McGregor links with Ewan News (www.ewan.pitas.com), which features all the facts. Virtual McGregor (www.enter.net/~cybernut/ewan) is big on articles, pictures and screen savers. On the downside, the severe white-on-black layout is hard on the eyes, and there seems to be a problem with the sounds pages.

EDDIE MURPHY
There don't seem to be many Eddie Murphy fansites, perhaps a reflection of his erratic career. Div's Crib (www.div.ca/eddies/) offers a no-frills biography, filmography and television credits. While this site isn't great on pictures, the sound clips include material from Murphy's *Saturday Night Live* routines. That's where it all started, folks.

GWYNETH PALTROW
The Temple of Gwyneth Paltrow (www.domaindlx.com/gwyneth/) greets visitors with a dollar bill featuring the star's face. Unfortunately, it's all downhill from there. Six clickable pictures and six articles. That's it.

JULIA ROBERTS
www.juliafan.com offers animated butterflies, psychedelic colour shifts and a quiz. The numerous sections include Julia's Family and Julia's Beaus. Fans who do not regard Roberts as a living goddess may want to skip the open letter to the star.

MOVIE SITES

AUSTIN POWERS IN GOLDMEMBER

The 'shagedelic' Austin Powers site (www.austinpow-ers.com) downloads accompanied by a still of Powers in his finest blue crushed velvet suit ('Loading up, baby!'). Features include a trailer, production information and pictures. Cool animated icons lead intrepid surfers to Austin's Pad, Foxxy Girl, Dr. Evil's Lair, Swinger's Lounge and Exclusive Baby! Austin Outtakes! Acceptably groovy.

DIE ANOTHER DAY

The entry page for www.jamesbond.com/ features Pierce Brosnan and co-star Halle Berry looking intense, with matching automatics. Impatient surfers should note that a site this suave isn't loading but 'accessing data'. Lots of it. Features include production information, sound clips, downloads and a link to the 007 40th anniversary site. Fans can also send a James Bond e-mail to their friends. The image bank is overly intricate in design, slowing down picture access for no good reason. Available in six languages.

LOST IN LA MANCHA

This acclaimed 'un-making of documentary' tells the story behind Terry Gilliam's ill-fated *The Man Who Killed Don Quixote*. The official website (www.smart.co.uk/lostinlamancha/) is smartly designed in red, black and white. Features include the production history, interviews with the directors and producer, contacts and a link to an online Gilliam fanzine. The stills gallery is outstanding, with some fine shots of French actor Jean Rochefort, perfect casting for Quixote. The production photographs include Johnny Depp attempting to ride a donkey. Essential viewing.

MONSTERS, INC.

This slick official site (www.disney.go.com/disneypictures/monstersinc/) features a letter 'M' with a roving, blinking eye. The lead characters, monocular Mike and furry Sully, flank a bedroom door, which opens to reveal the chosen option. There are the usual trailers, 'outtakes' and a link to the official Pixar site, giving curious visitors a chance to 'learn about the creators of *MI*'. Most fans will opt for the interactive *MI* Tour. Collect all the items and a big surprise awaits.

SPIDERMAN

Can he really do anything a spider can? Webslingers arriving at www.spiderman.sonypictures.com are greeted by the wall-crawling superhero, posing against the New York skyline, along with a couple of press puffs. Diehard fans will want to check out the semi-animated Introduction, which covers Peter Parker and the other major characters. The many, many features include Trailers, Making of…, Press Conference and Costume Evolution. Exploring the entire site would probably take longer than making the film.

STUDIO SITES

BUENA VISTA www.movies.go.com	**PARAMOUNT CLASSICS** www.paramountclassics.com
DIMENSION FILMS www.dimensionfilms.com	**PIXAR** www.pixar.com
DREAMWORKS www.dreamworks.com	**SONY PICTURES** www.sonypictures.com
FOX SEARCHLIGHT www.foxsearchlight.com	**20th CENTURY FOX** www.foxmovies.com
LION'S GATE www.lionsgate-ent.com	**UIP** www.uip.com
MGM www.mgm.com	**UNIVERSAL PICTURES** www.universalpictures.com
MIRAMAX www.miramax.com	**WALT DISNEY** www.disney.go.com/disneypictures/
NEW LINE www.newline.com	**WARNER BROTHERS** www.movies.warnerbros.com
OCTOBER FILMS www.focusfeatures.com	

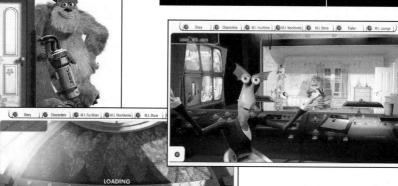

Awards and Festivals

The 74th American Academy of Motion Picture Arts and Sciences Awards ('The Oscars') and Nominations for 2001: Kodak Theater, Los Angeles, 24 March 2001

• **Best Film:** *A Beautiful Mind.*
Nominations: *Gosford Park*; *In the Bedroom*; *The Lord of the Rings: The Fellowship of the Ring*; *Moulin Rouge!*.
• **Best Director:** Ron Howard, for *A Beautiful Mind.*
Nominations: Robert Altman, for *Gosford Park* Peter Jackson, for *The Lord of the Rings: The Fellowship of the Ring*; David Lynch, for *Mulholland Dr.*; Ridley Scott, for *Black Hawk Down.*
• **Best Actor:** Denzel Washington, for *Training Day.*
Nominations: Russell Crowe, for *A Beautiful Mind*; Sean Penn, for *I Am Sam*; Will Smith, for *Ali*; Tom Wilkinson, for *In the Bedroom.*
• **Best Actress:** Halle Berry, for *Monster's Ball.*
Nominations: Judi Dench, for *Iris*; Nicole Kidman, for *Moulin Rouge!*; Sissy Spacek, for *In the Bedroom*; Renée Zellweger, for *Bridget Jones's Diary.*
• **Best Supporting Actor:** Jim Broadbent, for *Iris.*

Nominations: Ethan Hawke, for *Training Day*; Ben Kingsley, for *Sexy Beast*; Ian McKellen, for *The Lord of the Rings: The Fellowship of the Ring*; Jon Voight, for *Ali.*
• **Best Supporting Actress:** Jennifer Connelly, for *A Beautiful Mind.*
Nominations: Helen Mirren, for *Gosford Park*; Maggie Smith, for *Gosford Park*; Marisa Tomei, for *In the Bedroom*; Kate Winslet, for *Iris.*
• **Best Animated Feature:** *Shrek.*
Nominations: *Jimmy Neutron: Boy Genius*; *Monsters, Inc.*
• **Best Original Screenplay:** Julian Fellowes, for *Gosford Park.*
Nominations: Guillaume Laurant & Jean-Pierre Jeunet, for *Amélie*; Christopher Nolan, for *Memento*; Milo Addica & Will Rokos, for *Monster's Ball*; Wes Anderson & Owen Wilson, for *The Royal Tenenbaums.*
• **Best Screenplay Adaptation:** Akiva Goldsman, for *A Beautiful Mind.*
Nominations: Daniel Clowes & Terry Zwigoff, for *Ghost World*; Rob Festinger & Todd Field, for *In the Bedroom*; Fran Walsh & Philippa Boyens & Peter Jackson, for *The Lord of the Rings: The Fellowship of the Ring*; Ted Elliott & Terry Rossio and Joe Stillman and Roger S H Schulman, for *Shrek.*

• **Best Cinematography:** Andrew Lesnie, for *The Lord of the Rings: The Fellowship of the Ring.*
Nominations: Bruno Delbonnel, for *Amélie*; Slawomir Idziak, for *Black Hawk Down*; Roger Deakins, for *The Man Who Wasn't There*; Donald M McAlpine, for *Moulin Rouge!.*
• **Best Editing:** Pietro Scalia, for *Black Hawk Down.*
Nominations: Mike Hill and Dan Hanley, for *A Beautiful Mind*; John Gilbert, for *The Lord of the Rings: The Fellowship of the Ring*; Dody Dorn, for *Memento*; Jill Bilcock, for *Moulin Rouge!.***Best Original Score**: Howard Shore, for *The Lord of the Rings: The Fellowship of the Ring.*
Nominations: John Williams, for *A.I. Artificial Intelligence*; James Horner, for *A Beautiful Mind*; John Williams, for *Harry Potter and the Sorcerer's Stone*; Randy Newman, for *Monsters, Inc.*
• **Best Original Song:** 'If I Didn't Have You' by Randy Newman, from *Monsters, Inc.*
Nominations: 'May It Be' by Enya, Nicky Ryan and Roma Ryan, from *The Lord of the Rings: The Fellowship of the Ring*; 'There You'll Be' by Diane Warren, from *Pearl Harbor*; 'Until...' by Sting, from *Kate & Leopold*; 'Vanilla Sky...' by Paul McCartney, from *Vanilla Sky.*
• **Best Art Direction:** Catherine Martin (art) and Brigitte Broch (set), for *Moulin Rouge!.*
Nominations: Aline Bonetto (art direction) and Marie-Laure Valla (set direction), for *Amélie*; Stephen Altman (art) and Anna Pinnock (set), for *Gosford Park*; Stuart Craig (art) and Stephenie McMillan (set), for *Harry Potter and the Sorcerer's Stone*; Grant Major (art) and Dan Hennah (set), for *The Lord of the Rings: The Fellowship of the Ring.*
• **Best Costume Design:** Catherine Martin and Angus Strathie, for *Moulin Rouge!.*
Nominations: Milena Canonero, for *The Affair of the Necklace*; Jenny Beavan, for *Gosford Park*; Judianna Makovsky, for *Harry Potter and the Sorcerer's Stone*; Ngila Dickson, for *The Lord of the Rings: The Fellowship of the Ring.*
• **Best Sound:** Mike Minkler, Myron Nettinga and Chris Munro, for *Black Hawk Down.*

Opposite: Russell Crowe in Ron Howard's Oscar-winning *A Beautiful Mind*

Nominations: Vincent Arnardi, Guillaume Leriche and Jean Umansky, for *Amélie*; Christopher Boyes, Michael Semanick, Gethin Creagh and Hammond Peek, for *The Lord of the Rings: The Fellowship of the Ring*; Andy Nelson, Anna Behlmer, Roger Savage and Guntis Sics, for *Moulin Rouge!*; Kevin O'Connell, Greg P Russell and Peter J Devlin, for *Pearl Harbor*.
• **Best Sound Effects Editing:** George Watters II and Christopher Boyes, for *Pearl Harbor*.
Nominations: Gary Rydstrom and Michael Silvers, for *Monsters, Inc.*.
• **Best Make-Up:** Peter Owen and Richard Taylor, for *The Lord of the Rings: The Fellowship of the Ring*.
Nominations: Greg Cannom and Colleen Callaghan, for *A Beautiful Mind*; Maurizio Silvi and Aldo Signoretti, for *Moulin Rouge!*.
• **Best Visual Effects:** Jim Rygiel, Randall William Cook, Richard Taylor and Mark Stetson, for *The Lord of the Rings: The Fellowship of the Ring*.
Nominations: Dennis Muren, Scott Farrar, Stan Winston and Michael Lantieri, for *A.I. Artificial Intelligence*; Eric Brevig, John Frazier, Ed Hirsh and Ben Snow, for *Pearl Harbor*.
• **Best Animated Short Film:** *For the Birds*, by Ralph Eggleston.
Nominations: *Fifty Percent Grey*, by Ruairi Robinson and Seamus Byrne; *Give Up Yer Aul Sins*, by Cathal Gaffney and Darragh O'Connell; *Strange Invaders*, by Cordell Barker; *Stubble Trouble*, by Joseph E Merideth.
• **Best Live Action Short Film:** *the accountant*, by Ray McKinnon and Lisa Blount.
Nominations: *Copy Shop*, by Virgil Widrich; *Gregor's Greatest Invention*, by Johannes Kiefer; *A Man Thing*, by Slawomir Fabicki and Bogumil Godfrejow; *Speed for Thespians*, by Kalman Apple and Shameela Bakhsh.
• **Best Documentary Feature:** *Murder on a Sunday Morning*, by Jean-Xavier de Lestrade and Denis Poncet.
Nominations: *Children Underground* by Edet Belzberg; *LaLee's Kin: The Legacy*, by Susan Froemke; *Promises*, by Justine Shapiro and B Z Goldberg; *War Photographer*, by Christian Frei.

• **Best Documentary Short:** *Thoth*, by Sarah Kernochan and Lynn Appelle.
Nominations: *Artists and Orphans: A True Drama*, by Lianne Klapper McNally; *Sing!*, by Freida Lee Mock and Jessica Sanders.
• **Best Foreign-Language Film:** *No Man's Land* (Bosnia and Herzegovina).
Nominations: *Amélie* (France); *Elling* (Norway); *Lagaan* (India); *Son of the Bride* (Argentina).
• **Honorary Awards:** Sidney Poitier, Robert Redford.
• **Gordon E Sawyer Award:** Edmund M Di Giulio, for 'technological contributions [which] have brought credit to the industry'.
• **Jean Hersholt Humanitarian Award:** Arthur Hiller.

The 43rd Australian Film Institute Awards: 16 November 2001

• **Best Film:** *Lantana*.
• **Best Actor:** Anthony LaPaglia, for *Lantana*.
• **Best Actress:** Kerry Armstrong, for *Lantana*.
• **Best Supporting Actor:** Vince Colosimo, for *Lantana*.
• **Best Supporting Actress:** Rachael Blake, for *Lantana*.
• **Best Director:** Ray Lawrence, for *Lantana*.
• **Best Original Screenplay:** Robert Connolly, for *The Bank*.
• **Best Screenplay Adaptation:** Andrew Bovell, for *Lantana*.
• **Best Cinematography:** Donald M McAlpine, for *Moulin Rouge!*.
• **Best Production Design:** Catherine Martin, for *Moulin Rouge!*.
• **Best Editing:** Jill Bilcock, for *Moulin Rouge!*.
• **Best Music:** Cezary Skubiszewski, for *La Spagnola*.
• **Best Costumes:** Catherine Martin & Angus Strathie, for *Moulin Rouge!*.
• **Best Sound:** Andy Nelson, Roger Savage & Guntis Sics, for *Moulin Rouge!*.
• **Best Young Actor:** John Sebastian Pilakui, for *Yolngu Boy*.
• **Best Foreign Film:** *Crouching Tiger, Hidden Dragon* (Hong Kong/Taiwan/USA).
• **Best Documentary:** *Facing the Music*,

produced and directed by Robert Connolly and Robin Anderson.
• **Best Short Fiction Film:** *The Big House*, by Rachel Ward.
• **Best Animated Short:** *Living With Happiness*, by Sarah Watt.
• **Byron Kennedy Award:** Ian David.

The 52nd Berlin International Film Festival: 17 February 2002

• **Golden Bear for Best Film:** *Sen To Chihiro No Kamikakushi* (*Spirited Away*); and *Bloody Sunday* (UK).
• **Silver Bear, Jury Grand Prize:** *Halbe Treppe* (*Grill Point*)
• **Silver Bear for Best Director:** Otar Iosseliani, for *Lundi Martin*.
• **Silver Bear, Best Actor:** Jacques Gamblin, for *Laissez-Passer*.
• **Silver Bear, Best Actress:** Halle Berry, for *Monster's Ball*.
• **Blue Angel Prize:** Annette K Olesen, for *Sma Ulykker* (*Minor Mishaps*).
• **Alfred Bauer Prize** (for a debut film): *Baader*.
• **Silver Bear for Individual Artistic Contribution:** The ensemble of actresses in *Huit Femmes*.
• **Golden Bear for Best Short Film:** *At Dawning*.
• **Jury Prize (Silver Bear) for Short Films:** *Bror Min* (*Brother of Mine*), by Jens Jonsson.
• **Premiere First Movie Award:** *Beneath Clouds*, by Ivan Sen
• **Special Mentions:** *The Laramie Project*, by Moises Kaufmann; and *Chen Mo and Meiting*, by Liu Hao.
• **Wolfgang Staudte Award:** *Wesh Wesh, Qu'Est-Ce Qui Se Passe?*, by Ralph Ameur-Zaimeche.
• **CICAE** (international confederation of art cinemas):
• **Panorama:** *Piñero*, by Leon Ichaso.
• **Forum:** *Elaman Aidit* (*Mothers Of Life*), by Anastasia Lapsui and Markku Lehmuskallio.
• **German Arthouse Cinemas Guild:** *Halbe Treppe* (*Grill Point*), by Andreas Dresen.
• **Gay Teddy Bear Award, Best Feature:** *Walking on Water*, by Tony Ayres.
• **Gay Teddy Bear Award, Documentary:**

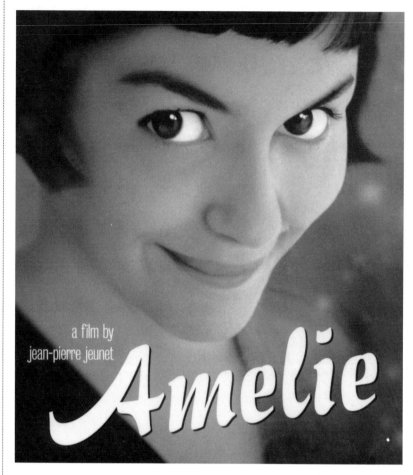

a film by
jean-pierre jeunet
Amelie

Alt Om Min Far (All About My Father) by
Even Benestad.
• **Peace Film Prize**: *A Moment Before the
Eruption*, by Avi Mograbi.
• **Ecumenical Jury Prize** (in competition):
Bloody Sunday.
• **Panorama Audience Award**: *Im Toten Winkel.
Hitlers Sekretaerin (Blind Spot. Hitler's Secretary)*,
by Andre Heller and Othmar Schmiderer.
• **Piper Heidsieck New Talent Awards**:
• **Best Actor**: Hugh Bonneville, for *Iris*.
• **Best Actress**: Dannielle Hall, for
Beneath Clouds.

*Jury: Mira Nair (president), Nicoletta
Braschi, Peter Cowie, Lucrecia Martel,
Claudie Ossard, Raoul Peck, Declan Quinn,
Oskar Roehler, Kenneth Turan*

The 22nd Canadian Film Awards ('Genies'): Toronto, Ontario, 7 February 2002

• **Best Film**: *Atanarjuat (The Fast Runner)*.
• **Best Director**: Zacharias Kunuk, for
Atanarjuat (The Fast Runner)

• **Best Actor**: Brendan Fletcher, for *The
Law of Enclosures*.
• **Best Actress**: Élise Guilbault, for *La
Femme qui boit (The Woman Who Drinks)*.
• **Best Supporting Actor**: Vincent Gale, for
Last Wedding.
• **Best Supporting Actress**: Molly Parker,
for *Last Wedding*.
• **Best Screenplay**: Paul Apak Angilirq, for
Atanarjuat (The Fast Runner).
• **Best Cinematography**: Pierre Gill, for
Lost and Delirious.
• **Best Editing**: Norman Cohn, Zacharias
Kunuk and Marie-Christine Sarda, for
Atanarjuat (The Fast Runner).
• **Best Art Direction**: Ken Rempel, for
The War Bride.
• **Best Music**: Chris Crilly, for *Atanarjuat
(The Fast Runner)*.
• **Best Original Song**: Ron Sexsmith for
'Love is Free' from *The Art of Woo*.
• **Best Costumes**: Howard Burden, for *The
War Bride*.
• **Best Sound Editing**: Stephen Barden,
Kevin Banks, Joe Bracciate, John Sievert
and Virginia Storey, for *Treed Murray*.
• **Best Overall Sound**: Todd Warren, Todd

Beckett, Herwig Gayer and Bisa Scekic, for
Treed Murray.
• **Claude Jutra Award for Best First
Feature**: Zacharias Kunuk, for *Atanarjuat
(The Fast Runner)*.
• **Best Feature-length Documentary**:
Westray, by Kent Martin and Paul Cowan.
• **Best Animated Short**: *The Boy Who Saw
the Iceberg*, by Marcy Page and Paul Driessen.
• **Best Live-Action Short**: *The Heart of the
World*, by Guy Maddin and Jody Shapiro.
• **The Golden Reel Award for Box-Office
Performance**: *Nuit De Noces*.

The 55th Cannes Film Festival Awards: 15-26 May 2002

• **Palme d'Or for Best Film**: *The Pianist*
(Poland/France), by Roman Polanski.
• **Grand Prix du Jury**: *The Man Without a
Past* (Finland), by Aki Kaurismaki.
• **Best Actor**: Olivier Gourmet, for *The
Son* (Belgium).
• **Best Actress**: Kati Outinen, for *The Man
Without a Past*.
• **Best Director**: Paul Thomas Anderson,
for *Punch-Drunk Love* (USA); and Im
Kwon-Taek, for *Chihwaseon* (South Korea).
• **Best Screenplay**: Paul Laverty, for *Sweet
Sixteen* (UK).
• **Palme d'Or for Best Short**: *Eso Utan*
(aka *After the Rain*) (Hungary), by
Peter Meszaros.
• **Jury Prize for Best Short**: *The Stone of
Folly* (Canada), by Jesse Rosensweet, and
A Very Very Silent Film (India), by
Manish Jha.
• **Prix du Jury (Fiction)**: *Divine
Intervention* (France/Morocco/Germany),
by Elia Suleiman.
• **Camera d'Or** (for first feature): *Bord de Mer*
(aka *Seaside*) (France), by Julie Lopes-Curval.
• **Special 55th Anniversary Prize**: *Bowling
for Columbine* (USA), Michael Moore.

*Jury: David Lynch (president), Bille August,
Christine Hakim, Claude Miller, Raul Ruiz,
Walter Salles, Sharon Stone, Regis Wargnier,
Michelle Yeoh.*

Below: Gosford Park highlighted Robert Altman's assured direction of the ensemble cast

The 27th Deauville Festival of American Cinema: 31 August-9 September 2001

- **Grand Prix for Best Film**: *Hedwig and the Angry Inch*, by John Cameron Mitchell.
- **Jury Prize**: *Ghost World* by Terry Zwigoff.
- **Grand Prix for Best Short**: *The Good Things*, by Seth Wiley.
- **Jury Prize for Best Short**: *Mental Hygiene*, by Lori Silverbush.
- **Critics' Award**: *Hedwig and the Angry Inch*.
- **Audience Award**: *Jump Tomorrow*, by Joel Hopkins.
- **Cine Live Award**: *Hedwig and the Angry Inch*.
- **Canal Plus Short Film Award**: *Frank's Book*, by R A White.
- **Honorees**: Joel Silver, Julianne Moore, Christopher Walken.

The 14th European Film Awards ('The Felixes'): Tempodrom Theatre, 1 December 2001

- **Best European Film**: *Le fabuleux destin d'Amélie Poulain* (*Amélie*) (France), by Jean-Pierre Jeunet.
- **Best Director**: Jean-Pierre Jeunet, for *Amélie*.
- **Best Actor**: Ben Kingsley, for *Sexy Beast*.
- **Best Actress**: Isabelle Huppert, for *The Piano Teacher*.

- **Best Screenplay**: Danis Tanovic, for *No Man's Land*.
- **Best Cinematography**: Bruno Delbonnel, for *Amélie*.
- **Best Short Film**: *Je t'aime John Wayne* (UK), by Toby MacDonald.
- **Discovery of the Year** (Fassbinder Award): Achero Manas, director of *El Bola* (Spain).
- **Best Documentary** (Prix Arte): *Black Box BRD (Black Box Germany)* (Germany), by Andres Veiel.

People's Awards:

- **Best Actor**: Colin Firth, for *Bridget Jones's Diary* (UK).
- **Best Actress**: Juliette Binoche, for *Chocolat*.
- **Best Director**: Jean-Pierre Jeunet, for *Amélie*.
- **Best Non-European Film**: *Moulin Rouge!* (Australia/USA).
- **Achievement in World Cinema**: Ewan McGregor.
- **Lifetime Achievement Award**: Monty Python.

The 27th French Academy ('Cesar') Awards: 2 March 2002

- **Best Film**: *Le fabuleux destin d'Amélie Poulain* (*Amélie*).
- **Best Director**: Jean-Pierre Jeunet, for *Amélie*.
- **Best Actor**: Michel Bouquet, for

Comment j'ai tué mon père.
- **Best Actress**: Emmanuelle Devos, for *Sur mes lèvres* (*Read My Lips*).
- **Best Supporting Actor**: André Dussollier, for *La Chambre des officiers* (*The Officers' Ward*).
- **Best Supporting Actress**: Annie Girardot, for *La Pianiste*.
- **Most Promising Young Actor**: Robinson Stévenin, for *Mauvais genres*.
- **Most Promising Young Actress**: Rachida Brakni, for *Chaos*.
- **Best First Film**: *No Man's Land*.
- **Best Screenplay**: Jacques Audiard and Tonino Benacquista, for *Sur mes lèvres*.
- **Best Cinematography**: Tetsuo Nagata, for *The Officers' Ward*.
- **Best Production Design**: Aline Bonetto, for *Amélie*.
- **Best Editing**: Marie-Josèphe Yoyotte, for *Le peuple migrateur*.
- **Best Music**: Yann Tiersen, for *Amélie*.
- **Best Costumes**: Dominique Borg, for *Le Pacte des loups* (*Brotherhood of the Wolf*).
- **Best Sound**: Cyril Holtz and Pascal Villard, for *Sur mes lèvres*.
- **Best Short**: *Au premier Dimanche d'août*, by Florence Miailhe.
- **Best Foreign Film**: *Mulholland Dr.* (USA).
- **Honorary Cesars**: Anouk Aimée, Jeremy Irons, Claude Rich.

The 22nd Golden Raspberries ('The Razzies'): The Abracadabra Theatre, Santa Monica, 23 March 2002

• **Worst Film:** *Freddy Got Fingered*.
• **Worst Actor:** Tom Green, for *Freddy Got Fingered*.
• **Worst Actress:** Mariah Carey, for *Glitter*.
• **Worst Screen Couple:** Tom Green & Any Animal He Abuses in *Freddy Got Fingered*.
• **Worst Supporting Actress:** Estella Warren, for *Driven* and *Planet of the Apes*.
• **Worst Supporting Actor:** Charlton Heston, for *Cats & Dogs*, *Planet of the Apes* and *Town & Country*.
• **Worst Director:** Tom Green, for *Freddy Got Fingered*.
• **Worst Screenplay:** Tom Green and Derek Harvie, for *Freddy Got Fingered*.
• **Worst Remake or Sequel:** *Planet of the Apes*.

The 59th Hollywood Foreign Press Association ('Golden Globes') Awards: 20 January 2002

• **Best Picture – Drama:** *A Beautiful Mind*.
• **Best Picture – Musical or Comedy:** *Moulin Rouge!*.
• **Best Actor – Drama:** Russell Crowe, for *A Beautiful Mind*.
• **Best Actress – Drama:** Sissy Spacek, for *In the Bedroom*.
• **Best Actor – Musical or Comedy:** Gene Hackman, for *The Royal Tenenbaums*.
• **Best Actress – Musical or Comedy:** Nicole Kidman, for *Moulin Rouge!*.
• **Best Supporting Actress:** Jennifer Connelly, for *A Beautiful Mind*.
• **Best Supporting Actor:** Jim Broadbent, for *Iris*.
• **Best Director:** Robert Altman, for *Gosford Park*.
• **Best Screenplay:** Akiva Goldsman, for *A Beautiful Mind*.
• **Best Original Score:** Craig Armstrong, for *Moulin Rouge!*.
• **Best Original Song:** 'Until…,' from *Kate & Leopold*, by Sting.
• **Best Foreign Language Film:** *No Man's Land* (Bosnia and Herzegovina), by Danis Tanovic.
• **Cecil B DeMille Award:** Harrison Ford, for his 'outstanding contribution to the entertainment field'.
• **Best TV Film or miniseries:** *Band of Brothers*.

The 22nd London Film Critics' Circle Awards: The Dorchester, London, 13 February 2002

• **Best Film:** *Moulin Rouge!*.
• **Best Actor:** Billy Bob Thornton, for *The Man Who Wasn't There*.
• **Best Actress:** Nicole Kidman, for *Moulin Rouge!* and *The Others*.
• **Best Director:** Alejandro González Iñárritu, for *Amores Perros*.
• **Best Screenwriter:** Ethan and Joel Cohn, for *The Man Who Wasn't There*.
• **Best British Film:** *Gosford Park*.
• **Best British Director:** Gurinder Chadha, for *What's Cooking?*
• **BestBritish Screenwriter:** Richard Curtis, Andrew Davies and Helen Fielding for *Bridget Jones's Diary*.
• **Best British Actor:** Ewan McGregor, for *Moulin Rouge!*.
• **Best British Actress:** Judi Dench, for *Iris*.
• **Best British Supporting Actor:** Paul Bettany, for *A Knight's Tale*.
• **Best British Supporting Actress:** Helen Mirren, for *Last Orders* and *Gosford Park*.
• **Best British Newcomer:** actor Colin Farrell.
• **Best Foreign Language Film:** *Amélie* (France).
• **Dilys Powell Award:** Eon Productions.

Presenters: Carol Allen, James Cameron-Wilson, Mariella Frostrup, Paul Gambaccini, Marianne Gray, Karen Krizanovich, Barry Norman, George Perry, Dee Pilgrim, Simon Rose and Jason Solomons

The 27th Los Angeles Film Critics' Association Awards: 15 December 2001

• **Best Picture:** *In the Bedroom*.
• **Best Actor:** Denzel Washington, for *Training Day*.
• **Best Actress:** Sissy Spacek, for *In the Bedroom*.
• **Best Supporting Actor:** Jim Broadbent, for *Iris*.
• **Best Supporting Actress:** Kate Winslet, for *Iris*.
• **Best Director:** David Lynch, for *Mulholland Dr*.
• **Best Screenplay:** Christopher Nolan, for *Memento*.
• **Best Foreign-Language Film:** *No Man's Land* (Bosnia and Herzegovina).
• **Best Cinematography:** Roger Deakins, for *The Man Who Wasn't There*.
• **Best Music:** Howard Shore, for *The Lord of the Rings: The Fellowship of the Ring*.
• **Best Production Design:** Catherine Martin, for *Moulin Rouge!*.
• **New Generation Award:** John Cameron Mitchell, for *Hedwig and the Angry Inch*.
• **Best Animation:** *Shrek*, by Andrew Adamson and Vicky Jenson.
• **Best Documentary:** *The Gleaners and I*, by Agnès Varda.
• **Douglas Edwards Independent/ Experimental Film/Video Award:** *The Beaver Trilogy*, by Trent Harris.
• **Special Citation:** Joe Grant
• **Career Achievement:** Ennio Morricone.

93rd National Board of Review Awards: 5 December 2001

• **Best Film:** *Moulin Rouge!*
• **Best Director:** Todd Field, for *In the Bedroom*
• **Best Actor:** Billy Bob Thornton, for *Bandits*, *The Man Who Wasn't There* and *Monster's Ball*
• **Best Actress:** Halle Berry, for *Monster's Ball*
• **Best Supporting Actor:** Jim Broadbent, for *Iris* and *Moulin Rouge!*
• **Best Supporting Actress:** Cate Blanchett,

for *The Lord of the Rings: The Fellowship of the Ring*, *The Man Who Cried* and *The Shipping News*.
• **Best Foreign Film**: *Amores Perros* (Mexico), by Alejandro González Iñárritu.
• **Best Documentary**: *The Endurance: Shackleton's Legendary Antarctic Expedition*, by George Butler.
• **Best Animated Feature**: *Shrek*.
• **Best Screenplay**: Rob Festinger & Todd Field, for *In the Bedroom*.
• **Best Production Design/Art Direction**: Grant Major, for *The Lord of the Rings: The Fellowship of the Ring*.
• **Special Achievement Award In Filmmaking**: Peter Jackson, for *The Lord of the Rings: The Fellowship of the Ring*.
• **Best Ensemble Performance**: The cast of *Last Orders*.
• **Best Breakthrough Performance**: Naomi Watts, for *Mulholland Dr.*; and Hayden Christensen, for *Life as a House*.
• **Directorial Debut**: John Cameron Mitchell, for *Hedwig and The Angry Inch*.
• **Humanitarian Award for the Advancement of Social Reforms and the Promotion of Human Welfare through Film**: Arthur Cohn.
• **William K Everson Award for Film History**: Martin Scorsese, for *Il mio viaggio in Italia*.
• **Career Achievement Award**: Jon Voight.
• **Billy Wilder Award for Excellence in Direction**: Steven Spielberg
• **Career Achievement for Excellence in Film Music Scoring**: John Williams

The 36th National Society of Film Critics' Awards: New York, 5 January 2002

• **Best Film**: *Mulholland Dr.*
• **Best Actor**: Gene Hackman, for *The Royal Tenenbaums*.
• **Best Actress**: Naomi Watts, for *Mulholland Dr.*
• **Best Director**: Robert Altman, for *Gosford Park*.
• **Best Supporting Actor**: Steve Buscemi, for *Ghost World*.

• **Best Supporting Actress**: Helen Mirren, for *Gosford Park*.
• **Best Screenplay**: Julian Fellowes, for *Gosford Park*.
• **Best Cinematography**: Christopher Doyle and Mark Li Ping-bin, for *In the Mood for Love*.
• **Best Documentary**: *The Gleaners and I*, by Agnès Varda.
• **Best Experimental Film**: *Waking Life*, by Richard Linklater.
• **Special Citation**: Faith Hubley, 'for a career devoted to exploring animation's art and soul'.
• **Film Heritage Award**: *My Voyage to Italy* (*Il mio viaggio in Italia*), by Martin Scorsese.

The 67th New York Film Critics' Circle Awards: 13 December 2001

• **Best Film**: *Mulholland Dr.*
• **Best Actor**: Tom Wilkinson, for *In the Bedroom*.
• **Best Actress**: Sissy Spacek, for *In the Bedroom*.

• **Best Supporting Actor**: Steve Buscemi, for *Ghost World*.
• **Best Supporting Actress**: Helen Mirren, for *Gosford Park*.
• **Best Director**: Robert Altman, for *Gosford Park*.
• **Best Screenplay**: Julian Fellowes, for *Gosford Park*.
• **Best Cinematography**: Christopher Doyle and Mark Li Ping-bin, for *In the Mood for Love*.
• **Best Foreign Film**: *In the Mood for Love*, by Wong Kar-wai.
• **Best Non-Fiction Film**: *The Gleaners and I*, by Agnès Varda.
• **Best Animated Film**: *Waking Life*, by Richard Linklater.
• **Best First Film**: *In the Bedroom*, by Todd Field.
• **Special Award**: *Lola and Bay Of Angels*, by Jacques Demy.

The 2001 Orange British Academy of Film and Television Arts Awards ('BAFTAs'): Odeon Leicester Square, London, 24 February 2002

• **Best Film:** *The Lord of the Rings: The Fellowship of the Ring.*
• **Orange Audience Award:** *The Lord of the Rings.*
• **David Lean Award for Best Direction:** Peter Jackson, for *The Lord of the Rings.*
• **Best Original Screenplay:** Guillaume Laurant & Jean-Pierre Jeunet, for *Amélie.*
• **Best Adapted Screenplay:** Ted Elliott, Terry Rossio, Joe Stillman & Roger S H Schulman, for *Shrek.*
• **Best Actor:** Russell Crowe, for *A Beautiful Mind.*
• **Best Actress:** Judi Dench, for *Iris.*
• **Best Supporting Actor:** Jim Broadbent, for *Moulin Rouge!.*
• **Best Supporting Actress:** Jennifer Connelly, for *A Beautiful Mind.*
• **Best Cinematography:** Roger Deakins, for *The Man Who Wasn't There.*
• **Best Production Design:** Aline Bonetto, for *Amélie.*
• **Best Editing:** Mary Sweeney, for *Mulholland Drive.*
• **The Anthony Asquith Award for Best Music:** Craig Armstrong, for *Moulin Rouge!.*
• **Best Costumes:** Jenny Beavan, for *Gosford Park.*
• **Best Sound:** *Moulin Rouge!.*
• **Best Special Visual Effects:** *The Lord of the Rings.*
• **Best Make-up/Hair:** *The Lord of the Rings.*
• **Alexander Korda Award for Best British Film:** *Gosford Park.*
• **Best Foreign Language Film:** *Amores Perros* (Mexico).
• **Best Short Film:** *About a Girl,* by Janey de Nordwall, Brian Percival & Julie Rutterford.
• **Best Animated Short:** *Dog,* by Suzie Templeton.
• **Carl Foreman Award for British Newcomer:** director Joel Hopkins and producer Nicola Usbourne, for *Jump Tomorrow.*
• **Michael Balcon Award for contribution to British Cinema:** stunt director Vic Armstrong.

• **BAFTA Fellowships:** Warren Beatty, James Ivory, Ismail Merchant and Ruth Prawer Jhabvala.

Host: Stephen Fry

23rd Sundance Film Festival: Park City and Salt Lake City, Utah, 18-20 January 2002

• **The Grand Jury Prize** (best feature): *Personal Velocity,* by Rebecca Miller.
• **The Grand Jury Prize** (best documentary): *Daughter from Danang,* by Gail Dolgin and Vicente Franco
• **Best Performance:** The ensemble cast of *Manito.*
• **Best Direction:** Gary Winick, for *Tadpole.*
• **Best Direction** (documentary): Rob Fruchtman and Rebecca Cammisa, for *Sister Helen.*
• **Best Cinematography:** Ellen Kuras, for *Personal Velocity.*
• **Best Cinematography** (documentary): Daniel Gold, for *Blue Vinyl.*
• **Audience Award** (best feature): *Real Women Have Curves* by Patricia Cardosa.
• **Audience Award** (best documentary): *Amandla! A Revolution in Four Part Harmony* by Lee Hirsch.
• **World Cinema Audience Award:** *Bloody Sunday* by Paul Greengrass; and *The Last Kiss* by Gabriele Muccino.
• **Short Filmmaking Award:** *Gasline* by Dave Silver.
• **Waldo Salt Screenwriting Award:** Gordy Hoffman, for *Love Liza.*
• **Freedom of Expression Award:** *Amandla! A Revolution in Four Part Harmony* by Lee Hirsch.
• **Special Jury Award:** America Ferrera and Lupe Ontiveros, for *Real Women Have Curves.*
• **Special Jury Award** (documentary): *How to Draw a Bunny* by John Walter; and *Senorita Extraviada* by Lourdes Portillo.
• **Special Jury Award for Originality:** *Secretary* by Steven Shainberg.
• **Latin American Cinema Award:** *The Trespasser* by Beto Brant.

The 58th Venice International Film Festival Awards: 8 September 2001

• **Golden Lion for Best Picture:** *Monsoon Wedding,* by Mira Nair.
• **Golden Lion for Best Picture, Cinema Del Presente Competition:** *L'Emploi du temps* (*Time Out*), by Laurent Cantet.
• **Best Director:** Babak Payami, for *Raye Makhfi* (*Secret Ballot*).
• **Best Actor:** Luigi Lo Cascio, for *Luce Dei Miei Occhi* (*Light of My Eyes*).
• **Best Actress:** Sandra Ceccarelli, for *Luce Dei Miei Occhi* (*Light of My Eyes*).
• **Best Screenplay:** Alfonso Cuarón and Carlos Cuarón, for *Y Tu Mamá También* (*And Your Mother Too*)
• **Grand Jury Prize:** *Hundstage* (*Dog Days*), by Ulrich Seidl.
• **Grand Jury Prize, Cinema Del Presente Competition:** *Le Souffle* (*Deep Breath*) by Damien Odoul; and *Haixian* (*Seafood*), by Zhu Wen.
• **Luigi De Laurentiis Award for Best First Feature:** *Kruh In Mleko,* by Jan Cvitkovic.
• **Marcello Mastroianni Award for Emerging Actor or Actress:** Gael Garcia Bernal and Diego Luna, for *Y Tu Mamá También.*
• **Golden Lion Lifetime Achievement Award:** Eric Rohmer.
• **Silver Lion For Best Short Film:** *Freunde* (*The Whiz Kids*), by Jan Krueger.
• **FIPRESCI International Critics Awards:** *Savage Innocence* (*Wild Innocence*), by Philippe Garrel.
• **Cinema Del Presente and Critics Week Films:** *Le Souffle* (*Deep Breath*)
• **Future Film Festival Prize for Best Special Effects and Best Use of Digital Technology:** *A.I. Artificial Intelligence,* by Steven Spielberg.
• **Special Mention:** *L'Anglaise et le Duc* (*The Lady and the Duke*), by Eric Rohmer.
• **Critics' Week:** *Tornando A Casa* (*Sailing Home*), by Vincenzo Marra.

Jury: Nanni Moretti (president), Jeanne Balibar, Amitav Ghosh, Taylor Hackford, Cecilia Roth, Jerzy Skolimowski and Vibeke Windelov.

In Memoriam

JAMES BERNARD

Born: 20 September 1925 in Nathia Gali, India.
Died: 9 July 2001, in London.
• A protégé of Benjamin Britten, James Bernard won an Oscar for co-writing the story of acclaimed thriller *Seven Days to Noon* (1950) but his break into film music came via his work on a BBC Radio production of *The Duchess of Malfi*. His spinechilling score for *The Quatermass Xperiment* (1955), limited to strings and percussion, was supplemented by the full orchestral works for such evergreen Hammer classics as *Dracula* (1958), *She* (1965), *The Devil Rides Out* (1967) and *Frankenstein Must Be Destroyed* (1969). After retiring to Jamaica, he returned to London in his final decade and provided the Photoplay/Channel 4 restoration of Murnau's *Nosferatu* with a stupendous new score, premiered at the Royal Festival Hall in 1997.

PAUL CHUBB

Born: 14 January 1949 in Arncliffe, Sydney, New South Wales.
Died: 9 June 2002 from complications after surgery for cardiomyopathy, in Newcastle, New South Wales.
Real name: Paul Dunford.
• A popular, chubby character actor in his native Australia, Chubb made his biggest impact in the starring role of *The Roly Poly Man* (1994) and also made a sharp impression in such local successes as *Bliss* (1985), *The Coca-Cola Kid* (both 1985), *Golden Braid* (1990) and *Cosi* (1995). His last film was *Dirty Deeds*, with Bryan Brown and Toni Collette.

HILDEGARD KNEF

Born: 28 December 1925 in Ulm, Germany.
Died: 1 February 2002 from a lung infection, in a Berlin hospital.
Full name: Hildegard Frieda Albertine Knef.
• Actress Hildegard Knef began her film career in Nazi-controlled German cinema. Her later performance as a concentration camp survivor in *The Murderers are Among Us* (1946) drew international acclaim. Knef co-starred in a handful of Hollywood films, notably the taut Cold War thriller *Diplomatic Courier* (1952), directed by Henry Hathaway, and *The Snows of Kilimanjaro* (1952), co-starring Gregory Peck, Susan Hayward and Ava Gardner. Knef's later films include Billy Wilder's *Fedora* (1978), a lament for the lost 'golden age' of movies, and *The Sacrifice* (1986), the final film by director Andrei Tarkovsky.

JENNY LAIRD

Born: 13 February 1917 in Manchester.
Died: 31 October 2001.
• Character actress Jenny Laird made a handful of films in between her many stage appearances. She played Ethel in *Just William* (1939) and Sister Honey in the Michael Powell-Emeric Pressburger classic *Black Narcissus* (1946).

PHILIPPE LÉOTARD

Born: 28 August 1940 in Nice, France.
Died: 25 August 2001 in Paris, of respiratory failure.
• A strong, often surly presence in scores of French movies, actor Philippe Léotard got his break into films with director François Truffaut, who cast him in *Domicile conjugal/Bed and Board* (1970) and *Two English Girls* (1971). Léotard had one of his best roles in the Paris-set crime drama *La Balance* (1982) as a 'good' pimp forced to turn informer when the police harass his prostitute lover (Nathalie Baye). His performance deservedly won him a Best Actor Cesar Award, the French equivalent of an Oscar.

JAY LIVINGSTON

Born: 28 March 1915 in McDonald, Pennsylvania.
Died: 17 October 2001 in Los Angeles, of pneumonia.
Real name: Jacob Harold Levison.
• Songwriter Jay Livingston enjoyed a fruitful creative partnership with Ray Evans. Under contract to Paramount from 1945-55, the duo produced songs

for the studio's top comedy stars, notably Bob Hope. *The Paleface* (1948) featured the tune 'Buttons and Bows', which netted Livingston and Evans their first Academy Award. 'Mona Lisa', composed for the otherwise forgettable *Captain Carey, USA* (1950), brought a second. Livingston shared his third Oscar with Evans for 'Que Sera, Sera', sung by Doris Day in *The Man Who Knew Too Much* (1956).

LINDA LOVELACE

Born: 10 January 1949 in the Bronx, New York City.
Died: 22 April 2002 in Denver, Colorado, from injuries sustained in a car crash.
Real name: Linda Susan Boreman.
• Porn star Linda Lovelace achieved a brief celebrity, and notoriety, with *Deep Throat* (1972), the first 'fashionable' hardcore feature film. Made for $24,000, *Deep Throat* has supposedly grossed over $600 million worldwide, of which Lovelace saw virtually nothing. She attempted a more mainstream film career with the softcore sex comedy *Linda Lovelace for President* (1975). The movie flopped and Lovelace reinvented herself as an anti-pornography campaigner.

BILL McCUTCHEON

Born: 23 May 1924 in Russell, Kentucky.
Died: 9 January 2002 in Ridgewood, New Jersey, of 'natural causes.'
• Character actor Bill McCutcheon was known to millions of children as *Sesame Street*'s Uncle Willy, a role he played between 1984 and 1992. His film credits include bit parts in *W.W. and the Dixie Dancekings* (1975), *Steel Magnolias* (1989) and *Family Business* (1989). However, his biggest claim to movie infamy was a supporting role in the wretched *Santa Claus Conquers the Martians* (1964).

DOROTHY McGUIRE

Born: 14 June 1918 in Omaha, Nebraska.
Died: 13 September 2001 of heart failure at St John's Hospital in Santa Monica, California.
• An accomplished, unshowy actress, Dorothy McGuire projected a gentle, compassionate screen persona, attractive without a hint of predatory glamour. Her best film is probably *The Spiral Staircase* (1945), an atmospheric murder-mystery. McGuire received an Academy Award nomination for her performance in Elia Kazan's *Gentleman's Agreement* (1947), a worthy, if dated, attack on anti-Semitism.

SPIKE MILLIGAN

Born: 16 April 1918 in Ahmaddnagar, India.
Died: 27 February 2002 near Rye, East Sussex, of liver disease.
Real name: Terence Alan Milligan.
• Acclaimed as the father of postwar British humour, comedian-writer-performer Spike Milligan peaked early in his career with BBC Radio's *The Goon Show* (1951-60). However, his largely verbal humour, surreal and unstructured, seemed ill-suited to the cinema. Milligan starred in a couple of modest comedies for MGM, the best of which was *Postman's Knock* (1962). He also made quirky cameo appearances in otherwise mainstream comedies, notably *Watch Your Stern* (1960), *What a Whopper!* (1962) and *The Magnificent Seven Deadly Sins* (1971). He played 'straight' acting roles in *Suspect* (1960) and *The Three Musketeers* (1973), acquitting himself with modest distinction. He also appeared as his own father in *Adolf Hitler, My Part in His Downfall* (1972), based on his best-selling autobiography. The Monty Python team, who acknowledged their debt to Milligan, gave him a bit part in *The Life of Brian* (1979).

DUDLEY MOORE

Born: 19 April 1935 in Dagenham, Essex.
Died: 27 March 2002 in New Jersey, from pneumonia, as a complication of progressive supranuclear palsy.
• A gifted musician and capable actor, Dudley Moore is best known for his cele-

brated comedy partnership with Peter Cook. Established during the swinging sixties, Moore and Cook took their double act to the big screen in the Faustian comedy *Bedazzled* (1967), which proved a patchy vehicle for the duo. Moore had an early shot at solo stardom with *30 is a Dangerous Age, Cynthia* (1967), an unsuccessful romantic comedy. Much to his surprise, Moore achieved Hollywood stardom in *10* (1979), Blake Edwards' comedy of middle-aged angst and lust. Audiences responded to his 'Cuddly Dudley'/'Sex Thimble' persona. Unfortunately, Moore's later films were generally feeble and only *Arthur* (1980) proved a major success. By the time of *Arthur 2: On the Rocks* (1988), Moore's star status had faded.

PEGGY MOUNT

Born: 2 May 1918 in Southend-on-Sea, Essex.
Died: 13 November 2001 in London, after a long illness.
• A distinguished actress and comedienne, Peggy Mount played the archetypal mother-in-law from Hell in the farce *Sailor Beware!* (1956), a role she'd created on the stage. This new-found celebrity led to parts in a run of mostly indifferent screen comedies. Exceptions included *The Naked Truth* (1958), co-starring Dennis Price, Terry-Thomas and Peter Sellers, and the amiably surreal *One Way Pendulum* (1964).

GEORGE NADER

Born: 19 October 1921 in Pasadena, Colorado.
Died: 4 February 2002 in California, of pneumonia.
• Actor George Nader found movie immortality - of a kind - as the star of *Robot Monster* (1953), a zero-budget science fiction 'shocker.' Playing opposite a

stuntman in a gorilla suit and diving helmet, Nader kept an admirably straight face. Under contract to Universal-International, Nader also appeared in *Away All Boats* (1956), a reasonable World War II adventure. However, his best film was the British-made *Nowhere to Go* (1958), a downbeat crime drama co-starring Maggie Smith.

BILL PEET

Born: 29 January 1915 in Indiana.
Died: 11 May 2002.
Full name: William Barlett Peet.
• An exceptional artist, animator and screenwriter, Bill Peet spent nearly 30 years with Walt Disney, working on *Snow White and the Seven Dwarfs* (1937) and *Pinocchio* (1940). Peet designed many of the leading characters for *Dumbo* (1941), arguably Disney's greatest achievement, *Song of the South* (1946) and *Peter Pan* (1953). He also devised the story for *101 Dalmatians* (1961), based on the Dodie Smith book.

FRANÇOIS PÉRIER

Born: 10 November 1919 in Paris.
Died: 28 June 2002.

Real name: François Pilu.
• A veteran of over 100 films, French actor François Périer is best known for his role as Heurtebise, the angel of death-cum-chauffeur, in Jean Cocteau's *Orphée* (1950). Périer also appeared in Jean-Pierre Melville's *Le Samourai* (1967) and Costa-Gavras' *Z* (1969).

JULIA PHILLIPS

Born: 7 April 1944 in New York City.
Died: 1 January 2002 in West Hollywood, California, of cancer.
Maiden name: Julia Miller.
• Best known as the author of the Hollywood-bashing memoir *You'll Never Eat Lunch in This Town Again* (1991), producer Julia Phillips was an ambitious, fiercely driven talent which self-destructed. During the mid-1970s, husband-and-wife team Julia and Michael Phillips hit the big time with *The Sting* (1974), *Taxi Driver* (1976) and *Close Encounters of the Third Kind* (1977). Phillips was the first female producer to share in a Best Picture Academy Award, for *The Sting*. Later, she blamed the male-dominated Hollywood establishment for undermining her career, yet her well-publicised cocaine abuse also played a part.

BRYAN PRINGLE

Born: 19 January 1935 in Glascote, Staffordshire.
Died: 15 May 2002.
• A character actor specialising in lugubrious roles, Pringle made memorable contributions to *Saturday Night and Sunday Morning* (1960), *Lawrence of Arabia* (1962) and *The Boy Friend* (1971). The RADA-trained actor also turned up in Terry Gilliam's *Brazil* (1985) and Peter Greenaway's *Drowning By Numbers* (1988), adding a touch of humanity to the surreal goings-on.

FRANCISCO RABAL

Born: 8 March 1925 in Aguilas, Spain.
Died: 29 August 2001 from pulmonary complications while flying home from the Montreal Film Festival.
Real name: Francisco Valera.
• Beginning his film career as an on-set electrician, Rabal blossomed into an accomplished actor. He worked with such acclaimed directors as Luis Buñuel (*Nazarin* 1959, *Viridiana* 1961, *Belle de Jour* 1967), Michelangelo Antonioni (*The Eclipse* 1962) and Pedro Almodóvar (*Tie Me Up! Tie Me Down!* 1990). Rabal had one of his best roles in *The Holy Innocents* (1984), an affecting 1960s tale of life in rural Spain under the Franco dictatorship. His sensitive performance earned him the (shared) Best Actor prize at the 1984 Cannes Film Festival. His daughter is the actress-singer Teresa Rabal and his son the filmmaker Benito Rabal.

YVES ROBERT

Born: 19 June 1920, in the Loire valley, France.
Died: 10 May 2002.
• A character actor who became a successful director, Yves Robert often touched on the theme of childhood. *The War of the Buttons* (1962), remade in Ireland 30 years later, features rival gangs of schoolboys who regularly do battle in the local sandpit. Two of Robert's biggest hits were remade in Hollywood, with depressing results. *The Tall Blond Man with One Black Shoe* (1972) became *The Man with One Red Shoe* (1985), a now-forgotten Tom Hanks vehicle. *Pardon mon affaire* (1976) turned into the Gene Wilder hit *The Woman in Red* (1984). Yves Robert's last films included *My Father's Glory* and *My Mother's Castle* (both 1990), based on the early years of Marcel Pagnol.

REGINALD ROSE

Born: 10 December 1920, in New York City.
Died: 19 April 2002.
• Writer Reginald Rose enjoyed his biggest success with *Twelve Angry Men* (1957), an ingenious, if schematic, jury-room drama starring Henry Fonda. Based on his 1954 teleplay, the film brought Rose to the attention of Hollywood. He subsequently scripted *Man of the West* (1958), a psychological 'adult' Western starring Gary Cooper and Lee J Cobb. He later penned a series of slick action movies, including *The Wild Geese* (1978) and *Who Dares Wins* (1982), which packaged fading star names with half-arsed political comment and gory violence.

HERBERT ROSS

Born: 13 May 1927 in Brooklyn, New York.
Died: 9 October 2001 in New York, from heart failure.
• An accomplished choreographer and competent director, Herbert Ross was always stronger on solid craftsmanship than inspiration. After Broadway experi-ence, he choreographed the Hollywood films *Carmen Jones* (1954), *Doctor Dolittle* (1967) and *Funny Girl* (1968). He then made an inauspicious directing debut with *Goodbye Mr Chips* (1969), a lumbering musical remake of the much-loved 1939 film. He did better with a series of deftly handled comedies based on Broadway hits: *The Owl and the Pussycat* (1970), *Play It Again Sam* (1972), *The Sunshine Boys* (1975) and *The Goodbye Girl* (1977). Ross' most ambitious project was the Dennis Potter-scripted 'anti-musical' *Pennies from Heaven* (1981), starring Steve Martin and Bernadette Peters. This Depression-era tale of a frustrated sheet music salesman contrasts the feel-good movie musicals of the period with the grim reality of the protagonists' lives.

HAROLD RUSSELL

Born: 14 January 1914 in Sydney, Nova Scotia, Canada.
Died: 29 January 2002 in Needham, Massachusetts, from a heart attack.
• An Oscar-winning amateur actor, Harold Russell was serving as a para-trooper during World War II when he lost both hands in a grenade explosion. Opting to be fitted with hooks rather than artificial hands, Russell achieved unexpected fame when he co-starred in William Wyler's *The Best Years of Our Lives* (1946), the story of ex-soldiers read-justing to civilian life. Russell played Homer Parrish, who fears that his loyal girlfriend will be unable to deal with his disability. Russell's touching, unselfcon-scious performance was rewarded with a Best Supporting Actor Academy Award, and a unique second Oscar, 'for bringing hope and courage to his fellow veterans.' Having pursued a successful career as a public relations executive, Russell returned to films in *Inside Moves* (1980), an offbeat drama centring on a Los Angeles bar filled with disabled regulars.

In 1992, Russell sold one of his awards to pay his wife's medical bills.

SHIRLEY RUSSELL

Born: 11 March 1935 in Woodford, Essex.
Died: 4 March 2002.
Maiden name: Shirley Kingdon.
• One of the film industry's best costume designers, Shirley Russell specialised in authentic period detail. Married to director Ken Russell for 20 years, she came up with a striking art deco look for *Women in Love* (1969), developed and refined in *The Boy Friend* (1971) and *Valentino* (1977). She also made a crucial contribution to *The Devils* (1971), her husband's best film, designing nuns' habits that didn't look fresh off the rack. On the downside, her outlandish costumes for *Tommy* (1975) and *Lisztomania* (1975) have dated as badly as the films themselves. Following the flop biopic *Valentino*, the Russells went their separate ways, both professionally and personally. While Ken hit a serious career slump, Shirley thrived, working on *Yanks* (1979), for which she won a BAFTA, *Reds* (1981), *Greystoke* (1984) and *Hope and Glory* (1987).

GEORGE SIDNEY

Born: 4 October 1916 in Long Island City, New York State.
Died: 5 May 2002 in Las Vegas, Nevada, of complications of lymphoma.
• A specialist in jaunty Technicolor musicals, director George Sidney spent most of his career with MGM, home of wholesome family entertainment. Sidney's accomplished, if lightweight, films for the studio include *Bathing Beauty* (1944) with swimming star Esther Williams, *Anchors Aweigh* (1945) starring Gene Kelly and Frank Sinatra, *The Harvey Girls* (1946) with Judy Garland, *Annie Get Your Gun* (1950), *Show Boat* (1951) and *Kiss Me Kate* (1953) in 3D. Taking a break from musicals, Sidney directed the stylish swashbuckler *Scaramouche* (1952), noted for its epic duel sequence. Quitting MGM in 1955, Sidney made a production deal with Columbia, though films such as the long-delayed *Pal Joey* (1957) proved disappointing. Sidney's best Columbia movie is the exuberant musical *Bye Bye Birdie* (1963), starring Ann-Margret and Dick Van Dyke. Sidney then retired from films after the British-made *Half a Sixpence* (1968).

CHARLES SIMON

Born: 4 February 1909 in Wolverhampton.
Died: 19 May 2002, of pneumonia.
• Active in showbusiness over eight decades, character actor Charles Simon lent a touch of octogenarian class to films such as *Shadowlands* (1993), *Topsy Turvy* (1999) and *102 Dalmatians* (2000).

KIM STANLEY

Born: 11 February 1925 in Tularosa, New Mexico.
Died: 20 August 2001, of uterine cancer, in Santa Fe, New Mexico.
Real name: Patricia Beth Kimberley Reid.

• An exceptionally gifted stage actress, Kim Stanley made an impressive film debut in *The Goddess* (1958), a savage anti-Hollywood satire, but showed little interest in a movie career. In Bryan Forbes' British-made *Seance on a Wet Afternoon* (1964), Stanley's unsettling performance as a mentally unhinged medium earned her a deserved Academy Award nomination. After nearly two decades away, Stanley returned to the screen in *Frances* (1982), a biopic of ill-fated Hollywood star Frances Farmer (Jessica Lange). Transcending the superficial, melodramatic script, Stanley won another Oscar nomination for her role as Farmer's disturbed mother.

GUY STOCKWELL

Born: 16 November 1934 in Hollywood, California.
Died: 6 February 2002 in Prescott, Arizona, of 'undisclosed causes.'
• The older brother of Dean Stockwell, actor Guy Stockwell never achieved the same success in films, despite his severe good looks. Under contract to Universal in the 1960s, he gave a strangely mannered performance opposite Charlton Heston in *The War Lord* (1965), an unusual medieval romance. Stockwell also appeared in the Hitchcockian thriller *Blindfold* (1966), starring Rock Hudson, and two cut-price adventure movies, *Beau Geste* (1966) and *The King's Pirate* (1967). 20 years later, a much heavier Guy Stockwell co-starred in Alejandro Jodorowsky's truly bizarre *Santa Sangre* (1989), playing the hero's grotesque knife-throwing father.

DAVID SWIFT

Born: 1919 in Minneapolis, Minnesota.
Died: 31 December 2001 in Santa Monica, California, from heart failure.
• Producer-writer-director David Swift began his film career in Walt Disney's animation department. He later wrote and

directed Disney's ultra-wholesome live action films *Pollyanna* (1960) and *The Parent Trap* (1951), both starring Hayley Mills. Moving into the big league, Swift made the marital farce *Good Neighbour Sam* (1964) for Columbia, and the satirical musical *How to Succeed in Business Without Really Trying* (1967) for United Artists.

RICHARD SYLBERT

Born: 16 April 1928 in Brooklyn, New York City.
Died: 23 March 2002 in Woodland Hills, California, of cancer.
• An outspoken perfectionist, Richard Sylbert was the production designer of choice for leading directors John Huston, Elia Kazan, Sidney Lumet, John Frankenheimer, Roman Polanski and Mike Nichols. His sets for Frankenheimer's *The Manchurian Candidate* (1962) include the surreal brainwashing room, which rotated through 360 degrees. Sylbert won Academy Awards for *Who's Afraid of Virginia Woolf?* (1966) and *Dick Tracy* (1990), widely contrasting examples of his craft. Long associated with Paramount, Sylbert briefly ran the studio's film division, from 1975 to 1978.

JOHN THAW

Born: 3 January 1942 in West Gorton, Manchester.
Died: 21 February 2002 in Wiltshire, from cancer of the oesophagus.
Full name: John Edward Thaw.
• In contrast to his high-profile television work, notably *The Sweeney* and *Inspector Morse*, actor John Thaw's film credits are relatively minor. His early big screen appearances include *The Loneliness of the Long Distance Runner* (1962), *Praise Marx and Pass the Ammunition* (1968) and *Dr Phibes Rises Again* (1972). The two *Sweeney* film spin-offs (1976 and 1978) are disappointing, completely fumbling

the material's cinematic potential. Thaw later appeared in a couple of Richard Attenborough's epic biopics, the impassioned *Cry Freedom* (1987) and the patchy, superficial *Chaplin* (1992).

LAWRENCE TIERNEY

Born: 15 March 1919 in Brooklyn, New York.
Died: 26 February 2002 in Los Angeles, from pneumonia.
• Lawrence Tierney was an imposing 'B' movie actor whose tough-guy image seemed very much part of his own personality. Tierney got a modest film break with *Dillinger* (1945), a superior low-budget gangster movie. Cast in the title role, Tierney looked believably ruthless, if low on charm. He played another murderous sadist in *Born to Kill* (1947), a tough *film noir* directed by Robert Wise. After years of relative obscurity, the actor found an unlikely patron in the form of movie buff-turned-filmmaker Quentin Tarantino. A big fan of Tierney's performance in *Dillinger*, Tarantino gave him a co-starring role in *Reservoir Dogs* (1992), playing seasoned crime boss Joe Cabot. Despite a few personal differences with the novice writer-director, Tierney delivered a first-rate performance of great authority.

LINDEN TRAVERS

Born: 27 May 1913 in Durham.
Died: 23 October 2001.
Real name: Florence Lindon-Travers.
• Actress Linden Travers did her best film work with trains, notably in Alfred Hitchcock's *The Lady Vanishes* (1938), playing Mrs Todhunter. Her most infamous role came in the ersatz gangster movie *No Orchids for Miss Blandish* (1948), recreating a part she'd played on the London stage in 1942. Despite all the negative publicity, Travers cited the film as her personal favourite.

DOROTHY TUTIN

Born: 8 April 1930 in London.
Died: 6 August 2001 of leukaemia, at the Edward VII Hospital in London.
• RADA-trained stage actress Dorothy Tutin made few film appearances, something she regretted in later life. Following her screen debut as Cecily in Anthony Asquith's *The Importance of Being Earnest* (1952), Tutin appeared in *A Tale of Two Cities* (1957), *Cromwell* (1970), Ken Russell's *Savage Messiah* (1972) and *The Shooting Party* (1984). *Savage Messiah* depicted the unconventional relationship between artist Henri Gaudier (Scott Anthony) and writer Sophie Brzeska (Tutin), 20 years his senior. Restrained by Russell's standards, the film benefited greatly from Tutin's sensitive, and sensual, performance.

ROBERT URICH

Born: 19 December 1946 in Ohio.
Died: 16 April 2002, of synovial cell sarcoma, a rare form of cancer.
• Robert Urich was a highly successful television actor, starring in *Vega$* (1978-81), *Spencer: For Hire* (1985-88) and *Lonesome Dove* (1989), among others. Urich's occasional film roles never

achieved the same popularity. Making his big screen debut as one of the vigilante cops in *Magnum Force* (1973), he co-starred in Alan Rudolph's offbeat thriller *Endangered Species* (1982) and the uneven science fiction spoof *Ice Pirates* (1984).

DERMOT WALSH

Born: 10 September 1924 in Dublin.
Died: 26 June 2002.
• Blessed with saturnine good looks, actor Dermot Walsh appeared in several Gainsborough melodramas, including *Hungry Hill* (1946) and *Jassy* (1947). Walsh's best film, however, was John Gilling's period shocker *The Flesh and the Fiends* (1959), starring Peter Cushing.

LEW WASSERMAN

Born: 15 March 1913 in Cleveland, Ohio.
Died: 3 June 2002 in Los Angeles, California, from a stroke.
Full name: Lewis Robert Wasserman.
• One of Hollywood's most powerful agents and producers, Lew Wasserman is credited with creating the modern block-buster. As head of MCA-Universal, Wasserman oversaw such box-office hits

as *The Sting* (1973), *Jaws* (1975) and *E.T. The ExtraTerrestrial* (1982).

BILLY WILDER

Born: 22 June 1906 in Sucha, Austria.
Died: 27 March 2002 in his Beverly Hills home, Los Angeles, California, of pneumonia.
Full name: Samuel 'Billy' Wilder.
• Billy Wilder was one of the truly great writer-directors, producing at least four classics of the American cinema: *Double Indemnity* (1944), *Sunset Boulevard* (1950), *Ace in the Hole* (1951) and *Some Like It Hot* (1959). His best films are sophisticated, ironic, cynical, witty, vulgar, compassionate and blackly funny. Wilder had a gift for investing his flawed lead characters with a real humanity, even Walter Neff (Fred MacMurray), *Double Indemnity*'s murderous insurance sales-man. He won seven Academy Awards, including Best Picture, Best Director and Best Screenplay for both *The Lost Weekend* (1945) and *The Apartment* (1960). Wilder's career declined after the early 1960s, though many rate the much re-edited *The Private Life of Sherlock Holmes* (1970) as a melancholy masterpiece.

WILLIAM WITNEY

Born: 15 May 1915 in Lawton, Oklahoma.
Died: 17 March 2002
• Director William Witney made over 60 films during his 40-year career. Confined to the low-budget end of the industry, he worked on some of the best-loved Saturday morning serials, including *The Adventures of Captain Marvel* (1941), and a handful of intriguing second features. Following a long stint with 'B' factory Republic Pictures, Witney directed several films for AIP, including *The Cool and the Crazy* (1958), a tale of marijuana madness. After several years in television, he briefly returned to feature films with *I Escaped from Devil's Island* (1973), starring Jim Brown, and the blaxploitation parody *Darktown Strutters* (1975).

IRENE WORTH

Born: 23 June 1916 in Fairbury, Omaha, Nebraska.
Died: 10 March 2002 in New York, from a stroke.
• An acclaimed stage actress, Irene Worth made few film appearances. She won a British Film Award for her performance in Anthony Asquith's *Orders to Kill* (1958), a downbeat World War II drama. She then made a suitably imperious Queen Elizabeth I in the spaghetti swash-buckler *Seven Seas to Calais* (1962), taking no nonsense from Rod Taylor's unlikely Sir Francis Drake. Returning to her theatrical roots, Worth played Goneril to Paul Scofield's King Lear in Peter Brook's 1970 film of Shakespeare's tragedy, based on their 1962 stage collaboration. In the downbeat epic *Nicholas and Alexandra* (1971), the actress stood out in the all-star cast as Tsar Nicholas II's mother, coolly resentful of Tsarina Alexandra's influence over her naïve son. Later credits include *Lost in Yonkers* (1993) and *Onegin* (1999).

Index

Names of films and videos appear in the index in *italics*. Page references for illustrations appear in **BOLD**.
The last separate word of an individual's name is used as the index entry. Thus Robert De Niro appears within 'N' as Niro, Robert De